CATALAN CINEMA

The Barcelona Film School and the New Avant-Garde

Catalan Cinema

The Barcelona Film School and the New Avant-Garde

EDITED BY ANTON PUJOL AND
JAUME MARTÍ-OLIVELLA

UNIVERSITY OF TORONTO PRESS
Toronto Buffalo London

© University of Toronto Press 2024
Toronto Buffalo London
utorontopress.com

ISBN 978-1-4875-4450-8 (cloth)   ISBN 978-1-4875-4452-2 (EPUB)
                                 ISBN 978-1-4875-4453-9 (PDF)

Toronto Iberic

Library and Archives Canada Cataloguing in Publication

Title: Catalan cinema: the Barcelona Film School and the new avant-garde /
  edited by Anton Pujol and Jaume Martí-Olivella.
Names: Pujol, Anton, editor. | Martí-Olivella, Jaume, editor.
Series: Toronto Iberic ; 85.
Description: Series statement: Toronto Iberic ; 85 | Includes bibliographical
  references and index.
Identifiers: Canadiana (print) 2023055265X | Canadiana (ebook)
  20230552730 | ISBN 9781487544508 (cloth) | ISBN 9781487544522
  (EPUB) | ISBN 9781487544539 (PDF)
Subjects: LCSH: Motion pictures – Spain – Catalonia – History.
Classification: LCC PN1993.5.S7 C38 2024 | DDC 791.4309467–dc23

Cover design: Alexa Love
Cover image: Pere Portabella's *Nocturn 29* (1968) © Films 59

We wish to acknowledge the land on which the University of Toronto Press operates. This land is the traditional territory of the Wendat, the Anishnaabeg, the Haudenosaunee, the Métis, and the Mississaugas of the Credit First Nation.

University of Toronto Press acknowledges the financial support of the Government of Canada, the Canada Council for the Arts, and the Ontario Arts Council, an agency of the Government of Ontario, for its publishing activities.

  Canada Council   Conseil des Arts
        for the Arts   du Canada

Contents

Illustrations   vii

Acknowledgments   ix

   Introduction   3
   ANTON PUJOL AND JAUME MARTÍ-OLIVELLA

Part One: The Mavericks and the Barcelona School

1 Future Seeds: Some Considerations on the Cinema around Barcelona 92   43
   ÀNGEL QUINTANA

Part Two: The Jordà Legacy

2 The Hunter and the Monkeys: Jacinto Esteva, Joaquim Jordà, and the Legacy of the Barcelona School   65
   ESTEVE RIAMBAU

3 Jordà's Last Trilogy: Situationist Turn and Subject Transformation   80
   IGNASI GOZALO-SALELLAS

4 The Militant Cinema of Joaquim Jordà: The Essay Film as Form   102
   STEVEN MARSH

Part Three: The Portabella Nexus

5 Economies of Sound: Labouring Europe in Pere Portabella and Carles Santos   125
   SARA NADAL-MELSIÓ

6 Pere Portabella's Radical Theatricality: A Political Gaze over Two Transitions   145
   JAUME MARTÍ-OLIVELLA

7 Traversing the Real with the Reel: Infrapolitical Spectrality in Pere Portabella's *Vampir.Cuadecuc* and Albert Serra's *Història de la meva mort*   171
   TERESA M. VILARÓS

Part Four: The New (Post) Avant-Garde

8 Beyond Melancholy: The Post-Avant-Garde Cinema of José Luis Guerín   207
   JOSEP MARIA CATALÀ DOMÈNECH

9 On the Threshold of the Diegetic World: Optical and Haptic Visuality in *Elisa K*   231
   EVA BRU-DOMINGUEZ

10 Watching Novels and Reading Films: Deleuzian Affects in Catalan Cinema   255
    ANTON PUJOL

Part Five: Minimalism and Beyond

11 Formal Disruption, Minutiae, and Absence in the Films of Jaime Rosales   283
    AGUSTÍN RICO-ALBERO

12 Identity Kit: Where to Meet Isaki Lacuesta   299
    JOSETXO CERDÁN AND MIGUEL FERNÁNDEZ LABAYEN

Contributors   333

Index   339

Illustrations

5.1　Film still from *Die Stille vor Bach* showing a pair of hands on blood-smeared sheet music　138
7.1　Clapperboard with the words "El proceso" from *Vampir. Cuadecuc*　175
7.2　Black-and-white photograph of the 1970 production of *Ronda de mort a Sinera*　179
7.3　Photograph of the cover of *Le Petit Journal* (1893) with a drawing of the Liceu stalls being hit by the bomb　181
7.4　Black-and-white screenshot from *Vampir.Cuadecuc* showing a woman sitting in a Liceu opera box　182
7.5　Black-and-white screenshot showing a letter with the drawing of a bomb　182
7.6　Colour film still from *Història de la meva mort* showing Vicenç Altaió as Casanova　192
7.7　Colour film still from *Història de la meva mort* showing Vicenç Altaió as Casanova　194
7.8　Black-and-white screenshot from *Història de la meva mort* showing Eliseu Huertas as Dracula　195
9.1　Black-and-white screenshot showing Elisa's school from the outside　238
9.2　Black-and-white screenshot showing the indoor puppet theatre　239
9.3　Black and white screenshot showing Elisa travelling on the train with her two siblings　239
9.4　Black-and-white screenshot showing the children visiting the museum of automata　242
9.5　Black-and-white screenshot showing Elisa's siblings looking at a miniature Ferris wheel　242

viii   Illustrations

9.6   Black-and-white screenshot showing a cafe from the outside with the family seen through large glass panes   244
9.7   Black-and-white close-up of Elisa's brother attempting to fix the iron ring that attaches the swing's chain to the frame   245
9.8   Colour screenshot showing a cafe from the outside with an adult Elisa sitting opposite her father   246
9.9   Colour screenshot of Elisa's face while holding a cup of coffee   250
9.10 Colour close-up of Elisa's lower front neck area   250
9.11 Colour close-up of Elisa's bare feet as she walks over the shards of a broken mirror   251
9.12 Colour underwater image, featuring bright oxygen bubbles and a human figure diving   252

Acknowledgments

To Mark Thompson, our unrelenting editor, Barbara Porter, Charles Stuart, and the team at University of Toronto Press for their help and support. To Jaume Martí-Olivella and to the contributors to this volume. Special thanks to Helena Gomà and Pere Portabella for their assistance. To all my friends and colleagues – they know who they are, and I thank them for always being there. And to three very special people: Roberta Johnson, for believing in me more than I ever did; Rick Carpenter, for being the best life partner anyone could have; and *la meva mare*, for everything and then some.

Anton Pujol

To Belen and Manel, for bringing so much joy to my life. To Anton Pujol, the co-editor of this volume, for his unflinching belief in the project. To the Center for the Humanities of the University of New Hampshire, for the Senior Faculty Fellowship that made possible the initial research for this volume.

Jaume Martí-Olivella

CATALAN CINEMA

Introduction

ANTON PUJOL AND JAUME MARTÍ-OLIVELLA

Catalan Cinema: The Barcelona School and the New Avant-Garde is a collection of essays that bridges two cinematic groups: the Barcelona Film School (Escola de Barcelona, EdB from now on) in the late sixties and early seventies and contemporary Catalan cinema. The different authors in the volume articulate similarities and differences as well as highlight points of connection through their choice and analysis of various film-makers from each group. The cinematic achievements of the two groups share aesthetic and political premises that are the basis for this volume. The goal of this project is to establish a critical territory where the two historical times and their cinematic expressions are considered together. In so doing, we propose to merge two concepts employed by Steven Marsh, one of the contributors to this volume, in his 2020 description of Spain's alternative cinema. Marsh suggests "a spectral historiography" in order "to map a genealogy" of Spain's experimental film.[1] We think our volume could also be viewed as "a spectral genealogy," as a way of defining those (in)visible traditions within Catalan cinema that always happen at the margins of any canonical national tradition. And yet, unlike Marsh's study, our volume is clearly anchored in a national history. Indeed, our critical goal is not only to establish a possible common genealogy but also to articulate and interrogate two parallel epochal crises in need of theoretical and political interpretation. Needless to say, that notion of (in)visibility also points towards the fact of the scarcity of critical attention

---

1 See pages 3 and 6 in Steven Marsh's 2020 volume *Spanish Cinema Against Itself: Cosmopolitanism, Experimentation, Militancy*. In fact, the three elements of Marsh's subtitle are central to most of the films studied in this book.

paid to Catalan cinema in general within the American academia. In that sense, this volume appears as a pioneering effort to address such a critical gap.

Despite a very promising beginning, Catalan cinema became almost extinct after the Spanish Civil War (1936–9), and the subsequent repression of Catalan culture carried out by Franco's dictatorship obliterated most of Catalan culture, particularly cinema. The sixties brought about a partial regime opening – politically known as "la apertura" – that offered the possibility of an alternative cinematic product. In Madrid, that alternative consolidated in what was to be known as "el nuevo cine Español" (New Spanish Cinema) that was loosely based on the Italian neorealist cinematic boom of the previous decade. The break from the folklore-infused, extremely conservative Franco fare in the film sector of Madrid in the early sixties was made possible by three events that took place in the earlier decade: the support from the Instituto de Investigaciones y Experiencias Cinematográficas, or IIEC; the arrival of José María Escudero to the Dirección General de Cinematografía; and the conference titled Conversaciones de Salamanca in May 1955, organized by Basilio Martín Patino, where he clearly articulated the need for a new Spanish cinema. In his famous speech during the same Salamanca conference, Juan Antonio Bardem declared that "el cine español es: políticamente ineficaz, socialmente falso, intelectualmente ínfimo, estéticamente nulo e industrialmente raquítico" ("Spanish cinema is politically inefficient, socially false, intellectually paltry, aesthetically inept andindustrially stunted"; Bentley 140). Among the participants' demands were "the codification of censorship criteria" (a problem that did not get resolved until two decades later) and a need to improve "protection quotas, distribution of films and the establishment of a special category for films of particular artistic merit" (Higginbotham 28). Although the conversations did not yield any tangible results, they did start a dialogue and crack open a door to envision new projects. The best exponents of this cinematic trend are the early works of Miguel Picazo (1927–2016), Carlos Saura (1932–2023), Francisco Regueiro (b. 1934), Manuel Summers (1935–93), and Mario Camus (1935–2021) around the early sixties that continued in the footsteps of José Antonio Nieves Conde (1916–2006), Juan Antonio Bardem (1922–2002) and Luis García Berlanga (1921–2010). These young film-makers were politically critical of the Franco regime, were socially aware of class distinctions, and openly criticized the powers that prevailed in Spain at that time, mostly the aristocracy and the Catholic Church.

Introduction 5

In Barcelona, a decade later, a similar impulse led by Joaquim Jordà to break with the cinematic status quo took a rather different form, more in tune with British pop art and Free Cinema while clearly sharing some of the tenets from the French Nouvelle Vague. The equivalent of the Salamanca conference was held in Sitges during October 1967. According to Higginbotham:

> The Sitges Conference was a product of the extraordinary energy of the Barcelona Film School. Jordà had announced at the Pesaro (Italy) Film Festival that "today it is not possible to speak freely of reality in Spain, so we're trying to describe its imaginary life." That he spoke in French underlined the strong sense of nationalism felt by the Barcelona film-makers and their efforts to distinguish themselves as separate and distinct from Madrid and the New Spanish Cinema. The Sitges manifesto denounced any effort to make films within the established industry, with or without state subsidy as collaboration with a corrupt system. (66)

Jordà's manifesto was a template for the goals of the EdB that he published later. His objectives for the School encompassed both the economics and the artistic side of cinema. They included self-financing and co-operative system of production, teamwork, formal preoccupation referring to the field of the structure of the image and the structure of the narrative, experimental and avant-gardist in character, subjectivity, characters, and situations different from those of the cinema of Madrid, and the use of non-professional actors among others (MacKenzie 156). At the outset, apart from the film-makers, there were also film critics and historians involved with the EdB, including Román Gubern, and, according to Alberto Mira, it was the director of photography Néstor Almendros who "had just started his collaborations with Eric Rohmer and who, in a historical 1965 visit brought to Barcelona the fresh influence of the nouvelle vague" (116).

Quickly shut down by the Spanish Guardia Civil (Civil Guard), the Sitges meeting clearly set out the film-makers' avant-garde position vis-à-vis the Francoist establishment. It also structured a radically different aesthetic and industry credo than the New Spanish Cinema had launched a decade earlier. Marvin D'Lugo summarizes the ideological break with Madrid:

> At its core, these "positions" voiced by members of the Barcelona School represented a critique of everything dominant Spanish cinema stood for. The essence of that critique was the ideological cleavage between cosmopolitan, universalist culture in Barcelona, strongly identified with the

intellectual and artistic currents of the rest of Europe, and the Francoist Castilianism of Spanish culture and film which was, in their eyes, provincial and anachronistic. (133)

Although the EdB is invariably part of the perennial Madrid-Barcelona ideological and cultural dichotomy, the group was never Catalan-centred. While some of the films were in Catalan, shot in Barcelona, or dealt with Catalan-speaking artists, the film-makers usually avoided local politics (except in the case of Pere Portabella's political films). Instead, the backlash in both Catalan and Spanish circles against the EdB stemmed from the group's social status as rich young artists, most of whom were offspring of the very conservative Catalan bourgeoisie. Ángel Llorente, writing of the EdB, remarks:

> Se sumergió así en un sueño creado por la comodidad y el snobismo, con el que se enterraron en una nueva y brillante torre de marfil, tan inútil y antisocial en el fondo como la de nuestro intelectualismo tradicional.
>
> (They submerged themselves in a dream made possible by privilege and snobbism in which they buried themselves in a new and shining ivory tower, albeit as useless and antidemocratic as [Spanish] conservative intellectuals.) (Riambau and Torreiro 190)[2]

Joan Ramon Resina goes a step further and writes that

> Even in Barcelona, this adventure [EdB] achieved little less than private repercussion. Aesthetically the films of the School strived to be cosmopolitan, but did not even manage to become local, except in the narrowest sense: a neighbourhood affair in the upper-class districts of Sarrià and Sant Gervasi. (3)

There is also the issue that the EdB never did fully coalesce as a true group, let alone as an organization. As José María Nunes wrote about the School:

> Y nunca se crearon acuerdos, normas ni obligaciones mutuas, no hubo ni una sola convocatoria de reunión; hablábamos cuando nos encontrábamos como antes de que inventáramos la Escuela, de lo que pensábamos hacer, de las ideas que tenías, de cómo unos podrían colaborar con el otro, como cualquier grupo de amigos con entusiasmo por lo que les hace sentirse compañeros.

---

2 Unless otherwise specified, all translations are the authors'.

(There were never agreements, norms, mutual obligations, not even a meeting announcement. We would talk when we would meet, as we used to do before we invented the School. We would talk about what we were about to do, about our ideas, about collaborating with each other as any group of close friends do, making them feel as colleagues.)

Each of the film-makers developed their own personal trajectory. The close similarities in their films was due mainly to their need to innovate, to create a new cinematic language, and to follow their own impulses.

Esteve Riambau and Casimiro Torreiro, in their seminal *La Escuela de Barcelona: El cine de la "gauche divine,"* criticize the neglect that the "Escola de Barcelona" has suffered throughout Spain at all levels, from the cultural leaders to the critics: "No anda el cine español, y mucho menos el catalán, tan sobrado de logros auténticos como para permitirse el lujo de menospreciar la memoria de este movimiento inclasificable e irrepetible" ("Spanish, and let alone Catalan, cinema, have not been successful enough as to afford to ignore the memory of such an unclassifiable and unique movement"; 30). Whether right or wrong in their assessment, the films produced by this group are usually ignored by both audiences and scholars. These movies are very difficult to find since they have been rarely commemorated in any festival nor has there been a DVD release of the most important films, except for those of Pere Portabella. One important exception, as noted by Jaume Martí-Olivella (2011), was the "Film in Catalunya. 1906–2006" series held at the Lincoln Center in New York in 2007, which included a tribute to the Barcelona School. The series presented a selection of twenty-five films that spanned Catalonia's entire modern cinematic output. Perhaps the main reason behind this (in)visibility should be found in the fact that Catalonia's official culture had mostly disregarded cinema in its attempt to create a national narrative, a fact that will be considered in the first chapter of our volume. Other reasons for lack of engagement with audiences are varied: the difficulty for the regular cinemagoer to connect with the films; the disparity among the films of the group; or the film-makers' own playful disregard for developing engaging narratives. The lack of connection with audiences is, according to D'Lugo, the key reason for the historical neglect. He writes that "the Barcelona School seemed disengaged from its potential audiences by virtue of its strong commitment to a reconceptualization of the visual aesthetics of cinema" (138–9). He then enumerates the main influences of the group:

[They] embraced a more cosmopolitan Europeanism whose modernity was evident as much in the settings and characters they depicted as in the thematic foci, inspired by the recent works of Antonioni, Godard, and Resnais. One particular feature of the modernity the group embraced was the emulation of a glossy, fashion magazine style and chic television advertising techniques. (138)

The modernist connection is fully explored by Jean-Paul Aubert in *Seremos Mallarmé. La Escuela de Barcelona: Una apuesta modernista*, published in 2016. The title references Joaquim Jordà's slogan from 1967 when he proclaimed that "Si no nos dejan ser Victor Hugo, seremos Mallarmé" ("If they do not allow us to be Victor Hugo, we will be Mallarmé"). The French poet Stéphane Mallarmé (1842–98), whose work anticipates modernism, fits perfectly with the aesthetic goals of the EdB since, as Alex Ross writes about the French poet, the "activity of avant-garde artists often resembled rival expeditions into uncharted polar regions. The goal was to discover novel spheres of expression: the unspoken word, the unpainted image, the unheard sound." Aubert establishes a similar claim when he concludes that the EdB yearns for "an artistic proposal that can yield new perspectives" (231), and Santos Zunzunegui, in "Extraterritorial Portabella," draws a conclusion about the film-maker that could be easily applied to all the members involved with the School. He writes that Portabella's goal is to explore "the limits of the expressible" and the artist always "questions the commonplace habits that guarantee an orderly access to meaning." The common thread around the films produced in the EdB sphere is the search for a new way to express their reality and to devise new aesthetic paths regardless of what their ultimate objective might be. Whether narratively, aesthetically, or politically, the directors want to shatter whatever expectations the spectator might have.

Another distinctive characteristic was the School's attempt to move away from the notion of transparency, defined by André Bazin as the basic trademark of classic narrative cinema. Instead, the cinema produced by the School's major players such as Joaquim Jordà (1935–2006), Pere Portabella (b. 1929), Jordi Grau (1930–2018), Jacinto Esteva (1936–85), José María Nunes (1930–2010), and Vicente Aranda (1926–2015) foregrounded the cinematic apparatus in a way that made the viewer conscious of its performative nature. Thus, many of their films had a very loose script and avoided traditional studio locations. A fundamental, and unmistakable, aspect of the cinema of the Barcelona School is its aesthetics. Most of the films give pre-eminence to the image and its preponderance over the scripted text, as can be seen in the early films of the group: Vicente Aranda's *Fata Morgana* (*Left-Handed Fate*, 1965), Jacinto Esteva Grewe and Joaquim Jordà's *Dante no es únicamente severo*

(*Dante Is Not Only Harsh*, 1967), Gonzalo Suárez's *Ditirambo* (1967), Carles Durán's *Cada vez que...* (*Every Time That...*, 1968), Pere Portabella's *Nocturno 29* (1968). Pere Portabella was adamant about defining the need for minimalism in cinema, as it was already made clear in other visual arts:

> Sin tener una imagen previa al rodaje, es inútil tratar de extraerla de la realidad. En la realidad siempre existen todas las posibilidades. Es necesario vaciarla de sus contenidos habituales y darle una nueva significación; es la única manera de salvarse del descriptivismo, que es uno de los peores males del cine español.
>
> (Without having an image previous to the shooting of the film, it is useless to try and rescue it from reality. Reality contains all the possibilities. It is necessary to empty it from its habitual content and give it a new significance, that is the only way to escape from being descriptive, which is one of the worst problems of Spanish cinema.) (Riambau and Torreiro 244)

Portabella's radical non-narrative position might explain his aesthetic conflict with other school practitioners who, like Joaquim Jordà, were still inclined to have a scripted textual basis in their films.

Another defining characteristic was the avoidance of any national film stars. Again, following in the footprints of the Nouvelle Vague, many of the lead actors and actresses of their films were foreign names who had rarely been seen on national screens. And they were mostly treated as media figures or as publicity models rather than flesh-and-blood characters. All in all, the Barcelona School emerged as a complex and cosmopolitan movement that brought back some of the principles of the pre-war avant-garde and merged them with the most important aspects of the European new cinemas of the time. It distanced itself clearly from the neorealist and descriptive Spanish new cinema of the late fifties and early sixties and also from the few commercial films produced by a highly debilitated Catalan cinema industry. Unfortunately, as usually happens with most avant-garde artistic undertakings, it also distanced itself from reaching a large audience. And yet, its historical importance and its enormous influence on the current Catalan cinematic avant-garde clearly merits a critical analysis that has been rather lacking so far.

Some notorious exceptions to this critical void are the volumes of Riambau and Torreiro, and Aubert, mentioned above. There is also "The Barcelona School," a special issue published by *Hispanic Review*. In her editorial preface, "The Invisible Tradition: Avant-Garde Catalan

Cinema under Late Francoism," Sara Nadal-Melsió, who also contributes to our volume, writes:

> "Political cinema is about the absence of the people." This paraphrase of Gilles Deleuze could serve as an epigraph to the present volume. Avant-Garde Catalan cinema thematizes not just the lack of visibility of a people but, more significantly, makes of such an absence and silence a powerful cinematic trope with which to counteract the political vacuum created by Late Francoism. (1)

The historical absence and silence suffered by Catalan culture under Franco is thus thematized in the many absences portrayed by a series of films which constitute "an invisible tradition" that nevertheless has shaped the current blossoming of a new Catalan cinema whose minimalist, polyglossic, and post-national idiom cannot be understood without a serious analysis of its indebtedness to the Barcelona School and all its ramifications. Deleuze is also the central focus of David Vilaseca's *Deleuze no es únicamente severo: Time and Memory in the Films of the Escola de Barcelona*. Vilaseca uses Deleuze's books on Cinema and argues that the films of the EdB

> cannot be understood unless we consider them in relation to the aesthetic and philosophical framework which Deleuze defines as characteristic of the new European cinemas of the post-war period: a framework which does away with the sensory-motor schema which had dominated Hollywood film, aiming at a radical undermining of traditional subjective and cinematic practices by, among other means, its revolutionary representation of memory and time. (135–6)

Vilaseca's and Nadal-Melsió's approach offers an ideal transition to move to the contemporary Catalan film-makers because they emphasize a common thread between the film-makers of the EdB and their contemporary counterparts: a disregard for the sensory-motor schema in favour of narratives that question and challenge more than disclose.

The works on cinema by Deleuze (*Cinema 1* and *Cinema 2*) and his work, along with Guattari, on minor and/or minoritarian art loom large when analysing the works by the Catalan film-makers in this volume. Several cinema scholars dealing with contemporary film-makers have used Deleuze to articulate the problems the films present. For example, Bingham uses Deleuze's cinema theories to analyse *Honor de cavalleria* (*Honour of the Knights*, 2006) and show how Serra's film "is a text scarred by lack, by absences" (44). Lee Carruthers and Teresa Vilarós also use Deleuze to elucidate Serra's films, as do Megan Saltzman and Javier Entrambasaguas and Jacques Terrassa to frame Guerín's works. Lourdes Monterrubio and Manuel Broullón Lozano also lean on the French philosopher for Lacuesta, and Pujol for Marc Recha, and Rubén Hernández for Portabella, among many others.

The presence of Deleuze's philosophy in scholarship researching the members of the EdB and the younger Catalan generation is far from coincidental, and we need to revisit two important areas for this volume. First, Deleuze and Guattari's concept of the minor or minoritarian that they developed in *Kafka: Toward a Minor Literature* relates to any artistic expression that appears opposite to hegemonic discourses, and it invariably affects Catalan cinema. The minoritarian framework developed by Deleuze and Guattari is not about numerical minorities. Instead, they characterize minor arts as involving the deterritorialization of language, the connection of the individual to a political immediacy, and the collective assemblage of enunciation (*Kafka* 18). Minor or minoritarian is, or it is perceived as, a counter discourse to the constant and homogeneous system. In our case, the Catalan film-makers and the avant-garde works that they are producing appear opposite to the Spanish language and the Spanish state (and all it represents in terms of socio-economic policies) and to more commercial or accepted filmic practices. A minor art, or any other enunciative expression, is immediately connected with politics. "Each individual intrigue" (17) inevitably echoes a political cause embedded in an asymmetric relationship with a majority, and the political tension is always present. By using the oeuvre of Kafka, a Prague Jew who wrote in German, Deleuze and Guattari "connect the political structures of minorities to the formal experimentations typical of the modernist avant-garde" (Bogue 168). The minor/minoritarian position that the Catalan film-makers inhabit is due to not wanting to follow the major line of expression (neither politically nor artistically). Instead, they strive to create their own "expression machine" (Deleuze and Guattari, *Kafka* 28). Their films "break forms, encourage ruptures and new sproutings" (28) because in order for them to exist they have to draw their own territory out of a map that does not yet exist.

The break from old systems that the Catalan film-makers experiment with is parallel to the disruption that Deleuze used to separate his two books on cinema: the change from the Movement-Image to the Time-Image. Amy Herzog explains Deleuze's transition from movement to time:

> The emphasis shifts from the logical progression of images to the experience of the image-in-itself. What we find here are pure optical and sound

situations (opsigns and sonsigns), unfettered by narrative progression, and empty, disconnected any-space-whatevers. This move from "acting" to "perceiving" carries over to the characters in the film, who cease to be "agents" and become, instead, "seers."

Most of the EdB films and the contemporary film-makers that are studied here follow very similar characteristics to the ones explained above. Their films rely heavily on optical and sound situations that undermine classical narratives where characters just experience their environment but fail to act. Not surprisingly, the films analysed in this volume are rarely shown in theatres or on television. Rather, they can be seen in museums, as part of exhibits, or in very specialized film retrospectives simply because they require a different kind of spectatorship. The audience is asked to fill in the blanks and to try (and often fail) to disambiguate the narratives while facing the many other challenges that the directors from the EdB and the younger generation pose.

Beyond that pervasive Deleuzian theoretical framework, we should add the importance of Jacques Rancière's work, especially his post-Brechtian conflation of theatricality and politics and his essential notion of dissensus as a way of conceptualizing the emerging dissenting voices of the most unheard and unrepresented parts of the body politic. Indeed, Rancière's work becomes another critical paradigm that looms large in chapters 4 and 6 of this volume. Another influential critical voice is that of Michel Foucault, whose fundamental critique of Western disciplinary institutions together with his biopolitical approach can be heard throughout this book. The spectral deconstructive criticism developed by Jacques Derrida will be the essential theoretical framework that holds together the parallel reading of Pere Portabella and Albert Serra in chapter 7. Chapter 8 will rely on the paradoxical nature of the symbolic function, as described by Slavoj Žižek, to uncover José Luis Guerín's nostalgic cinematic output, while chapters 9 and 12 will both reference the new phenomenological approach to visual culture developed by theorists such as Vivian Sobchack, Laura U. Marks, Thomas Elsaesser, and Malte Hagener. Finally, the anthropological work on primitivism carried out by Claude Lévi-Strauss will also be a central framework in the elucidation of Isaki Lacuesta's cinema in chapter 12 of our volume.

The main focus of this book will be the cinema produced by several Catalan directors who have already achieved national and international recognition and who, in many cases, have expressed their direct relationship with some of the members of the "invisible tradition" that coalesced around the Barcelona School. The "invisible tradition" is also articulated in the film journal *Nosferatu*, when Joaquim Jordà was asked why the new batch of Catalan directors is still following the avant-garde tendency that Jordà and the EdB had initiated over fifty years ago. The interviewers wonder if it is due to their low budgets ("cine pobre") or if there is also something else. He answers:

> Esta tradición arranca en los años veinte y es común a la producción artística catalana, con J.V. Foix, Salvat-Papasseit. Pero es una tradición tan sorprendente y tan libre como podía serlo en Madrid en aquellos mismos años. Yo no creo que sea una cuestión privativa.
>
> (The [avant-garde] tradition starts in the twenties, with the works of J.V. Foix and Salvat-Papasseit and it has since been an intrinsic part of any Catalan artistic production. But it is a surprising and free tradition that it could have also taken place in Madrid around the same time. I do not think it is a budgetary issue.) (Riambau, Salvadó Corretger, and Torreiro 57)

Jordà also mentions that, as a professor of film at the Pompeu Fabra University in Barcelona, he developed friendships with Marc Recha and Isaki Lacuesta, who were also his students, and he was well acquainted with most younger film-makers. Thus, Jordà's role as a mentor for the younger generations cannot be underestimated – it is another thread in the invisible tradition that joins the two groups. Roman Gubern, a distinguished cinema scholar, recently stated that the new generation of Catalan film-makers are a second chapter of the Barcelona Film School. He added that, "Son una constelación, estrellas independientes pero que se ven como conjunto" ("They are like a constellation, independent stars that are seen as a group"; Elola). Regardless of the reasons or the origins, the avant-garde attitude that the EdB presented, whether politically or aesthetically motivated or both, appears inexorably in the contemporary Catalan cinema that the present volume explores.

The relationship between the EdB and contemporary film-makers that our volume explores focuses on works by Jordi Cadena (b. 1947), Judith Colell (b. 1958), José Luis Guerín (b. 1960), Marc Recha (b. 1970), Jaime Rosales (b. 1970), Isaki Lacuesta (b. 1975), and Albert Serra (b. 1975) as well as the late works of Joaquim Jordà and Pere Portabella. Thus, we have organized the contributions to this volume as a genealogical map that offers a reading through the two historical times and their possible connections. Unfortunately, there is only one woman film-maker in our list since, until very recently, Catalan cinema was dominated almost exclusively by male directors.

The five parts of our study suggest a lineage that is both critically visible and yet historically (in)visible in the sense of any traditional historiography. Part 1, "The Mavericks and the Barcelona School," offers a necessary analysis of one of the previously mentioned invisibilities within Catalan cinema: the institutional one. Indeed, the lack of official support for local cinematic production in the years prior to the Barcelona Olympic Games of 1992 contributed largely to the obscurity of a cultural activity deemed almost irrelevant in the national building project. And yet, these very years saw the emergence of a group of maverick directors, with more or less clear connections with the Barcelona School, who produced a number of remarkable films that managed to set the foundations for the current avant-garde revival. Part 2, "The Jordà Legacy," explores the cinematic output of one of the key figures in bridging the two historical times: Joaquim Jordà. Indeed, Jordà's fundamental role as one of the main theorists and practitioners within the Edb is by now quite well documented, and our volume elucidates the complexity of his transitional years and his militant cinema, and the enormous impact that his most recent work has had on the new auteurist generation of Catalan film-makers explored in this book. Part 3, "The Portabella Nexus," focuses on the second most important linking element between the two avant-gardes considered here, namely, the persistence of Pere Portabella's cinematic vision and his uninterrupted reclaiming of a radical narrativity in front of any commercial concession. Portabella's political reading of the two historical transitions and his direct impact on some of the most iconoclastic new Catalan directors, such as Albert Serra, is explored in this section. Part 4, "The New (Post) Avant-Garde," analyses the work of Jordi Cadena and Judith Colell, José Luis Guerín and Marc Recha, who are among the most salient figures within the current generation of Catalan film-makers whose works are clearly indebted to the spirit of the Edb. Finally, part 5, "Minimalism and Beyond," explores the innovative and multimedia cinematic production of Jaime Rosales and Isaki Lacuesta, two of the most prolific hybrid stars in that new constellation described by Roman Gubern.

Of the many connections described between the two historical groups, we could emphasize the "auteuristic" designation which invariably their films receive. Thus, Santos Zunzunegui (2012), writing about Portabella, argues that his cinema "strategically articulates a complex notion of 'authorship' through its double relationship: between film and other artistic practices, and between film and politics," it is "always linked to the exploration of avant-garde expressive forms" and "eccentric to the cinema of his time." We can easily extrapolate Zunzunegui's ideas about Portabella and apply them to the younger film-makers analysed in this volume. Whether intentional or not, and whether we want to call it "auteuristic," "art cinema," or "avant-garde," the young film-makers create films that are very much a particular way of interpreting their world that is reminiscent of the EdB. And yet, some contributors to this volume take exception with the use of the term "avant-garde" because of its very specific historical connotations or try to connect this new cinema to yet another hidden tradition, that of Catalonia's cinematic amateurs. Most critics, both within and without this volume, tend to reinforce the political and cultural link between the EdB and the current production. In his analysis of Albert Serra's *Honor de Cavalleria* (*Honour of the Knights*, 2006), for instance, Adam Bingham writes that the film explicitly references "a number of pre-eminent directors from the first wave of European art cinema" (38), the same directors that strongly influenced the directors of the EdB: Antonioni, Bresson, Dreyer, or Godard to note the most significant names. Later on, Bingham summarizes the director's style: "Serra rejects the devices of continuity editing and other stylistic norms as rigorously as he eschews any dramatic import in the narrative: no POV shots or other subjective identification techniques, no analytical decoupage, a Bressonian "automatism" of 'model' and performance and only one instance of non-diegetic music" (42).

Matt Zoller Seitz, in his *New York Times* review of Serra's film, simply wrote that the film "is a virtual definition of the phrase 'acquired taste.'" The same characteristics that Bingham enumerates can easily be found in most of the films of the EdB and the younger film-makers, such as Recha, Lacuesta, or even in those of Portabella himself. Throughout their dramatic films, both groups strive to depict scenarios that confound and frustrate the audience. In his seminal article on Pere Portabella, Steven Marsh writes that "the director's style, both within individual films and in his overall career, is marked by discontinuity. The films themselves are jagged, fractal, collages of apparently disconnected sequences, complete with jarring, atonal, and often incongruous soundtracks" (553–4). He goes on: "these are films distinguished by their gasps, by the yawning spaces to be filled in, by the dots to be joined" (554). And Portabella still remains faithful to his earlier style. Jordan and Morgan-Tamosunas, while assessing the director's *Pont de Varsòvia* (*Warsaw's Bridge*, 1989) write that, "Reminiscent of Godard and reflecting the style and context of the vanguard films of the old Escuela, this dense, complex, unfriendly feature confirmed that Portabella's film style had not evolved significantly since the 1970s" (178). Although damning with faint praise, it is an accurate description of both the films of the EdB and those of the new generation of film-makers discussed in this volume. The style of the films falls into an avant-garde, auteuristic, or artistic cinema. The directors rely on self-consciousness and ambiguity, while employing techniques that disturb the spectators' usual mode of watching a film. David Bordwell, in *Narration in the Fiction Film*, devotes one chapter to the kind of film-making we are discussing in this volume. In "Art-Cinema Narration," Bordwell analyses films by Fellini, Antonioni, Bergman, Rohmer, and others in an attempt to categorize what these directors are trying to accomplish. Bordwell refers to them as "Art" because they stand opposite the mainstream cinema of the time, they do not intend to be commercial, and the old narrative prerogatives are ignored. According to Bordwell, art cinema is "concerned less with action than reaction, the art cinema presents psychological effects in search of their causes" (208). In order to achieve their usual "marked self-consciousness" (209), the directors flaunt "Stylistic devices that gain prominence with respect to classical norms – an unusual angle, a stressed bit of cutting, a striking camera movement, an unrealistic shift in lighting or setting, a disjunction on the sound track, or any other breakdown of objective realism which is not motivated as subjectivity – can be taken as the narration's commentary" (209). Film-makers from both the EdB and the current generation certainly use a similar toolbox to create their films. This is evidenced in what appears to be a constant searching for the avant-gardist frame of mind, to innovate, to create something different, and to look for new ways to narrate. Although the younger generation do not claim the EdB as an influence or model to follow, their films do follow a similar pattern when it comes to the discordant elements, the non-narrative plots, the ellipsis, the silences, the ambiguity, and the constant need for the audience to accept their ambivalent choices.

As it is probably clear by now, the films analysed in this volume are challenging and they require a different kind of spectatorship. In an article about Lacuesta that could easily summarize the films of the EdB and the contemporary avant-garde films discussed here, Eulalia Iglesias reminds us that "La filmografía de Isaki Lacuesta nos resitúa en esta voluntat de considerar el cine como un arte cuyos potenciales no merecen ser encorsetados por ningún apriorismo estético o industrial" ("Isaki Lacuesta's filmography compels us to reconsider cinema as art. Its potential does not deserve to be restrained by any aesthetic or commercial apriorism"; 45). The following chapters discuss films whose aim is their own, always singularly expressed. Their respective directors rewrite cinema's rules by filming narratives as they see fit, regardless of the consequences, be they an empty cinema or the critics' silence. We have discussed several threads around the invisible tradition that unites the two generations of film-makers. And although we cannot pinpoint exactly where their intentions originate, their refusal to adapt to any sort of conventions and determination to create a cinema that it is truly their own emerges as the sturdiest unifying thread.

This volume is divided into five parts, which present an overview of the most innovative cinema produced in Catalonia since the celebration of the Olympic Games in Barcelona in 1992. It is thus fitting that the first part, "The Mavericks and the Barcelona School," be devoted to the cinema of a group of maverick directors who took the torch of the Barcelona School avant-garde at a time when Catalan cinema was in a rather precarious cultural position. Part 1 thus includes Àngel Quintana's chapter 1, "Future Seeds: Some Considerations on the Cinema around Barcelona 92," which offers a thorough overview of the developing and difficult years of Catalan cinema once the experimentation of the Barcelona School was a thing of the past and the scarce attempts at a commercial cinema did not find much success in the box office. In his essay, Quintana analyses the cultural and historical context surrounding the Barcelona 1992 Olympic Games while underlining the fact that cinema production had not been considered an important part in the revamping of the Catalan cultural landscape. And yet, as Quintana argues, it will be the effort of a group of maverick directors, working from the margins, together with the recovery of essential figures from the Barcelona School, such as Joaquim Jordà and Pere Portabella, that planted the seed for a new cinematic language that reconnected with the avant-garde trends of the past and formulated new versions of the essay cinema while expanding the traditional boundaries between the documentary and the narrative genres. This new cinematic impulse consolidated itself with the creation of academic programs at the end of the nineties. The arrival of Agustí Villaronga's iconoclastic imaginary, of Marc Recha's transgressive minimalism, and of José Luis Guerín's spectral poetics, among others, completely transformed the face of a Catalan cinema that was beginning to find its place in the international film festival circuit. The impact of these maverick directors became institutionalized, as it were, with the incorporation of Joaquim Jordà, José Luis Guerín, and even Marc Recha as instructors and mentors in the Master in Creative Documentary program at the Pompeu Fabra University in Barcelona, which was soon to become one of the most productive centres in the history of contemporary Catalan cinema.

The second part of our volume, "The Jordà Legacy," focuses on the fundamental role played by the multifaceted figure of Joaquim Jordà, arguably the most influential film-maker in the development of a more militant and alternative cinematic language in Catalonia. In chapter 2, "The Hunter and the Monkeys: Jacinto Esteva, Joaquim Jordà, and the

Legacy of the Barcelona School," Esteve Riambau, the current director of the Filmoteca de Catalunya, studies the significance of Jordà's 1990 *El encargo del cazador* (*The Hunter's Request*), which constitutes both a homage and a critique of his old friend, Jacinto Esteva, with whom he co-directed *Dante no es únicamente severo* in 1967, one of the early and better-known landmarks of the Barcelona School. In Riambau's own words, the film "is a cross between a funeral eulogy for a friend who has departed, an unrelenting criticism of the most frivolous faction of the Barcelona School, and a preview of what Jordà's final films would be: each one based on up-close views, more or less agreed-to by the people portrayed, of the intimate details of their lives, normally fragile or even marginal" (Riambau and Torreiro 91–2). Still espousing the free spirit of his early years, Jordà was a very different director when Dària Esteva, Jacinto Esteva's daughter, approached him with the unedited materials of the film her father had shot in Africa. As Riambau comments, Jordà's experiences as a translator, screenwriter, and, more importantly, the time as a militant director working close to the Italian Communist Party had distanced him both personally and ideologically not only from Esteva, but also from most of the old members of the Barcelona School. In fact, again in Riambau's words, Jordà used *El encargo del cazador* "to settle the score" (73) with what he considered "the superficiality of the leftist opposition to Franco's regime" (74) and to document his own political disappointment. Ultimately, as Dària Esteva said, the film became "a live autopsy" (76) not only of her deceased father but of an entire movement, that of the Barcelona School. And yet, as Riambau's essay makes clear, the legacy of that school and its brand of transgressive cinema lives fully in a film that signals Jordà's return to the forefront of the most innovative cinema to be produced in Catalonia.

Ignasi Gozalo-Salellas's essay "Jordà's Last Trilogy: Situationist Turn and Subject Transformation," which is chapter 3 of this volume, starts precisely by positing the privileged position achieved by Joaquim Jordà and his cinema among the new generations of Catalan film-makers. In his study, Gozalo-Salellas focuses on the last seven years of Jordà's career while arguing for the existence of what he terms "a situationist trilogy" formed by *Mones com la Becky* (*Monkeys Like Becky*, 1999–2000), *De nens* (*About Children*, 2003), and *Veinte años no es nada* (*Twenty Years Is Nothing*, 2004). According to Gozalo-Salellas, such a trilogy constituted the director's response to a societal divide between "the sphere of spectacularity and simulation" and one of the "situated lives" (81). In front of the market logic of globalization imposed by an institutional Barcelona, Gozalo-Salellas argues, the city offers a movement of micromanagement that relies on what David Harvey, building on the work by Henri Lefebvre, called "the right to the city" (Harvey 2008). In this context, one saw the emergence of a series of artistic practices aimed at disrupting the grand narratives and sensible to the social realities hidden behind them. In Jordà's case, as Gozalo-Salellas has it, it meant a reappearance from the margins with a cinematic gaze cast on building up a Foucaldian critique of some of our central disciplinary institutions. Thus, in *Mones*, Jordà, relying on his own mental illness, offered a scathing vision of our psychiatric order, whereas in *De nens*, he unveiled the limitations of a justice system permeated by media prejudgement, and, in *Veinte años*, he rallied for a historical memory that could undermine the effects of the political silence first imposed by Francoism and then agreed by the different parties during the Spanish Transition. Ultimately, Gozalo-Salellas argues, Jordà's situationist cinema aims at "the construction of a collective conscience that appropriates the audiovisual device as a social tool" (83).

"The Jordà Legacy," the second part of our volume, ends with chapter 4, Steven Marsh's essay "The Militant Cinema of Joaquim Jordà: The Essay Film as Form," which focuses on the films *Numax presenta… (Numax presents…*, 1979) and *Veinte años no es nada* (2004). According to Marsh, the first of these two films constitutes a "performative intervention" (102) that creates a discordant statement at the heart of the Spanish Transition. Against the official narrative of political agreement built on the silence about the past, Jordà's film becomes an enactment, a "re-presentation" of the collective gesture of political rejection carried out by the workers of the Numax factory in Barcelona between 1977 and 1979. Shot in 1979 with the money left from the strike fund, the film documents and performs a strike and an occupation that had already ended but whose effects lingered since the film, as stated by Marsh, "points to a critique of traditional working practices as determining and conditioning life" (102). Both the film's lingering effects and its diegetic open-endedness will be underlined and echoed in the sequel *Veinte años no es nada*, where Jordà reunites many of the protagonists of the *Numax* event more than twenty years later. Considered together, Marsh argues, both films "highlight[] a rupture in the everyday continuum – the norm – marked by representational politics" (102) in order to create "a filmic site of the demos, as a voice of those habitually excluded from the discourse of democracy" (102–3). In doing so, Marsh continues, Jordà manages to reconfigure militant cinema by asserting a double challenge to the cinematic and the political establishments during Francoism and the Spanish Transition. Relying on Foucaldian notions of biopolitics and Toni Negri's autonomism, Jordà's films follow these workers beyond the factory walls while recording their collective critique of the political consensus, in a gesture that seems to anticipate historical events like the Indignados (or 15-M) Movement or the Catalan Independence Process as massive expressions of alternative political and vital desires.

Dissonance, both in its acoustic and political sense, will be at the heart of Sara Nadal-Melsió's essay "Economies of Sound: Labouring Europe in Pere Portabella and Carles Santos," which is chapter 5 and the first piece in "The Portabella Nexus," the third part of this volume. As Nadal-Melsió states, "the fact that European sovereignty is exclusively economic, and that it functions fundamentally by tempering transnational fiscal dissonances, will underline my discussion" (125). In order to ground textually that discussion, Nadal-Melsió revisits the musical concept of the "wolf," which the Baroque tuners used to refer to "the dissonant and resilient sound produced by any attempt to temper and harmonize an instrument" (126). In this sense, the wolf, Nadal-Melsió suggests, "smuggl[es] a figure of dissent" that "travels nested in the apparent harmony of cultural legacy" (126). Armed with such an overarching metaphor, Nadal-Melsió addresses "the political agency of dissonance" (126) in Carles Santos's 2006 restrospective ¡Visca el piano! (*Hooray for the Piano!*) and Pere Portabella's *Die Stille vor Bach* (*The Silence before Bach*, 2007), a film that marked Portabella's return to the experimental and avant-garde roots of his Barcelona School days. Ultimately, Nadal-Melsió contends "that the wounded sovereignty of Catalonia constitutes a vantage point from which to make the 'wolf' audible again, to listen to the incomplete harmonization that lies at the dead centre of Europe" (127).

Appropriately enough, Nadal-Melsió relies on an apparently minor historical anecdote, the fact that Santos and Portabella shared a cell after their arrest in October 1973 as members of the Assemblea de Catalunya, to provide yet another linking metaphor of an aesthetic and political nexus that has united these two artists throughout their long careers. Santos's performance of an entire Bach sonata on an out-of-tune piano within the Modelo jail in Barcelona, moreover, "deployed the disharmony of the 'wolf' to militantly intervene in the biopolitical regime of a Francoist prison, by forcing a listening that fell far outside the signifying references of the space where it resonated" (128). Dissonance and dislocation are also at the heart of Portabella's *Die Stille vor Bach*, a film that starts precisely with a preamble showing a wheeled player piano performing the Goldberg Variations on an empty hall at the Miró Foundation in Barcelona. As Nadal-Melsió aptly puts it, with this prelude, Portabella moves back and forth at the same time by recalling Bach and the early cinema of attractions in "a strategic use of anachronism [...] that serves as a playful model for a dislocation of Europe's cultural capital that the film as a whole proposes" (134). What Portabella's film achieves is to make Europe's historical discontinuities "audible and visible, in an attempt to bring life to a legacy that may still yield some political momentum" (135). This emphasis on sound, movement, or transit is always couched in Portabella's "larger governing assumption that historical conditions must be understood as material conditions" (136). That is why the entire film is punctuated by "the everyday sounds of labour" (136), which constantly disrupt any harmonizing narratives. Ultimately, Portabella's film, as it was the case in Santos's performance, reminds us that "the emancipatory potential of an aesthetic phenomenon is contained in its ability to transport us elsewhere" (136). In the case of *Die Stille vor Bach*, Nadal-Melsió concludes, "it serves as the meeting place for a political community that is still to come, for an absent Europe" (136–7).

This Europe that is yet to come will also occupy the central metaphorical place in Portabella's film, *Informe general II: El nuevo rapto de Europa* (*General Report II: The New Abduction of Europe*, 2016), the extraordinary sequel to his groundbreaking documentary of the political transition: *Informe general sobre algunas cuestiones de interés para una proyección pública* (*General Report on Issues of Public Screening*, 1976). Indeed, Pere Portabella occupies a privileged position in any study of the possible (dis)continuities between the legacy of the avant-garde and the free-spirited cinematic practice of the Barcelona School and the current upsurge of experimental films in Catalonia. Like Joaquim Jordà, his cinematic career spans the two historical moments while becoming one of the most influential figures in both times. Appropriately, thus, chapter 6 in this volume, Jaume Martí-Olivella's essay "Pere Portabella's Radical Theatricality: A Political Gaze over Two Transitions," focuses on one of Portabella's most important aesthetic (dis)continuities, his capacity to animate or dislocate iconic references in order to create new cultural understandings. As pointed out in Nadal-Melsió's essay, this gesture refers back to the early "cinema of animation." In Portabella's hands, however, it will be the entire "archive" that becomes animated as it is shown in his self-conscious extended panning of Picasso's *Guernica* at the early stages of his *Informe general II*. With his "animation" of that emblematic painting and all the archival references embedded in it – Francoism, the Spanish Civil War, Nazi Germany, Euskadi's identity, and the centrality of bull(fights) in the Spanish cultural imaginary – Portabella aims at the need to reinterpret any work of art and any museum as a "container" of art's transgressive energies. Alongside that continuity, Martí-Olivella also explores the political aspect of Portabella's dissonance, which adopts Jacques Rancière's notion of "dissensus," to chronicle the two parallel popular uprisings in Spain: the 15-M (or Indignados) Movement and the Catalan Independence Process. Both movements are presented by Portabella as an expression of civil society retaking the public space and reclaiming the political institutions that have stalled within a stagnant parliamentary democracy. Portabella's film stages itself inside the Reina Sofía museum in Madrid in order to cover the international symposium entitled "The Abduction of Europe" that was being held there. The film also dislocates that privileged staging by incorporating the political demonstrations that are happening in the square outside the museum itself, and, in so doing, it visualizes the director's rejection of the traditional binary politics based on the public/private divide. Thus, echoing the historical intervention of his first *Informe general*, Portabella "is very conscious that our historical time is defined by the emergence of a new political subject created by dissident popular movements which have already positioned themselves in the public space" (155). Considered together, Portabella's two *Informes* offer an impressive view of the commonality and, at the same time, the enormous distance between those two historical transitions.

Chapter 7 contains Teresa M. Vilarós's "Traversing the Real with the Reel: Infrapolitical History in Pere Portabella's V*ampir.Cuadecuc* and Albert Serra's *Història de la meva mort*," the third and final essay in "The Portabella Nexus" part of our volume. Vilarós's study also spans the two historical moments mentioned above. This time, however, Portabella's aesthetic (dis)continuities and his cinematic legacy will be considered in terms of his direct impact on Albert Serra's very singular brand of experimental film. Both directors, as seen through Vilarós's critical lens, share a peculiar "spectrality" that stems from the very nature of the cinematic medium and expands itself onto the political domain. Thus, when considering Portabella's 1970 *Vampir.Cuadecuc*, Vilarós argues that the film unfolds as a spectral, X-ray-like imaging of a particular time (1970), a place (Catalonia and the Burgos trial) and a certain cinema (vampire-themed cinema). In other words, as Vilarós also suggests, the film relies on a symbolic appropriation of the figure of the vampire as a stand-in for General Franco and Francoism. The absent presence of the dictator will permeate the entire film, as it will be the case in Portabella's 1977 *Informe general*, which, as mentioned in chapter 6, started with Portabella's camera spectral visit to Franco's mausoleum in the Valle de los Caídos. Once again, Portabella resorts to movement/animation in his anachronistic temporal dislocations and his playful superimpositions. A playfulness that Vilarós interprets in the director's own name when she writes:

> It is no wonder that Portabella's last name in Catalan literally and appropriately means a beautiful (-bella) gate (Porta-). The movie opens a door from where we can, on one hand, glimpse and attempt to make sense of the beautiful though darkly humorous quality of vampire cinema, and, on the other hand, take a quick though stark glance at the spooky, non-laughable political reality of Francoism during the Burgos trial. Enacting a series of eerie transpositions, a mirroring between his own name and the surname of both Jesús Franco and the Spanish dictator, General Francisco Franco, Portabella opens the door and unhinges time so that the two "Francos" can consistently traverse time in an extended nebula.
>
> Portabella's movie is a house of mirrors, and one that displays the constant intertwining between real and reel. (178)

Relying on Jacques Lacan's "logic of phantasy," Vilarós's essay then tackles the Portabella imprint in Albert Serra's peculiar adaptation of Giacomo Casanova's memoir *Histoire de ma vie*. With the transposition between life and death in the film's title, Serra's *Història de la meva mort* (*Story of My Death*, 2013) foregrounds the spectral nature of his undertaking. Despite their common use of the Dracula figure, the two films will explore different, perhaps even opposite, time dislocations. In fact, there will be no linear time progression in Serra's movie. Here, as was the case in Portabella's film, the materiality of life and history will be spectrally and infrapolitically inscribed. As Vilarós puts it:

> Serra, similarly to what Pere Portabella did with *Vampir.Cuadecuc*, gives a fantasmatic materiality to two of the most immaterial concepts, death and pleasure. [It] does so by spectrally decoupling the figure of the gayest of lovers, Casanova, to the saddest of all figures, Dracula. That is, through the presentation of Casanova, the ultimate embodiment of living pleasure, not as one figure, but two (always already dead ones): Casanova as himself, and Dracula as Casanova (and vice versa). Both doomed to bear, as Richard Brody once stated, the "quiet weight of world-historical conflict." (190)

Ultimately, Vilarós summarizes, "In forcing the encounter between a creepy-laughing Casanova and a stiff Kantian-like Dracula touched by a whiff of existential anguish, *Història de la meva mort* shines a surprising light onto the fate of modern (and contemporary) history" (194).

"The New (Post) Avant-Garde" and "Minimalism and Beyond," the third and fourth (and last two) sections of our volume, focus on the analysis of a series of Catalan directors who, like Albert Serra, have already achieved national and international recognition and who, in many cases, have expressed their direct relationship with some of the members of the "invisible tradition" that coalesced around the Barcelona School, most especially with Joaquim Jordà and/or Pere Portabella. Chapter 8 brings us to Josep Maria Català Domènech's "Beyond Melancholy: The Post-Avant-Garde Cinema of José Luis Guerín," which is the first essay in the third section of our volume. In it, Català, following T.S. Eliot's reading of Dante's *Divine Comedy*, interrogates the process that takes a man to express an idea through visionary images. Given the current hybridization between technology and subjectivity and given the possibility to recover pre-modern positions opened up by modernity's failure, Català argues, contemporary cinema is poised to find new visionary ways to contemplate reality. The new documentary genre is placed in a privileged position to engage in this new way of seeing. This is the context wherein the cinema of José Luis Guerín must be considered. It is because of this new context, precisely, that Català takes issue with the notion of any direct genealogy between the Barcelona School and its connection with the historical avant-gardes and the current upsurge of experimental cinema in Catalonia. For Català, the current post-avant-garde moment is characterized not by any possible continuity implied by the use of the "post" qualifier but by the radical difference of the two historical moments and, in cinematic terms, by the fact of the different adscription to formalism. Whereas the Barcelona School embraced formalism as its essential component, the formalism of the new directors is the result of their radical subjective transformations. Guerín's cinema, Català writes, cannot belong to the avant-garde because it is too intimate and subtle and because it is not focussed on the future. Instead, it is devoted to contemplate how the past always reappears in the scars of the present, as epitomized in Guerín's highly acclaimed *En construcción* (*Work in Progress*, 2001), a film whose power, according to Català, relies on its capacity to dismantle the modernist narrative of progress. Guerín's cinema emblematizes the paradoxical nature of contemporary documentary cinema, Català suggests, because it is a cinema of the real, because it feeds directly on reality, it paradoxically expresses in a way more relevant than any other medium the process of subjectivation. To further explain that paradoxical nature of Guerín's documentary cinema, Català relies on Slavoj Žižek's statement regarding the symbolic functions as those that produce at the same time a reality loss while becoming the only possible access to reality itself. In Guerín's case, moreover, the predominant emotion of his visionary cinema is that of melancholy, the kind of melancholy that implies a subversion of temporality where past and present get superimposed onto each other as an expression of the inner reconfiguration of the subject. Following Kristeva, Català adds, Guerín's melancholy becomes "a visionary epistemology" (224). The two parallel films *Unas fotos en la ciudad de Sylvia* (*Some Pictures in Sylvia's City*, 2007) and *En la ciudad de Sylvia* (*In Sylvia's City*, 2007) perfectly illustrate this visionary melancholy since they capture the caducity of a reality that the gaze cannot retain but as a memory and therefore dies at the very moment of being seen. Ultimately, as Català suggests, death becomes a central vision in Guerín's cinema, which is framed by two suicides, the fictitious one represented in *Los motivos de Berta* (*Berta's Motives*, 1985), the director's first film, and the real one of his neighbour, the musician depicted in *Recuerdos de una mañana* (*Memories of a Morning*, 2011), one of Guerín's last productions. In this sense, *Recuerdos* seems to condense Guerín's cinematic universe, the one that combines and subverts the traditional voyeuristic gaze of the cinematic medium with the visionary capacity of an epiphanic documentarist. And that is why, ultimately, it is this melancholic and visionary gazing that distances the director from the epic forms of the traditional avant-gardes, destined to change the world by means of a frontal attack against its own representation.

Chapter 9 gives us Eva Bru-Dominguez's essay "On the Threshold of the Diegetic World: Optical and Haptic Visuality in *Elisa K*." In it, she offers a complex and rich reading of the real-life couple Colell's and Cadena's cinematic adaptation of Lolita Bosch's short novel *Lolita Kiseljak* (2005), a story of rape and trauma amidst the Catalan bourgeoisie. The dyadic structure of a film shot with four hands and with a stylistic clash clearly sought by the two directors not only calls attention to the cinematic form but also, as displayed in Bru-Dominguez's reading, requires a dual take on the analytical response to it. Thus, building on Vivian Sobchack's and Laura U. Marks's new phenomenological approach to visual culture, Eva Bru suggests that *Elisa K* does indeed fluctuate between the "optic" and the "haptic" modes of visual representation. Historically, Bru argues, *Elisa K* needs to be seen in the current Catalan context: "Its focus on memory echoes the widespread concern with historical and cultural discontinuities in Catalan cinema […] and the recovery of the collective's fractured and unwritten past" (232). Thus, following the path opened by Joaquim Jordà and other new Catalan documentary directors, *Elisa K* is also a private story of illness and trauma that contains a public statement regarding the country's own mental health and/or memory loss. Moreover, the film's formal self-consciousness arises from its being "in line with the interests of the film-makers of the Barcelona School" (233). Thus, special attention is given to Jordi Cadena's lifelong relationship with visual and conceptual art and to his direct allusion to the Catalan avant-garde with the inclusion of Joan Brossa, the poet, playwright, and visual artist, who was one of the founding members of *Dau al Set* and a frequent collaborator in Pere Portabella's early films, in his most experimental feature film *Es quan dormo que hi veig clar* (*It Is When I Sleep That I See Clearly*, 1988). Besides, as Bru-Dominguez's essay foregrounds, *Elisa K* is rich in references to the early "cinema of attractions," another crucial aesthetic and historical connection that defined the Barcelona School, as we have already indicated. In this context, Bru relies on Giuliana Bruno's notion that cinema "'incarnates [the] ability to "animate"; it is a machine that activates lifelike (e)motion'" (240) to focus on the significant sequence during the film inside the Tibidabo museum of toy automata that figures the violence to come. As the author writes, "The brutality enacted by these mechanical figures anticipates both the sexual abuse that Elisa will be subject to and the visual dynamics that are later to be established" (241). Beyond this Portabella-like use of "animation" and formal self-consciousness, Bru-Dominguez suggests that the recurrent framing through doors, windows, and mirrors displayed in *Elisa K* recall the notion formulated by Elsaesser and Hagener of "a threshold between diegetic realms [that] problematizes the relationship between spectator and screen[; ...] the window-cum-mirror in *Elisa K* is also indicative of 'an arrangement that hides something or someone by dividing a space'" (243). Thus, if the first half of the film is dominated by a detached optic visuality, its second part, shot by Judith Colell, relies heavily on a haptic approach that will bring the viewer into close proximity to Elisa and her mental and body reactions during her traumatic bout when the memory of that early sexual violence surfaced in her consciousness. To close her analysis, Bru-Dominguez moves from the private to the public, from the personal to the collective, by invoking Diana Taylor's performative approach to trauma. Such a passage from the personal to the social is made possible, Bru argues, by the "reversibility in haptic viewing, which entails 'making oneself vulnerable to the image'" (248). This spectatorial engagement requires empathy, mimesis, and, ultimately, affect. At the end, as the author concludes, "As haptic criticism would have it, we might have learned to look with our senses and with our culturally and historically specific bodies. Moreover, through empathy and mimesis, we might even have dug deep into our unconscious and unearthed some unpalatable memories on the way, for *Elisa K* primarily is a film about re-establishing continuities between past and present, and therein lies its relevance in our present-day context, where, urged by the primacy of making space for the enforced gaps in our history, culture, and society, the recovery of lost memory has become a crucial endeavour" (252).

Anton Pujol's "Watching Novels and Reading Films: Deleuzian Affects in Catalan Cinema," is chapter 10 and closes "The New (Post) Avant-Garde" section in our volume. It explores Marc Recha's *El cielo sube* (*Heaven Rises*, 1991), the first feature film of one of the champions of minimalism within the new Catalan experimental film. Recha's film is a cinematic adaptation of Eugeni d'Ors's *Oceanografia del tedi* (*Oceanography of Tedium*, 1916), an unclassifiable fiction described by Pujol as "a fragmented and ambiguous [avant-garde] text [...], constantly forcing readers to adapt to a narrative of 'affects' in the Spinozan sense" (255). Pujol's reading is mapped out as a triple encounter: the actual clash of affects in d'Ors's text, the cinematic encounter between this text and Recha's film, and the clashes and continuities with the Barcelona School. Throughout his essay, Pujol's critical apparatus will draw heavily from Deleuze's and Guattari's concept of affect. Moreover, Pujol emphasizes d'Ors's humour and ambiguity as crucial distancing techniques while recalling critic Jaume Vallcorba's definition of Tedi as "'a playful textual impertinence'" (257). Arguably, it will be this impertinent confrontation with the reader's/viewer's comfort zone that will attract Marc Recha to the project of making a film out of d'Ors's text. Like *Tedi*, Pujol writes, Recha's "*El cielo sube* defies categories. It is a hybrid that recalls such cryptic works of the Barcelona School as Esteva and Jordà's *Dante no es únicamente severo* (*Dante Is Not Only Harsh*, 1967) and Pere Portabella's *No compteu amb els dits* (*Don't Count with Your Fingers*, 1967) and *Nocturno 29* (1968), to name a few (258). Indeed, the film echoes d'Ors's distancing techniques by inserting chapter titles on screen which "force the disoriented spectators to reckon with watching a novel and reading a film" (258). This formal self-consciousness is then reinforced by Recha's inclusion of "a greenish scratch" on the black and white celluloid to make the film "look old and worn" (258). In this way, echoing the gesture of the Barcelona School directors, Recha's film "challenges us to re-evaluate the passive process of watching a movie from its first scratched frame right up to the closing credits" (259). For Pujol, both d'Ors's text and Recha's film may be seen in terms of a kind of "coenaesthesia" that he equates to the notion of affect, central to Spinoza and Deleuze. Moreover, as Pujol recalls, "In Deleuze's reading of Spinoza, a body is constituted, like a work of art, by its capacity to be affected" (261). That is why, he concludes, "Coenaesthesia, short of psychotic distress, is the ideal state since the body is open to receive affects" (261). This open body is akin to the "body without organs," the recurrent notion in the work of Deleuze and Guatari, for whom a body without organs "is not opposed to the organs but to the 'organic organization of the organs'" (264). That is the basis for their valorization of the "lines of flight" that go beyond, that "deterritorialize," any "still signifying" within works of art. And that is why Anton Pujol reads the end of d'Ors's *Tedi* like this:

> At the end of the second part, Author caves in; he swims to the surface. To make matters worse, his hand signs the Cross. [...] The contrary forces, the affects, are stripped off. [...] The third part opens with Author quoting Catholic verses in Spanish to indict himself as an old man. He is perhaps also signalling two discourses (Spanish and Catholic/religious) that have been notorious in Catalonia at certain moments in history for their re-territorializing impulses. (264–5)

Recha's radical minimalism found a perfect vehicle in the cinematic adaptation of d'Ors's text. His *El cielo sube*, according to critic Carlos Heredero, is "'an audiovisual essay more than a narrative film'" (268). For Pujol, moreover, Recha's film is an illustration of the time-image concept formulated by Deleuze, where "'the emphasis shifts from the logical progression of images to the experience of the image-in-itself'" (268). Recha's film, he continues,

> creates in the spectators' experience the affective equivalent of what transpires between Author and his own experience. Author and spectators are motionless subjects experiencing intensive expressive movements. The decentred interval occupied by words in d'Ors's text is now occupied by Recha's hazy shots, fragmentary editing, and the seemingly scratched film. (270)

To conclude, Pujol writes, "in his first long feature film, Recha uses a written text to challenge (deterritorialize) cinema. He creates a new, hybrid narrative that the spectators must piece together, but the irrational cuts and affection-images they see on screen cannot be made coherent" (272). His gesture is a direct echo of the Barcelona School imprint, since, as suggested in Aubert's *Seremos Mallarmé* (2016), Deleuze's central notion of the time-image arose precisely from his close analysis of the French Nouvelle Vague, the movement with the utmost influence on the Catalan directors of the Barcelona School.

Chapter 11, "Formal Disruption, Minutiae, and Absence in the Films of Jaime Rosales" by Agustín Rico-Albero, is the first essay in the last section of our volume entitled "Minimalism and Beyond." In it, Rico-Albero considers the production of Catalan film-maker Jaime Rosales in the context of the economic crisis that started in 2008 and plunged Catalonia and Spain into a period of social, cultural, and political unrest.

Rosales's minimalist aesthetics, in tune with the most relevant cinematic approach within recent Catalan cinema, focuses on the impact of that crisis. Catalan directors "will explore the significance of [...] stylistic emancipation and the rejection of homogeneity in the context of Catalonia's struggle for self-determination" (284). Following the Barcelona School trademark, Rico-Albero adds, "Rosales's films subtly reflect the political and social situation without explicitly being political" (284). Echoing Martí-Olivella's notion that Rosales's cinema captures social "forms of (in)visibility," Rico-Albero zooms into two of Rosales's films: *Las horas del día* (*The Hours of the Day*, 2003) and *Hermosa juventud* (*Beautiful Youth*, 2014). He analyses how they manage "to render invisible subjects visible" (285). Both films, moreover, are set in depressed urban landscapes that directly visualize the economic crisis. In this sense, Rico-Albero writes, "It could be argued that *The Hours of the Day*, as it was released in 2003, anticipated frustration about a lived reality in which society is far from cohesive, stable, or equal as expressed through the weariness and exasperation that saturates the minutiae of the protagonist's daily life, and through the duality of the protagonist's characterization and his acts of violence" (287). Following Pere Portabella, Jaime Rosales's formal choices always call attention to themselves by employing a fragmentary mode of storytelling which always requires the active attention and participation of the spectator in decoding the film's narrative. And, if Portabella's *Vampir.Cuadecuc* (1971) disrupted and dislocated the horror genre, Rosales's *The Hours of the Day* defamiliarizes the psycho-killer genre by presenting the killer's actions in a minimalist matter-of-fact format that renders them more disconcerting and routine. An apparent banality that again echoes another fundamental gesture of the Barcelona School, as Rico-Albero writes: "Using this violent act as an extreme resolution of the monotony of the protagonist's daily routine is reminiscent of some Escola de Barcelona films, like the documentary *Lejos de los árboles* (*Far from the Trees*, 1972), by Jacinto Esteva, which focussed on boredom as a means to challenge the disconnect between tough lived realities and the cheerful sheen of the regime's touristic propaganda" (290). Shot almost a decade after his first film, *Hermosa juventud* is again a portrayal of everyday life, but the brutal effects of the economic crisis are now brought to the film's foreground as we encounter a working-class couple in their twenties struggling to survive in a Madrid suburb during the austerity measures imposed by then ruling Partido Popular. Instead of resorting to violence, the couple will turn to pornography in order to make ends meet. As in his previous films, Rosales will experiment formally by inserting several instances of popular digital communication juxtaposed with a rather conventional narrative format. He suggests that this symbolizes a "'trivialization of human experience' [...] in an environment where what matters is the quantity of images, not what they portray" (292). Unlike the graphic violence displayed in *The Hours of the Day*, *Beautiful Youth* will make visible a more insidious kind of violence, the one that Rosales himself describes as "'the most conspicuous,'" that is, "'the social violence associated with not being able to find a job'" (293), which the director considers a form of structural violence akin to "'social terrorism'" (293). From this perspective, Rico-Albero considers that Rosales's denunciation of the devastating effects of neo-liberalism in Spain may be drawing a parallel with films such as Vicente Aranda's *Fata Morgana* (1966) or Pere Portabella's *Nocturno 29*, where these two film-makers from the Barcelona School were also reflecting on the changes in Catalonia and Spain brought about when neo-liberalist capitalism was initially welcome. And yet, again echoing the Barcelona School's "(a)political principles," Rico-Albero writes, "the director does not explicitly question the current political climate in Spain" (294). Instead, he tries to reflect the fact that "'they were completely detached from politics'" (294), as he learnt by interviewing a lot of unemployed young people while casting his film. And yet, the film is a profound political statement that adds to a very solid cinematic corpus, which, in Rico-Albero's words, "embodies a trend towards keeping alive a cinema that rebels against a dominant capitalist film industry and against an endemic system in a subtle way and with an absence of an explicit reflection on the issues" (295).

Chapter 12, "Identity Kit: Where to Meet Isaki Lacuesta," co-written by Josetxo Cerdán and Miguel Fernández Labayen, is the closing piece in our volume. It analyses the work of Isaki Lacuesta, one of Catalonia's most prolific new directors, and his roots in the Creative Documentary Program from the University Pompeu Fabra in Barcelona, where he studied under the guidance of José Luis Guerín and Joaquim Jordà. Cerdán and Fernández Labayen offer an anthropological approach to the director's cinematic production while studying it in the context of Catalonia's own cinematic and political culture. They also consider Lacuesta's public projection and the way his cinema has evolved. In fact, they claim that unlike the traditional vision of Lacuesta as a chameleonic and volatile author there is an inner logic to his work that they suggest may be best understood when seen from the perspective of Claude Lévi-Strauss's notion of the *bricoleur*. To this end, the essay is divided into four sections: the first is devoted precisely to present Lacuesta as *bricoleur*; the second attempts to insert his work within a revised version of the historiography of Catalan cinema; the third considers the effects of some of the most prominent public positions of the director in recent cinematic and political debates; while the fourth and last studies some of Lacuesta's films and how they reflect the director's own evolution. Thus, the first section considers Lacuesta's first feature films, *Cravan vs. Cravan* (2002) and *La leyenda del tiempo* (*The Legend of Time*, 2006), and his cinematic place in between the new avant-garde and the search for a genuine popular culture.

A distinctive quality of such a search, the two co-authors claim, was Lacuesta's penchant for a primitivism that can be related to Lévi-Strauss's work. Unlike the high-culture tradition of art for art's sake, primitivism does not respond to any given tradition but engages in a direct dialogue with the materials employed. It is an art of the present. And yet, it also falls into the realm of the mythical time and its structural repetitions, its constant recovery of the traces of the past. Lacuesta's entire production may be seen from this perspective, if one considers, for instance, the two films which have earned him the Concha de Oro (Golden Shell) in Spain's most prestigious film festival, the San Sebastián International Film Festival: *Los pasos dobles* (*Double Steps*, 2011) and *Entre dos aguas* (*Between Two Waters*, 2018). Lacuesta is also a *bricoleur* because he has always been able to work "with what he has" at any given point in time, and this is his most defining and enduring characteristic despite the common critical claims that consider him a clear instance of high-culture authorism.

In the second section, the essayists consider the process of institutionalization of contemporary Catalan cinema and its two major tools: the prestige acquired in international film festivals and the lineage established with the Barcelona School, the most famous movement in the context of Catalan independent cinema. The authors take issue with this lineage, which, they claim, is often predicated on the simple fact of the presence of the towering figure of Joaquim Jordà in both historical periods, and with the almost exclusive centrality given to the Barcelona School in this institutional narrative. Instead, they suggest revisiting the diversity of the different cinematic cultures in Catalonia in order to better understand the inner logic of Lacuesta's production. In this sense, instead of referring to Miquel Porter i Moix and his traditional "top-down" history of Catalan cinema, they propose to consider, following Malte Hagener's concept of a European transnational cinema rooted in the avant-garde, other phenomena, such as, in the Spanish and Catalan case, the culture of cine clubs and the important presence of an amateur cinema. The latter, they claim, has been doubly marginalized, both by the official historiography and by some of the historical attempts to describe it. In the case of Isaki Lacuesta, moreover, one needs to consider how his *bricoleur* approach connects him directly with the amateur practices despite his constant will to bring them to bear in the industrial circuits. In so doing, the authors also point out the importance of the contact zones and the hybridization processes that have truly shaped Catalan cinema and its current utterances. Ultimately, Cerdán and Fernández Labayen argue that the best way to approach Lacuesta's work is not only through his genealogical relationship with the Barcelona School but taking into account his capacity to articulate a "ludic experimentation" (310) that allows him to travel through and thus unsettle all the established cinematic categories: amateur, militant, bourgeois, or industrial.

In their third section, the authors analyse Lacuesta's public commitment before, during, and after the Indignados (or 15-M) Movement in Spain. When the Indignados Movement against the economic crisis exploded, Lacuesta got directly involved in it. Another issue that put Lacuesta in the eye of the hurricane was his very public and very visible reaction towards the critical bias against his films and those of other *auteurs*, as they were derogatorily defined by several critics who were publishing in Spain's major newspapers. This bias exploded after Lacuesta won the Golden Shell in San Sebastián for his film *Los pasos dobles* in 2011. Such a critical controversy fuelled the desire to produce a film that used all the worst Spanish stereotypes to create a parody of the action cinema championed by the traditional critics. The result was *Murieron por encima de sus posibilidades* (*They Died Beyond Their Means*, 2015), which, unfortunately, got bad reviews from those old negative critics and from some of Lacuesta's own followers, who considered it too grotesque an attempt at firing back.

The last section of the essay starts with a reflection on the possibility that we have entered a third stage, beyond Deleuze's time-image and time-movement, one that is characterized by the inscription of the human body. Beyond the cinematic and theoretical impossibility to recover "the people," Lacuesta's cinema, the authors claim, will focus on the experiential, the sensible, and the living person. This new fascination for the surface and vulnerability of the human body, which Thomas Elsaesser and Malte Hagener underline as a salient characteristic in the cinema of the last twenty years, is clearly at work in Lacuesta's production. The passage from those evanescent traces to the current materiality of the bodies that populate the Catalan director's films may be clearly inscribed when considering together *La leyenda del tiempo* and its sequel, *Entre dos aguas*, and yet, Lacuesta's attraction for an almost tactile treatment of the cinematic surfaces was already at work in his *Teoría de los cuerpos* (*The Bodies' Theory*, 2004). The importance of the body as a human cartography will also be transposed to the human vision reflected upon places that do not exist, or are not allowed to exist. Productions like *Lugares que no existen* (*Goggle Earth 1.0* 2009), *Dejà vu 1. Paisatges que desapareixen* (*Dejà vu 1. Disappearing Landscapes*, 2003), and *La desaparición* (*The Disappearance*, 2012) all share what the authors call "Bodies and geographies [...] or their cartographies, [which] also inscribe the history, embodying it even when it might be invisible" (326–7).

The essay closes with a brief analysis of *Entre dos aguas*, the sequel of *La leyenda del tiempo* with which Lacuesta won the Golden Shell in San Sebastián for a second time in 2018. As an index of the new materiality of the film, the authors focus on the importance of the tattoos on the bodies of the two brothers, Isra and Cheito. If, in the first film, the young Isra wanted a tattoo as a way of growing up and eventually escaping the trauma of his father's violent death, in the present film, Isra's wish to cover his back with an allegorical inscription of that violent moment marks the weight of the past and the fact of the symbolic acceptance to carry it on his back. Unlike the elusive and mysterious tattoos that covered the skin of the characters in *La propera pell* (*The Next Skin*, 2016), in *Entre dos aguas*, the authors write, "the tattoos anchor biographies and embody traumas and happy moments (on the body of both brothers we see the name of the father but also of their wives and daughters). *Entre dos aguas* shows the rotundity of the bodies becoming present on screen and, as such, generating carnal thoughts that shake the spectators" (328). Ultimately, the film seems to condense the almost twenty years of Lacuesta's cinematic trajectory, where "carnality, geography, political commitment, and history become intertwined" (329) in the work of a *bricoleur* who is able to create a world filled with "a horizontal ethics, which places him in a carnal reverberation with all the human beings that inhabit his works" (329).

We would like to conclude this introduction with a brief mention of some significant absences in our volume. Especially that of Ventura Pons, one of Catalonia's best-known directors whose prolific cinematic output has encompassed some of the central genres that define Catalan cinema as a whole. Indeed, as it will be briefly discussed in chapter 1, Ventura Pons was instrumental in tackling and revitalizing the comedy genre during the eighties and later he would become the most important proponent of a very personal and theatrical mode of literary adaptations, which won him international recognition. In the context of our volume, however, it is his pioneering work as a documentarist with the groundbreaking *Ocaña, retrat intermitent* (*Ocaña, an Intermittent Portrait*, 1978) that deserves special attention. It would be hard to understand the historical moment of the transition between Francoism and the new democratic state in Catalonia and Spain without referencing a film that put the queer community in the cultural forefront for the first time on our screens. Most certainly, Ventura Pons's *Ocaña* joins Pere Portabella's *Informe general* and Joaquim Jordà's *Numax presenta*... as the three more important forerunners of the contemporary trend in radically creative and performative documentaries that have so largely contributed to the recovery of our historical memory. A historical memory that has also been at the centre of the most interesting products to emerge from the new academic programs, such as the Master in Creative Documentary at the Pompeu Fabra University, with figures like Carla Subirana or Neus Ballús. Finally, among the most recent developments in Catalan cinema, only hinted at in this volume, we need to mention the attention given to the new cinema of the real with a series of young women directors whose intimate gaze has become a trademark, one that can be best illustrated in the figure of Carla Simón and her multiple award-winning films *Estiu 1993* (*Summer 1993*, 2018) and *Alcarràs* (2022). Needless to say, the appearance of this new cinema of the real and the growing number of women directors in Catalonia fully deserves a critical attention that bypasses the possibilities of this volume.

WORKS CITED

Aubert, Jean-Paul. *Seremos Mallarmé. La Escuela de Barcelona: Una apuesta modernista*. Shangrila, 2016.
Bentley, Bernard P.E. *A Companion to Spanish Cinema*. Tamesis, 2008.
Bingham, Adam. "The Romance of Certain Old Clothes, or, They Don't Make 'em Like That Anymore; Honour de Cavalleria and Art Cinema's Last Stand."*Cineaction*, no. 75, 2008, pp. 34–45.
Bogue, Ronald. "Minoritarian + Literature." *The Deleuze Dictionary*, edited by Adrian Parr, Edinburgh University Press, 2005, pp. 167–9.
Bordwell, David. *Narration in the Fiction Film*. University of Wisconsin Press, 1985.
Broullón Lozano, Manuel. "Correspondencias fílmicas. La aportación de los cineastas a los estudios sobre el discurso cinematográfico Kawase-Lacuesta." "Investigar la Comunicación hoy. Revisión de políticas científicas y aportaciones metodológicas: Simposio Internacional sobre Política Científica en comunicación." *Comunicaciones*, vol. 2, 2013, pp. 491–504.
Cada vez que... Directed by Carles Duran, performances by Luis Ciges, Jaap Guyt, Joaquim Jordà, Daniel Martín, and Alicia Tomás, Filmscontacto, 1968.
Carruthers, Lee. *Doing Time: Temporality, Hermeneutics, and Contemporary Cinema*. State University of New York Press, 2016.
El cielo sube. Directed by Marc Recha, performances by Salvador Dolç and Corinne Alba, NOMA Films, 1991.

Dante no es únicamente severo. Directed by Jacinto Esteva and Joaquim Jordà, performances by Serena Vergano, Enrique Irazoqui, Romy and Susan Holmqvist, Filmscontacto, 1967.

Deleuze, Gilles. *Cinema 1: The Movement-Image*. Translated by H. Tomlinson and B. Habberjam, University of Minnesota Press, 1986.

– *Cinema 2: The Time-Image*. Translated by H. Tomlinson and B. Habberjam, University of Minnesota Press, 1989.

Deleuze, Gilles, and Félix Guattari. *Kafka: Toward a Minor Literature*. Translated by Dana Polan, U of Minnesota P, 1986.

– *What Is Philosophy?* Translated by Hugh Tomlinson and Graham Burchill, Verso, 1994.

Ditirambo. Directed by Gonzalo Suárez, performances by Gonzalo Suárez, Yelena Samarina, Charo López, and José María Prada, Carlos Boué, producer, 1967.

D'Lugo, Marvin. "Catalan Cinema: Historical Experience and Cinematic Practice." *Quarterly Review of Film & Video*, vol.13, no. 1–3, 1991, pp. 131–46. Taylor and Francis Online, doi.org/10.1080/10509209109361373. Accessed 9 September 2019.

Elisa K. Jordi Cadena and Judith Colell, directors, performances by Aina Clotet, Hans Richter, and Lydia Zimmermann, Obreron Cinematogràfica, 2010.

Elola, Joseba. "Son pocos, son valientes." *El País*, 10 February 2008. https://elpais.com/diario/2008/02/10/cultura/1202598001_850215.html. Accessed 3 September 2018.

Es quan dormo que hi veig clar. Directed by Jordi Cadena, performances by Joan Brossa, Núria Cano, Hermann Bonnín, and Ona Planas, Septimània Films, 1988.

Estiu 1993. Directed by Carla Simón, performances by Laia Artigas, Bruna Cusí, Paula Robles, and David Verdaguer, Inicia Films and Avalon P.C., 2018.

Fata Morgana. Directed by Vicente Aranda, performances by Teresa Gimpera, Marianne Benet, Marcos Martí, and Antonio Ferrandis, Palmiro Aranda and Antonio Rabinat, producers, 1965.

Galt, Rosalind. "Impossible Narratives: The Barcelona School and the European Avant-Gardes." *Hispanic Review*, vol. 78, no. 4, 2010, pp. 491–511. doi 10.1353/hir.2010.0011. Accessed 9 September 2018.

Guerín, José Luis, director. *En construcción*, performances by Juana Rodríguez Molina and Iván Guzmán Jiménez, Ovideo, S.A., 2001.

– *En la ciudad de Sylvia*, performances by Pilar López de Ayala and Xavier Lafitte, Eddie Saeta, S.A., 2007.

– *Los motivos de Berta*, performances by Silvia Gracia and Iñaki Aierra, P.C. Guerín, 1984.

– *Recuerdos de una mañana*, Seoul: JIFF, 2011.

– *Unas fotos en la ciudad de Sylvia*, performances by Pilar López de Ayala and Xavier Lafitte, Eddie Saeta, S.A., 2007.

Harvey, David. "The Right to the City." *New Left Review*, vol 53, 2008, https://newleftreview.org/issues/ii53/articles/david-harvey-the-right-to-the-city.
Hernández, Rubén. *Pere Portabella: Hacia una política del relato cinematogáfico*. Ediciones Errata Naturae, 2008.
Herzog, Amy. "Images of Thought and Acts of Creation: Deleuze, Bergson, and the Question of Cinema." *Invisible Culture: An Electronic Journal for Visual Culture*, vol 3, 2000, https://ivc.lib.rochester.edu/images-of-thought-and-acts-of-creation-deleuze-bergson-and-the-question-of-cinema/. Accessed 3 September 2018.
Higginbotham, Virginia. *Spanish Film under Franco*. University of Texas Press, 1988.
Jordà, Joaquim, director. *De nens*, performances by Marta Galán, Núria Lloansi, Xabier Robés, Mireia Serra, Carla Jiménez, and Oscar Albadalejo, Massa d'Or, 2003.
– *El encargo del cazador*, performances by Dària Esteva, Rosa María Esteva, Annie Settimó, and Romy, Institut del Cinema Català, 1990.
– *Mones com la Becky*, performances by João Maria Pinto, Marian Varela, Petra Alcántara, Montse Bustos, Juana Cabeza, and Ramsés Espín, Els Quatre Gats and La Sept Arte, 1999.
– *Numax presenta...*, performances by Walter Cots, María Espinosa, Mario Gas, Rosa Gavín, Víctor Guillén, and Joaquim Jordà, Asamblea de Trabajadores de Numax, 1979.
– *Veinte años no es nada*, performances by Blanca Galán, Josefa Sánchez, Fernanda Gázquez, Eulogio Roca, Josefina Altamira, and Emilia Fernández, Ovideo, 2004.
Jordan, Barry, and Rikki Morgan-Tamosunas. *Contemporary Spanish Cinema*. Manchester UP, 1998.
Lacuesta, Isaki, director. *Cravan vs Cravan*, performances by Frank Nicotra, Enric Cassasses, Eduardo Arroyo, Benecé Produccions, 2002.
– *Dejà vu 1. Paisatges que desapareixen*, 2003.
– *La Desaparición*, 2012.
– *Entre dos aguas*, performances by Israel Gómez Romero, Francisco José Gómez Romero, Filmax, 2018.
– *La Leyenda del Tiempo*, performances by Israel Gómez Romero, Makiko Matsumura, Francisco José Gómez Romero, Sagrera TV, 2006.
– *Lugares que no existen*. Goggle Earth 1.0, 2009.
– *Murieron por encima de sus posibilidades*, performances by Raúl Arévalo, Julián Villagrán, Albert Pla, Versus Entertainment, 2014.
– *La Propera Pell*, performances by Àlex Monner, Emma Suárez, Sergi López, BTeam Pictures, 2016.
– *Los pasos dobles*, performances by Miquel Barceló, Amassagou Dolo and Alan Cisse, Tusitala P. C., Bord Cadre Films and Televisión Española, 2011.
– *Teoría de los Cuerpos*, 2004.
Lejos de los árboles. Directed by Jacinto Esteva Grewe, Filmscontacto, 1961–71.

MacKenzie, Scott. *Film Manifestos and Global Cinema Cultures A Critical Anthology*. University of California Press, 2014.
Marsh, Steven. "The Legacies of Pere Portabella: Between Heritage and Inheritance." *Hispanic Review*, vol. 78, no. 4, 2010, pp. 551–67. JSTOR, www.jstor.org/stable/25790602. Accessed 29 Dec. 2020.
– *Spanish Cinema against Itself: Cosmopolitanism, Experimentation, Militancy*. Indiana University Press, 2020.
Martí-Olivella, Jaume. "Catalan Cinema: An Uncanny Transnational Performance." *A Companion to Catalan Culture*, edited by Dominic Keown, Tamesis, 2011, pp. 185–205.
Mira, Alberto. *Historical Dictionary of Spanish Cinema*. Scarecrow Press, 2010.
Monterrubio, Lourdes. "Tecnología digital y cine español contemporáneo (2000–2010). En busca de la modernidad Perdida." 27 November 2017. http://www.revistacomunicacion.org/pdf/n15/Articulos/A5_Monterrubio-Tecnologia-digital-y-cine-espanol-contemporaneo-2000-2010-En-busca-de-la-modernidad-perdida.pdf. Accessed 20 January 2018.
Nadal-Melsió, Sara. "Editor's Preface. The Invisible Tradition: Avant-Garde Catalan Cinema under Late Francoism." *Hispanic Review*, vol 78, no 4, pp. 465–8. DOI: www.jstor.org/stable/25790597, Accessed 9 September 2018.
Nunes, José María. "Recuerdos también de hoy, sobre la escuela de Barcelona." http://nunescine.es/id42.htm. Accessed 8 May 2018.
Ocaña, retrat intermitent. Directed by Ventura Pons, performances by José Pérez Ocaña and Paco de Alcoy, Prozesa, 1978.
Portabella, Pere, director, *Die Stille vor Bach*, performances by Alex Brendemühl, Feodor Atkine, Christian Brembeck, Daniel Ligorio, and Georgina Cardona, Films 59, 2007.
– *Informe general sobre algunas cuestiones de interés para una proyección pública*, Films 59, 1976.
– *Informe general II: El nuevo rapto de Europa*, Films 59, 2016
– *No compteu amb els dits*, performances by Mario Cabré, Natacha Gounkevitch, Josep Santamaría, Willy van Rooy, and Daniel van Goleen, Films 59, 1967.
– *Nocturno 29*, performances by Lucía Bosé, Mario Cabré, Anne M. Settimò, Ramón Julia, and Antoni Tàpies, Films 59, 1968.
– *Pont de Varsòvia*, performances by Paco Guíjar, Jordi Dauder, Carme Elias, Ona Planas, and Josep M. Pou, Films 59, 1989.
– *Vampir.Cuadecuc*, performances by Christopher Lee, Herbert Lom, Soledad Miranda, Jack Taylor, Maria Rohm, and Fred Williams, Films 59, 1970.
Pujol, Anton. "Visualizing Trauma – Marc Recha's *Dies d'agost*." *Studies in Spanish & Latin American Cinemas*, vol. 13, no. 2, 2016, pp. 177–94.
Rancière, Jacques. *Dissensus: On Politics and Aesthetics*. Edited and translated by Steven Corcoran. Continuum, 2010.

Resina, Joan Ramon. "Introduction." *Burning Darkness: A Half Century of Spanish Cinema*, edited by Joan Ramon Resina and Andrés Lema-Hincapié, State University of New York Press, 2008, pp. 1–7.

Riambau, Esteve, and Casimiro Torreiro. *La escuela de Barcelona: El cine de la "gauche divine."* Editorial Anagrama, 2006.

Riambau, Esteve, Glòria Salvadó Corretger, and Casimiro Torreiro. "'A mí la normalidad no me gusta.' Un largo encuentro con Joaquín Jordá." *Nosferatu: Revista de cine*, vol. 52, pp. 40–79, 2006. http://hdl.handle.net/10251/41456. Accessed 6 July 2017.

Rosales, Jaime, director. *Hermosa juventud*, performances by Ingrid García Jonson, Carlos Rodríguez, Inma Nieto, and Fernando Barona, Cameo Media, 2014.

– *Las horas del día*, performances by Alex Brendemühl, Vicente Romero, María Antonia Martínez, and Àgata Roca, Cameo Media, 2004.

Ross, Alex. "Encrypted: Translators Confront the Supreme Enigma of Stéphane Mallarmé's Poetry." *The New Yorker*. 11 April 2016. https://www.newyorker.com/magazine/2016/04/11/stephane-mallarme-prophet-of-modernism. Accessed 4 December 2018.

Saltzman, Megan, and Javier Entrambasaguas. "Immigration and Rhizomatic Itineraries of Resistance in the Global City: Reflections on Two Films: *Si nos dejan* and *Raval, Raval*." *Local Cities, Global Spaces: Towards a Multicultural Configuration of Spain*, edited by Ana Corbalán and Ellen Mayock, Fairleigh Dickinson University Press, 2014, pp.71–84.

Seitz, Matt Zoller. "Reflections of Don Quixote." Review of *Quixotic/Honor de cavalleria*, directed by Albert Serra, *The New York Times*, 21 September 2007, p. E8.

Serra, Albert, director. *Història de la meva mort*, performances by Vicenç Altaió, Luís Serrat, Eliseu Huertas, Andergraun Films, 2013

– *Honor de cavalleria*, performances by Lluís Carbó, Lluís Serrat Masanellas, and Jimmy Gimferrer, Albert Serra and Montse Triola, producers, 2007.

Terrasa, Jacques. "Les vanités enfouies: Signes et sédiments dans le film *En Construcción* de José Luis Guerin." *La ville, lieux et limites* 2, special issue of *Cahiers d'études romanes*, vol. 12, 2005, pp. 145–59. https://journals.openedition.org/etudesromanes/2585. Accessed 5 September 2018.

Vilarós, Teresa M. "Albert Serra's Digital Singularity." *Revista de Estudios Hispánicos*, vol. 52 no. 2, 2018, pp. 375–405. Project MUSE, doi:10.1353/rvs.2018.0060. Accessed 5 July 2018.

Vilaseca, David. *Queer Events: Post-Deconstructive Subjectivities in Spanish Writing and Film 1960s–1990s*. Liverpool University Press, 2010.

Vilaseca, David. "*Deleuze no es Únicamente severo*: Time and Memory in the Films of the Escola de Barcelona', *Queer Events: Post-deconstructive Subjectivities in Spanish Writing and Film, 1960s to 1990s*. Liverpool Scholarship Online, 20 June 2013. https://doi.org/10.5949/liverpool/9781846314674.003.0005.

Zunzunegui, Santos. "Extraterritorial Portabella." Translated by David Barba. MoMA.org. https://www.moma.org/interactives/exhibitions/2007/portabella/extraterritorial.html. Accessed 3 May 2018.
– "Pere Portabella: The Politics and Aesthetics of Auterism." *A Companion to Spanish Cinema*. Edited by Jo Labany and Tatjana Pavlović, Wiley Blackwell, 2016.

PART ONE

The Mavericks and the Barcelona School

1 Future Seeds: Some Considerations on the Cinema around Barcelona 92

ÀNGEL QUINTANA

1. When Barcelona Was Powerful

On 13 May 1989, Manuel Vázquez Montalbán, the renowned writer and cultural critic, published one of his journalistic essays against the hypothetical speculation that was being generated around Barcelona 1992. In those days, Vázquez Montalbán had become a privileged observer of what was called "olympic impulse." Instead of the official narrative that painted an immaculate process in the gestation of a "Barcelona that has power," he preferred to use his journalistic pieces as a means of establishing a clairvoyant intellectual and emotional distance. Thus, he appeared concerned about losing the fundamental idea that the 92 Olympic Games were the first chance that Barcelona had in order to grow democratically with the depth that a democracy acquires when the citizens participate in municipal policies. Instead, the political situation had transformed the organization of the Summer Olympics into a personal fight by a city mayor full of dreams – Pasqual Maragall – against the Spanish Socialist government, presided by Felipe González, who preferred to look to the South and to promote Expo 92 in Seville or the grand commemorations of the Quincentennial of the Discovery of the Americas. In the Catalan context, moreover, Maragall was also fighting against a Generalitat government, which, presided by Jordi Pujol, was trying to keep a low profile not to magnify a possible "socialist success." In the midst of all this, Vázquez Montalbán, wrote, "The Olympic Games have shown that the city of Barcelona is only able to grow by impulses and not because of developing plans that respond to its real needs and capabilities" (112).

Vázquez Montalbán's critical sharpness constituted a true antidote to the official discourse created in the media since October 1986, when José Antonio Samaranch proclaimed in Lausanne the candidacy of "la ville de Barcelona," which lasted until 9 August1992, when the Games were officially closed. And yet, during these six years, Barcelona underwent what many have considered the most intense urban transformation since the Cerdà Plan.[1] The city also experienced strong economic growth spurred by the collective illusion created by a project that gave it an enormous international visibility. Indeed, the Games had a huge impact in the international media which, after some time, resulted in the consolidation of Barcelona as a privileged tourist destination.

Today, after thirty-one years, the situation has changed and also the memory of the Games. Amidst the effervescence created by the independence movement, it looks like the shadows have darkened some aspects relating to the traditional 92 narrative. In a polemic article entitled "Matar al Cobi," Jordi Amat studied the way in which the new hegemonic Catalanism in 2012 had decided to erase the Games from its discourse: "The moment in which Catalonia's projection to the world achieved a climactic point thanks to its capital city. Today one barely remembers it or it begins to be negatively connoted" (2–5).[2] Beyond the political polemics, which are fed by a hegemonic change brought about by the breakdown of the Catalan left and the emergence of a transversal independence movement focussed on recovering other narratives and minimizing the Olympic ones, it is clear that the shadows generated around the 1992 event have resurfaced. However, in the possible critiques articulated around the contradictions of the historical moment, one tends to forget that one pending subject regarding Barcelona 92 is the study of its impact and repercussion in the cultural world. In the final pages of his volume entitled *La vocació de modernitat de Barcelona: Auge i declivi d'una imatge urbana*, Joan Ramon Resina considers in a critical way the different discourses generated by the 92 event and condemns the way culture was manipulated to turn the city of Barcelona into a big mall (312–13). And yet, in order to understand the position of those who managed the relationship of the Olympic Games with the cultural world at large, it may be very useful to look into the research carried out by the Centro de Estudios Olímpicos de la Universidad Autónoma de Barcelona. In a collective and multidisciplinary volume, Miguel de Moragas admits that against the urbanistic and economic successes of the city there remained the serious problem of the "difficulty of fitting culture as part of the central organization of the event" (106).

---

1 This is one of the conclusions reached by the architects and urban planners Oriol Bohigas, Jordi Borja, Mercè Tatjer, and Josep Maria Montané as shown in Pauné.
2 Unless otherwise indicated, all translations are mine.

In his article, de Moragas analyses the so-called Olimpiada Cultural that happened without any true repercussion.

Indeed, between April and August 1992 a series of pre-Games events were organized with the aim of giving Barcelona an essential role as a cultural capital. These events were, however, organized without any cohesiveness and with many gaps. Upon examination of the catalogue one finds the paradox of the non-existence of a single event devoted to cinema. Not a single cinematographic event related to Barcelona 92 was organized, and the only production to emerge from the Games was Carlos Saura's *Marathon* (1992), which became the official document of the Olympic Games. Instead, the celebration of the Quincentennial of the Discovery of the Americas, which took place the same year in Madrid, was accompanied by the polemics generated by the Spanish government's funding for the shooting of *1492* (1992), Ridley Scott's blockbuster casting Gerard Depardieu and Sigourney Weaver, which was awarded 200 million pesetas, half the amount of the entire budget destined to fund Spanish films that year. The funding of Ridley Scott's film was also detrimental to the possible support of another American production on the topic: John Glen's *Cristobal Colón, el descubrimiento* (*Christopher Columbus: The Discovery*, 1992), starring Georges Correface and Marlon Brando. It is true, however, that in 1992, Catalan cinema was considered a marginal product by the official culture.

Despite certain political gestures aimed at changing that situation, there was no audience that believed in its existence and it had not yet been considered as part of the tourist promotion of Barcelona, as latter happened with films such as Pedro Almodóvar's *Todo sobre mi madre* (*All about My Mother*, 1999) or Woody Allen's *Vicky, Cristina, Barcelona* (2008). It felt as if culture were somewhere beyond cinema, while the majority of the Catalan cinema professionals seemed to undergo an inferiority complex in front of the industrial boom of the sector in Madrid. Barcelona was regarded as a cutting-edge city in terms of its architecture, its plastic arts, its graphic design, its theatre, and its literature. But in this modernity cinema was absent because cinema was considered to exist only in Madrid. Thus, Catalan institutions started to change the concept of Catalan cinema for that of Catalan audiovisual and supported the role that TV3 (Catalonia's own television channel) began to have in the creation of a certain national imaginary. Another key factor that helps us understand the situation of the audiovisual surge in those years is that of the publicity industry. Around 1992, publicity had a big impact and became good business. An essential part of the audiovisual world took refuge in the publicity sector since it generated more jobs, was more profitable and secure, and was much less risky. The cinema produced in Catalonia around Barcelona 1992 was marginal both in terms of viewership and of cultural diffusion. Most productions released during those years have already been forgotten. What is worse is that the situation also showed the impotence of an industrial sector that saw many opportunities being lost.

And yet, beyond the chronicle of all those lost chances, the passing of time has shown that things were a bit more complex. Thus, amidst the failure of commercial productions, one saw how another kind of cinema was emerging from the margins of the system. Good cinema produced around Barcelona 92 was scarce, and yet, there were a series of interesting proposals that planted the seed for future developments. In order to understand this paradoxical situation, one needs to pay attention to the fact that artistic creation in Catalonia has always followed the urbanistic pattern. Thus, the country's artistic production has been created through impulse, often generated by adversity, silence, and forgetfulness. Despite its multiple failures, it is impossible to understand the relative boom of auteur cinema in Catalonia during the twenty-first century without studying some of its foundations during the Barcelona 92 events. Some chances were lost, but their loss implied a discreet emergence of something different.

2. A Cinema without Industry

Between 1984 and 1985, the Conselleria de Cultura de la Generalitat de Catalunya was presided over by Joan Rigol, a member of the Unió Democràtica de Catalunya. His main political goal was to achieve a specific cultural deal that made Catalan culture more visible. In the design of this cultural deal cinema once more had no real place. In 1986, when the Olympic candidacy was confirmed, Joaquim Ferrer was in charge of the Conselleria de Cultura de la Generalitat and wanted to remedy this situation promising 300 million pesetas to fund the new cinematographic policies. Previously, in 1983, the Spanish government had approved a Royal Decree, known as the Miró Law, that aimed at a radical change in the means of production of Spanish cinema. The Miró Law introduced an early funding program according to a specific production and financing planning. The law gave full powers to a committee that decided the projects to be considered. It basically supported the production of projects based on prestigious works that already had cultural recognition and that came from other artistic fields, mostly literature. This model crashed with the policies undertaken in Catalonia, which, due to the weakness of the industrial cinema sector, could not find a good fit for them. In the first place, the Miró Law meant the death of a kind of commercial production of second-rank films (B movies) that had been the specialty of part of the small Catalan cinematographic industry (see Cerdán and Pena). Secondly, the administration's directives regarding production had a negative impact in Catalonia, especially given the distance between certain Catalan cultural politics and those espoused in Madrid at the time. Finally, one needs to take into account that the projects that distanced themselves from the established cultural frame faced many problems when considered by the committee (see Balló, Espelt, and Lorente 99). Thus, for instance, *Tras el cristal* (*Behind the Glass*, 1987), Agustí Villaronga's opera prima, received only minimal funding because it did not fit with the committee's policies. And yet, this film was a big success in the Berlin International Film Festival and had a much larger impact than most Spanish films funded by the state during those years.

With the arrival of Fernando Méndez Leite as general director of the ICAA (Institute of Cinema and Audiovisual Arts), tensions were eased. Méndez Leite created an evaluation subcommittee inside his department that was based in Barcelona. This generated more opportunities for the production of certain Catalan cinema projects. The goal was to try and increase the local production given the fact that the traditional quota of cinematic production in Catalonia – both in Spanish and in Catalan – had gone down from 25 per cent to only 18 per cent of the total production in Spain. According to data released by the Generalitat (Catalan government), the box office for both Spanish and Catalan films in Catalonia had dropped from 1636 million pesetas in 1981 to only 739 million in 1986 (see Bonet, Cubeles, and Miralles 63).

Between 1986 and 1988, Josep Maria Forn acted as the new general director of cinematography in the Generalitat. This facilitated the creation of a production process that was more in sync with the local cultural situation. As a result, many new projects were funded and the production of films shot in Catalan increased from only two in 1985 to a total of thirteen in 1988 (see Porter i Moix 371). Also in those years, a group of new Catalan film-makers reached the public scene. This group was called Nous Directors Catalans and was formed by Ferran Llagostera, Ignasi P. Farré, Albert Abril, Antoni Martí, Simó Fàbregues, Pere Vila, Antoni Verdaguer, Xavier Juncosa, Romà Guardiet, and Raul Contel. Many of these directors were able to obtain public funding in order to create their opera prima. Thus, in the years prior to the Olympic Games, films such as *Bar-Cel-Ona* (1987) by Ferran Llagostera, *Una nit a Casa Blanca* (*A Night at Casa Blanca*, 1987) by Antoni Martí, *Qui t'estima Babel?* (*Who Loves You Babel?*, 1987) by Ignasi P. Farré, *L'home de Neó* (*The Neon Man*, 1988) by Albert Abril, *L'escot* (*The Cleavage*, 1986) by Antoni Verdaguer, *Entreacte* (*Intermission*, 1989) by Manuel Cussó-Ferré, and

Solitud (*Solitude*, 1991) by Romà Guardiet reached commercial theatres. The very existence of such a heterogeneous group of films certifies the fact that new opportunities were created in order to reach a stable level of production. And yet, the ultimate oblivion of most of those films also shows their limited impact and their lack of success, both in local theatres and with international audiences. A new Catalan cinema that could break away from the legacy of the Spanish Transition years was being created. However, it was still necessary to establish a stronger intellectual basis that could bring about a more cohesive collective project in order to avoid too much dispersion. Catalan society at large was very oblivious of the inner battles between the different sectors of the cinema professionals in the country. The political class was not worried by the little impact achieved by a cinema that still found real problems to become visible beyond Catalonia's borders.

In the years prior to the Olympic Games, Catalan cinema was still depending on the commercial success of its social comedies. Ventura Pons entered this trend with *La rossa del bar* (*The Blond Girl at the Bar*, 1987) and, almost on the eve of the Olympic Games, achieved a certain degree of popular success with his comedy of errors *Què t'hi jugues, Mari Pili?* (*What Do You Bet, Mari Pili?*, 1991). Ignasi P. Farré signed *Un submarí a les estovalles* (*A Submarine on the Tablecloth*, 1991), inspired by Joan Barril's eponymous novel. The film's protagonist is an Arab immigrant who almost unwittingly finds his way into the country's political life. The renewal of the comedy genre in those years also saw a remarkable opera prima, Rosa Vergés's *Boom boom* (1990). This film attempted to break away from the traditional canon of the social comedy in order to look for a better fit with the ever-changing Catalan society around 92. At the same time, Francesc Bellmunt, who had enjoyed some commercial and popular success with his social comedies, left the genre to try his hand at a thriller by producing a kind of fable describing a hypothetical conspiracy within the COI (International Olympic Committee). The film was appropriately titled *El complot dels anells* (*The Rings Conspiracy*, 1988). On the other hand, the brand of historical cinema inspired by literary works continued to look for its place on Catalan screens with films like *Laura en la ciutat dels Sants* (*Laura in the City of Saints*, 1986) by Gonzalo Herralde, based on Miquel Llor's renowned eponymous novel, and *La teranyina* (*The Cobweb*, 1990) by Antoni Verdaguer, inspired by one of Jaume Cabré's early historical novels. There were also several attempts to continue the local cinema noir tradition with films like *L'amor és estrany* (*Love Is Strange*, 1988), by Carles Balagué, or *Manila* (1991), by Antonio Chavarrías. High-class erotic products could also find some box office response, as shown by Bigas Luna with his *Los amantes de Lulú* (*Lulú's Lovers*, 1990), a production that opened the director's way towards a commercial model that, supported by the Madrid cinema industry, found its culmination in his most popular film, *Jamón, Jamón* (*Ham, Ham*, 1992).

The main problem with the cinema produced during those years was the lack of industrial confidence in the projects. That scepticism was fed by the progressive disenchantment of the audience in front of a series of products with which they did not identify. Nevertheless, the number of films created around 92 was possible because of the funding policies of the Catalan government, although their presence and their distribution were less than remarkable. Indeed, most films released during those years have been already forgotten, with no will to revisit or to recover them. At the end of the eighties there were no university programs devoted to forming cinema professionals in Catalonia. It was precisely in 1992 that the first departments of audiovisual communication were established in Catalan colleges, and the ESCAC (Superior School of Catalan Cinema and Audiovisual) was not created until 1994. There was a feeling of being orphans from past historical referents but also a detachment from certain practices that were working on a voluntary basis, without being supported by any solid industrial grounding or counting with a well-formed professional sector. It was quite common to create producing companies in order to carry out a single project that had received official funding. Many of those companies would have to shut down after the failure of the released films at the box office. The best audiovisual professionals had been trained in publicity and continued to work in that field while cinema had lost its professional integration. Whereas the generation that produced films during the Spanish Transition years had been formed within the training system that existed in Barcelona during the sixties, the young directors of the eighties had only had an amateur training or were simply following their cinematic dreams.

In the midst of this context, it is curious to note how the future seed that was sowed during these years did not spring from any of the established models but came at the hands of a group of mavericks from the margins. These upstarts started to create a break from the traditional limits of the narrative and documentary genres while searching for other systems of authorial writing that, albeit indirectly, managed to set up a series of traits that ended up influencing the turn-of-the-century generation for whom the access to film schools was already a fully developed reality.

3. The Mavericks' Cinema

If we analyse the mavericks' *cinéma d'auteur* created around 1992, it seems easy to establish three categories. The first would be that of the film-makers with roots in the Catalan avant-garde of the fifties and sixties who came back with a film released in the midst of the new juncture. A case in point is Pere Portabella, a key figure in that avant-garde and a central case study in this volume, as may be seen in "Part Three: The Portabella Nexus." Portabella returned to cinema after thirteen years with his *Pont de Varsòvia* (*Warsaw's Bridge*, 1989), but he took another sixteen years to sign his new film, *Die Stille vor Bach* (*El silenci abans de Bach /The Silence before Bach*, 2007). Another important figure, also centrally featured in this volume, is that of Joaquim Jordà, who, after an intense period as a screenwriter, returned to film direction with his *El encargo del cazador* (*The Hunter's Request*, 1990), where he pondered over the remains of the Barcelona School, the movement he helped to create and which became one of his central pillars. This film, which will be analysed in depth in the next chapter by Esteve Riambau, allowed Jordà to continue his work as a director and made possible his ultimate role as teacher and mentor in the Master in Creative Documentary program established at the end of the nineties at the Pompeu Fabra University in Barcelona. Antoni Padrós, another key figure of the Catalan underground, tried his luck in this new environment with the film *Verónica L. (Una dona al meu jardí)* (*Veronica L. [A Woman in My Garden]*, 1990), co-written with Octavi Martí, but this approach to commercial cinema was to mark his last activity as an active film-maker. Alongside this return of some key referential figures, it is interesting to observe the emergence of new alternatives both in the field of narrative cinema, with the names of Agustí Villaronga and Jesús Garay in front, and in the field of the new essay-like documentary genre, where we can place the first works by José Luis Guerín and Manuel Cussó-Ferré. This period also saw how Jordi Cadena found new ways in his cinematic production.

It is also important to note that some of the essential titles in the cinema of this group of maverick directors achieved a notable presence at international festivals. Portabella's *Pont de Varsòvia*, for instance, made it into the Quinzaine des Réalisateurs in Cannes and Agustí Villaronga's *Tras el cristal* (*Behind the Glass*, 1986) opened at the Berlin International Film Festival. *El niño de la luna* (*The Child from the Moon*, 1989), also by Villaronga, took part in the official section of the Cannes Festival. Moreover, *Innisfree* (1990), by José Luis Guerin, competed in the section Un Certain regard also in Cannes while *L'última frontera* (*The Last Frontier*, 1992), by Manuel Cussó-Ferré, was seen in the Berlin Festival

Forum. Confronting the scarce international repercussion of the Catalan commercial model, this new cinema started to open up the way into the festival circuit. This created a path that would become essential in the later international expansion of the Catalan cinema produced in the first decades of the twenty-first century.

During the Spanish Transition years, Pere Portabella was elected senator by the leftist coalition, Entesa dels Catalans. His presence in the political arena distanced him from his life as a cinema director while turning him into an important analyst of the changes and transformations in the Left. In 1959, Portabella had created Films 59, the production company that made possible the shooting of Luis Buñuel's *Viridiana* (1961). After that, he started to create a series of iconoclastic works that related to the artistic and literary avant-garde of the time while articulating a sustained anti-Francoist narrative. In 1989, after a very long interval, Portabella returned to directing feature films and he did it with a strange film that tried to offer a synthesis of the unease created by the collapse of the ideological utopias, the commodification of culture, and the decline of the avant-gardes. *Pont de Varsòvia* was a curious asteroid that emerged in the midst of a cinema in crisis to try to underline the importance of previous references. These references, in Portabella's case, had always been those of a certain Catalan artistic avant-garde that covered a wide spectrum ranging from Joan Miró to the Informalists with Antoni Tàpies at the forefront, or the visual poetry created by Joan Brossa. Throughout his filmography, Portabella has not ceased to ask himself about the role of cinema in a time of artistic decline.

In 1989, the film-maker had seen how art and culture had set aside some of the avant-garde dreams and how the old anti-Francoist fights had begun to be forgotten in the political realm. *Pont de Varsòvia* is a work that recovers some of the lost radicality in the cinema of the time, especially concerning the formal drawbacks of the current cinematic currency. Portabella continues to break with narrativity, despite playing with some formal traits related to certain genres which the director himself sees with distrust. The result, in Santos Zunzunegui's words, is a work where "The artist evaluates and actively intervenes in a historical situation where the passion for television coexists with an unrestrained visit to museums which still show apparent forms of avant-garde art, in which cultural consumption is confused in a self-interested way with the accessibility of the works and where one tries to go against anything that questions the traditional ways that guarantee an ordered access to meaning" (41). *Pont de Varsòvia* was there, in the midst of the Olympic fever, to remind all the young film-makers to be that the commitment to the avant-garde tradition was an essential one.

As mentioned above, this return to the origins is also at work with another key film of the time, Joaquim Jordà's *El encargo del cazador*. Originally produced by Televisión Española, the film starts with Dària Esteve's request to shoot a film with and about certain unreleased material shot by his father in Africa. Dària is the daughter of director Jacinto Esteva, with whom Jordà had co-directed *Dante* at the early stages of the Barcelona School. Instead of organizing the material of the deceased director, Jordà took advantage of that request to create a peculiar portrait of the universe surrounding the Barcelona School. Jordà stages the director's decadence and death as a platform to move backwards in search of the traces left by something that had been erased. The result, according to Carles Guerra, is "a film that manages to walk on the razor's edge, always avoiding the fall into any unnecessary reckoning" (22). Like *Pont de Varsòvia*, *El encargo del cazador* establishes a sort of revival of the past that becomes a benchmark against any lack of memory while reclaiming something that was and has now been blurred by the shadows of time. The film also served to sow a future seed towards a new cinema that should carry on the avant-garde legacy of provocation to show that, beyond the industrial models promoted by the Generalitat, it was necessary to reclaim a rather (in)visible but important creative tradition which, from the margins, had managed to place Catalan cinema inside the artistic avant-garde. An (in)visible tradition, we should add, that becomes the main object of this volume.

This legacy had another chapter that ended up being a bit more complicated with the shooting of *Veronica L. (Una dona al meu jardí)* (1990) by Antoni Padrós and Octavi Martí. Since 1969, Antoni Padrós had been the author of a notable cinematic production created in the most absolute margins and distributed also only in marginal circuits, without any of his films ever reaching a commercial release. Some of his most emblematic titles, such as *Lock Out* (1973) and *Shirley Temple Story* (1976), had been recovered by important museums like the Tate Modern in London or the Centro de Arte Reina Sofía in Madrid. Padrós occupies a special place in the construction of an underground model in Catalonia under Francoism and during the transition. In 1990, with the help of then cinema critic Octavi Martí, Padrós embarked on a commercial production, *Veronica L.* The disputes among producers and other disagreements landed the film in a very limited commercial run and forced Padrós to abandon cinema until his project *L'home precís* (*The Precise Man*, 2012). Even if *Veronica L.* may look like a marginal film, it is important to underline that Padrós also tried to create his own revival and to have his own spot in the new cinematic space alongside Pere Portabella and Joaquim Jordà. All three of them tried to take advantage of the new juncture to reflect anew over the function of cinema as an avant-garde provocation.

All these examples stand in contrast to the desire of some new cineastes who wanted to establish another fictional model that brought to light strong images in order to create new visual atmospheres that could confront the supposed lethargy of the postmodern culture of the time. The two main proponents of this partially frustrated renewal of the fictional model were Agustí Villaronga and Jesús Garay. It all started in 1986 when a Catalan film, the previously mentioned *Tras el cristal*, by Agustí Villaronga, becamea scandal of sorts at the Berlin International Film Festival. In the film's prologue, a Nazi, formerly a torturer at a concentration camp, poses a young man in a posture that evokes Saint Sebastian. The Nazi caresses, hits, and tortures the youth while taking pictures of him. A short while after, the Nazi jumps to his death from the balcony of his apartment. From that moment on, the action of *Tras el cristal* takes place inside a room where the Nazi survives within an iron lung that his wife has imported from Germany. Then, a young man shows up in the house offering his services as caretaker, a fact that will soon develop into a tense power play between the two men. In her analysis of *Tras el cristal*, Pilar Pedraza states that

> The film deals with the depravation of children and the transformation of the victims into players of a perverse game as winners of their castrated victimizers whom they are condemned to replace unto eternity. It is a dark and pessimistic version of the universal game between victim and victimizer, with vaguely a direct mention of the Nazi camps where the guards' brutality and the humiliation of the inmates was given such a free rein. (23)

Despite being a film that explores the nature of evil, it also foregrounds themes such as child abuse or paedophilia that broke with any kind of hypothetical political correction. How could the cinema around 92 accept such an extreme film as Agustí Villaronga's opera prima? To try and answer this question, one needs to consider the film as a formal apparatus with great plastic energy, as an attempt to look for a narrative capable of shocking the spectator while transgressing some of the dominant aesthetic norms. The mid-eighties, when the film was shot, had seen the revival of a certain international auteur cinema that privileged form over content. The postmodern society born around 92 appears to be less sensitive to extreme situations than the previous one. During the Spanish Transition years, some films like Bigas Luna's *Bilbao* (1977) or *Caniche* (1978) had already signalled the way towards a moral incorrectness in their treatment of the power relations or sexual pathologies. *Tras el cristal* follows the same path but crosses a new frontier by showing the tension between victim and victimizer under Nazism.

Villaronga was thus betting on a radical *cinéma d'auteur* based on a fiction that could be competitive in an international market. The move turned out to be the right one and it got him the passport to carry out his second feature film project, *El niño de la luna* (1989), which was selected to take part in the official section of the Cannes Film Festival. And yet, Villaronga's proposal was perhaps a bit too risky for a production system where most films had serious amortization problems. In 1991, Villaronga started the pre-production work for his project to adapt Mercè Rodoreda's novel *La mort i la primavera* (*Death and Spring*). As in his previous films, Villaronga needed to build a complex world, based on a primitive aesthetics and inhabited by deformed beings. The design of such a universe was not possible given the precariousness of the existing cinema industry. The director had to put aside his projects during a certain time while taking refuge in commercial cinema.

A case relatively similar to that of Agustí Villaronga is that of Jesús Garay. The director, who was born in Santander but relocated to Barcelona, created an important diptych where one could foresee new possible aesthetic ways for Catalan cinema. The diptych was composed of *Més enllà de la passió* (*Beyond Passion*, 1986) and *La banyera* (*The Bathtub*, 1989). Both films start out as thrillers, although their narratives get blurred until they turn into an exploration of visual spaces and atmospheres. In the first film, Garay uses the story of a female singer who has lost her voice to create a universe marked by a series of ritual acts that progressively erase the rationality of the narrative. In *La banyera*, instead, we share the experience of a character who has lost his memory and who takes refuge in his bathtub as if it were surrounded by a hypnotic fluid that contains his obsessions. In both films, Garay explores a strange territory placed in between the vagueness of the senses, the frailty of memory, and the subtle borders that separate madness from sanity. The political juncture allowed him to shoot *La banyera* under good production terms, without the need to lower his cinematic ambitions (see Casas 53). Unfortunately, the project undertaken in these two films – and in his two earlier works, *Nemo* (1978) and *Manderley* (1980) – ended without any possible continuity. The director had to accept freelance work such as the adaptation of a novel by Simenon in *Els de davant* (*People in Front*, 1993) or work in television. The lack of public impact of Garay's two films with the audience of the time forced him to a certain creative silence. It also made clear the difficulty in creating a fiction that explored dense atmospheres in search of a new visual style that could break away from the imaginary established by Catalan cinema in those years.

This risky approach was the one also chosen by Marc Recha in his peculiar opera prima, *El cielo sube* (*Heaven Rises*, 1991), the adaptation of Eugeni d'Ors's *Oceanografia del tedi*, which will be the central piece of study in chapter 10 of this volume. The film portrays the ruminations of a man in a spa. This man fights his anxiety by meditating on the physical sensations he experiences while lying in a hammock, after having set his mind free of all other thought. Recha shot the film with a very low budget, but it allowed him to become one of the main voices in the new emerging Catalan cinema of the nineties. Another key narrative film of the time was the opera prima shot by Gerard Gormezano – who had previously worked with José Luis Guerín – *El vent de l'illa* (*The Island Wind*, 1988), which was based on an event that took place during the English occupation of the island of Minorca during the eighteenth century.

The renewal of the cinematic parameters by the new generations did not happen only within the limits of narrative cinema but expanded into a reformulation of the documentary genre and its frontiers with the essay cinema. This rewriting of the documentary genre emerged in a moment when the tradition of numerous documentaries shot during the Spanish Transition years had already been left behind. A moment, in fact, when there was practically no documentary being produced in the context of Spanish cinema. Thus, in the cinema around 1992, we cannot talk of any orthodox model but for the existence of an essay-like cinema that uses techniques close to the documentary genre. The important thing in this model was the search for alternative writing forms able to break away from fictional parameters in order to avoid the limitations imposed by commercial Catalan cinema.

The desire to break away from the traditional imaginary is also key to understand, for instance, the position undertaken by José Luis Guerín in his second feature film, *Innisfree* (1990). The director had started his career within narrative cinema with *Los motivos de Berta* (*Berta's Motives*, 1985), a film shot in the Castilian plains and structured as a coming-of-age fantasy depicting the experience of an adolescent girl in a hostile environment. Since that first film, Guerín's universe appeared very close to the director's cinephilia. His images made clear references to those created by Alexander Dovzhenko, Robert Bresson, or Victor Erice. *Innisfree* emerged as a kind of trip back to a cinephile's paradise, to the village of Cong in the Connemara region of Galway, Ireland, where John Ford shot *The Quiet Man* in 1950. Guerín's goal was to create a film about the cinematic ghosts who walked and lived in a small Irish village, to bring back to life the memory of those who were familiar with the shooting, while feeding multiple legends surrounding it. The result is not a documentary about what it meant to shoot at Innisfree, but an essay on cinema's evocative power, on its ghostly capacity, and on the presence of the shadows of the past in a given present. *Innisfree* built a very peculiar poetics that the director would further explore in *Tren de sombras* (*A Train of Shadows*, 1997). *Innisfree*, which was selected for the Un Certain Regard section at Cannes, suggested two essential breaks. The first was the desire to find beyond Catalonia's own borders a cinematic imaginary stripped from any signs of local colour. Throughout his career Guerín has been consistent in this approach and has shot most of his films abroad. The second desired break, as indicated by José Luis Fecé, had to do with Guerín's determination to locate his cinema "beyond the usual limitations surrounding the debates about cinema's realism or about the relationship between documentary and fiction, since his goal is neither the representation of the historical world (at least in its strict sense), nor to conform with the usual documentary modalities, the expositive and the observational" (see Fecé 309).

Alongside Guerín we can find the work of Manuel Cussó-Ferré, whose approach to documentary cinema in his film *L'última frontera* also relies on a move towards a more essay-like format and on the possibility of establishing a link with a series of artistic fields. Cussó-Ferré – an old member of the collective group of Nous Directors Catalans – created his second feature film around philosopher Walter Benjamin's death at Portbou, Catalonia. Benjamin's clandestine passage between Banyuls-sur-Mer, France, and Portbou together with his son and his Polish wife becomes the narrative centre of the film. The film uses this fact to analyse some elements in Benjamin's life and some of his personality traits. There are documentary techniques such as the use of the photographer Giselle Freund's voice-over or the inclusion of an interview with the art critic Jean Selz, who met Benjamin in Berlin. However, there are also artistic contributions such as Francesc Abad's installation dealing with the issue of borders and exile that establishes a direct link with the film's images.

In a manner quite close to that of Manuel Cussó-Ferré, we can find Jordi Cadena's essay-like film *Es quan dormo que hi veig clar* (*It Is When I Sleep that I See Clearly*, 1988). The first images of the film show us the poet J.V. Foix's burial in the rain, on 30 January 1987. We see these images while listening to a musical score written by Carles Santos, the composer who composed for many of Pere Portabella's films, as will be analysed in chapters 5 and 7 of this volume. From its starting point, it seems clear that Jordi Cadena's film – in a script co-written with the poet Carles Hac Mor – is trying to establish a link with the avant-garde legacy represented by the figure of J.V. Foix, but also by the figure of Carles Santos himself as a composer always connected with a certain cinematic model. In the film, Cadena weaves a small fiction around a cinema director – interpreted by the artist Carles Pazos – who wants to shoot a documentary dealing with the figure and the work of the Catalan poet. While researching his personality, the director becomes the victim of an obsession that forces him to take refuge in a mental clinic. Cadena interweaves this basic fictional plot with his own research of the archival images of the poet and his work, in an effort to find a way to convey his poetry on screen. Thus, *Es quan dormo que hi veig clar* is presented as an homage to the poetic legacy of J.V. Foix, the most acclaimed figure from the Catalan avant-garde, while also becoming a reflection on the possibility of creating another kind of cinema that establishes links with the past, and which also connects with the Barcelona School and with the most interesting elements both in poetry and in contemporary arts at work in Catalonia. In this sense, it is interesting to note how the film engages in different forms of collaboration with other artists and film-makers who were fighting for a new Catalan image other than that promoted by the Catalonia of the art design illustrated by the Cobi icon created by Mariscal. Thus, in the title credits of the film, we can find the presence of Joan Brossa or Antoni Tàpies, alongside directors such as Jesús Garay, Josep Antoni Salgot, Manuel Cussó-Ferré, and Gerard Gormezano, together with some resistant figures from the Barcelona School, such as that of Josep Maria Nunes.

4. Conclusion: To Sow the Seed

If one considers the box office returns of most of these films or simply their running times in commercial theatres, it is easy to speak of a certain failure in the cinema produced by this group of maverick directors. And yet, this very idea of failure could have been assigned to the cinema of the seventies around the Barcelona School. In both cases, the issue is not so much to be able to establish a solid industrial base, given the fact of Catalonia's scarce cinematic audience or the reality that most power within the cinematic institution had moved to Madrid, but to see how an alternative production was possible from the margins. It is from the perspective of this deeply assumed marginality that one must consider and admire the existence of a series of works that emerged around 92 Barcelona that ended up ignoring them. Besides, if one considers this reality from a historical perspective, it seems pretty obvious that the seed planted by the films shot by Portabella, Jordà, Guerín, Garay, Villaronga,

Cadena, Cussó-Ferré, Gormezano, and Recha became a fundamental one. That may explain why, almost ten years later, at the end of the nineties, one saw the emergence of the Master in Creative Documentary program at the Pompeu Fabra University in Barcelona. Its director, Jordi Balló, had the brilliant idea to look for a budgeting system, supported by ARTE and the Spanish Television, that made possible the revival of a documentary genre that had had almost no presence in Southern Europe in the last few years. Balló looked into the remaining figures from the Catalan avant-garde and, in the first season of the master's program, managed to count on the work of Joaquim Jordà and José Luis Guerín, and later with that of Marc Recha, who also directed a project. Beyond the direct filiation between the cinema around 92 and the documentary boom of the late nineties, one needs to consider the presence of several interesting linking elements. Many of the films produced during these years, for instance, tried their best to blur any genre borders and constantly searched for a new cinematic imaginary that fought against the dominance of television. These films also aimed for an auteur cinema model that could be competitive internationally while searching for a new gaze that would break away from any academic style. In 1992, there was no political juncture that paid any attention to the cinematic factor. This juncture did not come to be until a few years later, almost at the turn of the new millennium. Despite all of this, the very existence of a group of maverick directors who were willing to create works against the grain became an example and a true seed for the future of Catalan cinema.

Translated by Jaume Martí-Olivella

WORKS CITED

1492: The Conquest of Paradise. Directed by Ridley Scott, performances by Gérard Depardieu, Sigourney Weaver, Angela Molina, and Fernando Rey, Gaumont, 1992.

Amat, Jordi. *El llarg procés. Cultura i política en la Catalunya contemporánia (1993–2014)*. Tusquets, 2015.

— "Matar al cobi." *L'Hora*, 19 June 2013. http://www.noucicle.org/lhora/jordi-amat-matar-al-cobi/. Accessed 20 Dec. 2020.

L'amor és estrany. Directed by Carles Balagué, performances by Mario Gas, Eulàlia Ramon, and Muntsa Alcáñiz, Diafragma Produccions cinematogràfiques, 1988.

Balló, Jordi, Ramon Espelt, and Ramon Lorente. *Cinema català, 1975–1986*. Columna, 1990.

La banyera. Directed by Jesús Garay, performances by Muntsa Alcáñiz, Pep Munné, and Mercedes Sampietro, Manderley P.C., 1989.

Bar-Cel-Ona. Directed by Ferran Llagostera, performances by Ramon Madaula, Begoña Martí, and Alfred Luchetti, CPI, 1987.
Bilbao. Directed by Bigas Luna, performances by Àngel Jové, María Martín, and Isabel Pisano, Figaro Films and Ona Films, 1977.
Bonet, Lluís, Xavier Cubeles, and Joan M. Miralles. *La indústria del cinema a Catalunya*. Generalitat de Catalunya. Departament de Cultura, 2007.
Boom boom. Directed by Rosa Vergés, performances by Victor Laszlo, Sergi Mateu, Fernando Guillem Cuervo, and Àngels Gonyalons, Arsenal and Lamy Films, 1990.
Caniche. Directed by Bigas Luna, performances by Àngel Jové, Consol Tura, and Linda Pérez Ballardo, Figaro Films, 1978.
Casas, Quim. *Jesús Garay*. Filmoteca de Catalunya, 2009.
Cerdán, Josetxo, and Jaime Pena. "Variaciones sobre la incertidumbre (1984–2000)." *Historias del cine español*, edited by José Luis Castro de Paz, Via Láctea Editorial, 2005.
Christopher Columbus: The Discovery. Directed by John Glenn, performances by Georges Correface, Marlon Brando, Rachel Ward, and Catherine Zeta-Jones, Warner Bros, 1992.
El cielo sube. Directed by Marc Recha, performances by Salvador Dolz, Cornine Alba, and Ona Planas, Nofilms S.A., 1991.
El complot dels anells. Directed by Francesc Bellmunt, performances by Stephen Brennan, Ariadna Gil, Mònia Huguet, and Josep Maria Pou, Fair Play Produccions, 1987.
Els de davant. Directed by Jesús Garay, performances by Juanjo Puigcorbé, Estelle Skornik, and Ben Gazzara, La sept Arte, Redcom films, 1993.
De Moragas, Miguel. "La Olimpiada cultural de Barcelona en 1992: Luces y sombras. Lecciones para el futuro." *Investigación multidisciplinar y difusión de los estudios olímpicos*, edited by Emilio Fernández Peña et al., CEO. Centre d'Estudis Olímpics, 2012.
Die Stille vor Bach. Directed by Pere Porabella, performances by Alex Brendemühl, Feodor Atkine, Christian Brembek, and Daniel Ligorio, Films 59, 2007.
Las edades de Lulú. Directed by Bigas Luna, performances by Francesca Neri, Oscar Laroide, Javier Bardem, and Fernando Guillem Cuervo, Iberoamericana Films and Apricot Films, 1990.
El encargo del cazador. Directed by Joaquim Jordà, performances by Dària Esteban, Jacinto Esteban, Ricardo Bofill, and Luis Garcia Berlanga, Institut del cinema català and TVE, 1990.
Entreacte. Directed by Manuel Cussó-Ferré, performances by Vanessa Lorenzo, Fermí Reixach and Rosario Flores, Kronos Plays and Films S.A,1989.
L'escot. Directed by Antoni Verdaguer, performances by Laura Scott, Abel Folk, Ferran Rañé, and Mingo Ràfols, Ópalo Films, 1986.

És quan dormo que hi veig clar. Directed by Jordi Cadena, performances by Carles Pazos, Hermann Bonnin, Ona Planas, Mayte Caballero, and Núria Cano, Septimània Films, 1988.

Fecé, José Luis. "El tiempo reencontrado. Tren de sombras." *Imagen memoria y fascinación. Notas sobre el documental en España*, edited by Josep Maria Català, Josetxo Cerdán and Casimiro Torreiro, Ocho y Medio, 2001, pp. 307–12.

Guerra, Carles. "La mirada poliédrica de Joaquim Jordà." In *Nosferatu. Revista de cine*, no. 52, April 2006.

L'home precís. Directed by Antoni Padrós, performances by Xavier Tort, Antoni Padrós produccions, 2012.

Innisfree. Directed by José Luis Guerin, Virginia Films, Jose Luis Guerin P.C. and La sept cinema, 1990.

Jamón, jamón. Directed by Bigas Luna, performances by Penélope Cruz, Javier Bardem, Stephania Sandrelli, and Anna Galliena, Lola Films, Ovideo and Sogepaq, 1992.

Laura en la ciutat dels Sants. Directed by Gonzalo Herralde, performances by Angela Molina, Sergi Mateu, Terele Pávez, Juan Diego, IPC Ideas and Lauren Films, 1986

Lock Out. Directed by Antoni Padrós, performances by Rosa Morata, Marta Vives, and Rita Cemelli, Antoni Pradós produccions, 1973.

Manderley. Directed by Jesús Garay, performances by José Ocaña, Enrique Rada, and Joan Ferré, Manderlay.P.C., 1980.

Manila. Directed by Antoni Chavarrías, performances by Álex Casanovas, Laura Mañá, Mathieu Carrière, and Fermí Reixach, Oberon Cinematográfica and Quasar S.A., 1990.

Marathon. Directed by Carlos Saura, performances by Larry Bird, Michael Jordan, and Magic Johnson, Ibergroup S.A., 1992.

Més enllà de la passió. Directed by Jesús Garay, performances by Juanjo Puigcorbé, Patricia Adriani and Àngel Jové, Oberon, Institut del cinema català and Manderley, P.C., 1986.

Los motivos de Berta. Directed by José Luis Guerín, performances by Silvia Gracia, Arielle Dombasle, and Iñaki Aierra, Producciones cinematográficas Guerín, 1985.

Nemo. Directed by Jesús Garay, performances by Enrique Ibáñez, Maria Gorgues, and Santiago Tancón, Jesús Garay produccions, 1978.

El niño de la luna. Directed by Agustí Villaronga, performances by Maribel Martin, Lisa Gerard, Enrique Saldaña, and Gunter Meisner, Ganesh, 1989.

Pauné, Meritxell M. "Luces y Sombras de La Herencia Olímpica de Barcelona." *Urbanismopatasarriba*, 27 July 2012, urbanismopatasarriba.blogspot.com/2012/07/luces-y-sombras-de-la-herencia-olimpica.html?showComment=1343381493955#c8742158028431360015. Accessed 20 Dec. 2020.

Pedraza, Pilar. *Agustí Villaronga*. Akal, 2007.

Pont de Varsòvia. Directed by Pere Portabella, performances by Carme Elies, Josep Maria Pou, Jordi Dauder, and Ona Planas, Films 59, 1989.

Porter i Moix, Miquel. *Història del cinema a Catalunya, 1895–1990*. Generalitat de Catalunya. Departament de Cultura, 1992.

Què t'hi jugues Mari Pili? Directed by Ventura Pons, performances by Núria Hosta, Mercè Lleixà, and Núria Pàmpols, Els films de la Rambla, 1991.

The Quiet Man. Directed by John Ford, performances by John Wayne, Maureen O'Hara, Barry Fitzgerald, and Ward Bond, Republic films, 1950.

Qui t'estima Babel? Directed by Ignasi P. Farré, performances by Mercedes Sampietro, Assumpta Serna, and Mireia Tomàs, Produccions TA Barcelona and Lauren Films, 1988.

Resina, Joan Ramon. *La vocació de modernitat de Barcelona: Auge i declivi d'una imatge urbana*. Galàxia Gutemberg, 2008.

La rossa del bar. Directed by Ventura Pons, performances by Enric Majó, Núria Hosta, Ramoncín, and Loles León, Els Films de la Rambla and Lauren Films, 1987.

Shirley Temple Story. Directed by Antoni Padrós, performances by Rosa Morata, Dolors Duocastella, Montse Fontova, and Jesús Garay, Antoni Padrós produccions, 1976.

Solitud. Directed by Romà Guardiet, performances by Omero Antonutti, Núria Cano, Carme Samsa and and Pep Tosar, Quasar S.A., 1991.

La teranyina. Directed by Antoni Verdaguer, performances by Sergi Mateu, Fernando Guillén, Amparo Soler Leal and Jordi Dauder, Floc, 1990.

Tras el cristal. Directed by Agustí Villaronga, performances by David Sust, Gunter Meisner, and Marisa Paredes. T.E.M. Productores S.A., 1987.

Tren de sombras. Directed by José Luis Guerín, performances by Anne Céline-Auche, Juliette Gautier, and Ivon Orbain, Films 59, Institut del cinema català and Grup Cinema-Art, 1997.

Todo sobre mi madre. Directed by Pedro Almodovar, performances by Cecilia Roth, Marisa Paredes, Penélope Cruz, and Antonia San Juan, El Deseo, 1999.

L'última frontera. Directed by Manuel Cussó-Ferré, performances by Quim Lecina, Francesca Neri, and Blanca Martinez, Kronos Films, S.A., 1992.

Un submarí a les estovalles. Directed by Ignasi P. Farré, performances by Dina Souli, Ariadna Gil, and Rosa Maria Sardà, Institut del cinema català and Ixia Films, 1991.

Una nit a Casa Blanca. Directed by Antoni Martí, performances by Emma Vilarasau, Carles Pongiluppi, Miquel Cors, and Victor Israel, Serveis Video Empordà S.A, 1987.

Vázquez Montalbán, Manuel. *Obra periodística III. Las batallas perdidas*. Debate, 2015.

El vent de l'illa. Directed by Gerard Gormezano, performances by Simon Casel, Ona Planas, Mara Truscana, Anthony and Pilley, Gerard Gormezano produccions, 1988.

Verònica L. (Una dona al meu jardí). Directed by Antoni Padrós i Octavi Martí, performances by Sergi Mateu, Rosa Morata, and Karin de Villeneuve, Antoni Padrós produccions, 1989.

Vicky, Cristina, Barcelona. Directed by Woody Allen, performances by Rebeca Hall, Scarlett Johanson, Penélope Cruz, and Javier Bardem, Wenstein Company and Mediapro, 2008.

Viridiana. Directed by Luis Buñuel, peformances by Sílvia Pinal, Fernando Rey, and Paco Rabal, Films 59, 1961.

Zunzunegui, Santos. "Portabella extraterritorial." *Historias sin argumento]: El cine de Pere Portabella*, edited by Marcelo Expósito. Ediciones la Mirada, 2001.

PART TWO

The Jordà Legacy

2 The Hunter and the Monkeys: Jacinto Esteva, Joaquim Jordà, and the Legacy of the Barcelona School

ESTEVE RIAMBAU

It has often been argued that the Barcelona Film School's legacy was kept alive by film-makers such as the underground artist Antoni Padrós or the politically committed Llorenç Soler only to be handed over to the generation of Catalan film-makers that sprung up beginning in the 1990s. Objectively, however, it is difficult to set figures from that generation, like Agustí Villaronga, Jesús Garay, José Luis Guerín, Marc Recha, or younger members like Mercedes Álvarez, Isaki Lacuesta, and Albert Serra, alongside the figures that preceded them: Jacinto Esteva, Pere Portabella, José María Nunes, and Vicente Aranda. To start, the historical context is radically different: active from 1967 to 1970, the Barcelona School had no classrooms at all; rather, it was a one-of-a-kind movement with its own trajectory. It appeared under the Francoist regime as a reaction not only to the dictatorship but also to the politically dissident cinema that was being produced in Madrid at that time. Young film-makers like Basilio Martín Patino, Julio Diamante, Antxon Eceiza, and Miguel Picazo trained at the Official School of Cinema and were influenced by social realism. They wanted to emulate the Italian neorealist style that arrived very late in Spain since the regime's strict censorship was unwilling to tolerate a style of that sort. Their colleagues from Barcelona, on the other hand, looked to the French Nouvelle Vague – a much more recent and geographically proximate style – for a new aesthetic model, one that could be emulated without as much risk of censure: "If they do not allow us to be Victor Hugo, we will be Mallarmé," said Joaquim Jordà publicly, which meant in plain speak: "Since our censorship will not allow realism in cinema, we will do poetic films." And thus, the Barcelona Film School was born, with the support of José María García Escudero, the General Director of Spanish Cinematography, who said that "As long you do not include working class in your films, you will not have any problems." Both men were quite right.

Joaquim Jordà and Jacinto Esteva first met and worked as co-directors of *Dante no es únicamente severo (Dante Is Not Only Harsh)* in 1967. Before crossing paths with Esteva, Jordà – whose father was a Catalan notary close to Franco's ideology – had made a short film, *Día de los Muertos (Day of the Dead*, 1960), which was censored for showing the tombstones of Republican intellectuals in the Almudena Cemetery in Madrid. Jacinto Esteva Grewe also belonged to a high society Catalan family and had likewise directed two short documentary films as well as a feature-length documentary that were similarly restricted by the government. *Notes sur l'émigration. Espagne 1960 (Notes on Emigration, Spain 1960*, 1961) was filmed in three locations – Geneva, Barcelona, and Andalusia – to document the journey made by Spaniards who were forced to look for work in Switzerland while, at same time, Franco's regime began to promote Spain's appeal as a tourist destination internationally. *Notes on Emigration* was seized in Milan by a Spanish Nationalist commando, heavily re-edited, and later broadcast on Spanish national television as an example of actions taken by the regime's enemies. Esteva then chose the island of Ibiza to film *Autour des salines (Around the Salt Marshes*, 1962), where a worker's alleged death serves as the pretext to film the reactions of the man's friends on camera. Although it was screened at the Cannes Film Festival, this short film never made it onto the viewing circuit in Spain. Finally, the feature-length *Lejos de los árboles (Far from the Trees)* was filmed between 1961 and 1963, following the calendar of Spanish popular festivals that included animal torture and killing, psychological trances bordering on hysteria, or displays of self-inflicted physical punishment as religious penance. After re-editing the film several times, the final version that was ultimately presented to the censor board was shortened by thirty minutes due to many cuts (they were restored only after Spain return to democracy).

Once it became clear that it would be impossible for Esteva and Jordà to emulate Victor Hugo, they decided on a feature-length film that fully conveyed Mallarmé's spirit. Néstor Almendros, the Barcelona-born director of photography who had lived in Cuba during the first days of Castro's revolution and had already made his home in the France of the Nouvelle Vague working for Eric Rohmer and François Truffaut, led the way. It was he who suggested to his colleagues in Barcelona that they should embark upon the course of the newly formed School with an episodic feature-length film similar to *Six in Paris (Paris vu par...*, 1965), on which he had collaborated for Rohmer's section. However, the other directors did not follow through: Antonio de Senillosa and Gonzalo Suárez parted ways with the project while still in its earliest phase, and at some point before the final editing, Pere Portabella and Ricardo Bofill also left the production. Without their respective sections (Portabella's *No compteu amb els dits* [*Don't Count with Your Fingers*] and Bofill's *Cercles* [*Circles*]), all that was left was Esteva and Jordà's contributions, tucked in between a prologue and an epilogue reminiscent of Buñuel, that comprised the feature film which was to become the flagship of the Barcelona School. The result was a manifesto that combined homages to Jean-Luc Godard, the exaltation of the cosmopolitan city through which strolled the so-called *gauche divine*, Dadaist provocations, and a predominance of a pop aesthetic over any realist (or social, of course) critique.

Despite their friendship, the two film-makers' paths once again parted ways. Esteva remained active in making explicitly iconoclast fiction film such as the feature films *Después del diluvio* (*After the Flood*, 1968), *Metamorfosis* (*Metamorphosis*, 1970), and *Le Fils de Marie* (*Marie's Son*, 1971), the last of which was filmed in Catalonia but under Luxembourg's flag in order to avoid the censorship, which had turned yet more strict, even for films in which workers did not appear. For his part, Jordà also attempted to continue in fiction film with adaptations – ultimately abandoned – of novels by Witold Gombrowitz (*Cosmos*, 1967), Miquel Llor (*Laura in the City of Saints / Laura a la ciutat dels sants*, 1969), and Maria Aurèlia Capmany. The description of one of Capmany's books did lead, however, to a mid-length film: *Maria Aurèlia Capmany parla d'Un lloc entre els morts* (*Maria Aurèlia Capmany Talks about "A Place among the Dead,"* 1969). Jordà made the film, a documentary essay about a liberal intellectual, prior to his voluntary exile in Italy, where he would make a series of politically committed feature films: *Portogallo, paese tranquilo* (*Portugal, a Quiet Land*, 1969), *Il perchè del dissenso* (*The Reason of Dissent*, 1969), *Lenin vivo* (*Lenin Alive*, 1970), and *Spezziamo le catene* (*Let's Break the Chains*, 1971). Esteva visited Jordà during his first months in Italy, but his travels took a turn upon discovering in Africa a magnified and ancestral version of the rituals he had filmed previously in Spain. The result is two unfinished documentaries, *Mozambique* (1970) and *La isla de las lágrimas/Del Arca de Noé al Pirata Rhodes* (*The Island of Tears/From Noah's Ark to the Rhodes Pirate*, 1971), filmed consecutively, during each of the African expeditions Esteva undertook, with colonization and slavery firmly in the background of both films. Of all the material filmed, only five hours were preserved, unedited and with no sound, during which the camera focuses on flayed buffaloes, monkeys strung up in trees as bait for big game hunting, burials and witchcraft rituals. The footage survives as Esteva's premature cinematic testimony. He remained connected to Africa through the creation of a safari company in the Central African Republic, ruled at the time by the dictator Jean-Bédel Bokassa.

Jordà returned to Spain shortly before Franco's death and promptly applied his talent for writing, which he had essentially developed as a translator, to a new career as a scriptwriter. In 1979, he returned to film-making with *Numax presenta... (Numax Presents...)*, a documentary about a cooperative-management experiment at a factory taken over by its employees. With the support of the new democracy, workers could now appear on screen, since Marx, or perhaps Antonio Labriola or Georges Sorel, had substituted Victor Hugo. More importantly, the new film-makers with whom he came into contact when he began teaching in the Master of Documentary Film Programme at the University of Pompeu Fabra in Barcelona in the late 1990s applauded Jordà's first documentary. Lacuesta and Álvarez enrolled in classes he taught, while Guerín took the lead on one of the first documentary film projects *En construcción (Work in Progress*, 2001) at the university and Recha filmed *Pau i el seu germà (Pau and His Brother*, 2001) with Jordà as the scriptwriter. With Nuria Villazán as co-director and J.A. Pérez Giner as producer, Jordà's *Mones com la Becky (Monkeys Like Becky*, 1999) was his other contribution during that time at Pompeu Fabra. The film centres on a critique of the Portuguese psychiatrist and neurosurgeon Egas Moniz, winner of the Nobel Prize in Medicine in 1949 for inventing the lobotomy, a palliative technique designed to assuage the aggression that certain psychiatric patients presented, but which also effectively eliminated the person's personality. The film was conceived at its outset as a fictional project starring Fernando Fernán Gómez; however, difficulties financing the film, as well as the Portuguese resistance to criticism of a national hero, who had appeared on the back of the 10,000 escudo bill, meant that the project became a documentary. The in-patient residents at a psychiatric asylum enact Moniz's story, and Jordà makes a personal appearance in the plot by including images of the procedure he underwent to remove a clot that had caused him to suffer a cerebral stroke. Whereas in *Dante* he had filmed the scalpel about to tear an eye in homage to *Un chien andalou*, this time he provided a close-up view of his sick body and the medication he took as an act of empathy and solidarity with the psychiatric patients who appear in *Monkeys Like Becky*.

From that moment on, Jordà's personal transformation – prompted by a disease that forced him to retrain his brain while granting him new inspiration as a film-maker – became the motor and the unifying thread of a particular style in Catalan cinema.[1] Young film-makers,

---

[1] I referred to it as such in the title of an article published in the magazine *Nosferatu*, no. 9, June 1992, an issue dedicated to Garay, Guerín, Jordà, and Portabella.

finding themselves on the professional sidelines of a precarious industry, followed a particular style: one that weaved documentary work and fiction, joined conventional narrative and an experimental style that, although commonly recognized as a distinguishing element of the Barcelona School, in fact owed more to a shared transgressive desire than to any direct influence. The power of the unifying thread that stitched its way along unconventional paths is demonstrated by the fact that the only fiction film that Jordà filmed at that point, *Un cos al bosc/Un cuerpo en el bosque* (*A Body in the Forest*, 1996), does not shine as brightly as his following documentary-essay work. In the documentary *Més enllà del mirall/Más allá del espejo* (*Beyond the Mirror*, 2006), he looked to Lewis Carroll's *Alice Through the Looking Glass* to find his own reflection in the portrayal of two girls with sensory deficits. A blind young lady and a girl who suffers from agnosia (inability to recognize objects using the senses) became part of the singular characters that appear in Jordàs's works: characters who are injured or disabled but always rebellious. Other examples would be the pederast Vicente Tamarit, who appears in *De nens/De niños* (*About Children*, 2003); amid the corruption problems in the development of the Barcelona neighbourhood of El Raval; or the former *Numax* workers who reappear in *Vint anys no són res/Veinte años no es nada* (*Twenty Years Is Nothing*, 2004), an affecting testimony to the passage of time; and, of course, Jacinto Esteva in the earlier *El encargo del cazador* (*The Hunter's Request*, 1990). The latter is the essential link between the Barcelona School and new generations of film-makers. It anticipates various elements that Jordà will bring back to the screen in *Monkeys Like Becky*: the borders between madness and art – painting and writing in Esteva's case, theatre in the case of the in-patient residents in the 1999 film; the abyss that opens up to death, which Jordà shares following his own illness; the destruction of the accompanying myths – the self-destructive film-maker and the award-winning neurosurgeon who eliminated patients' personalities; and lastly, the allusions to Africa thanks to the journeys Esteva undertook there and the reference to Becky the monkey, Moniz's test subject for the lobotomy procedure.

The Hunter's Request was filmed in 1990, almost three years prior to the publication of the book[2] in which Casimiro Torreiro and myself defended the Barcelona School – a movement reviled by some, ignored

---

[2] *Temps era temps: L'Escola de Barcelona i el seu entorn*, Departament de Cultura, Barcelona, 1993. There was a later edition, corrected and modified: *La Escuela de Barcelona. El cine de la "gauche divine,"* Anagrama, Barcelona, 1999.

by others, and at that time, downplayed by those who were, in effect, its driving forces. The film was, in fact, Daria Esteva's initiative. Upon her father's death in 1985, Daria Esteva had taken to heart the desire he expressed in his will that she keep his work alive: "Make sure that they don't forget me," Jacinto had asked her. With this goal in mind, Daria Esteva contributed the images previously filmed in Africa and the pages of the unfinished novel, *El elefante invertebrado* (*The Invertebrate Elephant*), so that Joaquim Jordà, his friend and co-producer of *Dante*, could edit them and, hopefully, end the feeling of waste – waste of time, and waste of talent – that she felt regarding her father's important but unfinished work. Jordà declined her first proposal but acquiesced to filming a piece about Esteva in which Daria ended up playing a crucial role. This was the origin of *The Hunter's Request*, a cross between a funeral eulogy for a friend who has departed and an unrelenting criticism of the most frivolous faction of the Barcelona School. It would be a preview of what Jordà's final films would be, each one constructed around peeping into other people's lives, laying bare intimate details of their fragile, even marginal, existence.

The film-maker has shared the details about this posthumous encounter with the friend he had not seen since the late 1960s. Jordà had one final chance in 1984, when Esteva invited him to the opening of his exhibition, *Cien dibujos y pinturas* (*A Hundred Drawings and Paintings*), at an art gallery in Madrid. Several of Esteva's latest pieces were being displayed, some of them painted with organic materials with the express desire that they actually decay and not withstand time. Others were full of tormented figures, similar to Goya's etchings but drawn with markers or created through a variety of techniques, and with content as apocalyptic as the great master's. Later his art turns darker. For example, next to an amalgam of faces grouped together, it reads: "Camina, pero deja caminar: también existen muñecas de colores … pero hay que pintarlas" ("Walk, but let walk: there are also colourful dolls … but they must be painted"; 1983). Later, in 1985, he painted three human faces beneath the invocation: "Cristo nuestro señor. Padre y madre a los 7 años el día de tu primera comunión" ("Lord, Our God. Father and Mother, at 7 years old, the day of your First Communion"). Perhaps it is the autobiographic invocation of that boy who, in *Dante*, at age thirty-one, does not understand why they force him to get out of bed to go to school. He also invoked his African excursions in a horrific work, *Hipopótamo sin raíces* (*Rootless Hippopotamus*, 1983). Meanwhile, *Virgen María* (*Virgin Mary*, 1985) examined religious beliefs that were also featured in his last feature film, *El hijo de María* (*Mary's Son*) from the perspective of fertilization, which also appears in the drawings *Maternidad*

4 (*Maternity 4*, 1985) and *Publicidad de píldoras anticonceptivas* (*Advertising for Birth Control Pills*, 1985).[3]

Despite his friend's letter, Jordà did not go to the meeting: "I'm not sure, but I finally decided not to go because I really don't want to talk about it again and relive years that are long gone" (Jordà in Riambau, Salvadó, and Torreiro 67). In fact, not many people attended the vernissage and there was hardly any media coverage. And yet, that would have been their last chance to meet, since Esteva died in September the following year, and Jordà apologized for missing this chance in his obituary:

> I spent many days and many nights with Jacinto, more nights than days (since he was not an early riser) over several years. We drank together. Together we made the film, *Dante*, together we started that "mess" later called the Barcelona School [...]; we laughed about it together; we travelled together after making the film; and we lived through the death of our film editor, Joan Oliver, who died standing at the moviola and to whom we dedicated the film. Then we stopped seeing each other. He made a few more films that made a bit of a stir, and I made a few others that made none at all. He went to Kenya, or somewhere, and I went to Italy. But there was always a chance that this mutual absence was only temporary, and that some fortunate encounter would put an end to it. And now that chance is gone. And it hurts. [...] I guess the best show that anyone could hope to experience is to attend his own burial, or the funeral rites that follow the wrongs we lived. I like to imagine that Jacinto is able to do this. And I wish I could hear his laughter, that scratchy laugh made hoarse by alcohol. "What are these crazy guys saying!"[4]

Much of the same heartfelt and nostalgic spirit, as well as a sceptical and sarcastic tone, are present in the film that Jordà later dedicated to Esteva. But several more years would pass before Daria Esteva, during a memorial event at the University of Barcelona in late 1988, shared the legacy that Esteva's friend, Jordà, seemed to be the best-suited to carry out "the hunter's request" to finish his work, although ultimately in his own style.

---

3 Property of Daria Esteva and displayed in the exhibit "Jacinto Esteva: A l'ombra de l'últim arbre" ("Jacinto Esteva: Under the Shadow of the Last Tree"), curated by Esteve Riambau in the Filmoteca de Catalunya, Barcelona, 2014. The exhibit's virtual catalogue can be consulted at http://www.filmoteca.cat/web/la-filmoteca/publicacions/llibres-i-catalegs/cataleg-virtual-de-lecposicio-jacinto-esteva-a-lombra-0.
4 Joaquim Jordà, "Lo compararon con Nicholas Ray ..." *El País*, 12 September1985, p. 25.

Once again, Jordà explained his strategy:

> The request to be in charge of material belonging to someone who had died had a necrophilic aspect that discouraged me. [...] As I tried to get over this feeling, another idea took hold of me: why not turn the material into a biographical essay about Jacinto? Instead of working with dead material, I would try to bring its author back to life. (Jordà, "El encargo del cazador" 100–1)

The process consisted of accumulating information and testimonies in order to develop the Freudian concept of the "familial romance": "When an abundance of neurotic behaviours manifest in one family group, an inappropriate distribution of parental roles must be considered. The psychoanalyst's task will be to determine what the appropriate balance would be," Jordà continues, before clarifying, "So I decided to treat the people I interviewed as 'characters' in a script written by reality, and to treat the accumulation of documentary material as the structural elements of an action film" (100). Upon Manuel Pérez Estremera's initiative and with the Institute of Catalan Cinema's executive support and produced by Spanish public television, the film was finished in June 1990, with a final cut leaving the film at some forty minutes shorter than Jordà originally planned.[5]

The Hunter's Request establishes a relation with its characters that is reminiscent of the relationship that Jaime Chávarri establishes with the characters in his *El desencanto* (*The Disenchantment*, 1976), a documentary that examines Francoist poet Leopoldo Panero and his family against the backdrop of the decline of the dictatorship. Jordà carefully analysed Chávarri's group dynamics, rather than reverting to his first-person involvement like he did in *Monkeys Like Becky*. His documentary about Jacinto Esteva transcends the everyday dimension of its characters. Rather, it bestows upon them a metaphoric air thanks to interviews contextualized through the important staging that Jordà was to repeat in his subsequent work. The film's structure also added to this transcending of reality, conceived of as "a journey to the land of the dead" (Jordà in Riambau, Salvadó, and Toreiro 63). It retells the myth

---

5 The testimonies that were not used include one by film-makers Jaime Camino and Vicente Aranda or Eve, one of Esteva's lovers, and the comedian José Luis Coll. Part of his adventure in the Central African Republic was also cut, along with testimonies by Romy and Omar about gambling, as well as Daria Esteva's explanation of her father's relationship with dogs. The version that was finally shown does not, however, change the overall meaning.

of Orpheus and Eurydice with the difference that this time around they are not lovers, but instead father and daughter. It is also the daughter who goes in search of her departed parent in an Inferno where the fear of being forgotten is just one of its many horrors.

The hunter's death drive and his final request are explicitly present in the film's opening scenes. Daria visits the Esteva family mausoleum and reads the letter in which her father ask,: "If I go to Africa this week and the plane crashes, I beg you to go through my writings, patiently when you have time, and publish them. Even if only for the sake of a dead man's vanity." The anthropologist Manuel Delgado, who organized Esteva's memorial event at the University of Barcelona and is the author of the excellent essay on *Far from The Trees* (see Delgado), remarked that day that "one never returns unharmed from the journeys to find oneself and sometimes, like in Jacinto's case, one never returns at all." With these scenes as a preamble, the film's arc is already delineated; it foreshadows the conclusion of a simultaneously biological and mythological trajectory. In its first section, *The Hunter's Request* presents the testimonies of Jacinto's siblings, Carlos and Rosa, and the architect Ricardo Bofill as well as Annie Settimó, his first wife and the mother of his two children, Jacinto and Daria. But it quickly introduces the first shadows of his alcoholic addiction, as narrated by Dr. Pozuelo. The next section traces his importance as a film-maker.

Several directors appear and explain Esteva's work and persona: Pere Portabella, the film-maker who became Annie Settimó's partner following her separation from Esteva; the Portuguese director José María Nunes, who calls Esteva "mi amo" ("my boss"); the cinematographer Manel Esteban – who refers to him as "a gentle monster"; and Francisco Ruiz Camps, the manager of the company that produced Esteva's films, who compares Esteva's work as a film-maker to that of "a painter who painted with very expensive brushes." We are in the thick of the Barcelona School years. While Jordà was a founding member of the School, he later critically distanced himself, and in the film he settles the score relentlessly. At that time, members of the Barcelona School gathered in the Boccaccio club with writers, editors, photographers, architects, and models from the Barcelona bourgeoise, with the slogan "Life was better [when we were] against Franco." Twenty-five years later, Jordà invites some of the survivors to another fashionable locale to let them impersonate themselves as a group, with frivolous banalities that the camera records in a long and majestic travelling shot that shows them anonymously, as ghosts in the shadows, while photographs of their younger selves confront their present selves, showing their personal exposure to the inexorability of time. Jordà filmed the shot at the beginning and at the end of the evening – the shot is much longer in the first version of the film – and he did not include the later take, when alcohol had made the scene even more pathetic, out of compassion. Unquestionably, this is revenge for the same wrongs – the censorship imposed by Franco's regime, but also a certain superficiality of the leftist opposition to the dictatorship coupled with a personal sense of political disappointment – that drove him to exile in the late 1960s and with that, his definitive abandonment of the Barcelona School. But it was also the door that, in the film, opens onto the abyss that Jacinto Esteva slid into.

In the next scene, a series of unidentified friends gather at the Stork Club, another fashionable venue of the times, and the character's dark side is revealed in a second lateral travelling shot, much tighter this time and layered with troubling repetitions. This sombre portrayal, still blurry, grows in the presence of his women. Romy, the model and actress with whom he lived for nineteen years, refuses to be filmed inside what had been her home, which is chock-full of hunting trophies. She explains that she voluntarily had her gallbladder removed in order to accompany Jacinto in his nocturnal alcoholic binges. During one of those nights, he committed sexual violence as an act of love. Then, Ana Ventosa, his final partner, admits that she served him drinks on binge drinking nights, and explains that until the day she brought her toothbrush to the apartment, he did not ask her to bring her suitcases. Lastly, Annie Settimo's memory of what their relationship was is already too far lost in time, and the film leads into one of the final African adventures.

Lacking the budget necessary to film in natural settings, Jordà filmed Jacinto and Annie's daughter in the Barcelona Zoo as the site for her narrating the outlandish story of Ebra Safaris, the leading elephant-hunting company that ultimately failed, due to the prevailing corruption in Bokassa's regime. Jacinto Esteva and José Antonio Moreno, the company's founders, were imprisoned and the company was seized because a minister wished to keep for himself their seven tons of ivory. Julio Garriga, another of the company's members, recovered the valuable inventory at the very last moment. The hunters' revenge was to buy diamonds directly from miners and move them out of the country, illegally, and then drop them over Sudanese territory from a small airplane. The plan was never put into action, but it was worthy of a James Bond film.

The Hunter's Request continues to portray Esteva's gambling addiction. This time it is his friend Omar who, in front of the green felt and amidst cheerful allusions to guns, tells the tale of never-ending card sessions with judges, lawyers, policemen, and businessmen with millions of pesetas on the table, which he would then collect and take to the bank. This scene is the unquestionable last step before Jordà's film descends into hell. A fortuitous encounter between film-maker Luis G. Berlanga and Jacinto Esteva in an airport, where the latter was transporting his adolescent son's ashes after cremation in Madrid, provides Daria with the opportunity to retell her brother's suicide by cyanide in his mother's home. A psychiatrist diagnoses the motives: Jacinto Jr. admired his stepfather, Pere Portabella, but interpreted as a betrayal his role in organizing President Josep Taradellas's return to Catalonia following his exile, a rejection of the communist attitude that he had supported until then. For the psychiatrist, suicide is a second paternal failure. For Daria, on the other hand, it was "an aesthetic choice" that her brother carried out in competition with his biological father. Jordà explores this wound further, and at this point in the film introduces a tape-recording in which her father's imagined voice reminds her "that it was you and not Jacinto who should have taken the cyanide." She knew that it was Jordà's own voice, distorted, and in the film she does not take this interpellation seriously; she does, however, agree with Ana Ventosa that Jacinto could not get over the loss of his son, and this feeling drove him to self-destructive behaviour. He tried, in vain, to find a way out of this black hole by travelling to Africa again, and following new medical treatment, but bit by bit, he isolated himself in his Barcelona home, giving himself over to writing, painting, and caring for his dogs. "You can't deceive the ghosts using the same tricks," Daria claims, as the film moves on to the failure of the 1984 painting exhibit in Madrid mentioned earlier.

This is the exact moment when Jacinto Esteva appears physically in *The Hunter's Request*. Jordà achieves this appearance by means of images filmed by Benito Rabal for a 1984 Spanish Television program about the borders between painting and madness, entitled *What Are We Doing Here?*, a title that in Spanish employs a play on words (*¿Qué pintamos aquí?*) evoking existential questioning of the human condition. Benito/Paco Rabal, the film-maker's dear friend and star of *After the Flood*, acts as presenter. Jacinto prepared conscientiously for this interview, but the crew postponed the filming by a day, and by the next morning, Jacinto had fallen back into the abyss. The result, in Daria's words, is "a live autopsy" that she herself could not bear; as such, she did not attend the final two days of filming, unlike her friend Ana Ventosa, who became fascinated and who, according to Daria in the film, "was used like the wall in a handball game." Jacinto's interventions, as presented by Jordà in the film, are more distilled than in Benito Rabal's original interview, and they transmit an even more delirious – and depressing – sensation, as he speaks on topics ranging from surrealism to the difference between humans' and animals' relationship with the real and the affective, to the justification for killing old elephants in order to guarantee protein in the natives' diet.

The result is devastating. Jordà shows no pity in portraying his friend's decadence in transgressing boundaries that he, too, perhaps perceived but would never have dared to cross. These images bear no likeness even to those of Leopoldo Panero, the Francoist poet's disobedient son, in his appearance at the end of *The Disenchantment*, which fully contradicts the narrative told by his mother and brothers about the figure of the absent father. Jacinto Esteva, at the end of *The Hunter's Request*, cannot be critical because he is not in his right mind. He is, simply, a vulnerable instrument in Jordà's hands, just as his other characters will be in further films: the psychiatric patients in *Monkeys Like Becky*, the convicted pederast in *De nens/De niños*, the workers-cum-bank robbers in *Twenty Years Is Nothing* or the young women with disabilities in *Beyond the Mirror*. It is a ghostly apparition that achieves its dramatic effect but that, according to Daria's testimony in the film, "would be less painful if Jacinto hadn't died a short time after. He was in the last stretch, and the path towards his death was clear." Jordà illustrates that fact with another travelling shot. It is no longer lateral, like the one that shows the debris from the fallout of the Barcelona School and the *gauche divine*; rather, it is head-on and subjective, with Jacinto's drunken voice (or is it another impersonation by Joaquim?) and fragments of images filmed in Africa, reminiscent of the Vovodó River, in the Central African Republic, that Esteva would cross never to return, emulating the protagonist of the novel *Heart of Darkness* by Joseph Conrad.

In contrast to this use of metaphor, *The Hunter's Request* presents an abundance of extremely physical details: Esteva's death wish and cowardice in suicide, the self-destructive spiral of gin and cocaine, his body barely covered by a robe or a towel, his feet so swollen he couldn't even wear shoes, and, finally, the bathroom where his corpse was discovered, preceded by a second subjective travelling shot. And here is where metaphor makes its appearance, with Esteva's favourite Great Dane named Socrates, after the Greek philosopher who committed suicide with poisonous hemlock. The noble pet died a week later. Daria explains that her father believed that "that dog was the reincarnation of my brother, which made him a little unsettling in my eyes, and because of the whole story behind him, I had to bury him myself."

The film ends with a final artistic turn in which Daria confronts her father's legacy, in a letter in which he begs her "not to fall down the slippery slope of common sense;" and also with the impossibility of carrying out "the hunter's request." As she mentions, following the unfinished novel and the university homage, Jordà's film is the third frustrated attempt to do so, since "it is impossible to explain someone by trapping him in a film, because it's like freezing him, and that's not how real life is." Speaking directly to the camera, she delivers her final, ominous sentence: "I've had it with people talking about Jacinto," a fitting ending to Jordà's project of cinematic exorcism.

Epilogue: During the past seven years, as Director of the Filmoteca de Catalunya, I have worked with Daria Esteva to preserve her father's filmography by rescuing some material that was given up for lost. Together we curated the exhibition *Jacinto Esteva, a l'ombra de l'últim arbre* (*Jacinto Esteva, Under the Shadow of the Last Tree*, 2014), which reflected the filmmaker's choice to end his life journey by crossing the Vovodó River. The exhibit was accompanied by a retrospective of his restored films, and for the first time, some of his early paintings were included in the exhibit. We also edited his complete filmography on DVD, and in the near future, we will write a book that, perhaps, will allow us to close the circle.

Translated by Anton Pujol

WORKS CITED

Cercles. Directed by Ricardo Bofill, performances by Serena Vergano, Salvador Clotas, and Romy, Tibidabo Films, 1966.
Delgado, Manuel. "El arte de danzar sobre el abismo." *Imagen, memoria y fascinación: Notas sobre el documental en España*, edited by Josep Maria Català, Josetxo Cerdán, and Casimiro Torreiro, Consejería de Cultura, Junta de Andalucía, 2001, pp. 221–30.
El desencanto. Directed by Jaime Chavarri, Elías Querejeta PC, 1976.
En construcción. Directed by José Luis Guerín, Ovideo and La Sept Arte/INA, 2001.
Esteva Grewe, Jacinto, director. *Autour des salines*, Filmscontacto, 1962.
– *Después del diluvio*, performances by Francisco Rabal, Mijanou Bardot, and Francisco Viader, Filmscontacto, 1968.
– *Le Fils de Marie*, performances by Núria Espert, Romy, Ramón Eugenio de Goicoechea, and Serena Vergano, Filmscontacto, 1971.
– *Lejos de los árboles*, Filmscontacto, 1961–71.
– *Metamorfosis*, performances by Romy, Marta May, Marta Mejías, and Carlos Otero, Filmscontacto, 1970.
Dante no es únicamente severo. Directed by Jacinto Esteva Grewe and Joaquim Jordà, performances by Serena Vergano, Enrique Irazoqui, Romy, and Hannie van Zantwyk, Filmscontacto, 1967.

Notes sur l'émigration: Espagne 1960. Directed by Jacinto Esteva Grewe and Paolo Brunatto, 1961.

Jordà, Joaquim. "A quien una vez compararon con Nicholas Ray ..." *El País*, 11 Sept. 1985. https://elpais.com/diario/1985/09/12/cultura/495324002_850215.html. Accessed 20 Dec. 2020.

- "El encargo del cazador." *Nosferatu. Revista de cine*, June 1992, pp. 100–1.

Jordà, Joaquim, director. *De nens*, performances by Marta Galán, Núria Lloansi, Xabier Robés, Mireia Serra, Carla Jiménez, and Oscar Albadalejo, Massa d'Or, 2003.

- *Día de los Muertos*, UNINCI, 1960.
- *El encargo del cazador*, performances by Dària Esteva, Rosa María Esteva, Annie Settimó, and Romy, TVE and Institut del Cinema Català, 1990.
- *Il perchè del dissenso*, Unitelfilm, 1969.
- *Maria Aurèlia Capmany parla d'"Un lloc entre els morts,"* Los Films de Formentera, 1969.
- *Més enllà del mirall*, Ovideo, 2006.
- *Numax presenta...*, performances by Walter Cots, María Espinosa, Mario Gas, Rosa Gavín, Víctor Guillén, and Joaquim Jordà, Asamblea de Trabajadores de Numax, 1979.
- *Portogallo paese tranquilo*, Unitelfilm, 1969.
- *Spezziamo le catene*, Unitelfilm, 1971.
- *Un cos al bosc*, performances by Rossy de Palma, Núria Prims, Ricard Borràs, and Joan Masdeu, Sogedasa, Els Quatre Gats and Els Films de l'Orient, 1996.
- *Veinte años no es nada*, performances by Blanca Galán, Josefa Sánchez, Fernanda Gázquez, Eulogio Roca, Josefina Altamira, and Emilia Fernández, Ovideo and Unicamente severo Films, 2004.

Lenin vivo. Directed by Joaquim Jordà and Gianni Toti, Archivio Audiovisivo del Movimento Operaio e Democratico, 1970.

Mones com la Becky. Directed by Joaquim Jordà and Núria Villazán, performances by João Maria Pinto, Marian Varela, Petra Alcántara, Montse Bustos, Juana Cabeza, and Ramsés Espín, Els Quatre Gats and La Sept Arte, 1999.

No compteu amb els dits. Directed by Pere Portabella, performances by Mario Cabré, Natatcha Gounkevitch, and Willy van Rooy, Films 59, 1967.

Paris vu par .... Directed by Claude Chabrol, Jean Douchet, Jean Luc Godard, Jean Daniel Pollet, Jean Rouch, and Eric Rohmer, performances by Stéphane Audran, Johanna Shimkus, Micheline Dax, and Barbet Schroeder, Les Films du Losange, 1965.

Pau i el seu germà. Directed by Marc Recha, performances by David Selvas, Nathalie Boutefeu, Marieta Orozco, and Alicia Orozco, Oberon Cinematográfica and JBA Production, 2001.

¿Qué pintamos aquí? Directed by Benito Rabal. TVE, 1984.

Riambau, Esteve. "Una cierta tendencia del cine catalán." *Nosferatu. Revista de cine* June, 1992, pp. 16–25.
Riambau, Esteve, curator. "Jacinto Esteva. A l'ombra de l'últim arbre." Barcelona: Filmoteca de Catalunya, 2014.
Riambau, Esteve, and Casimiro Torreiro. *La Escuela de Barcelona. El cine de la "gauche divine."* Anagrama, 1999.
– *Temps era temps: L'Escola de Barcelona i el seu entorn*, Departament de Cultura, 1993.
Riambau, Esteve, Gloria Salvadó, and Casimiro Torreiro. "A mí, la normalidad no me gusta." *Nosferatu. Revista de Cine*, April, 2006, pp. 40–79.
Un chien andalou. Directed by Luis Buñuel, performances by Simone Mareuil and Pierre Batchef, 1929.

3 Jordà's Last Trilogy: Situationist Turn and Subject Transformation

IGNASI GOZALO-SALELLAS

In 2020, Joaquim Jordà had become practically a mythical figure, especially for the newer generations of Catalan documentarists and for the rest of Spain. Throughout his nearly fifty years of cinematographic work – whether as an actor, screenwriter, or director – his career underwent various turns and long periods of ostracism. After nearly a decade of leading the Barcelona School in the 1960s – more with his ideas than with his camera work – Jordà chose a political turn in his cinematography that, due to political and economic motives, took him first to first and later to Portugal. He returned to a newly democratic Spain where he would, to all intents and purposes, develop into the role of screenwriter for other film directors such as Vicente Aranda, among others, and television too. Although he directed a few works during the long period of the 1980s and 1990s, Jordà would not reappear with full force until the twenty-first century. In spite of the fact that he died in 2006 at the age of seventy-one, the final seven years of his long career were nevertheless the most politically and cinematographically prolific and interesting. *Mones com la Becky* (*Monkeys like Becky*, 1999–2000), *De nens* (*About Children*, 2003), and *Veinte años no es nada* (*Twenty Years Is Nothing*, 2004) form a type of situationist trilogy that would be the best representation of his influential contribution to Catalan and Spanish film, especially for the documentary genre.[1]

---

1 Jordà continued to work on two films afterwards, films of lesser importance due to his partial participation. His final work was *Más allá del espejo* (*Through the Mirror*, 2006), which we will consider a biographical conclusion to his career as well as a type of coda to the trilogy. A few years later, *Morir de dia* (*Dying by Day*, 2010) was produced posthumously, directed by Laia Manresa and Sergi Dies but following Jordà's idea. That was the film Jordà always wanted to do but could not.

More than thirty years after his beginnings as a director of the School of Barcelona, Joaquim Jordà reappears with unexpected strength on the new documentary scene in 1999 thanks to the Creative Documentary Master's Programme at the Pompeu Fabra University. That later cinema fit in a time of social change. The contemporary Spanish period has been conditioned by the clash between two forms of living reality: on the one hand through the sphere of spectacularity and simulation, and on the other a critical way of living (in) the public sphere that we will call "situated lives."[2] These two models became extremely visible in Barcelona at the turn of the new century: the institutional model, increasingly connected to the market and enhancing the figure of the "user" rather than the "citizen." In contrast, an everyday way of life dragged into precarious social unrest. Cities and daily lives thus were at the centre of the operations of social hegemony and counter-hegemony of that period. The battle between the symbolic and the real shifted from the national narrative – the state – to micro-geopolitical policies – the city, that, paradoxically, imported some of the planetary globalization logics. There appears a critique of the neo-liberal "glocal association'" idiosyncratic elements – the local – and the dynamics of governance imposed by the market – the global.

In terms of cultural genres, early collapse symptoms of the opulent institutional narrative model appeared during the first decade of the twenty-first century, through a mode of action that merges the social and the artistic in the form of the documentary film. Several spontaneous, non-programmatic cultural expressions of situationism emerge to denounce the superficial narrative model that institutions have given to the market. A problematic relationship such as art and activism seems to be reconciled with specific practices that combine political criticism with expressive poetics and artistic interventions.[3] In several Spanish cities, particularly in Barcelona, some critical artistic practices – from activist art practices in videography, or documentary, to performances and visual poetry – appeared against the "city-product'" model appealing to the social.

---

2 Referring to the notion of "situation" that the Situationist International movement proposed to the philosophical debates in the 1960s in France, in dialogue with other authors such as Henri Lefebvre.
3 It is not a specifically contemporary movement. The most famous historical precedent is the European Situationist movement that took place in the 1950s and the 1960s as a way of intervening in the social sphere in the cities, and to which Jacques Rancière alludes in *The Politics of Aesthetics: The Distribution of the Sensible* (2013).

In that context, and from the margins of the Catalan cinema, Jordà reappears. Almost a total unknown for the young generations of filmmakers in Barcelona, however, not so for the veterans of both the film industry and political militancy. His response to the 2000s will be a trilogy about contemporary disciplinary institutions. Whereas *Monkeys Like Becky* is a critical review of psychiatric techniques and centres, *About Children* proposes a different gaze on Barcelona based on the diversity of institutional control devices within the framework of contemporary cities – media, police, justice, and local political power. *Twenty Years Is Nothing* closes the series by facing the issue of political oblivion in contemporary Spain as the result of the "pact of silence" between the two sides of the war and its ideological legacy.

This trilogy builds a performative practice by highlighting the political regime that governs contemporary cities and by appealing to a new "citizen-spectator." In this cinema the camera is just one element in the game but not the starting point. Jordà considers the camera both as a cinematic device – the gaze – as well as an agent of transformation – the body.[4] This new mode of "documentality" imposes on itself a critical subjectivity over the issue of forms, and escapes the discussion between fiction and non-fiction – film or documentary, film or television technologies, documentary film or television reportage (even among observational or situational techniques), and ethnographic or sociological approaches. By contrast, this new wave opens the possibility of a collective consciousness by appropriating the audiovisual device as an activator of underlying subjectivities.

Some features in Jordà are a constant, like the self-consideration as a non-formalistic director. He believes in the need for situations. The director is entirely aware of his lack of interest for the formal aspect of cinema:

> Yo me preocupo más por la mise en place de la escena y el plano, que no por cómo lo captará la cámara. Organizo la situación y después me retiro. Podría irme a tomar un café y regresar cuando todo esté hecho.
>
> (I'm more concerned with the mise en place of the scene and the shot than by how the camera will shoot it. I organize the situation and then I withdraw from it. I could even go to have a coffee and come back once it's all done.) (Guerra, "Joaquim Jordà")

---

[4] Several other documentaries that emerged from the same educational program (MA in Creative Documentary at the UPF, Barcelona) have put the focus on rethinking the discursive function of the documentary genre. Isaki Lacuesta, Mercedes Álvarez, Neus Ballús, Marc Recha, Carla Subirana, and José González Paco Toledo are some of the most outstanding names.

In each experience of this style of cinema, sociology plays an essential role by opening the path of active participation to the recorded communities and, thus, the construction of a collective conscience that appropriates the audiovisual device as a social tool.

Monkeys Like Becky: Insanity and "Parrhesia"[5]

During the last decade of his philosophical work, Michel Foucault observed the necessity of taking a turn toward the interior of the subject. This was of particular importance in moments of historical urgency like the one in which he lived the final years of his life given the ravages that AIDS was causing in society at the time; it was a repairing and ethical turn, quite distinct from the question of power that had occupied his second philosophical period – starting with *Discipline and Punish* (1995) and throughout concepts such as "microphysics of power" or "disciplinary society." The "technologies of the Self" that take a central place in the third and final era in Foucault's work – *The Care of the Self: The History of Sexuality Volume 3* (1990), *The Hermeneutics of the Subject* (2005), *The Courage of Truth* (2012), essentially – will become the main conceptual apparatus as much as an exercise in reparation and healing against the exertions of power. If we think of the unpolished sequences that Jordà will show us without any ambiguities from the director himself, we should understand the film in its entirety as the willingness to place oneself in the shoes of the patients – and actors in the film – as a form of caring, as much personal as it is interpersonal.

In the first scene presented in the mental hospital, the wide-angle lens of the Steadicam captivates us with a hypnotizing tour through the interior of a psychiatric ward. The exposition of an almost empty space is interrupted by some of the film's future protagonists. As the camera ascends the staircases and travels the hallways, it passes various patients whose stories, finally, are collected and told. Through myriad voices, the camera presents a great variety of personalities, silhouettes, and maladies. Among them, we see Jordà himself, walking around. One of the voices faces the camera, and then faces Francesc, a key character in the patient community. While Jordà appears in the distance at the moment of filming, Francesc bitterly shares with us his experiences at the psychiatric centre with the disciplinary pharmacological regime that is regularly applied to the patients' bodies via prescriptions – there

---

5 I quote this concept from Foucault and Pearson's work on the ancient Greeks in *Discourse and Truth*.

are quite a few pills on the dining table, the neurological space of the centre.

Jordà enters into play, sharing the scene with Francesc and conversing with him. He describes to him what his psychiatric diagnosis is, the aftermath of the blood clot that he suffered years prior, which the director explains using the real operation images described earlier. A certain consequence of the *verfremdungseffekt* – distancing effect – is searched for by a montage that juxtaposes scenes in black and white – real situations between the members of the psychiatric community – and in colour – those that portray the level of representational narration: that is, archival images, mise en scènes, or theatrical reproductions. This is accomplished in such a way that various levels of rupture of the documentary representation code occur: the border between camera and character, and the border between director and film. "We're a bit alike," Jordà says to his favourite character, Francesc.

Another scene defines the expertise of Jordà's modus operandi. On foot and almost off-camera, Jordà faces about a dozen members of the Malgrat community who, sitting in a circle, are waiting for the director's instructions. The exercise consists of introducing themselves to the group and briefly explaining relevant biographical aspects of each character. The moment creates a space of confusion between the real and the performed, between the therapeutic and the theatrical. Each testimonial highlights the limits between the regimes of representation of the real and fiction. A second protagonist of the collective practice, whose presence we sense, introduces herself to the group, and later on tells a sentimental story: "I knew a boy …" The centre's spokeswoman, giving him a dubious look, chimes in: "This is a real story, you know." A third person feels incapable of reproducing the story: "it's really serious …," to which the spokeswoman reminds her what role she should play – Doctor Moniz's wife – and that she should tell a story, "whatever you want." The variety of biographies, however, does not hide shared characteristics, such as an inability for normalized communication or the vague limits in their stories between fiction and reality.

The character in the documentary that best incarnates the fuzzy barrier is the Portuguese actor who plays Moniz. Diagnosed as manic-depressive, the actor follows the camera on the visit to a psychiatric hospital that Moniz frequented in the past. In front of the camera, he shares his experience in another psychiatric centre in 1978 in the form of a documental testimony. A few voice-over reflections make us more aware of the protagonist's illness, called the "ailment of happiness," which could also be defined as the state of well-being with one's self. If this is manifested in the Portuguese actor through his desire to share his emotions and keep himself artistically active, the so-called ailment manifests itself in the psychiatric centre's characters as a drive to open up oneself and put oneself on display as a form of individual and group therapy – that which Foucault termed "parrhesia": "free speech" in the Greek tradition, not freedom of expression but rather honesty with oneself, without manipulation and with the purpose of a common good. "It's a completely different view of the world," an off-screen voice says. "I live very well with it [the illness] because, thankfully, I work in the theatre." Therefore theatre – as a space for "permanent catharsis" – facilitates a better living for these patients: the "art of living" of the Presocratic Greeks (Foucault and Pearson).

Jordà takes the provocation of situations to the limit. The theatrical recreation of Moniz's life that he presents to the patients is carried out and will be filmed from the opening of the documentary. Jordà shows us the characters reflected in the mirror, putting on makeup, in a type of double mask – the patient pretending to be an actor, the actor playing the role of the doctor. The performance does not seem to slow down at all in the actors and in their specific movements. The camera is situated at a relative distance, head-on, showing an artificial mise en scène, one that is theatrical with obvious interpretive flaws and lacking verisimilitude. Even so, we quickly notice the ease with which some of the centre members are able to transform the assigned interpretive role to very personal performances – a direct result of their different concerns. The end result of the performance is altered by these improvisations that seek an escape, a break.

We can observe the therapeutic effect and liberating aspect of exposing one's self in front of the camera in the group's satisfaction as they return by bus from a group outing they take to the Barcelona Zoo. "Filming in front of a camera is just like talking to a normal person," Montse says. For another member, it's something more; it's "like a dream. I had always dreamt that one day I'd do something I enjoyed." The result is an enriching experience that enables both the patients and the performers to exorcise some of their most intimate ghosts and go on a lyrical and heartbreaking harangue against society about the need for therapy, for individual as much as collective attention, and for dialogue between the ill and the community of caretakers.

About Children: The Law of Public Trial

Let us consider the second film of the trilogy, *About Children*, as the exact moment of Jordà's situationist turn. This second film transitions the space of control from the psychiatric centre to the institutions that govern the city of Barcelona – that is, the media, legal system, police, and, fundamentally, the municipal government. Within this space, Jordà faces the challenge of showing specific lifestyles breaking free from those generalizations and stigmas produced by the media's public voices. He does it by creating a performative practice – the film itself, containing the participation of some of the city's residents – that appeals to a new receiving subject, which we will call the "citizen spectator." Jordà directs his message to the citizen spectator, elaborating it from the contradictions of the political regimes that rule modern-day cities. In an interview, Jordà explains how the desire for creating this situationist audiovisual artefact is produced:[6]

> Regresé a Barcelona después de mi infarto cerebral [...]. Instalado aquí percibí algo que estaba ocurriendo, un barrio que guardaba algo muy catastrófico, y de ese algo no se hablaba, había como misterios, como secretos y como miradas enfrentadas, veías que alguien no se hablaba con alguien, gente que vivía en la misma calle, o extrañas enemistades. Una ciudad dividida en dos, entonces apareció el libro de Arcadi Espada y acudí a su presentación. Vi al autor y a algunos de los personajes de la historia, y me impresionó el dolor con que contaban los hechos.
>
> (I returned to Barcelona after my brain stroke [...]. Once settled here I noticed something that was happening, an entire neighbourhood that was hiding something rather catastrophic. Nobody was talking about it. There were mysteries, secrets, and confronting gazes of sorts. You could see people not talking to each other despite living in the same street or strange enmities. A city split in two. Then Arcadi Espada's book was published and I attended its presentation. I saw the author and some of the characters in the story and was impressed by the pain inscribed in their narrative of the facts.) (Seifert and Castillo)

---

6 Jordà explains at one point in *About Children* that the title ended up being what it was because his original and favourite idea, "A Child's Game," was already taken: "Everybody played like children: Todos jugaban como niños: district attorneys, journalists, everyone. They're playing children, like children, with children, and in a really infantile manner they're playing the judges."

The film *About Children* is a portrait of various social classes: it is the portrait of Raval, a neighbourhood in a never-ending social crisis; of Barcelona, a city undergoing excessive growth; and of Spain, a country in the middle of a housing bubble. It is also, finally, a reflection on the universal temporality of global cities fatigued by the dynamics of neo-liberal urbanity and marketing. To that end, Jordà tackles an uncomfortable topic: what will become the famous paedophilia case of Raval, a case that the media covered usually resulting in a virulent effect upon the accused. In that case, the hegemonic media aligned with the institutional version of the case by supporting the "cleansing" reform that attacked the lifestyle of a self-managing and self-sustaining community, of Raval. As Carles Guerra affirms, the film brings to light two "cleansing" processes: "a story of moral regeneration that combines with one of urban regeneration, all of which occurs right in the heart of Barcelona at the beginning of the twenty-first century" (Guerra, "Joaquim Jordà").

Jordà initiates a tough political exercise, converting the film into an apparatus and an event at the same time: an apparatus in that it is a vigilant eye of what is real and represented; and an event whose transformative presence has effects upon social reality and as such, modifies the deliberate tale. From the beginning the camera monitors all institutions that are part of the topic – justice, medicine, media, and modern urbanism – with a patient and dialectical lens, and offers a heart-rending portrait of the moral determinism that state apparatuses exercise over accused people. Discursive and transformative, the film demands attention from the spectator's conscience. Yet above all, it modifies the reality within which it operates; as a consequence of the documentary, certain security measures and police protocols had to be re-evaluated.[7]

It is a film that lasts nearly three hours, resulting in an amalgam of different cinematographic techniques: observational cinema – the marathon courtroom sessions as well as images of the neighborhood's co-existing realities; testimonial cinema – numerous interviews at different parts of the conflict; and, as tends to be the director's habit, theatrical cinema – with fictionalized sequences of passages that are only orally documented. The result is a variable artefact, based on

---

[7] Ten years later, another apparatus of audiovisual discourse will pick up the tradition of practice of audiovisual experiences: *El taxista ful*, a collective film that denounces work conditions in the city.

the hybridity of languages and tactics. As part of his ethical position towards institutions of power, Jordà does not set anything up before filming. Instead, right from the beginning, he opts to film the lengthy hearings of the accused as nothing more than a way to document the judicial process. The film equipment in the courtroom is faced with a predetermined condemning environment: a contemptuous judge, accusatorial glances made by lawyers with haughty attitudes, and the accusations of disrespect from witnesses like journalist Arcadi Espada. Jordà, going against what tends to be recommended when filming, decides to keep almost a full hour of the judicial hearing in the final production: on a much smaller scale, it will serve as a perfect metaphor for the macro-dynamics of institutional power that reads verdicts upon an entire community.

The director does not renounce fictitious representation as pedagogical art. Introducing blasphemous interpretations and irreverent actions, the director situates the spectator – the spectator is also a member of society – in front of a double standard that is hidden behind the Raval case: that is, a few acts of sexual violence massively condemned, but whose details and language are silenced by moral prudishness. In front of a scene of self-inflicted anal sex, the spectator feels both symbolic violence and shame at the same time, all of which is a consequence of a self-reflective act of performativity.

Oriol Bohigas, main ideologue of the project of urban transformation for the "Olympic" Barcelona, explains to the assistant director, Laia Manresa, what are his expectations for the city's remodelling. Two concepts stand out from the rest of the conversation: "hygiene" and "sociability." Bohigas, referring to the barely half-completed urban plan, tells the journalist:

> I think it will function well. Mostly from the point of view of hygiene and sociability, there isn't much doubt. But we'll see if the architecture turns out pretty or ugly. Ultimately, this is the problem you never see ahead of time. (Jordà, *De nens*)

His words give off an immense disinterest about the effects of the enormous architectural changes that will happen in the neighbourhood, and they make clear his obsession for what is "sanitary"; it is all about cleansing the neighbourhood.

A central role of the film's conceptual thread is provided by Manuel Delgado's reflections about the city of Barcelona – as, for example, in his extensive work as a social anthropologist who specializes in urban anthropology. In one of those moments, Delgado refers to the very concept in question:

> Han conseguido lo que ellos llaman 'higienizar' el barrio, que no consiste sino en abrirlo en canal, en llenarlo de cortafuegos justamente para que lo que ocurre en su seno sea 'vigilable' y pueda contribuir a lo que ellos sueñan: una ciudad coherente consigo misma. Pero una ciudad puede ser incluso según cómo cohesionada pero no coherente, y menos Barcelona.
>
> (They've achieved what they call "to sanitize" the neighbourhood, which is nothing other than splitting it in half and filling it with fire barriers precisely aimed at a better surveillance of what happens inside. This will contribute to their dream: a city with inner coherence. And yet a city may certainly be cohesive but never coherent, especially, the city of Barcelona.)

Throughout the film, the original problem – a premeditated and obstructed discursive construction – is supplanted by a new concept for Barcelona: hatred. Delgado justifies the urban politics of the city's socialist governments with a hatred

> of death, which is dread at the same time, facing exactly that: the city or, better yet, the urban space. What moves, what's agitated, what happens. And in El Raval too many things happened, many of which were less than desirable [...]. That's why they're hoping to do away with it.

"Hatred" is a term that appears with rare force in the city's debate of the time. Delgado accuses the powers of hating the city at the street level, the real city, while the general unrest that is created by the difference-neutralizing urban politics creates a new hatred: hatred of the designed city. A tension is made evident between two gazes fed by the same mechanism: the creation of an antagonistic "other" and the negation of the "self," whether it be through the strategy of erasure – the institutional strategy – or through collective confrontation – between neighbours, both activist and artistic.[8] The film insists upon

---

8 A significant number of written essays emerged in the 2000s, coming out of this hatred of the planned city. One year after the film, the editor Bellaterra published *La otra cara del Fòrum de les Cultures, S.A.*, which was analysed earlier; it was published with other texts from the Espai en Blanc group, Manuel Delgado, and citizen associations like the FAVB (Federació de Veïns de Barcelona [Federation of Neighbours

the antagonism between the two sides of the conflict: the neighbourhood and the city institutions. Delgado emphasizes this:

> Es como si hubiera dos ciudades. Por una parte, está la ciudad planificada, la ciudad de los diseñadores, de los políticos, de los arquitectos. Una ciudad que existe en la paz absoluta de los planos, de las maquetas. Es una ciudad soñada. Y luego, al margen, de espaldas o contra esa ciudad que es la de los planos, la de los políticos y de los diseñadores urbanos, lo que hay es la ciudad. Que es otra cosa: las prácticas, los hechos, los acontecimientos, los imprevistos, los conflictos, las luchas, las miserias, alguna grandeza de vez en cuando [...]. Lo que la caracteriza es que, de hecho, es opaca. No es que sea invisible, sino que de hecho es inexplicable, vive demasiado de la complejidad que nunca deja de generar como para que ni tan siquiera sea comprensible a los ojos de un urbanista que, por encima de cualquier cosa, lo que desea es que la ciudad sea eso: cuadriculada, pacificada y especialmente sumisa.

> (It is as if there were two cities. On the one hand, there is the planned city, the city of the designers, the politicians, and the architects. It is a city that exists in the absolute peace of plans and models. It is a dreamed city. And then, on the margins, behind, or against this planned city that belongs to the urban designers and the politicians, there exists the real city. And that is something else altogether: the practices, the facts, the events, the unforeseen actions, the conflicts, the struggles, the miseries, and the sparse grandiose things happening from time to time [...]. What characterizes this city is that it is opaque. It is not a question of being invisible, so much as the fact that it is inexplicable. It lives so immersed in the complexity that it never ceases to generate that it is impossible to be grasped by the gaze of the urban planner, who, beyond anything else, desires only that a city be gridded, pacified, and especially submissive.)

Jordà understands the complex reality of this neighbourhood, and, as a result, he looks for the conflicting views about the neighbourhood's

---

of Barcelona]) or the Associació d'Afectats 22@. In the following decade, Manuel Delgado himself wrote two relevant works regarding the matter: *La ciudad mentirosa. Fraude y miseria del 'Modelo Barcelona'* (2010) and *Ciudadanismo: La reforma ética y estética del capitalismo* (2016). A lesser lauded work by the press, but a very valiant one nonetheless, is the collection *Odio Barcelona*, edited in 2008 by Melusina. In the text, authors like Javier Calvo, Llucia Ramis, Hernán Migoya, Agustín Fernández Mallo, and Eloy Fernández write about the city with unprecedented harshness.

transformation models, giving as much a voice to the urban institutions as he does to the members of the neighborhood's social net. A municipal worker is unequivocal in his defence of his model: "In order to save a person's life, sometimes you have to remove different parts." Those words legitimize a process that is sold as decisively successful given both its flexibility and the same consensus various "experts" all around the world arrive at. Because of it, the municipal employee says, "Ciutat Vella – a city district that includes the El Raval neighbourhood – is a miracle. Fifteen years in the life of a city is just a drop of water. For just one person or for a family, it's a lot, but for a city it's nothing!" In contrast, Iñaki García, spokesman of El Lokal – a community space in El Raval – offers a different insight into the neighbourhood: "there are many Barcelonas, it's a place where there's a lot of life, and there's a lot of conflict. The main difficulty is the administration's willpower, as well as that of the city; to gulp down the conflict, and there's a lot of hesitance to do so."

Figures appear on screen that break the logic of concentration. Octavi Aleixandre might not seem like a part of the neighbourhood, but he presents himself as an urban consultant, and later as a representative of the Raval Roundtable, or Taula del Raval, an association that arose out of the rift with the neighbourhood's official association. Aleixandre affirms that the Raval case "constitutes the first case, and until now the only effort to criminalize the neighbourhood movement by the actual powers responsible for the reform of Ciutat Vella." Furthermore, he recalls how the text *El Raval: Historia de un barrio servidor de una ciudad* was published in 1980; in it, representatives of the neighbourhood movements during the Spanish Transition offered the grassroots mobilization for "the conservation of an urban tapestry, architectural patrimony, and social structure," after which would come the Special Plan of Interior Reform of the neighbourhood, which the institutions had already written.[9]

---

9 At this point, it is interesting how Jordà, through his interviews, is able to get the city hall representative to agree to explain the model of the 70s and beginning of the 80s, when the neighbourhood movements opposed the urban plan of the local institution and redacted the "popular proposals, with urban experts from the left. [...] That same year, the left won the first municipal election, and those experts that were involved with neighbourhood platforms became experts with power, with the capacity to make decisions at the municipal level. City hall took possession of those proposals and transformed them into the famous PERI: special plans for the interior reform of Raval, Casco Antiguo, and Barceloneta" (Jordà, *De nens*). We see, then, how once again institutions absorb the energy of grassroots movements. To some extent,

Jordà's film uses the same technique that another non-fiction director, José Luis Guerín, used in *En construcción* (*Work in Progress*, 2001): filming the neighbourhood walls over and over, as they are full of critical messages about the treatment of El Raval. From the physical dimensions of the wall arises a space in which the anger and resistance of the old neighbourhood are transmitted. Moreover, it is the embodiment of hatred for the future design. The messages vary: "rising anger," "Fuenteovejuna, all for one!," "we don't want profiteers in our neighbourhood!" One deserves particular attention: "The Xino neighbourhood is punk." In just four words, and without arguing against anyone, the message reclaims an attitude – punk – and a memory – calling the neighbourhood by its old name, Xino, as opposed to the contemporary urban marketing strategy of El Raval. An image of a sad clown in a mural that looks like it's bleeding will be chosen by the director for the film poster.

If Guerín's above-mentioned film is centred upon building a poetic tale based on the dialectic between past and future, between an interior and an exterior, between tradition and the market, *About Children* proposes a thorough look into the dynamics and workings of present-day power. Carles Guerra considers the film to be a "counter-device," much like a mirror that reflects a widespread "device of power held up by a constellation of institutions (urbanism, social services, education, law enforcement, and health services, as well as the media, which repeats and spreads its headlines)" ("Joaquim Jordà" 54). Guerra's words are not all that different from how the writer Sergi Pàmies defined the film in an article in *El País*:

> Es una forma de ficción si admitimos que la justicia también lo es. La carne de cañón podría localizarse sobre el mapa y coincide, casualmente, con el tejido más vulnerable del barrio (ese que, en otro documental, inspiró el En construcción, de José Luis Guerín). Las diferencias entre lo que se demuestra y lo que se castiga pone en evidencia el sistema. Dentro de la sala, la ley será sentencia. Fuera de ella será expropiación.
>
> (It is a form of fiction if we accept that justice is also that. The cannon fodder might be placed on a map that casually coincides with the most vulnerable layer within the neighbourhood (the same that inspired another

documentary film, *Work in Progress*, by José Luis Guerín). The differences between what is shown and what gets punished betrays the system's position. Within the courtroom, the law will be the sentence. Outside of it, it will be an expropriation.)

In *Ideología y aparatos ideológicos del Estado*, Louis Althusser (2004) describes the ideological state apparatuses as the limbs that ideologically arm and hold up the state. By filming the discreet but always constant shadows of journalists working on the case, Jordà reminds us that the first judgment is not issued by the judges but by the media outlets.[10] These are partially to blame for the consequences that the interpretation of events had on the neighbourhood's everyday life. Such is also the case with the negligence of the courts and the police, for whom the sentencing is already done before the fact. It is not that way in the film due to the fact that the scene in the courtroom represents

> texto y pretexto. Texto porque constituye un argumento y pretexto por que sirve para escarbar en esa transición en la que los mismos que con la llegada de la democracia proponían cambios radicales tuvieron que ejecutar, ya desde el poder, traumáticas cirugías urbanas.
>
> (Text and pretext. Text because it constitutes an argument and pretext because it allows to dig into the Transition, where those who upon the arrival of democracy used to propose radical changes were the same ones who, once already in power, had to carry out traumatic urban surgeries). (Pàmies)

The vast mosaic of elements that Jordà arranges throughout the film problematizes the new subject of contemporary politics – the city – distancing it from pure and uniform identities, posing it as multifaceted and made up of various layers, and reclaiming both the history and the memory of spaces as a type of antidote to the social and historical "cleaning up" of a neighbourhood; when all is said and done, this is

---

10 *About Children* is, above all, a self-critical exercise with informative deontology. Giving voice to the journalist that uncovered the case's irregularities, Arcadi Espada (in *Raval, del amor a los niños*), the film questions deontological malpractice as well as the pact between real powers – the press, law enforcement, and politicians – that try to hide the various miscommunications happening in the case. In Espada's own words, "the problem is spreading the failures with heroism. It's worse still to disguise corruption with heroism" (Pàmies).

what the El Raval case and the urban operation that is justified after the controversy are all about.

Twenty Years Is Nothing: Against Forgetting Memory

Twenty Years Is Nothing (2005) concludes the trilogy after *Monkeys Like Becky* and *About Children*. Above all, it aims to close the fantasy of the so-called Spanish democratic period, gathering together a group of former factory workers from the late 70s two decades later. *Twenty Years Is Nothing* is, in that sense, a way to repair with dignity the aftermath of an inconclusive utopia – liberty and revolution – that was pitched in an earlier movie, *Numax Presents...* (1979).

Numax presents... is an exceptional case within the cinematic Spanish landscape at the time. Directed between 1979 and 1980 by Joaquim Jordà and produced under a cooperative structure, *Numax presents...* took up a form of cinematographic artwork that was no longer merely a technology of observation or representation but also served to stimulate collective productions and community tactics. The film takes place at Numax – an appliances factory in Barcelona – and tells of the workers' collective decision to resist the closure of the factory by taking it over themselves. The film is part of the cultural production of Workers Autonomy inspired by the Italian workerism.[11]

The director considered the film as a repoliticization of subjectivities that went through the "disidentification" of old ideological labels, and by avoiding production structures close to labour unions:

> En Numax todos los personajes terminan por liberarse de una condición proletaria que no habían asumido voluntariamente. La película se realizó en un ambiente militante, con una estructura militante, pero sin militantes.
>
> (In Numax all the characters end up freeing themselves of a proletarian condition that they had not assumed willingly. The film was made in a militant environment, with a militant structure, but without militant persons.) (Guerra, "Joaquim Jordà")

---

11 Originally emerging in Italy as "Operaismo," "Autonomism" was a sort of connection between social and political left-wing organizations. In this attempt, the movement approached art and other cultural practices such as media, literature, and post-structuralism. As Franco Berardi writes, within that context "artistic experimentation and subversive political intention began to merge, taking back a similar direction that the American underground had already tried in other conditions" (114). The goal was social transformation of culture and ways of life through autonomy.

In a similar reading, the philosopher Marina Garcés describes it as "a process of radically autonomous politicization that is not explained by ideology but by the capability of invention and creation of common life" (Guerra, "Joaquim Jordà"). *Numax* not only explained how workers collectivized social ownership – economic production in socialist systems – but also the circulation of bodies and unstable subjectivities.

As we can imagine, labour unions rejected the movie, but it interested some civil society sectors that were not explicitly part of any organization because it promoted an estrangement effect: the film moves from its initial euphoria to a story of desertion. First, the workers have a goal: try to maintain the workers' power inside the factory until a final consideration. As Jordà stated, "we abandon that simulated power and go to live" (Guerra, "Joaquim Jordà"). The words of the director talk about the displacement of the tight and political subject to the claim for life, bodies, and enjoyment.

The film concerns the construction of subjectivity – what we will call "subjectivization." The ethical decision to participate in the strike is, first of all, an individual dilemma, and a way of problematizing what one does, and what "the world in which oneself lives" is. We could argue that the goal of this community is both self-management – the pragmatic economic conditions – but also self-governance in a more political meaning, by promoting what Foucault calls "new forms of subjectivity through the refusal of this kind of individuality which has been imposed on us for several centuries" ("Subject and Power," 785). As Moreno-Caballud points out, "The whole process of making the film is part of the film itself: the film-maker and the workers have thrown themselves into an open-ended process in which knowledge is not neutral, but produced through the interactions of the different subjectivities at play" (65).

The question of "subjectivization" as a commitment is crucial to several characters as part of this liberation process from any aprioristic condition. Women represent the central process of "subjectivization" in the movie and emerge as representatives of the group. They lead the assembly and explain the collectivization process as well as express their political thoughts. Take, for example, the old nun who – following Foucault's desire of "creating one's self as a work of art" that "implies that one refuses given subjectivities, imposed by knowledge and power systems," and relates the kind of relation that everybody has to oneself as "a creative activity" ("On the Genealogy of Ethics," 351) – decides to leave her religious habit and participate in the workers' collectivization at Numax. In the memorable final sequence of the film, a large group of people are dancing and enjoying themselves. We do not notice anything unusual until the interviewer – the director – appears in front of the camera, joining the party. By interviewing different characters, Jordà breaks the limits between sender and receiver, between observer and actor, and between creator and object. At a given moment he interviews a woman, who answers warmly but with conviction, "I will not work ever again in my life, or at least I will try not to." Suddenly, we realize that this is not a party but a happy ending, that that space is not a disco but a factory hangar. It is, in the end, a film about workers' autonomy.

It is not a trivial fact that the film was forgotten in the Catalan Film Library under the category of "Unknown director" for more than thirty years. But in the 2000s the Catalan institution accepted Jordà's legal ownership of the production and decided to do a remake of Numax. In *Twenty Years*, Jordà resumes the story and makes a critical retrospective of the Spanish Transition and its legacy through those characters that decided to abandon the factory and also the coming capitalist life in the early eighties. This second film represents a desire to live a moral life. It is again an expression of joy, as Pierre Hadot qualified the ancient Stoics' idea of "gaudium," or happiness, understood not as pleasure but as virtue (232–42). *Twenty Years* demonstrates how art sometimes precedes the social by articulating situated tactics of intervention based on a moral commitment upon the social sphere.

During the making of the second film, Jordà explains that upon finishing the production of *Numax Presents...*, he had the feeling that the topics of the film would demand a new chance to speak in the future. The constant echo of the inconclusive past and interrupted memory is already felt in the title, which references the song "Volver" by Carlos Gardel.[12] The film belongs to a body of documentary work that in the 2000s sought to revise Spain's recent history – looking as far back as the Civil War as well as the more recent Spanish Transition (1975–8, or 1982) in a trendsetting way. Due to its investigative and revealing nature, it uses tools like archives, testimonies, and revisiting history. In Spain's case, we can go so far as to say that in the 90s, the arts were ahead of

---

12 The phrase that is used as a title in the film appears in the third and last stanzas of Gardel's song: "Returning with a wrinkled forehead / The snowflakes of time covered my temples with silver / Feeling that it's nothing more than a breath of life / That twenty years is nothing / How restless the glances, wandering in the shadows / It looks for you and names you / Living with a soul that you must cling to / To a sweet memory / And crying yet again." It is important to emphasize that it is not the only title that was proposed for the film, as Laia Manresa explains in *Joaquín Jordà*. At one of the beginning stages, the director considered the title "Lost Illusions," in reference to the novel with the same title by the French author Honoré de Balzac.

their time, capable of perceiving a still-latent social unrest, articulating visual intervention tactics in the social realm, questioning the historic debt within our collective memory. Authors of video art, like María Ruido and Marcelo Expósito, share the interest in the question at hand with conceptual artists, like Antoni Muntadas, and politically driven film directors, like Jordà himself.

Cinematographically, *Twenty Years* begins as one would expect: by reproducing the images that ended the film *Numax presents...* and the factory experience. The celebration – the party – is the connecting thread that brings *Twenty Years Is Nothing* together. In that sense, if the closing party was a collective experience, a bitter farewell that nevertheless carried hopes, now it is a reunion, a celebration of resistant memory. Each of our characters – Pedro, Carlos, el Roca – arrives at the reunion by car and melts into embracing arms. The images of the Numax party are placed in between each of the different testimonies, like a dialogue between eras: one person talks about the school where he teaches, another from her own elementary school, and another from the bar she manages. All of them display a disenchantment with the self-regimenting institutions – the so-called 78 Regime – as much as the fragility of the utopia that they all shared. "I have the feeling that the only change that's possible with democracy is that, before it, I couldn't speak; now they let me, but they don't listen to me." It seems that the sequence of testimonies speeds up without an end in sight, but the movie stops at a different moment: two former strikers, one of whom is named Pepi, run into each other on a train. Pepi's narrating voice tells us about the only absent figure, Juan, who takes shape in the movie thanks, once again, to the archival images. The low-quality video images, recorded by a local television station – Granollers – and obtained by Jordà, retell in a confusing way what happened in that fateful year of 1985: Juan and Pepi's attempted bank robbery, carried out due to their political convictions. Indeed, one of them belongs to a small communist faction, which we learn through their lawyer from the time. This, in effect, alters the film's reception. We sense a movie within another movie. With these frenetic and erratic images, Jordà does not seek the spectacularity of the crime genre, but rather he disentangles the pact between the narrator and spectator that had been accepted until that point as organic. The exceptionality of the images, both narrative and historic, demands from that very moment the acceptance of the reunion as full of pain, taboos, willingly forgotten moments, and self-criticism.

The lawyer and activist Mateo Seguí discusses "transgression of reality and legality" to explain the conduct of certain dissidents of the time, like Juan and Pepi. The images that mix with the story at that moment allow us to visualize the two sides of what happened – the robber and the civil government, personified in the space of the robbery. These are also the two sides of the narrated and archived history of Spanish democracy: the losers and the winners, the dissidents and the State. The destiny of these particular lives, which time erases, comes undone in the reunion that Jordà sets up. Memory not only reunites through the bodies that made it possible, and not even just across the large screen on which the old film plays, but it is also incarnated in the encounters between different generations, parents and their children, present and not absent from the first part: Numax. In that way, Jordà's last edited sequence centres on the reactions of X, the mute-deaf son of a former member of Numax who has already died, who for the very first time sees the images of his father's lived experience twenty-five years earlier. The worth of the sequence resides precisely in the difficulty of transmitting that memory, due to material motives – the fact that the son is both deaf and mute makes it impossible for him to have an explicit sensory reception – as well as historical ones. Luckily, the son's absence of memory is saved by the archival function of whatever historical document, which, in this case, is the film *Numax presents*.... In the last instalment of the trilogy, the film becomes a saving device working against the device of forgetfulness, as much material as it is narrative, that the State imposed for generations concerning its recent past.

Coda

Jordà represents the insurgent voice against power. In any period. Contrary to the very consensual discourse about the Spanish Transition that has been narrated by official actors and historians, Jordà reappears in the theatres at the very beginning of the "'78 Regime" crisis to repair the whole period by denouncing several ideological apparatuses all over the period. I would like to refer to his films as practices of what Foucault described as "arts of living." That is to say, as ethical actions of transmission: values, ideologies, commitment. Against the State's communicative apparatuses, his movies transmitted modes of life and ways of resistance through the visual arts.

As a result, I propose to read them as neo-situationist practices based on the materiality of their mostly urban experiences. Procedures rather than products, situations rather than narratives, they shared two features that the situationist movement emphasized in the fifties and sixties: the desire for play and transformation. Like Guy Debord's "dérive," these practices became the symptom of social discontent by creating and fostering fluid situations and unexpected incursions into an alien world. Practically forgotten twenty-five years on, their legacy re-emerged as an "excess" for the political order. Hegemonic media, through symbolic representations of euphoria and happiness, neutralized the symptom[13] – everyday life practices – and embodied the leading actor of the national obsession for the "fantasy of normalcy" during the Spanish democratic regime. His last cinematography demonstrates how artworks – both in their process and material result, whether literature or any other formal practices – sometimes offer us a spark that the social sphere is not able to ignite. The "art of living" is thus that explicit expression of enjoyment, or, in other words, the political and existential need of becoming a subject through the arts.

WORKS CITED

Althusser, Louis. *Ideología y aparatos ideológicos del Estado*. Translated by José Sazbón and Alberto J. Pla, Quinto Sol, 2004.
Berardi, Franco. "¿Qué Significa Hoy Autonomía?" *UninomadaSUR*, 28 Nov. 2018, uninomadasur.net/?p=708. Accessed 20 Dec. 2020.
Delgado, Manuel. *La ciudad mentirosa: Fraude y miseria del "Modelo Barcelona."* Catarata, 2010.
– *Ciudadanismo: La reforma ética y estética del capitalismo*. Catarata, 2016.
El taxista ful. Directed by Jordi Sol, Zip Films and Televisió de Catalunya, 2005.
En construcción. Directed by José Luis Guerín, Ovideo TV, 2001.
Espada, Arcadi. *Raval, del amor a los niños*. Anagrama, 2000.
Foucault, Michel. *Discipline and Punish: The Birth of the Prison*. Translated by Alan Sheridan, Vintage Books, 1995.
– *The History of Sexuality, Vol. 3: The Care of the Self*. Translated by Robert Hurley, Vintage, 1988.
– "On the Genealogy of Ethics: An Overview of Work in Progress." The Foucault Reader: An Introduction to Foucault's Thought, edited by Paul Rabinow, Penguin, 1984. pp. 340–72.
– "The Subject and Power." *Critical Inquiry*, vol. 8, no. 4, 1982, pp. 777–95. JSTOR, www.jstor.org/stable/1343197. Accessed 29 Dec. 2020.

---

13 In *The Sublime Object of Ideology*, Žižek refers to the symptom as an intrusive presence, "alien" to the system, a kind of excess for the social order.

Foucault, Michel, and Joseph Pearson. *Discourse and Truth: The Problematization of Parrhēsia*. Notes to the seminar given by Foucault at the University of California at Berkeley, 1983. Pearson, 1985.

Foucault, Michel, et al. *The Courage of Truth: The Government of Self and Others II; Lectures at the Collège de France, 1983–1984*. Michel Foucault Lectures at the Collège de France, 11, Palgrave Macmillan, 2005.

Foucault, Michel, Frédéric Gros, Graham Burchell, et al. *The Hermeneutics of the Subject: Lectures at the Collège de France 1981–1982*. Michel Foucault Lectures at the Collège de France, 9, Palgrave Macmillan, 2005.

Guerra, Carles. "Joaquim Jordà: Cine de situación." MACBA: Museu d'Art Contemporani de Barcelona. Macba, Sept. 2004. https://www.macba.cat/es/exposiciones-actividades/actividades/joaquim-jorda-cine-situacion. Accessed 20 Dec. 2020.

— "La militancia biopolítica de Joaquín Jordá." *Cinema Comparat/ive Cinema*, vol. 2, no. 5, 2014, pp. 50–5.

Hadot, Pierre. *The Inner Citadel: The Meditations of Marcus Aurelius*. Translated by Michael Chase, Harvard University Press, 2001.

Harvey, David. "The Right to the City." *New Left Review*, 53, September/October, 2008, https://newleftreview.org/issues/ii53/articles/david-harvey-the-right-to-the-city.

Jordà, Joaquim, director, *De nens*, Massa d'Or Produccions, 2003.

— *Más allá del espejo*, Ovideo TV and Únicamente Severo Films, 2006.

— *Mones com la Becky*, Els Quatre Gats Audiovisuals S.L., 1999.

— *Numax presenta…*, Asamblea de Trabajadores de Numax, 1980.

— *Veinte años no es nada*, Ovideo TV, 2004.

Manresa, Laia. *Joaquín Jordá: la mirada lliure*. Filmoteca de la Generalitat de Catalunya, 2006.

Moreno-Caballud, Luis. "Looking amid the Rubble: New Spanish Documentary Film and the Residues of Urban Transformation." *Studies in Spanish & Latin-American Cinemas*, vol. 11, no. 1, Jan. 2014, pp. 61–74.

Morir de día. Directed by Laia Manresa and Sergi Díes, Únicamente Severo Films and Estudi Playtime, 2010.

Pàmies, Sergi. "El barrio de los casos perdidos." *El país*, 9 Apr. 2004, elpais.com/diario/2004/04/10/babelia/1081552642_850215.html. Accesssed 20 Dec. 2020.

Pareja, Ana, et al. *Odio Barcelona*. Melusina, 2008.

Rancière, Jacques, and Gabriel Rockhill. *The Politics of Aesthetics: The Distribution of the Sensible*. Bloomsbury, 2013.

Seifert, Anuschka, and Adriana Castillo. "Entrevista a Joaquín Jordá." *Revista Lateral*, vol. 2004, no. 114, 2004. https://www.ipce.info/es/library/journal-article/entrevista-joaquin-jorda. Accessed 20 Dec. 2020.

Vidal Artigas, Jaume. *El Raval: Història d'un barri servidor d'una ciutat*. Associació de veïns de ciutat vella, 1980.
Vv.Aa. *La otra cara del Fòrum de les Cultures*, S.A. Bellaterra, 2004.
Žižek, Slavoj. *The Sublime Object of Ideology*. Verso, 2009.

4 The Militant Cinema of Joaquim Jordà: The Essay Film as Form

STEVEN MARSH

Numax presenta... (*Numax presents...*, 1980) is a singularly *democratic* Joaquim Jordà film. I refer to its democratic form as discordant, out-of-synch with the dominant narrative concerning the "democracy" under negotiation at the time of its production. The film documents the dispute, subsequent strike, occupation, and self-management by a group of workers of a domestic appliance factory in the centre of Barcelona between 1977 and 1979. Shot in 1979, at the initiative of the workers themselves and financed by what remained of the strike fund, the film is a performative intervention in the period of transformation of the Spanish state from dictatorship to liberal democracy. By "performative" I allude to its title, the suggestion within it of a presentation; the dotted coda that hangs off the title suggestive of both an ellipsis and of open-endedness, of unfinished business, of the inconclusive, of an uncertain future lying ahead. The film offers up a dense set of temporal relations at odds with its time; a counter-current flowing surreptitiously to shape its formal diegesis; it points to a critique of traditional working practices as determining and conditioning life. Significantly, *Numax presenta...* is a re-presentation; it was shot after the announcement that the conflict at its heart – the collective self-operation of the factory – was over, a fact made explicit in its opening sequence. Both *Numax presenta...* and its 2004 sequel *Veinte años no es nada* (*Twenty Years Is Nothing*) are events in the sense that both films, like performative linguistic speech acts, enact what they signify (with no effort to edit out, mask, or conceal the lapses and time lags involved). The event-ness of the films is key to their distinctive politics. It highlights a rupture in the everyday continuum – the norm – marked out by representational politics. Not only do the two films mark telling moments in an alternative history of democracy of the Spanish state, they are also exemplary of the formation, the forging, of a filmic site of the demos, as a voice of those habitually excluded from the discourse of democracy. In this vein I will argue here that Jordà reconfigures militant film so as to pose a challenge to conventional and enduring assumptions regarding both the cinematic and political regimes as conceived during late Francoism and the Spanish Transition.

Numax presenta... is staged in the present yet only after the event of its action. It is thereby paradoxically a documentary articulated through a fictional strategy. The film itself under workers control is a literal re-presentation that seeks therein to shape its own character, its own autonomy as demos, not only – as in the industrial dispute – from the official representatives of trade unions but also from the institutional exigencies of film-making. Factory workers whose daily task involved operating machines in order to shape objects extraneous to their needs and aspirations would, in this introductory declaration of intentions, give shape to their lives in the form of the film. Shape, of course, is – beyond the purview and criteria of critical discourse – a synonym for form. This chapter seeks to address questions of form – form, that is, that exceeds the limits and limitations of formalism as traditionally conceptualized in the history of cultural theory; form which is marked and conditioned by temporal-historical, social, and ideological factors. Re-enactment is arguably the form of these essay films. This chapter considers thus the relation between cultural and political form at a historical juncture when both, as we will see, were in crisis. Nonetheless, the form of *Numax presents...* is marked by an alternative shaping to that – the discourse – of the dominant narrative of the time "period" of the production of *Numax presenta....* Its historical framing, its extra-filmic reference – the Spanish Transition – is notable for establishing the rarely questioned ideology of consensus, the dominance of which is such that it has only recently been critically re-evaluated in terms of dissensus.[1]

Numax presenta... is a film about organized working-class action that departs from the conventions and confines (at least those defined

---

[1] It is precisely in respect to form that these films might be seen in relation to others that focus on the question of labour. They are shaped by a particular genre in which the complex and intimate experience of industrial alienation in turn connects Jordà to films as different from one another in time and geography as Rainer Werner Fassbinder's 1972 TV series *Eight Hours Don't Make a Day*, the films of Chris Marker and the Groupe Medvedkine of the late 1960s, and Pedro Pinho's *The Nothing Factory* (2017). The word "dissensus" is very much associated with Jacques Rancière, as is the use of the term "demos," which is also deployed in this essay. However, Rancière's contribution to the theoretical framework of this essay, while informing it, is not at its centre.

and practised within Spain) of most militant cinema. Jordà himself has observed that "es una película militante que rompe todos los esquemas de las películas militantes de aquel momento" ("a militant film that breaks all the moulds of militant film of that moment"; Jordà, "Nosferatu" 56). In a 2014 article about the film-maker, Carles Guerra quotes Jordà from an interview carried out ten years previously to argue that the film's claim to militancy is grounded in "biopolitics": "[P]rimero los trabajadores parten de un objetivo intentan mantener el poder obrero dentro de la fábrica, hasta que se impone una segunda reflexión. Al final, abandonamos ese simulacro de poder y vamos a la vida" ("The workers first began with the objective of keeping workers' power within the factory, until a second reflection took hold. In the end we abandoned that simulacrum of power and opted for life itself"). Guerra continues,

> A partir de este punto la gestión política pasa a ocuparse de algo más que la economía, los horarios o las condiciones laborales. Se ocupará de la vida dejando el terreno preparado para una militancia que, recordando el curso impartido por el filósofo francés Michel Foucault en los primeros meses del año 1979 – justo en el momento que se filma *Numax presenta...*–, será de corte biopolítico.
>
> (From that point on, politics becomes more significant than economics, working hours, or labour conditions. Life is spent preparing the terrain for a militancy that, to recall French philosopher Foucault's course offered in the first months of 1979 – at the very moment that *Numax presenta...* was being filmed – was of a biopolitical nature.) ("La militancia biopolítica de Joaquín Jordá" 52)

It is in such statements that we can see the influence of Jordà's involvement with *Autonomía*, a significantly different project to that of Foucault's thought though not altogether unconnected to it – more biopolitical than disciplinary. During his years in exile in Italy Jordà had met (and planned a filmed interview with) Toni Negri, one of the ideologues of *Autonomia*. Negri was, of course, also influenced by biopolitics. Upon his return to Barcelona Jordà came into contact with Spanish/Catalan *autonomistas* such as Santiago López Petit, who were critical of what they termed the "authoritarian Left"[2] (particularly the Communist

---

2 I think here of the book López Petit wrote with José Antonio Díaz Valcárcel in 1974 (*Crítica de la izquierda autoritaria en Cataluña. 1967–1974*).

Party (PCE/PSUC), but also other groupings such as the LCR, who were active in the Numax occupation).[3] Jordà had clearly travelled a long way from the time of the 1970 *Lenin vivo (Lenin Alive)*, which he co-directed with Gianni Toti.[4] One of the many interesting things about *Veinte años no es nada*, the sequel to *Numax presenta...*, is that we learn how the fragmentation and dispersal of the Numax collective after the end of the occupation mirrors (in some ways) that of the Lotta Continua, Potere Operaio, and other Italian workerist groups who would from 1973 onwards form Autonomia Operaia. These groups share with their counterparts in Numax a rejection of traditional working-class representatives as hopelessly compromised – and institutionalized – with the State apparatus (itself in crisis), a rejection of salaried work (which many of the members of the Numax collective express in the party that marks the end of the occupation and the film), and even the recourse to armed struggle by a minority element of the Italian workerists. Much of this critique of representation manifested itself (particularly in the case of Potere Operaio) in terms of formal practices. I want then to map the complex relations (noting the departures, the non-correlations) between formal filmic practices and the form of politics practised by the workers themselves. Jordà's earlier work as a traditional militant film-maker at the service of the Communist Party (that of *Lenin vivo* [1970] and *Portogallo, paese tranquillo* (*Portugal, a Quiet Land*, 1969]) brings with it a change in formal practice. If form is historically marked, then questions of form (political and artistic) and those of crisis are perhaps relevant to the year *Numax* was shot. The period 1977–8 witnessed unprecedented upheaval in Italy among workers and students – notably in Bologna – inspired by the extra-parliamentary left in opposition to the State, which counted on the complicity of the Italian Communist Party (the PCI). It also saw corresponding repression on the part of the State in collaboration with extreme right-wing paramilitaries. Likewise, the critique of capitalism and the reformist Left expressed in *Numax presenta...* came at precisely the same time as in Spain leftist political parties (in particular the PCE/PSUC) and the trade union movement were negotiating their legalization, that is their incorporation into the orbit of the State and its institutions. In this sense, *Numax presenta...* is a political intervention in direct opposition to the political moment of its production that has left, in turn, a legacy that

---

3 LCR (Liga Comunista Revolucionaria), the Spanish section of the Fourth International, founded by Trotsky.
4 Jordà offers a critique of Helena Lumbreras' cinema, as exemplary of the type of militant film he had come to reject (https://www.macba.cat/es/numax-presenta-2779).

goes beyond mere historical anecdote. *Numax presenta...* is the story of those left out of political discourse, of those who have no voice in the historical process – the order of discourse – but who, irrespective of their status, act politically so as to give shape to their lives. Their struggle is within a tradition of workers taking control of production, indifferent to the connivance between union bureaucrats and management (from the shop floor to the national stage), from which they are excluded.

Autonomía Obrera extends the idea of work beyond the factory walls. Or rather society becomes the factory, within which transformation is as much about individuals – notably questions of subjectivity and desire – as it is about institutional change or economic demands. While *Numax presenta...* coincides with and offers a commentary on the Spanish Transition, it also provides a rare critique of the dominant consensus of the time, at odds with what proved to be the outcome of the negotiations that would bring into existence what, following the mobilizations of the 15 May 2011 (15-M) movement, would come to be known as the Regime of 1978, and most significantly – for working-class organization – it provides a rare example of a critique *en directo* of the Moncloa Pacts at the very moment of their negotiation. The film thus marks a convergence of a historical moment with a contemporaneous local action at odds with that moment but also, like the 15-M, it posits an alternative: the desire to change the way – the form – of life of its protagonists, to break with – via rejection and refusal – the grinding alienation of the factory and the assembly line even if self-management brought about a consciousness of the realities of capitalist production.

If *Numax presenta...* constitutes a critical intervention in the Spanish Transition, it is also a film that combines within its own structure different forms of representation: re-enactment, theatre, real archive footage material, photographs, newspaper clippings, and oral testimony. Representation is the key word here not only of cultural critique but also of the political moment. The word "transition," until recently discursively established within Spain as synonymous with democracy, is just the most glaring example of the politics of representation. But within that discourse and simultaneous with the filming, class representation (the trade unions and the PCE/PSUC), the official doctrine of representation that remains in place today, was being forged. The groundwork for monopolizing the definition of democratic discourse – an order that has been firmly policed ever since to the exclusion of the demos – was being established.

The first two thirds of *Numax presenta...* is punctuated by staged sketches that Jordà shot with the assistance of theatre director and writer Mario Gas and his workshop actors that recount the history of the Numax factory (the dubious Nazi past of the company's German owners who arrived in Catalonia in the aftermath of the Second World War, the asset stripping prior to their flight and decampment to Brazil, the ongoing dispute that commenced two years previous to the shoot, and the complicity of the official Left and the union bureaucracy with the process).[5] Theatre is a mode that has interested Jordà in later films too.[6] The combination of the seemingly incompatible registers of theatre and film contribute to the discordant tone. Clearly, an element of this involves Brechtian distanciation. There is an effort on Jordà's part to correlate the alienation of factory work with that of cultural work, to unravel and expose its mechanics on screen. This, though, in turn produces a seepage that unfolds to reveal other aspects of political and filmic practices. In a film whose initial – and expressed – intent was a collective enterprise, it is noteworthy that Jordà shot the staged commentary at his own initiative and without the assistance or participation of the Numax workers. Indeed, this points to a disruption of the paradigm in modern film theory that would suggest a tension arising from the de facto equality established between the collectivity and the film auteur.

That said, substantial sections (and arguably the film in its entirety) of *Numax presenta...* are also staged, but within the setting of the factory itself.[7] The ostensibly naturalist style of filming contrasts with the evident artifice of the theatre production. Shot in colour (the factory sequences are mostly in black and white), the theatrical interjections within the diegesis draw attention to their fake quality (a belly dancer, a tightrope walker, a juggler, the proscenium stage setting itself, the stilted text articulated in the mouths of the jobbing actors). Meanwhile, the workplace "stagings" are more ironic and integrated within the factory environment. Emblematic of this is a shot of one of the workers delivering a pre-prepared speech while framed within a cubicle. The camera slowly withdraws to reveal the man seated on a toilet, one of a

---

[5] There is an interesting parody of the historical figure of Communist Party General Secretary Santiago Carrillo in one of the theatrical sketches that deploys the rhetorical figure of the metonym. Carrillo, celebrated for having returned illegally to Spain prior to the legalization of the PCE disguised with a wig, is initially identified in the sketch by his absurd head garment.

[6] I think here of the important part played by theatre in films such as *Mones com la Becky* (*Monkeys Like Becky*, 1999) and *De Nens* (*About Children*, 2003).

[7] For Jacques Rancière "there is no political life, but a political stage" ("Thinking of Dissensus" 4).

line of identical stalls. As he finishes and stands to pull up his trousers, he rounds off his scatological diatribe with the commonplace: "una imagen vale más que mil palabras" ("one image is worth more than a thousand words"). Sequences such as this one mirror the set of shots that introduce the film: a written text, establishing the background, the motives, and the terms of the film as part of the collective project, read by a single worker in a medium shot that expands to incorporate a surrounding circle of applauding workers, followed in turn by a lengthy, looping tracking shot that opens up the space of the shop floor and the mass meeting of the occupiers, a shot that captures in its arc the machinery, the factory layout, the assembled self-managing workers. Both instances are stylistic components – formal elements – of the film as a whole: the factory dispute and the form by which it is articulated in filmic language. Both highlight, bring to the surface, the tension and the stress lines between the visual effect and the written text, the image and the word.

In the interview with Guerra, Jordà disavows the specificity of mise en scène in favour of what he calls narrative technique. In particular, in striking contrast to the worker Jordà films in the toilet cubicle, the director claims a disinterest in the image altogether. He insists he does not look through the camera viewfinder during the shoot, leaving questions of visual composition to the judgement of the operator and the cinematographer (https://www.macba.cat/es/arte-artistas/artistas/jorda-joaquim/numax-presenta). Disingenuous though this may be (mise en scène – a term whose origins lie in theatre – is fundamental to Jordà's work), it does say something regarding the form of the essay, the essay film in particular, and, indeed, form itself. Whatever else form is, it is not immovable, it is flexible. Moreover, the traditional dichotomy between form and content proves (and, once more, this returns us to performativity) to be false. In an echo (albeit a contradictory one) of the worker's bathroom sentiments, the antecedents of the essay form do indeed lie in the written word rather than in the image. But the essay is also the form of crisis, it is perhaps crisis writing itself. I will return to this point in the conclusion of this chapter.

If theatre is important to the cinema of Jordà, it is also important to the thinking ofRanciére in his definition of politics, both in the literal and the metaphorical sense of the term. As I suggested in the very first paragraph of this chapter, the title of the film *Numax presenta…* contains the suggestion of a performance. Rancière, meanwhile, conceives politics as organized in terms of a staging of the way power is perceived. While I do not wish to suggest any direct influence of Rancière on Jordà, the theatrical interludes contribute to this element of staging. What is often presented as fly-on-the-wall documentary (particularly in the case of the mass meetings or assemblies) turns out to be re-enactment. This is more explicitly the case when the workers recollect the beginnings of the dispute: the first meetings, the roughing-up of one of the managers, the breaking of an office window in one of the protests, the alternation between the direct testimony and its fictional recreation. But it is also there at the very end of the film, precisely when we are most led to believe in its naturalism. In the final sequence, the only one in which Jordà himself – a self-parodic signature – appears (though we occasionally hear his voice asking questions earlier), the workers celebrate the end of the occupation. A group of workers form the band that performs the music that accompanies the farewell bash, notably the tango *Adios muchachos*, popularized by Carlos Gardel. Jordà, meanwhile, circulates, microphone in hand, and interrogates the workers as to their future plans. Someone shouts out the question "¿Qué opinas de Lamas?" ("What do you think of Lamas?"), Lamas being the supervisor who had earlier been beaten by the female workers. In jocular fashion, one of the older men assumes the role of Lamas and the women slap him around. Within the representation, at the very moment when the film displays its apparatus, that is, when it is at its most Godardian (with the presence of Jordà, armed with the film-making sound apparatus, conducting interviews), the workers themselves re-represent, they act out, an instant of their own narrative, a narrative that exemplifies its politics of refusal in its refutation of the dominant idea of the Spanish Transition as modelic, as peaceful and consensual.

That this should come in the final sequence of the film is significant. The film is bookended (in two sequences that are marked out by being shot in colour) and given form precisely by the kind of performativity I mentioned at the beginning of the chapter; it is brought into being, instituted or constituted by it at the very moment when a new state is being born under the auspices of a Constitution. *Numax presenta...* thus functions as an antagonistic alternative to the official historical narrative, but this is characterized by the absorption of the film's thematic substance into its form. The traditional binary collapses and the two critical dichotomous terms become indistinguishable precisely at a moment in conflict with the conjuncture. While the film is marked by a style that reflects both the concept of collectivity – the workers (who financed the film) and the act of speaking for themselves – it also gives performativity a sense that links the theatrical notion of performance to the linguistic version. The first sequence – the reading of a written text (an essay within an essay) – is a declaration of intentions and it is one that poses a challenge to the institution of film itself; it institutes a counterinstitution, one that vies with the parodic narrative of professional actors provided by Mario Gas's troupe on an actual stage.

In the age of neo-liberalism, the words "democracy" and "demos," from which it derives, have taken on particular formal connotations. One of the interesting things about *Numax presenta…* is that the year it was shot – 1979 – coincides with the arrival on the world stage of neo-liberalism as a dominant discursive political and cultural formation.[8] The scenario of the demos, a word much deployed nearly thirty years later, is the disputed stage upon which the struggle of the film is acted out. Demos, the domain of the excluded, what Rancière calls "the part that has no part" (*Dissensus* 70) – literally and metaphorically frames the film. The complications of autonomous production under capitalism, self-organization, self-governance, and control, not only of "the means of production" but also over one's life, are the themes of the discussions staged throughout the film. This is in direct contrast to the parallel negotiations regarding and, more to the point, defining the limits of democracy that were taking place at the same time in Madrid. Thus, the formal organization of the film – its central trope, which gives voice to the hitherto voiceless[9] – corresponds to the wider antagonisms, their discourses and definitions, debated beyond the frame of the screen. This too makes the film a political – militant – intervention, an event.

In spite of Jordà's disavowal, style is an important feature of *Numax presenta…*. The use of colour in the introductory and final sequences of the film denotes actuality, the *now* of the conflict and the film itself; their common coincidence in time at the beginning and end of the film, is in contrast with the repetition and recreation of the dispute itself (almost – though not quite – in sepia-style). Given the use of colour to shoot the

---

8 I refer specifically to the 1979 election victory of Margaret Thatcher in the UK that signalled the end of the "post-war consensus" form of politics practised in Western Europe and North America (the neo-liberal experiment had, of course, been operating for several years previously in Latin America, most notably in Chile). The period 1978–9 was, to recall Guerra's earlier comments, the year of Foucault's lecture series on biopolitics and neo-liberalism at the Collège de France.
9 A significant number of the workers, and the majority of the leadership of the occupation, are women and most (though not all) of the film is shot in Castilian. Many of these workers are immigrants or the children of immigrants who have moved to Catalonia from other parts of the Spanish state. In the different assemblies both Castilian and Catalan are used with nobody objecting or even commenting on the fact. Indeed, at no stage in the film is the "national question" even mentioned. Jordà was not indifferent to Catalan nationalism, certainly in the later stages of his life, but that interest does not figure in these films.

theatrical episodes, a sense of disruption to the form itself develops; a disruption, moreover, that is historicized by the formal innovation.

Transformation in *social forms*, meanwhile, is what exercised – and continues to exercise – the autonomists in their endeavours to take the struggle of the factory to the wider world beyond. Filmic, historical, political, and social forms are marked by limits and barriers to which disciplinary concerns subject them in the same way as aesthetic forms. There is a transference inherent in the idea of transformation. The *placing* of *Numax* within the city of Barcelona is realized filmically by the shots of the hazy silhouette of the Sagrada Familia – emblematic of the Barcelona skyline – against which the group of women workers discuss the situation as they smoke on the roof or the terrace of the factory. Form is of course many things that work within and without the text: tropes, figures, genres, among them. *Numax presenta…* is part of the factory film genre, its essay form a mode of film-making that Jordà specialized in throughout his career. Prior to embarking on his Communist Party-sponsored projects, the director had made what is arguably a performative essay in which Catalan writer Maria Aurèlia Capmany discusses her novel *Un lloc entre els morts*.[10] Jordà's essays are defined by filmic speech acts that challenge the traditional separation of form from content. At the same time they historicize form; text and context entwine, align, and integrate with each other.[11]

Veinte años no es nada (2004)

Jordà's question to the Numax workers regarding their future at the party with which the film culminates is met with a unanimous refusal to contemplate a future devoted to salaried labour and assembly-line factory work: in what is paradigmatic of the autonomists' rejection of work gives rise to a dissensus.

---

10 *Maria Aurèlia Capmany parla d'Un lloc entre els morts* (*Maria Aurèlia Capmany Talks about a Place among the Dead*, 1969).

11 Although very different film-makers, this is something Jordà shares with Jean Rouch, a pioneer of the essay and the ethnographic film. Re-enactment, blurring the divisions between fiction and documentary film, are characteristics of the work of Rouch. Rouch would also abandon traditional objectification inherent in anthropological study to make his subjects active participants in his films, to express themselves in their own voices. Another connection between Jordà and Rouch is that of Africa itself. Jordà's 1990 biopic of his friend and collaborator from the Escuela de Barcelona, Jacinto Esteva, *El encargo del cazador*, is the result of his initial interest in the late 1960s in making a film about the anti-colonial struggles in Angola and Mozambique, a project that failed but led indirectly to *Portogallo, paese tranquillo*.

Twenty-five years after *Numax presenta...*, Jordà, as if in response to the open-ended coda appended to the title of the earlier film, and so as to provide concrete answers to his original question, sought out the protagonists of the earlier film and persuaded them to participate in a second production. The relation between the historical moment and the filmic diegesis in *Numax presenta...* is marked by a concentrated, saturated, and complex set of contradictions that bind and hold in abeyance the collective and the conjuncture. *Veinte años no es nada*, on the other hand, is about the dispersal and the consequential singularity of each individual experience. While the collective has evaporated, in the previous film's logic of reenactment, the staged reunion of *Veinte años no es nada* carves out a return. Although there is no theatrical narration, it is clear that many of the encounters are set up for the purposes of the film. The very evident differences in the filmic compositions of *Numax presenta...* and *Veinte años no es nada*, wittingly or not, have a relation (if not exactly a correspondence) with the shifts in the political forms that the passage of time has wrought. The point is important. Dissensus and dispersal raise formal questions too. At the heart of the displacement is a paradox: a contradictory condensation.

Once more, while these films are not reducible to the conjuncture alone, there is a relation between their on-screen interiority and the off-screen exteriority. Just as *Numax presenta...* has a discordant relation to its historical moment that prompts its internal debate, so too *Veinte años no es nada* is highly conscious of its place in relation to the broader world. These films, though, are not allegories of their respective periods. Their exemplary quality is as exceptions; they are allusive symptoms of their times rather than metaphors. They are films that, in their very different ways, give voice to the unheard, those excluded from dominant discourse; to recall Rancière, to the part that has no part.

If the first film was inspired by the collective experience (almost nobody is identified, except by their first names and in passing, even in the credits of the film), the focus of the second, two and a half decades later, is on the stories of the individuals. The shift of subjectivities is a notably distinguishing factor between the two pieces. Names, in this second film, are used throughout. The traditional notion of the working class as concentrated in one place is dislocated; mobility and individualization prove the characteristics of *Veinte años no es nada*. The common experience shared by the individuals now atomized points to a new and different sense of crisis, a crisis of collective action. The point, however, is how such abstraction – the relation between time and individual/collective experience – might be filmed. Although there is no repetition of the theatrical commentary of *Numax presenta...*, the entirety of *Veinte años no es nada* is in a sense staged, corseted within the parameters of its predecessor. The film establishes a scenography. As well as being a film about the evolution of a group of once-militant workers, it is a film about a film, a metafilm. *Numax presenta...* is screened during the reunion dinner of *Veinte años no es nada*. The condition of film-making itself – its essayistic quality – is wrapped within the interrogation of the concept of political militancy in the era of neoliberalism. As Jordà's penultimate film (he would die in 2006), it also brings to an end the director's trajectory as a militant film-maker; it points to a conclusion of sorts, a drawing together of life and representation in a very personal expression of biopolitics.

There is, though, an element that disrupts – a further dislocation – any tidy, sentimental ending: the demos, that which has been left out of discourse, the remainder, not only of that which is rendered surplus to needs but discounted altogether, excluded from the count, offsets succinct calculation. The labour market itself in these two and half decades between the two films has changed dramatically. By 2004 many of the benefits for workers of the Moncloa Pacts, for which the representatives of the working-class movement had willingly sacrificed their labour power in exchange for benefits – most notably stable employment, job security – had been whittled away in the name of corporate exigency. Unemployment had rocketed and created an army of alternative labour that threatened the conditions and security of salaried workers. Though never articulated as such in the film, the discourse of precariousness is characteristic of the post-1979 period. Meanwhile, autonomism emphasizes creative resistance, self-education, and re-education. It is about reclaiming the time that would otherwise be given up to work for oneself. If the initial project of *Numax presenta...* concerned the crises prompted by collective self-management, *Veinte años no es nada* is about what each of the protagonists subsequently went on to make of their own lives; much of which deals with new and different forms of waging the struggle that Numax initiated. Autonomism concerns refusal; it is about refusing to conform to the discipline – the bodily discipline – imposed by the rules of everyday life, a rejection of temporal and spatial order, symbolized by the regulatory conditions of the daily routine of factory work. Discipline has extended to the world beyond the factory walls and even beyond the frontiers of the human body. Paradoxically, though – and herein lies the nub of the film, the contradiction at its centre – *Veinte años no es nada* is also a film about losing the collective spirit. Indeed, a significant part of the film focusses on individuals who now work, if not exactly for themselves, at least alone (the taxi driver, the artisan, the schoolteacher, the owner of a bar, the sales rep).

Precariousness, given material form in the uncertain future contained in the title of *Numax presenta...*, is what distinguishes the labour market of 2004 but it also characterizes other aspects of life, such as housing and affective relations. The body is more fragile. We get a sense of this early on in the film with Emilia, a woman who heralds from León (and who says "Cataluña ha sido como una universidad" ["Catalonia has been like a university"]).[12] Now she runs a bar which, after many years, she is in danger of losing owing to speculation and gentrification. Meanwhile, another former Numax employee, Blanca, works as an elementary schoolteacher of evidently underprivileged, marginalized children in Cordoba. Blanca's charges and Emilia's situation point to a shift in historical temporality governed by new uncertainties.

Time enfolds in this second film; the apertures in its creases are revealed by promiscuous plundering of archive material, memories, and testimonials. Time also reveals the presence and the uneven shifts, the new forms of protest and new subjects of resistance. *Veinte años no es nada* was released at a significant historical juncture. While not as emblematic as 1979, 2004 is also a watershed year. Arguably it is the year when the street and the public square become singular sites of struggle. It is the moment of the anti-globalization movement and when popular mobilization first pose a serious threat to the institutions of 1978 in Spain. The year is also the one in which the demos took centre stage in political struggle and began to effect real change.[13] The year prior to the making of the film was marked by what is arguably the world's largest ever mass mobilization in opposition to the second Gulf war. In Spain the ¡No a la guerra: otro mundo es posible! moment (it had developed out of the anti-globalization movement, itself a response to neo-liberalism) had momentous effects. A year after the US-led invasion, the Aznar government was brought down after the exposure of its deception following the commuter train bombings by Islamic militants on 11 March 2004 during the general election campaign. This led to protests outside the headquarters of the ruling party and a sudden reverse in the predicted vote. *Veinte años no es nada* was of course made quite independently and prior to these events – the fact it emerged in the same year is coincidence and no mention is made of them in the film –

---

12 Marina Garcés titles her interview with Jordà with an echo of this phrase: "Numax was like a university for us."
13 Two years later in 2006 Garcés would collaborate with Jordà's old Autonomist comrade Santiago López Petit to write an article titled "El 11-M y la nueva politización" on the events surrounding the 11–14 March 2004 protests. http://espaienblanc.net/?page_id=518.

but in light of the politics of the two films, it is perhaps relevant. This is particularly so given that the anti-globalization movement is arguably heir to Autonomía, with which Jordà had once been associated.[14]

The period between the first film and the second sees a world transformed unimaginably for the participants in both pieces. The Cold War has ended, and neo-liberalism, whose symptoms were signalled by Foucault in 1979, has seemingly triumphed.[15] If *Numax presenta...* turned on the collective experience, *Veinte años no es nada*'s focus on the life stories of the individuals gives rise to a tension here between the autonomist refusal of the factory model and the neo-liberal conceptualization of the individual. Carlos, who features in the final moments of the earlier film and who now works as a taxi driver in the streets of Barcelona, captures this ambiguous change in conversation with two of his erstwhile workmates: "Hay mucha individualización" (There is a lot of individualization"), he says, lamenting the contemporaneous absence of solidarity that his generation experienced in the late 1970s. There is a desire for "una forma de vida diferente" ("a different way of life"), to cite one of the women who formerly worked at Numax. The irony regarding the formation of political subjectivity is pointedly made in the respective soundtracks: while the first film ends with a tango, the second culminates with a screening of the original film followed by a collective rendition of "The Internationale."

Reminders abound of the social factory beyond the confines of the old traditional Fordist model of industry. If, in the first, the Sagrada Familia appears shrouded in cloud, its grey outline providing the backdrop to the ongoing debate filmed in black and white, in the second it is shot in glorious colour as Carlos, the taxi driver, points it out to his Italian clients. Tourism, always important to the national economy, has replaced manufacturing. The city and colour provide the visual signs of changing times, but, as the singing of "The Internationale" suggests, *Veinte años no es nada* also has a particular soundscape. Sound, music, and speech are key elements of both films. The tango of the first film is countered in the second with another Gardel tango, "Volver" ("Return"), giving its title a double meaning: the passage of time and a return to the past. Title

---

14 I refer here to the influence of thinkers such as Toni Negri on the anti-globalization movement.
15 Neo-liberalism in Catalonia was, of course, enthusiastically embraced by the ruling nationalist coalition Convergencia i Unió, which, albeit under different guises, has governed the region for most of the post-dictatorial period. Its historical leader Jordi Pujol is currently awaiting trial on multiple corruption charges.

aside, tango is a genre tinged with affect, with desire, loss, and pain; the affective inflections of biopolitics.[16] There is an aspect of oral history in the second film, while verbal debate is at the heart of the first. If, as I suggested earlier, the camera captures those voices, there are other implications too. The reunion takes place in a Barcelona restaurant, and one of the first people introduced is the deaf-mute son of one of the workers, now dead, who participated in the original dispute. There is a hint here of Plato's *Phaedrus*, when Socrates distinguishes between the writing and speech: "they have no parent to protect them; and they cannot protect or defend themselves." While clearly the philosophical point is different, it is striking that the figure here is both an "orphan" and a figure who lacks the power of speech. We might read into this a somewhat different configuration: film qua writing, the mute orphan as demos. This idea might be reinforced by another example. A yawning absence in the film is that of Juan Manzanares. A silent figure who died prematurely of liver disease, he is represented in the film by his loquacious former lawyer. One of the interesting features, given the previous reference to Plato and my reading of the presence of the mute boy, is that the interview with the lawyer provides the sole occasion in *Veinte años no es nada* for Jordà himself to appear on screen.

In a film about legacy, a film constructed around testimony, the figure of the deaf-mute heir to the class struggle is charged with symbolic and affective power: he is in a sense an exemplary case of the (literally) voiceless, the demos that is the focus of Rancière's work. Amid the sonorous and auditory continuum in the film (and in many ways both films are oral and musical accounts), he represents a silence, a void or gap in the discursive narrative, a certain formal autonomy or supplement in the absence of his deceased father. In an affective gesture that exceeds the confines of the body, as the screening of *Numax presenta...* comes to an end, he wipes away the tears rolling down his cheeks as if the whale bones that line the corset of the confines of the metafilm had failed to fully contain its interior content within its corporeal limits. It is perhaps significant that Carlos, the taxi driver who a quarter of a century earlier at the party that marked the end of the occupation of the Numax factory and the film played drums and thus maintained the regulatory, even beat of the musical arrangement, is tapping out the rhythm of an alternative order. It is apt then that he now passes the time when he is without passengers interacting with language tapes. This is

---

16 "Veinte años no es nada" is, of course, itself the title of another Carlos Gardel tango.

not only an autonomist use of working hours for his own benefit but a technological self-education in oral expression.

While individualizing what was a collective struggle, the film centres upon questions of affect. Juan Manzanares is spoken of with greater dignity and understanding by his partner Pepi (Josefa Sánchez), one of the more vocal participants in the film of the original dispute, than by his lawyer. A key figure whose story occupies a significant proportion of this second film – she now runs a shop in Barcelona selling her own artisan products – she and others took up arms in the aftermath of Numax and held up banks at gunpoint to sustain their militancy. Pepi talks movingly about Juan, his life and his death: "era muy humano, extremadamente humano, muy sensible" ("He was very humane, extremely humane, very sensitive"). We learn from television archive material the story of Juan's final robbery in 1985 of a branch of the Banco de Sabadell in Valls, in which Pepi did not participate. Manzanares took the employees hostage, demanded the presence of the then minister of the interior, José Barrionuevo, and shot and seriously wounded the then civil governor of Tarragona province, Vicente Valero, who entered the bank in *representation* of Barrionuevo, as a supplement and a substitute.[17] There is an interesting correlation here with the artifice of the theatrical stage re-enactments of history in *Numax presenta*.... Providing an interestingly skewed perspective on cultural memory, the archival television footage embedded within the filmic text of *Veinte años no es nada* posits two immediacies, two *nows*, two present moments, as events viewed (by us, the spectators) in hindsight. The *now* indexed by the sequences shot in colour of the initial and final sequences of *Numax presenta*... is echoed (with concomitant distance or remove) here. The immediacy of the figure of the direct witness of the 1979 film is articulated through reminiscence, by the rhetoric of defeat, in a register of melancholia condensed in the collective singing of "The Internationale."

Demos refers to the uncounted or the unrecounted, that which has been left out of written accounts of history, that has been institutionally muted and not permitted a voice of its own. A trace though remains in the spoken word, this condition of oral testimony, in the fragments of memory that provide another kind of legacy unrepresented in statistics

---

17 In a singular irony Barrionuevo would himself later be tried and convicted of terrorist offences for instigating the kidnapping of Segundo Marey by state-sponsored paramilitaries. Sentenced to 108 years in prison, he was pardoned after less than two months of incarceration by the government of José María Aznar. Valero was interviewed separately, as an aside, inserted within *Veinte años no es nada*.

or official narratives. The voiceless demos is, in this sense, empowered by such an inheritance. The performative quality of the lived remembrance of the witnesses themselves is there in the conscious act of disputing versions of memory that by 2004 had become one of the dominant academic and political discourses in Spain.[18] *Veinte anos no es nada* ends with an intriguing image of inheritance and legacy. While in 1979 Jordà had asked the Numax workers about their future plans, in 2004 he does not have the same opportunity. The final shot of the film frames a child of around three, apparently Carlos' young daughter, her doll in one hand, the fist of the other raised, while the collective, their backs turned to her, sing the revolutionary hymn. Seemingly overdetermined, clichéd, even perhaps opportunistically staged, it is an image of the militant future, of struggles yet to come.

Conclusion: The Essay as the Form of/for Crisis

This rather forced ending, theatrically set up as a reaffirmation, is the visual image, the incarnation, of the open-ended "…" that hangs off the end of the title of *Numax presenta…*, the pending, ongoing, and future resistance in a different configuration. Earlier I cited filmic texts set in the factory, very much apart from one another and, in turn, from Jordà's films by time. Both the Fassbinder TV series and the Portuguese *The Nothing Factory* are fictions, Jordà's films are – in theory at least – documentaries.[19] The way they broaden to incorporate fictional strategies facilitates the undoing of film's claim to naturalism; they provoke a formal rupture of the conventions of fiction and non-fiction, or that suggested by Jordà himself, between word and image; they enact crisis. The cinematic essay is the form of crisis that, in turn, generates something unassimilable – like the demos itself – an excess or supplement within critical practice itself. The crisis the essay form aptly responds to is political crisis, not as a passive correlation but as an active intervention, as a subjective participant in an act of resistance. In this refusal there is a performativity that links protest with theatricality.

---

18 In a further instance of "performance" that recalls the parody of Santiago Carrillo in *Numax presenta…* the lawyer who represented the factory workers during the dispute and who has since become a chef (and was responsible for preparing the dinner) makes his appearance in disguise before removing the bulky headpiece hiding his true identity.

19 Although fictionalized, *The Nothing Factory* is in fact based on real events. Clearly very different, but related to this, is the fictional/performative strategy employed by Joshua Oppenheimer in *The Act of Killing* (2012).

For anyone who has been involved in grassroots politics in Spain over the last two decades, it is a strange and slightly unnerving sight to see video artist and activist Marcelo Expósito presiding over that most theatrical of stages and the most institutional of institutions, the Spanish Congress. However, as – at the time of writing – fourth in the hierarchical chain of house speakers and member of Parliament for the formation En Comú Podem this has indeed happened in recent years. En Comú Podem – the Catalan sister organization of Podemos – is very much part and product of the 15-M movement and the mass mobilizations of 2011 that saw the central squares of almost all Spanish cities occupied by protesters.

In 2004, the same year as *Veinte años no es nada,* Expósito, based (if not born) in Barcelona, released an hour-long video essay that exemplifies the kind of formal filmic engagement with politics that this chapter has sought to demonstrate in Jordà's work. Expósito depicts the evolution and operation of the social factory and does so by focussing directly on the work of one of the original autonomists, Paulo Virno (who appears in the film). *Primero de Mayo (la ciudad-fábrica)* (*May First: The City-Factory*) was shot largely in the city of Turin, at the site of one of Fiat's most emblematic factories now transformed into a commercial centre. Former factory workers and immigrants, recruited as private police, battle against their excluded cohorts, the unemployed, music techies, wifi geeks, punks, situationists, and other outcasts from society who seek to resist the speculators. This staging of the demos is a sign of neo-liberalism's brutal conquest of space and the resistance to it, the anti-globalization movement that in time would give rise to the worldwide revolts of 2011. Gerald Raunig describes *Primero de Mayo (la ciudad-fábrica)* in the following terms reminiscent of the apparent shift that has taken place between *Numax presenta...* and *Veinte años no es nada*:

> Marcelo Expósito's video ... outlines a complex introduction to the shift from the Fordist paradigm of the factory to the post-Fordist paradigm of virtuosic cognitive and affective labour. He takes as his model the Fiat factory Lingotto, a proud centre of automobile production in the 1930s and now – having been transformed into a multifunctional hotel and conference centre – a hotbed of the service industry and an example of the *fabbrica diffusa*. (The operaist term refers to the factory that has been diffused into the city, into the private spheres, into the forms of life.)

With this in mind, I want to conclude with reference to what Laura Rascaroli has called "the potentiality of all essay films to question and challenge their own form" (300). It is the essay as the critically shaping subject productive of its own subject matter via the performance of commitment, which points to a continuation of the militant tradition of film-making (of which Expósito is only one of Jordà's heirs). In the same volume as Rascaroli, Elizabeth Pazian and Caroline Eades describe the essay form as "dialectical thought that gravitates towards crisis. Thus it fosters the development of new forms" (8). There is within and between these two films a temporal dialogue and dialectic between enactment and re-enactment, between chronology and anachronology, a spectral relation between the militant event and its representation. That the two films discussed here focus on crisis (the collective crisis of the Numax dispute and the individual crises of its participants decades later) at two different moments of political crisis whose effects endure suggests a convergence that exceeds anecdotal coincidence, one that points to an openness to future political change and the filmic response to it.

WORKS CITED

The Act of Killing. Directed by Joshua Oppenheimer, 2012.
Eight Hours Don't Make a Day. Directed by Rainer Werner Fassbinder, 1972.
Foucault, Michel, *The Birth of Biopolitics: Lectures at the Collège de France, 1978–1979*, New York: Picador, 2020.
Garcés, Marina. "Numax, nuestra universidad. Conversación con Joaquim Jordà." *Revista Zehar* no. 58, 2006, pp. 10–13.
Guerra, Carles. Entrevista con Joaquim Jordà, 2004, https://www.macba.cat/es/arte-artistas/artistas/jorda-joaquim/numax-presenta.
– "La militancia biopolítica de Joaquín Jordá: The Biopolitical militancy of Joaquín Jordá." *Cinema Comparat/ive Cinema*, vol. 2, no. 5, 2014, pp. 50–5.
– "N for Negri: Antonio Negri in Conversation with Carles Guerra." *Grey Room*, no 11, 2003, pp. 86–109.
Hallward, Peter. "Staging Equality: Rancière's Theatocracy." *New Left Review*, vol. 37, 2006, pp. 109–29.
Jordà, Joaquim. "*Numax presenta...* y otras cosas." *Nosferatu. Revista de cine*, no. 9, 1992, pp. 56–9.
Jordà, Joaquim, director. *De nens*, performances by Marta Galán, Núria Lloansi, Xabier Robés, Mireia Serra, Carla Jiménez, and Oscar Albadalejo, Massa d'Or, 2003.
– *Lenin vivo*. Unitele Film, 1970.
– *Maria Aurèlia Capmany parla d'Un lloc entre els morts*, Los Films de Formentera, 1969.
– *Numax presenta...*, performances by Walter Cots, María Espinosa, Mario Gas, Rosa Gavín, Víctor Guillén, and Joaquim Jordà, Asamblea de Trabajadores de Numax, 1979.
– *Portogallo, paese tranquillo*, Unitele Film, 1969.

- *Veinte años no es nada*, performances by Blanca Galán, Josefa Sánchez, Fernanda Gázquez, Eulogio Roca, Josefina Altamira, and Emilia Fernández, Ovideo and Unicamente Severo Films, 2004.
Jordà, Joaquim, and Núria Villazán, directors. *Mones com la Becky*, performances by João Maria Pinto, Marian Varela, Petra Alcántara, Montse Bustos, Juana Cabeza, and Ramsés Espín, Els Quatre Gats and La Sept Arte, 1999.
López Petit, Santiago and José Antonio Diaz Valcárcel, *Crítica de la izquierda autoritaria en Cataluña, 1967–1974*, Ediciones de Ruedo Ibérico, 1974.
The Nothing Factory. Director, Pedro Pinho, 2017.
Pazian, Elizabeth A., and Caroline Eades, eds. *The Essay Film: Dialogue, Politics, Utopia*. Wallflower Press, 2016.
Primero de Mayo (la ciudad-fábrica). Directed by Marcelino Expósito, 2004.
Rancière, Jacques. *Dissensus: On Politics and Aesthetics*. Translated by Steven Corcoran, Bloomsbury Academic, 2015.
- "The Thinking of Dissensus: Politics and Aesthetics." *Reading Rancière*, edited by Paul Bowman and Richard Stamp, Continuum, 2011, pp. 1–17.
Rascaroli, Laura, "The Idea of Essay Film." *The Essay Film: Dialogue, Politics, Utopia*, edited by Papazian, Elizabeth, and Caroline Eades, Wallflower Press, 2016, pp. 300–5.
Raunig, Gerard. "Modifying the Grammar. Paolo Virno's Works on Virtuosity and Exodus." *Art Forum*, January 2008.

PART THREE

The Portabella Nexus

5 Economies of Sound: Labouring Europe in Pere Portabella and Carles Santos

SARA NADAL-MELSIÓ

I. The Wolf

A musical-becoming of sensibility and a global becoming of musicality have occurred, whose historiality remains to be thought about, all the more so since it is contemporaneous with an expansion of the image whose extent does not correspond to equivalent transformations in the perceptible realm.

Jean-Luc Nancy, *Listening* 12

In the context of the acoustic turn taken by contemporary art practices and culture at large, it seems pertinent to think about the specificity of sound as a mode of aesthetic production. Has the "musical-becoming" of our times changed the way in which we understand aesthetic processes of production? Can we treat acoustic processes of production and their discontinuities as blueprints onto which to project geopolitical processes of production at large? Is it possible to address Europe's failed sovereignty through a musical understanding of its public sphere? The privileged relationship of music to number – think of scores, partitions, and algorithms – provides a unique representation of the contemporary economic realities that shape, in an unprecedented manner, Europe's social and cultural legacy.[1] The fact that European sovereignty is exclusively economic, and that it functions fundamentally by tempering transnational fiscal dissonances, will underline my discussion.

---

1 Fredric Jameson comments on this analogy in his introduction to Jacques Attali's 1977 *Noise: The Political Economy of Music*. He reflects on the fact that Attali is a political economist rather than a musicologist (Attali vii).

I would like to begin by recuperating a Baroque musical concept that acquires a renewed meaning amidst contemporary aesthetic practices. In his book *The Fifth Hammer: Pythagoras and the Disharmony of the World*, Daniel Heller-Roazen describes the figure of the "wolf." "Wolf" is the name Baroque tuners gave to the dissonant and resilient sound produced in any attempt to temper and harmonize an instrument. As far as the relationship to number is concerned, the desire for absolute harmonization should be understood as an attempt to fully mathematize the world of acoustic phenomena: "Beyond the range of several reasonably pure fifths, for instance, the player will encounter that exceptional, yet unavoidable tone that the Baroque tuners called the 'wolf': the one note that must pay the price for the relative purity of all the others" (82). The lonely "wolf" Heller-Roazen evokes here cuts a striking figure in the presence of relentless efforts to harmonize sound. The fact that not all notes can be reconciled in harmony, or that musical codes are not all-encompassing, is materialized in the "wolf" as an acoustic emblem of resistance. In this way, the condensation of dissonance into a single note, the exception that tempers the rule of harmony as a universalizing system, doubles as a mechanism of transference that allows dissent to persevere. I am therefore not concerned with harmony or the purity of well-tempered sounds but rather with the figure of the "wolf" in its ability to transmit a dissonance that can be politically resituated every time it is performed. In the instances of transmission I will explore, a logic of preservation is at play: the wolf intensifies and retains an exceptional but necessary dissonance and allows for it to travel nested in the apparent harmony of cultural legacy. Thus the "wolf" is not just paying a price for an overall harmony but also, and more importantly, smuggling a figure of dissent into the uses of organized sound and its universalization in the Western public sphere.

The wolf will be my guide as I address the political agency of dissonance in the late musician and artist Carles Santos's 2006 retrospective ¡*Visca el piano!* and in Pere Portabella's 2007 experimental film *Die Stille vor Bach*. Both of these artists explore the role of sound and music in the production of a discontinuous European public sphere. In their work, acoustic dissonance cuts across and reorganizes economies and temporalities while acting as a challenge to a harmonic mode of representation. I will thus trace three moments where dissonance plays a role in the activation of political agency through resonance, and in the performative actualization of Europe's musical patrimony.

Because we are dealing with an immaterial form in movement, however, the political agency these works re-energize is intimately tied to their transit across specific temporalities and physical locations from which they borrow the materiality they themselves lack. These temporalities and places are not simply settings or contexts, but rather materialities that are called into being by the music itself, creating a loop or a transfer by which they activate one another in an expressive continuum. Europe is then not just the "location" for these aesthetic interventions, but the very thing that they construct and then destabilize. European sovereignty and its discontinuity are at the core of these artworks and take the shape of a "wolf" resisting harmonization.

As far as geopolitical contexts are concerned, the role of the peripheral is also relevant here: a Catalan film-maker and a Catalan musician take a sideways glance at Johann Sebastian Bach as a musical landmark that has been used to universalize European identity and its modes of cultural production. It will be my contention here that the wounded sovereignty of Catalonia constitutes a vantage point from which to make the "wolf" audible again, to listen to the incomplete harmonization that lies at the dead centre of Europe.[2]

In addition, the centrality of cinema as a site of encounters, collaboration, and composition is key to understanding the counterpoint between sound and image in the Portabella-Santos tandem. If, following Deleuze, Alain Badiou has argued that cinema names a "philosophical situation" because it allows for "an encounter between terms that are foreign to each other" (Badiou 202), the concrete relationship of music and cinema is an exploration of their difference, whereby each of the terms of the encounter highlights the exceptionality of the other one. Also passing through Deleuze, Steven Marsh has already spoken of the "disjunctive synthesis" at the heart of the Portabella-Santos collaboration ("The Legacies of Pere Portabella"). I wish to underline the exceptional and paradoxical nature of the cinematic as a visual environment for the political and experimental potential of this disjunction by following the "wolf" that, as an acoustic condensation of this same disjunction, bears witness to the discontinuous and dissonant ensemble, the organization of differences, that we call "Europe." The gesture is akin to understanding that Socrates learning to play the flute before his death is the mise en scène of a wordless and exceptional philosophical situation because it is conveyed in a medium other than the purely philosophical. Similarly, the dissonance of

---

2 This essay is part of a larger project entitled *Europe and the Wolf: Political Variations on a Musical Concept*, forthcoming with Zone Books. The manuscript proposes a musical reconfiguration of Europe as a temporal and acoustic rather than a territorial organization, through the work of Allora & Calzadilla, Tarek Atoui, and Anri Sala, in addition to Carles Santos and Pere Portabella.

Santos's "wolf" only resonates insofar it relates to the non-musical, to the silence of Portabella's image. It is in this way that this collaboration asks us to rethink cinema altogether: if cinema can only be thought in relation to other mediums, it is perhaps never itself. Or, to put it another way, cinema – but cinema as the name of the archive of different mediums that it is – bears its own wolf within it, a wolf that, fissuring it from within, opens up its historico-political potential.

II. Temperance and Chance: Carles Santos

The Catalan film-maker Pere Portabella recounts a story regarding avant-garde composer and virtuoso pianist Carles Santos's return to piano playing after a self-imposed hiatus. In 1973, Santos had decided to sell his piano, buy a motorcycle with the money he obtained, and record the piece *100km/h, 1, 2, 3*. The piece consists of footage of the pianist speeding on his motorcycle, fixated on an urgent endpoint.

Santos had decided to devote himself to clandestine political activities in order to put an end to Francoist rule in Spain. In October of the same year, he was arrested together with 113 members of the "Assamblea de Catalunya and incarcerated in the Modelo prison in Barcelona. As chance would have it, his cellmate was none other than Pere Portabella. On learning that somewhere in the prison building there was an abandoned piano, Santos decided it was time to play again. He then, and not without risk, proceeded to play an entire Bach sonata on a hopelessly out-of-tune piano. He had seemingly found a way to connect his virtuoso skill as a renowned pianist to the political dissonances of the Spain of his time. He had in this manner deployed the disharmony of the "wolf" to militantly intervene in the biopolitical regime of a Francoist prison, by forcing a listening that fell far outside the signifying references of the space where it resonated.

In this instance, the necessary simultaneity of the production of sound and its reception functioned at the same time as a call into presence of and a direct address to the dissident political community in the prison.[3] Those who listened may well have heard their dissent echoed

---

3 The act of playing has always been intimately connected to listening in Santos's conceptual output. The series "Piano intervinguts" (2006), for instance, presents an upright piano with two gigantic ears attached on each end. In 1973, he performed a number of "situacions de comunicació total o parcial o de no comunicació" for the *Informació d'Art Concepte* in Banyoles, Catalonia. In them, he complicated notions of performance (actor), recording (Magnetophon), and listening (public) in seventeen variations of their possible organizations (Santos 116).

and amplified in every out-of-key note Santos played, making sense of it as an acoustic and transient inscription of their collective being. Through Santos's action, the listening subject recognizes himself (the Modelo was a male-only prison) as a political subject by experiencing his own dislocation in the dissonant sounds of the out-of-tune piano. The political prisoner exists outside the bounds of the prison as a political actor; that is, elsewhere. Thus, the emancipatory and anticipatory potential of the aesthetic phenomenon, a deviation of Bach's music in this case, functions like a heterotopia. It transports the prisoners elsewhere, to a place that was not visible or audible before and that cannot be accounted for within the realm of the ideological and aesthetic modes of representation in place at a Francoist prison. Santos's performance triggers and in turn is triggered by what Theodor Adorno defines as "a desire for dissonances, and expression of a suffering, simultaneously autonomous and unfree subject" (*Introduction to Sociology* 221) – a political subject, he goes on to add, for whom music "is Utopia as well as the lie that Utopia is here now" (224).

Santos's intensity of resonance, his expansion of the physical and political space through the acoustic, implies a particular understanding of the aesthetic that, as we will see, he shares with Portabella.[4] Santos's sculptural expansion of space through the ability of sound to traverse walls and enclosures speaks to the emancipatory potential of the aesthetic phenomenon and calls for a redistribution of cultural capital understood as a closed archive. Both Bach's music and the physical resistance to it performed by Santos contain an ability to transport the listeners beyond the boundaries of ideological and aesthetic harmonization of cultural patrimony. The duration of Santos's performance – he did play an *entire* sonata uninterrupted – takes the form of an attack, and his mobilization of the "wolf" underscores the violence of his musical charge on Bach's temperance and the composer's association with harmonization. His choice of Bach is key.[5] Santos's relationship with

---

4 Aesthetic is always understood here quite literally as "aisthetis," what is perceptible and materialized.
5 It was Bach in *The Well-Tempered Clavier* who advocated on behalf of the new technology that resulted in a tuning of musical instruments that compromised a Renaissance pursuit of pure-fifths in favour of a system that eliminated wolf-tones and facilitated the development of modern tonality. Bach is the crucial figure in Baroque aesthetics

Bach is crucial to understand what Adorno might call his "musical conduct." If the loops that seem to adorn the first page of Bach's *The Well-Tempered Clavier* visualize a circular temperament where all keys sound in tune and produce a loop of call and response that harmonizes them, Santos is intent on reminding us that, despite Bach, and maybe because of him, not all sounds and the cultural capital they carry can be reconciled in harmony.

Santos's rendition both recalls Bach's towering figure in the dream of harmony and the fragility of such a dream in the context of Europe's cultural legacy.[6] With Bach's developments in harmony, which call musical modernity into being, dissonance is no longer something to be neutralized but rather something to be integrated into a larger system. Harmony becomes an ideological mystification that in turn echoes a fabular idea of Europe.

In addition, the connection of Bach both to imperial ideology and to subservient artistic labour holds the key to Santos's 1997 music theatre piece *La Pantera Imperial*. In this context, it is worth recalling that Bach's monumentality is a posthumous and anachronistic construction; in his lifetime, Bach was an overworked and underpaid church composer in the decentralized Lutheran denomination. His numerous letters to his employers are a testimony to the difficulties of his musical labour.

---

because he employs traditional forms – the fugue, most of all – in service of a modern technology and a modern harmonic system. His music resounds simultaneously forward and backward – itself a musical figuration that recurs constantly in his compositions.

6 Félix Fanés tells the story that Joan Brossa – a visual poet, early cinema fanatic, magician, playwright, mainstay of the Dau-al-Set, and principal instigator of a conceptual Catalan avant-garde – met Carles Santos in the Barcelona of the 60s. In such encounters Brossa called for a performance as a "carta de." The young avant-garde pianist and composer, who had studied with John Cage and was successfully introducing Fluxus noise-music to the hungry and stifled Spanish audience of the *tardofranquismo*, responded by playing Bach. The notoriously demanding Brossa responded to the virtuoso performance by simply asking, "I ara què?" ("and now what?"). One could say that Santos's lifelong engagement with Bach's music, his love-hate relationship with it, is a protracted attempt to answer this question.

Bach's monumental figure is *La pantera imperial* disembodied and materialized in a neo-Dadaist theatrical landscape that recalls a boxing ring. His overwhelming musical stature is broken down into a series of moving and threatening busts that fill a stage defined by an excess of bodies, voices, and sounds, fighting for harmonic ascendancy. The busts arrange and rearrange themselves into a number of variations, as does the music. The legacy of Bach is thus transformed into a situation, a violently anachronistic performance in which Santos takes up Adorno's challenge in the essay "Bach Defended against His Devotees." The violence of Adorno's critique, like Santos's, stems from a love of Bach as a transgressor, as a conflicted musical worker who, at times, transcended the emergence of specialized labour in his time, as well as its commodification. Through a radical exercise in the labour of advanced composition, Santos literally makes the dynamic unfolding of Bach's music both visible and audible, rescuing what is hidden in the truth-content of his work from cultural stagnation: "The entire richness of the musical texture, the integration of which was the source of Bach's power, must be placed in prominence by the performance instead of being sacrificed to a rigid, immobile monotony, the spurious semblance of unity that ignores the multiplicity it should embody and surmount" (Adorno, *Prisms* 145).

Santos's realization – i.e., interpretation *and* performance – of Bach's music also recovers a resistance to the commodity-character of music and of musical labour. By turning Bach's music into a theatrical situation where the composition, interpretation, performance, and listening of music cannot be compressed or separated, he transforms it into an event and a mode of immaterial production that challenges cultural commodification. Additionally, by framing his homage in the form of sacrilege, Santos actualizes Bach's legacy: "his legacy has passed onto composition, which is loyal to him in being disloyal; it calls his music by name by producing it anew" (Adorno, *Prisms* 146).

The question of the possibility of the new is intimately connected to an understanding of composition as a new mode of production in itself. Dissonance and multiplication introduce a differential that upsets the mode of production of the piece it intervenes in, by introducing the collective into divisions both of labour and authorship – as the two are quite clearly connected. Composition, therefore, has a relational value and is capable of producing the new, by pointing toward the limitations of representative modes of production.

Before we move onto the next section, let us stop for a moment and have a look at the space of the Fundació Joan Miró in Barcelona, where

Santos's retrospective ¡*Visca el piano!* takes place. The collection on view is a testimony to Santos's commitment to an aesthetic and political avant-garde. Two details, however, stand out in a way that is relevant to our discussion. A mechanical pianola moves through the space, filled with artefacts, forcing the audience to negotiate its transit through the exhibition carefully. In another room, Santos is working. He arrives every day to sit at his piano and practise for a few hours. Pere Portabella joins him to shoot a short movie, *No al No*, which collaboratively documents Santos working at the museum. The long-time collaborators engage once more in the visualization of labour through the durational complicities of the performative and the cinematic.

III. The Sounds of Labour, the Labour of Sound: Pere Portabella's *Die Stille vor Bach*

How then does collaboration, the putting together of distinct skills and epistemologies, become a form of composition? How does it provide us with a renewed theory of labour?

Pere Portabella's 2007 *Die Stille vor Bach* presents us with an extended reflection on these questions and locates them in a Europe with a very uncertain future. The film recovers the lessons of Catalan experimental production in the 70s and transposes them onto a larger geopolitical scale. As we have seen with Santos, the social and political imaginaries of Francoist Spain created a singular instance of dislocation in the Catalan avant-garde of the 1960s and 70s. The commitment to avant-garde practices, emerging from an established tradition in the Catalan context, pushed the envelope of political possibility by establishing an elective affinity and an affective transfer between the political and the aesthetic. Grup de Treball (Work Group), a heterogeneous Catalan art collective with a short lifespan (1972–6), affiliated predominantly with Marxist politics and conceptualist aesthetics, provides an excellent example of this double bind. Both Portabella and Santos were members of the collective.[7] Their collaboration in GdT provided both artists with an

---

7 To date, the GdT's documents have been used primarily to perform a much-needed historical correction, shedding light on peripheral and non-Anglo-American conceptualism, while at the same time insisting on a non-universalist approach to conceptualism as a philosophy of art. Here is the complete list of GdT's members: Francesc Abad, Jordi Benito, Jaume Carbó, María Costa, Alicia Fingerhut, Xavier Franquesa, Carles Hac Mor, Imma Julián, Antoni Mercader, Antoni Munné, Muntadas, Josep Parera, Santo Pau, Pere Portabella, Ángels Ribé, Manuel Rovira, Enric Sales, Carles Santos, Dorothée Selz, and Francesc Torres.

experimental platform in which to labour through the successes and failures of an ideological conceptualism.[8] The group's central preoccupation with artistic labour functions as a critique of capitalism under Franco and finds echoes in all of their subsequent output. The dissolution of the group after the end of Francoist rule also speaks to the centrality of its sociopolitical location and its strategic use of the mutual interference of aesthetic and political militancy. Once Franco died, so did GdT. The group's self-declared obsolescence is proof of the dependence of these two realms, the political and the aesthetic, in their militant practice. In fact, Portabella's creative capital was put to work in the writing of the Spanish Constitution, and later on, with the advent of the Delors Commission (1984–93), in thinking through the reinsertion of Catalonia and Spain into a complex European context, which was also in flux.

Die Stille vor Bach, Pere Portabella's return to film-making after more than a decade devoted primarily to political engagement, written in collaboration with Santos together with musicologist and theatre director Xavier Albertí, confronts the absences at the core of Europe and speculates on how to build a common identity that acknowledges those absences. Its political centre is articulated through a reflection on Europe's cultural legacy and acts as a counterpoint to the EU's championing of freedom of the market – that would in turn allow for the free movement of financial capital and eventually trigger the current free and unregulated circulation of debt. By contrast, in his film Portabella advocates for a legacy capable of containing the traces of Europe's violent history, together with the mourning and the labour it still

---

Here is a translation of the *Autodefinició del Grup de Treball*, 1975:

Heterogeneous grouping of individuals whose degree of union is established on the basis of a double articulation consisting in 1) ideological positions – implicit and explicit in the artistic practice, individual and collective, of the group, and in other types of articulated practice realized by the group – and 2) of the type of work in terms of the dialectical articulation of three types of practice: artistic practice, theoretical practice, and the practice of influence on and intervention in artistic and intellectual sectors. (Mercader, Parcerisas, and Valentí 42)

8 One of the better-known interventions of GdT consists of an anonymous list of the 44 professions of the 113 dissidents arrested at the Assamblea de Catalunya – both Santos and Portabella amongst them. The workers' catalogue was further developed in *Recorreguts* as a book project to be edited by the purchaser in the 1974 exhibition *Mostra d'art realitat*, and the profits from the sale of the piece were donated to the campaign Solidaritat amb el Moviment Obrer. The reflection on the status of the artists as worker was central to GdT.

demands, as a prerequisite to the construction of Europe as a possible community.

Die Stille vor Bach begins, silently and almost programmatically, with a white wall and ends with a blank screen. The naked presentation of the material conditions of film production is used to destabilize the mechanism of representation, conceptualizing the process of production instead – in an echo of the manifesto put forth by GdT. In the opening scene of the film, the camera pans over the silent white walls of a gallery space. By filming the scene in Josep Lluís Sert's Fundació Miró, emptied of all its paintings, Portabella opens the film by putting his Catalan avant-garde heritage to work. The scene speaks a sort of silent Catalan and echoes a collective and a legacy that at first sight is nowhere to be seen or heard. The slow camera movements and the film's silence are suddenly interrupted by the sound of the *Goldberg Variations*. The notes strike a disturbingly inhuman, but also funny, tone. The camera then searches for a diegetic source of sound and finds it in the form of a wheeled player piano. The camera follows the player piano and its twirling motions through the gallery space. When both camera and piano stop, we see a close-up of the musical scroll. The metronomic inscription of the music on the white scroll, itself a remediation of the musical score, brings to mind a mathematical algorithm and the pervasive fantasy of complete harmonization. Thus, it strikes a menacing chord by eliminating the human from this final equation. Throughout the film, Portabella speculates further on the cost of this equation in the context of a wounded European history.

In this prelude to the film and its protocols, Portabella engages not just Bach's music but also an early cinema of attractions. By going back in order to move forward, anachronism functions here as a dislocation of cultural legacy. The strategic use of anachronism is a constant in the film. The sequence of effacements the opening scene portrays – silence, absence, and anachronism – serves as a playful model for the dislocation of Europe's cultural capital that the film as a whole proposes.

Die Stille vor Bach consists of a non-narrative musical transport across Europe that structures itself across three centuries: eighteenth, nineteenth, and twenty-first; among three locations: a Barcelona museum, Leipzig, and Dresden; via three modes of sound production: silence, "found" noises, and formal music-making ; incorporating a variety of individual presences: booksellers, shop owners, truck drivers, Bach,

Bach's impersonator, Mendelssohn, Mendelssohn's butler, Mendelssohn's butcher, the present Cantor of St. Tomas, a cellist; and, most noticeably, the music itself, performed by soloists, collectively but not always in ensembles, and mechanically; also, featuring the compositions primarily of Bach, but also of Mendelssohn and Ligeti. The scenes of the film are not sutured. The space between spaces in the film, the sudden cuts it contains, reflect upon the production and transport of cultural and ideological meaning. Although the film moves from one century to another and one medium to another, from human bodies to machines and animals, from trains to rivers and roads, from computer screen to film screen and cell phone, it is movement as such that links and structures a sense of the common and foregrounds its absence.

Thus, the film is an extended political and aesthetic effort to put the legacies of European cultural capital to work and to set them in motion. The disenchanted realities of contemporary Europe after the fall of the Berlin Wall – which have only been redoubled by the more recent economic crisis – provide a context for a film that is as much a critique of Europe as it is a call for the reactivation of Europe's aesthetic and political legacies and practices. In the film, Portabella establishes aesthetics and politics as practices that mutually interrupt each other and that together interrupt the ideologies that have transformed them into products of cultural capital and thus consumption. Geographical markers, cultural capitals, and musical landmarks – the river Elbe, Dresden, Leipzig, and Bach's music – have indeed become culturally reified, yet their history contains discontinuities that the film makes audible and visible, in an attempt to bring life to a legacy that may still yield some political momentum.

Die Stille presents us with a Europe that is made out of cuts and interruptions and whose dissonance is the preferred mode of transmission for a cultural capital represented by Bach's music and echoed in absences located in the very heart of that European identity. That such a large part of the film takes place in Leipzig (though in three different centuries) is not just a matter of Bach's biography. It is in Leipzig that the revolutions of 1989 started under the banner "we are the people," which was a statement of the absence of one German collective and an echo of the 1968 graffiti "we are all German Jews." Bach's impersonator in Leipzig's Thomaskirche – a former academic in East Germany whose daily routine we follow – is a marker of the economic inequalities that followed Germany's reunification in 1990. The different temporalities the film inhabits establish a non-synchronic continuum that, in turn, allows for the incorporation of the past into the present.

European collectivity is thus enacted as a transformative transit between identities, temporalities, and physical conveyances. The aesthetic and political role of transit as a structural analogy linking the various elements of the film underscores Portabella's larger governing assumption that historical conditions must be understood as material conditions, which in turn can only be experienced in the shared contingency of work as a practice, and of art as the paradigmatic example of non-alienated work. The film asks the following questions: how much does a work of art cost? How many people work, and for how long, to transport art or simply to make it happen? Labour, transit, and cost are the material conditions Portabella insists we not forget.

In the same way, the use of direct sound emphasizes the finite duration of an action, the temporal materiality and the expenditure of labour it requires. Through this technique, which clearly references Jean-Marie Straub and Danièle Huillet's 1968 *The Chronicles of Maria Magdalena Bach*, music in the film is surrounded by everyday sounds and its interruptions. The aesthetic artefact is continually tampered with and this tampering, which often takes the form of the everyday sounds of labour in the movie, serves to create an alternative space that transforms the perception of what is given, and puts it back into motion. The situations the film records in real time and with direct sound function like moving ready-mades, or "sound sculptures," as Santos might put it. The constant reminder of duration; of the finite human temporality of work; of human effort, and its costs; of culture as human expenditure are the basis for both the militant politics and the conceptual aesthetics of *Die Stille*. The skill of Bach as a worker is as central to the film as the cultural capital of his legacy. The questioning of aesthetic autonomy and its avowed disinterestedness provides a mode and methodology for exploring political emancipation in all of Portabella's cinematic interventions – Immanuel Kant looms as large as Bach in the film. The emancipatory potential of the aesthetic is contained in its *sensus communis* and is by definition political. The power of reconciliation between orders and identities should be understood in this film as both a surplus to and an interruption of the representative nature of ideological apparatuses. The fact that the bodies that fill the screen – the Bach impersonator, the cellist, the musician, and the truck driver – are not just social constructs, but dignified workers who cannot be reduced to the product of their labour because via their "extended imagination" they participate in the aesthetic as a supplement is one of the critical points here. If, as with Santos, the emancipatory potential of an aesthetic phenomenon is contained in its ability to transport us elsewhere, in *Die Stille* it serves as the meeting place for a political community that is still to come, for an absent Europe that is not absent because it has disappeared but rather because it has never yet existed – as a single, homogeneous, self-identical political formation. The aesthetic functions here as both a relation and a movement, not as a product but as the making of a product. Activity in this context becomes participation and composition, not only for the actors/musicians but also for the audience, which participates by suturing the cuts of the film to produce meaning. The audience is given the chance to exercise a new European identity that may briefly seem possible because it never existed before.

Yet something is new in this film that was not present in Portabella's extraordinary production of the 60s and 70s: the use of myths or fables as yet another mode of transport by a film-maker who has insistently announced his rejection of narrative. After the very bleak 1989 film *Pont de Varsòvia*, the political "desencanto" with the Spanish Transition and its historical amnesia may have taught Portabella that a collective myth or a fable is a necessary tool not only for the construction of collectivity but also for the practice of a shared sense of accountability. Both *Pont de Varsòvia* and *Die Stille vor Bach* recover fable in the form of urban myths and anecdotes. *Die Stille* recovers the fable as a mode of transport, as a linking mechanism, because in the end the common always needs a story to be able to transform contingency, which is opaque, into experience, which can be shared. I am not referring here to historical narratives but to orally transmitted urban legends and myths as carriers of a condensed truth they merely point towards without fully disclosing. The urban legend of the discovery of Bach's *Saint Matthew's Passion*, wrapping a heart Mendelssohn's butler has just purchased in the market, is a wonderful example of Portabella's rediscovery of fable. This legend is sung, and not told, in the movie by a woman doing laundry. In the song, with lyrics by Xavier Albertí and a melody by Mendelssohn, the ambiguity of the German phrasing "Mendelssohn's butcher," which is also the butcher of Mendelssohn – and Mendelssohn did get butchered by Nazism – contains the trauma of Jewish extermination lodged in the Romantic building of the nation state and of fantasies of assimilation through high culture. The question of giving an account of something and being accountable for it is encapsulated in a song that establishes a link between all the historical moments in the film without subsuming them into a grand narrative or undoing their discontinuities.

In the face of Europe's traumatic history, *Die Stille* asks the question: What then can be done after this dislocation, this break in the historical continuum, has taken place, after the pages of Bach's *Passion* have

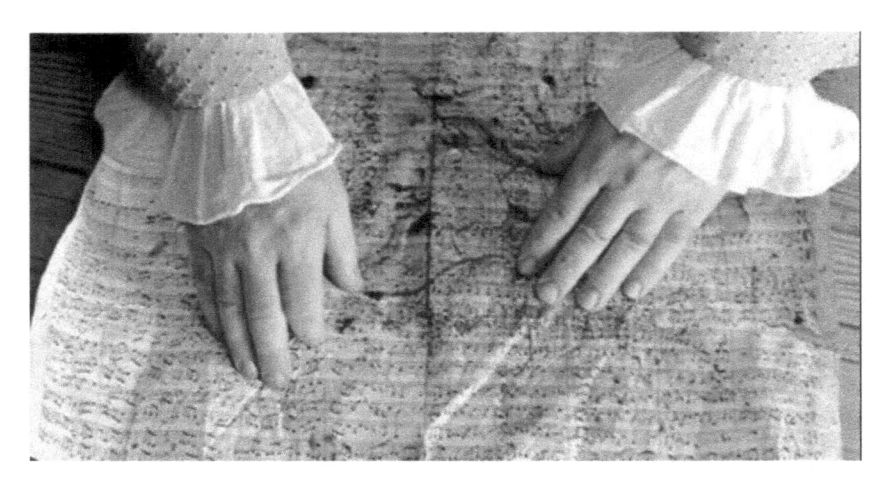

Figure 5.1 *Die Stille vor Bach* (2007).

been used to wrap up dead flesh (see figure 5.1)? In *Cinema 2*, Gilles Deleuze answers the question in this way: "Which is then the subtle way out? To believe, not in a different world, but in a link between man and the world, in love and life, to believe in this as in the impossible, the unthinkable, which nonetheless cannot be thought: "something possible, otherwise I will suffocate" (171).

This passage is echoed in *Die Stille* in a cafeteria conversation between two truck drivers, who are transporting musical instruments across the now open borders of the European Union. This ostensibly banal breakfast conversation is a reminder that the link between people can only be mediated with a relationship to the world, and that is exactly what happens when one of them creates an alternative space by playing the fourth Goldberg variation on a harmonica surrounded by the sound of other trucks passing by. This is cinema as the philosophy of everyday life at its very best. Music, which is man-made, provides a link to the world by interrupting the repetitive nature of work as labour, by establishing a passage through which to connect what has become disjointed. The scene is also a good example of the compositional complexity of the use of diegetic sound in the film.

The collaborative relation of sound and image, music and cinema, echoes the materiality of the creative process of the Santos/Portabella tandem. Composition and the redistribution of cultural capital is the key.[9] The encounter between music and cinema, between aesthetics and politics, produces a situation that is shared by all its participants/collaborators. In the words of Jacques Attali discussing the political economy of composition:[10]

> Composition – a labour on sounds, without a grammar, without a directing thought, a pretext for festival, in search of thoughts – is no longer a central network, an unavoidable monologue, becoming instead a real potential for relationship. (143)

This is what *Die Stille* is made of: the record of a relationship, the conjunction of two incomplete singularities in the making that manage to connect through a composition that interrupts the continuum of ideological narratives, namely, Bach's music. The link – music and cinema – needs to be constructed, because the real is made out of cuts. That is what the specificity of the cinematic brings to the table: cinema is made by cutting, as music is made through the syncopation of silence. The collective labour of composition, its socialization, demands an aesthetic practice of collaboration.

Film in Portabella is a practice, a collective practice. Portabella does not describe or depict situations in *Die Stille*, he creates them as events that are made possible and then recorded, locating himself between the

---

9 It is worth quoting Nancy again: "What distinguishes music, however, is that composition in itself, and the procedures of joining together never stop anticipating their own development and keep us waiting in some way for the result – or outcome – of their order, their calculation, their (musico)logic" (66).

10 Attali develops his argument on composition and new technologies with claims that echo Santos's experiments with recording technologies: "The new instrument thus emerging will find its real usage only in the production, by the consumer itself, of the final object, the movie made from virgin film. The consumer, completing the mutation that began with the tape recorder and photography, will thus become a producer and will derive at least as much of his satisfaction from the manufacturing process itself as the object it produces. He will institute the spectacle of himself as the supreme usage" (144). Attali wrote his text in 1977, and today's technologies give his words an anticipatory quality. In fact, the argument of Attali's entire text, which, as Fredric Jameson notes in his preface, is heavily influenced by Adorno, hinges on the premonitory and anticipatory nature of the acoustic. Attali's text in turn is clearly a reference for Nancy's *Listening*. Thus, the theoretical texts I reference in this essay are themselves an exercise in composition – albeit one that is not always acknowledged. For my part, I will return to the question of technology in the following section of this article.

before and after, which is the place of the blank screen and of silence in his film. We should not forget that Portabella belongs to a second avant-garde (late 60s and early 70s) that championed the "situation" over painting or the ready-made. To this, one should add John Cage's influence on conceptual art's "dematerizalization," as well as his movement towards sound understood broadly, beyond the musical and the representational.

IV. Acoustic Relation and Political Speculation

Carles Santos studied with Cage and was profoundly influenced by the experience. One of his most notorious performances as an artist and pianist echoes Cage's larger philosophical project, his emancipation of sound. In the 1973 film *Miró sculpteur* (Prévost and Santos), Santos undertook the action of completely destroying an upright piano inside an empty swimming pool. It was an attempt, he later explained, to learn to play the piano as if it were a new instrument. It was also a transformation of the piano into a conceptual object and the end-result of performance as the preferred artistic medium of the avant-garde he belonged to.

Santos's unmaking of the piano as a musical technology is relevant in the context of Europe's cultural identifications. The piano was not only the favourite mode of musical reproduction for the emergent capitalist bourgeoisie; it also represented the promises and failures of a class that once considered itself revolutionary. If we return now to the legend of Mendelsshon's discovery of Bach's *Saint Matthew's Passion*, it was clearly not enough that Mendelesshon "discovered" Bach; he had, above all, to play Bach on the instrument that defined the cultural habits of the bourgeoisie: the piano. The privatization of the instrument is part and parcel of the transmission of music, before the advent of recording techniques. Thus, the piano as technology plays a crucial role as a mode of production for the bourgeoisie in the development of capitalism.

The material assemblage of the piano itself, its technical complexity, which Aden Evens has called the "analytic instrument par excellence" (84), embodies the entire conceptual organization of the capitalist bourgeoisie. Evens describes the instrument as an assemblage: In its layout as interface, the piano keyboard asserts the well-tempered twelve-pitch system, the horizontal and vertical parametric orientation of the Western notational presentation, and "a logarithmic presentation of the whole orchestra" (85).

Together with the hegemony of the piano, the emergence of the orchestra and its spectacle is also connected to the rise of the bourgeoisie and its industrial economy. If harmony as a form of musical abstraction is related to number, the question of the score as an algorithm, and of the musician in an orchestra as a worker whose part has been mathematically allocated becomes extremely important and parallels the factory as capitalism's preferred site. Efficient labour and the mathematization of sound are intimately connected.

However, it would seem that thefantasy of a complete mathematization of sound is only possible in the abstraction of an economic equation. In this way, the representative mode is restricted to the visual and acoustic formulations of an economic reality. Ironically, as it stands, the European Union is fundamentally an exclusively economic form of government, where the market has taken over the state. Its efforts can be summed up as a "harmonization of the national economies whose levels of competitiveness are drifting drastically apart" (Habermas 3). Pythagoras's dream of absolute harmonization is finally encapsulated in the banking algorithms of a disintegrating Europe, rather than in music.

Nevertheless, the immateriality of the musical contains a compositional multiplicity of materialities, scales, and organizations that can serve as a model for a different conceptual organization. Both Santos and Portabella are as interested is questioning the commodification of Europe's musical legacy as they are in underscoring the compositional potential of the musical. Together, they propose a discontinuous transmission of Europe's cultural capital that highlights its differentials. A transmission where the figure of the "wolf" would no more be a disharmony to be avoided, but the place from which to build a different kind of harmony; one that is not predicated on the equality of the tones but on the extraordinary fact that geopolitical realities produce dissonant sounds and that we must train our ears to listen to them anew. Preservation and transmission appear here as two sides of the same coin. Europe's cultural legacy can only survive if it is continually tampered with and understood as a live performance that is as ephemeral as it is relevant.[11]

---

11 Is it hardly a coincidence that Portabella's latest film, his 2016 *Informe General II: El nuevo rapto de Europa*, signals Europe as a problem from the very beginning. The film is ostensibly a continuation of his 1976 *Informe General: Sobre algunas cuestiones de interés para una proyección pública*, his fictional documentary on the complex and

In the artistic and political practices of Santos and Portabella, acoustic dislocations function as indices to complex geopolitical realities that cannot be fully represented or fully signified. Thus, aesthetics and politics emerge as two incomplete orders of visibility that cross over each other like the hands of an interpreter of Bach at the keyboard; their complicity points towards the experience of a belief in the shared experience of collaboration. The situations presented by Santos and Portabella are made up of incomplete parts that connect through their incompleteness. There may be a place in these works for a harmony that cannot always be heard but can be practised: a collaboration and a transit between different spheres of knowledge and experience is at stake here. This collaboration is based in the incompleteness of music, art, and politics and calls for a transport between these different spheres, as well as a resituation of them. It relies on the anticipatory structure of the acoustic, whereby one sound always announces the next as well as in its composition of difference, whereby no sound is ever identical to another.

In the context of Europe's present crisis, where the pitfalls of its post-political and neo-liberal alliances have proven deaf to the refugee crisis, pandemics, or social contracts of any kind, the expression of wounded aspirations and unfulfilled political promises resonates anew and is unable to hide the current round of discontent. In Catalonia's fraught political present, in the midst of a failed renegotiation of its sovereignty, Europe is once again, and more than ever before, the name of a yet undefined promise. Europe has come to signify pure political expectation because the assumptions that held it together have been hollowed out. Similarly, Portabella and Santos interrupt the signifying impositions that Bach's legacy has been subjected to and empty them out of the representational myths that reconfigure form as content. Their artistic interventions rely not on the content of the artwork but on the longing for a content, as the expression of a political demand that takes the form of a void. In this way, possibilities emerge because the speculative space of the political is able to occupy that void.

Furthermore, the fact that the acoustic is not mimetic but relational, not concerned with representation or appearance but with the relations

---

changing political landscape during Spain's fraught transition to democracy after forty years of Francoism. His *Informe II* takes place in Spain and follows the country's political reactivation after the 15-M movement. However, the title of the film clearly indicates that the austerity policies and the social failures of contemporary Spain need to be understood within the frame of the European Union's neo-liberal loyalties.

established by the sonorous and its duration, underscores the potential of the medium in the construction of a communal political space – one that is based on difference as the prerequisite of any relation. In this way, the relational speaks to a movement of acoustic becoming still not bound by signification or identity, as the calling into being of absent community. Together, the immaterial and temporal nature of the acoustic also underscores the possibility of the new. The temporal spacing between a sound and its resonance, the movement of its vibration through space, always brings something other with it. For Nancy, "To sound is to vibrate in itself or by itself: it is not only, for the sonorous body, to emit a sound, but it is also to stretch out, to carry itself and be resolved into vibrations that both return it to itself and place it outside itself" (8).

Sound forever returns transformed, having folded the outside into the inside. The acoustic is, then, a site for encounters, for traces, and for differences. In Santos and Portabella's experimental practices, the acoustic functions as a model for a new organization of the aesthetic, one that it less stable than *mimesis* but more open to the political undertones of a musicalized labour, a performative *poiesis*.

In regard to cinema, Portabella's understanding of the image as a linking mechanism, as a creative and relational movement from and towards the non-cinematic, also underscores the durational aspect of film as a material labour of time. In this way, both the impurity and the temporality of the cinematic images echoes the dissonant musicality of the "wolf." Speaking about Jean-Luc Godard's treatment of sound, Badiou explains how the film-maker "transforms the sonic chaos into a murmur, like a sort of new silence made from the noises of the world" and continues to say that this silence allows us to hear "a secret the world were confiding" (Badiou 228). In the secret of Santos and Portabella's material impurity, their shared understanding of sound and image, it is still possible to hear Bach's wolf tones, this time untamed and in the form of a promise.

WORKS CITED

Adorno, Theodor W. *Introduction to the Sociology of Music*. Translated by E.B. Ashton, Continuum, 1976.
– *Prisms*. Translated by Samuel and Shierry Weber, MIT Press, 1967.
Attali, Jacques. *Noise: The Political Economy of Music*. Translated by Brian Massumi, University of Minnesota Press, 1985.
Badiou, Alain. "Cinema as Philosophical Experimentation." Philosophers on Film from Bergson to Badiou: A Critical Reader. Edited by Christopher Kul-Want, Columbia University Press, 2019.

Barthes, Roland. *The Responsibility of Form: Critical Essays on Music, Art, and Representation*. Translated by Richard Howard, University of California Press, 1985.

The Chronicles of Anna Magdalena Bach. Directed by Jean-Marie Straub and Danièle Huillet, performances by Gustav Leonhardt and Christiane Lang, Gian Vittorio, Jen-Luc Godard, and Jacques Rivette, producers, 1968.

Deleuze, Gilles. *Cinema 2: The Time-Image*. Translated by H. Tomlinson and B. Habberjam, University of Minnesota Press, 1989.

Delgado, Maria M. "Carles Santos: 'Music in the Theatre.'" *Taking It to the Bridge: Music as Performance*, edited by Nicholas Cook and Richard Pettenguill, University of Michigan Press, 2013, pp. 237–61. JSTOR, www.jstor.org/stable/10.3998/mpub.345788.17. Accessed 25 Oct. 2020.

Evens, Aden. *Sound Ideas: Music, Machines, Experience*. University of Minnesota Press, 2005.

Habermas, Jürgen. *The Crisis of the European Union: A Response*. Translated by Ciaran Cronin, MA Polity, 2012.

Marsh, Steven. "The Legacies of Pere Portabella: Between Heritage and Inheritance." *Hispanic Review*, vol. 78, no. 4, 2010, pp. 551–67. JSTOR, www.jstor.org/stable/25790602. Accessed 25 Oct. 2020.

Mercader, Antoni, Pilar Parcerissas, and Valentí Roma, eds. *Grup de Treball*, Exhibition catalogue, MACBA, 1999.

Miró sculpteur. Directed by Clovis Prévost and Carles Santos, Fundación Maeght, 1973.

Nancy, Jean-Luc. *Listening*. Translated by Charlotte Mandell, Fordham University Press, 2007.

Portabella, Pere. Director. http://www.pereportabella.com.

– *Die Stille vor Bach*. Performances by Alex Brendemühl, Feodor Atkine, Christian Brembeck, Daniel Ligorio et al., Films 59, 2007.

– *Informe general sobre algunas cuestiones de interés para una proyección pública*. Films 59, 1976.

– *Informe general II. El nuevo rapto de Europa*. Films 59, 2016.

– *Pont de Varsòvia*. Performances by Paco Guijar, Jordi Dauder, Carme Elias, Ona Planas, Josep M. Pou et al, Films 59, 1989.

Santos, Carles. ¡*Visca el piano!*, exhibition catalogue. ACTAR, 2006.

6 Pere Portabella's Radical Theatricality: A Political Gaze over Two Transitions

JAUME MARTÍ-OLIVELLA

Introduction: The Two *Informes* as a Whole: Towards an Aesthetic, Political, and Historical Contextualization

When posing the question of the possible continuities and legacies between the Escola de Barcelona and the current avant-garde cinematic output in Catalonia, one cannot help but refer to the towering figure of Pere Portabella. Indeed, Portabella, born in 1929, has given us a cinematic testimony that crosses both historical times and emerges as one of the most decisive illustrations of such a legacy. In this essay, I am going to focus on Portabella's two monumental documentary films: *Informe general sobre algunas cuestiones de interés para una proyección pública* (*General Report on Issues of Public Screening*, 1976) which became a true platform to articulate a political dialogue within the Left that was still impossible in the tense situation of early transition from Francoism to democracy in Spain, and *Informe general II: El nuevo rapto de Europa* (*General Report II: The New Abduction of Europe*, 2016), which chronicles what many actors have considered the second political transition fuelled by the upsurge of civic society and the rise of popular mobilizations that led to the Indignados (or 15-M) Movement and the Catalan independence process. Both films emblematize the transgressive spirit that was at the heart of the Barcelona School, while, at the same time, embodying Portabella's own estrangement from the School's most "fashionable" elements.[1] In order to do so, I would like to underline an essential aesthetic and ideological component that characterizes Pere Portabella's entire cinematic corpus. I am referring to its radical theatricality.

---

1 For a detailed study of the Barcelona School's formative years and its aesthetic components, see Riambau and Torreiro.

A radical theatrical performance that structures itself as a double and complementary understanding of a peculiar use of the traditional concept of the mise en scène with a post-Brechtian notion of performativity that encompasses both its artistic and its political value.

These two aspects of Portabella's performativity are clearly present in the two *Informes* just mentioned. Concerning the traditional notion of mise en scène, it might be helpful to recall here Louis Gianetti's definition:

> *Mise en scène* was originally a French theatrical term meaning "placing on stage." The phrase refers to the arrangement of all the visual elements of a theatrical production within a given playing area: the stage. [...] In movies, *mise en scène* is more complicated, a blend of the visual conventions of the live theatre with those of painting. [...] *Mise en scène* in the movies resembles the art of painting in that an image of formal patterns and shapes is presented on a flat surface and is enclosed within a frame. But cinematic *mise en scène* is also a fluid choreographing of visual elements that are constantly in flux. (Gianetti 48)

Gianetti's last statement leads us directly into one of the most paradigmatic sequences from *Informe General II*, the film by Pere Portabella which I consider one of the most important sequels ever produced in the context of both Catalan and Spanish cinemas. I am referring to the extended sequence inside the Reina Sofía museum in Madrid where Portabella's camera shows us frontally and almost conventionally Pablo Picasso's iconic 1937 *Guernica* painting. After that initial gaze, the camera focuses on the rails set up there to allow the movement of the director's Steadicam in what becomes a slow and detailed travelling shot that both visualizes and animates the formal details of Picasso's emblematic work. In this quasi-pedagogical shot, Portabella manages to invoke both the historical and the political context that was the background for his first *Informe general*, namely, the difficult transition from the Francoist system that was still in control of the most important and powerful institutions of the Spanish state, while, at the same time, he is introducing the aesthetic clues of his new *Informe*, which will be based on the mobility or, better put, on its capacity to portray the new-found life or "animation" of both the cultural archive and the very fabric of Catalonia's and Spain's body politic.[2] With his extended travelling shot

---

2 With the inclusion of the term "animation," I am referring to Portabella's and the Barcelona connection with the early animation cinema or "cinema of attractions," a

of Picasso's *Guernica*, Portabella invites us to see it as if for the first time while achieving a kind of animation of all the formal elements that constitute the painting as a fundamental historical and political symbol. With this camera movement, moreover, he is undermining the emblematic position of this painting (or any other painting or work of art) in an art museum understood as a closed cultural archive and not as an open centre of artistic creation and projection.[3] In doing so, Portabella manages both to defamiliarize the viewer's stance while appealing to his/her critical engagement in what constitutes another perfect example of his post-Brechtian performativity. In this way, Portabella continues to assert his unflinching political gaze, a political gaze that denounces the rigidity of most institutions of power, here represented by a Reina Sofía museum which Portabella uses as his theatrical background or his cinematic mise en scène for the first half of *Informe General II: El nuevo rapto de Europa*.

With the choice of the film's subtitle Portabella also indicates one of the activities that suggest a different use of the museum as an institution. In this case, with the obvious reference to the international 2014 winter symposium entitled "El nuevo rapto de Europa: Deuda, guerra y revoluciones democráticas" ("The New Abduction of Europe: Debt, War, and Democratic Revolutions") that was taking place at the Reina Sofía at the time. Portabella's film not only documents the conference as an act of collective awareness but also as an act of political mobilization in front of an economic regime that many people have perceived as the dismantling of Europe's welfare states. Ultimately, with his polysemic

---

critical connection that has been studied at length by Anna Cox in her "A New 'Cinema of Attractions'"? The Barcelona School's Exhibionist Loops," an essay included in the special issue on the Barcelona School published by *Hispanic Review* and edited by Professor Sara Nadal-Melsió, who also contributes to this volume.

3 The importance and impact of Portabella's "animation" of the Guernica symbols has reached other aspects of Spain's popular culture, as may be seen, for instance, in the "animation" and "appropriation" of the iconic Osborne bull advertising the Veterano brandy carried out by Sam3, the artist from Murcia who superimposed the *Guernica* to the cardboard bull near Santa Pola thus creating a double allegory, one against war and violence, as emblematized by Picasso's painting itself, and another one against the violent tradition of bullfighting, one of Spain's most controversial cultural manifestations (see Llanos and Rubio's). The very existence until today of ninety Osborne bulls by the Spanish roadsides is the result of a Supreme Court verdict to protect them as national cultural symbols after the Salvemos al toro (Let's Save the Bull) campaign carried out in 2007. For a discussion of this campaign in the context of Catalan filmmaker Bigas Luna's ironic deconstruction of the Osborne/Spanish bull stereotype in his 1992 film, *Jamón, jamón*, see Fouz Hernández. especially pp. 46–61.

performance from within the Reina Sofía museum, Pere Portabella reminds us once again that his cinematic political gaze always inscribes itself within and against the very centres of cultural and political power. Thus, if his 1976 *Informe* started from within the dark walls of the Valle de los Caídos, the most iconic monument of Franco's fascist regime, this second *Informe* takes off within the older walls of the Sabatini Palace, which so clearly symbolize the monarchical tradition that Francoism ended up restoring and that the museum's own name openly celebrates. On the other hand, by including the conference on "El nuevo rapto de Europa" and using this central slogan as the subtitle of his second *Informe*, Portabella is also clearly pointing towards one of the most substantial differences between the two films. Indeed, if in 1976 the director's political gaze focussed exclusively on the political transition to democracy in Spain, now, in 2016, while still concentrating on what many consider the second Spanish Transition, Portabella expands his political enquiry to encompass Europe as a whole.

This apparent divergence between the two *Informes* may nonetheless be read as a sign of inner continuity if one considers Portabella's two other feature films: *Pont de Varsòvia* (*Warsaw's Bridge*, 1989) and *Die Stille vor Bach* (*The Silence before Bach*, 2007), both of which already extended the director's gaze onto a European landscape. There is, moreover, an important parallelism that I want to underline between the "animation" of Picasso's *Guernica* that I have just described and the protracted and peculiar first sequence of *Die Stille vor Bach*. Just like he does in *Informe general II*, Portabella started *Die Stille* inside a museum. In this case, it was the Joan Miró Foundation in Barcelona where the viewer is invited to enter a completely empty room with impeccable white walls. Once inside this Oteiza-like empty space, Portabella surprises us with an odd mechanical piano that moves about the room as an animated robot, an automaton that is followed by the director's quasi-hypnotized camera while interpreting the first of Bach's *Goldberg Variations*. With this sequence, as Fèlix Fanés reminds us,[4] Portabella reinscribes his artistic avant-garde origins, the ones that connect his work to the painter Joan Miró's surrealism,[5] to the poet Joan Brossa's conceptual

---

4 See Fèlix Fanés' incisive reading of this sequence in his volume *Pere Portabella*, p. 86.
5 Portabella's connection with Joan Miró has been one of the director's staples throughout his work as may be seen in the two short films he dedicated to the Catalan painter: *Miró, l'altre* (*Miró, the Other*, 1969) and *Miró tapís* (*Tapestry Miró*, 1975). Today, Portabella's figure as a cinema director cannot be separated from his dedication to modern art and his political commitment. See, in this regard, Xavi Serra's chronicle of the recent retrospective exhibit dedicated to the director: *"Pere Portabella: Cinema, art i política."*

automatism, and to the ludic minimalism of Carles Santos, the great musician, composer, director, and performer, who owned both the idea and the physical object of that animated and robotic piano. Needless to say, this gesture of artistic rebellion and autonomy was one of the essential landmarks shared by the members of the Barcelona School. And yet, in Portabella's case, that rebellion started in his formal commitment to empty out the traditional narrative space in search of a new "image," as he himself declared:

> Sin tener una imagen previa al rodaje del film es inútil intentar rescatarla de la realidad. En la realidad existen siempre todas las posibilidades. Es necesaria vaciarla de su contenido habitual y darle un nuevo significado, esa es la única manera de evitar la descripción, que es uno de los peores problemas del cine español.

> (Without having an image previous to the shooting of the film, it is useless to try and rescue it from reality. In reality there are always all the possibilities. It is necessary to empty it from its habitual content and give it a new significance, that is the only way to escape from being descriptive, which is one of the worst problems of Spanish cinema.) (Riambau and Torreiro 244)

Thus, Portabella's peculiar rebellious gesture, as seen in the two examples mentioned above, revolves around a radical use of cinematic language. The director himself often uses this term when referring to his work, as may be seen in the following paragraph from his interview with José Enrique Monterde:

> En 1976 decido hacer *Informe general I* sobre una realidad en la que estaba totalmente implicado, no se trataba de hacer un documental, sino de utilizar la *radicalidad de mi lenguaje* para que tanto el actor como el espacio, sea éste vacío o un decorado, todo forme parte del conjunto, incluso la materialidad de la imagen.

> (In 1976 I decide to make *Informe general I* about a reality in which I was totally immersed. I did not want to make a traditional documentary. What I wanted was to use the *radicality of my language* so that both the actor and the space, be it an empty one or a prop, become part of a whole that incorporates also the materiality of the image.) (44; emphasis mine)

Indeed, Portabella uses this radicality as a kind of previous condition, as a forewarning to tell us that we are facing a cinematic discourse on the aesthetic, political, and historical reality that never gives up its own performative discursivity and that never strays too far from the Brechtian *Verfremdung* effect, as the reader is reminded in the *Pressbook* of his *Informe general II*: "[All of this] turns Portabella's films into "strange" artefacts, in the sense in which Bertolt Brecht's classical theatre produced "estrangement" effects on the spectator, who has to undergo the task of reconstructing the sense of the articulation of elements that form the film" (González np).

The aforementioned film's subtitle – "El Nuevo rapto de Europa" ("The New Abduction of Europe") – invites us to open another line of enquiry so that we can understand the global sense of Portabella's film. Doubtlessly, with this reference the director incorporates once again the world of classical culture, that is to say, the traditional canonical archive of the West, with a historical and political interpretation that is clearly contemporary and markedly critical in nature. Thus, if we pay attention to the double sense of the word "abduction," as it is described in classical mythology and specifically in the myth of Zeus and his abduction of the Phoenician goddess Europa, that which would be the base of the continent's name, we find that it means both "seduction" or "possession or rape." In fact, I believe Portabella's subtitle does not only reference the legacy of classical mythology but alludes to a book and a documentary film that explicitly analyse the artistic exploitation carried out by Nazi Germany during the Second World War. Both texts, the narrative and the cinematic one, chose the most critical definition of the term "abduction" since both are called "The Rape of Europe."[6] Ultimately, I believe that it is this most critical interpretation of the term "abduction" – that best describes the final goal of Portabella's film, which becomes an unsparing condemnation of the tearing apart of the social, economic, and political tapestry of an old European continent pushed to the limits by the ongoing attack from the neo-liberal forces of capitalist globalization that have become the hegemonic discourse in a rather weakened European Union. This strong political meaning was clearly recognized when *Informe general II: El nuevo rapto de Europa*

---

6 I am referring to *The Rape of Europe*, the book that earned Lynn H. Nicholas France's most prestigious award, the Legion of Honour, in 1994, and the documentary film with the same title based on Nicholas's text that was directed by Richard Berge, Bonni Cohen, and Nicole Newnham and released in the United States in 2007. In both cases, the choice of "rape" over "abduction" emphasizes their authors' strong criticism of such a sustained exploitation. Doubtlessly, both the verbal choice and the harsh critical message get reinscribed in Portabella's film.

premiered internationally at the Rotterdam International Festival in 2016, where the film was summarized in the following terms: "A cinematographic symposium on the current political crisis of parliamentary democracy and the nation-state, how neoliberalist capitalism thrives on this, and what is to be done. Arguably, the most important work of political cinema in a long time" (Rotterdam International Film Festival, Online Publicity) .

Besides confirming its fundamental political purpose, the presence of Portabella's film in the Rotterdam Festival also helped to underline another crucial element that was implicit in its genesis, namely, the director's will to establish a clear continuity with his initial political gaze over Catalonia and Spain, which became his 1976 *Informe general*. Portabella himself describes it both as a fact and as a surprise in his usual dialectical style:

> La sorpresa me llega cuando, tantos años después, al invitarme al Festival de Rotterdam con mi nueva película, me dicen que es fundamental proyectar también el primer *Informe* pues constituyen un *conjunto*. En cierto modo, aquel film, que podia ser considerado coyuntural en su momento, adquiere ahora otro valor.
>
> (The surprise arrives when, after so many years, upon the invitation to show my new film at the Rotterdam Festival, the organizers tell me that it is essential to also show my first *Informe* since they form a *cinematic whole*. In a way, a film that might have been considered tied to a specific historical moment, acquires now a different value.) (Monterde 44; emphasis mine)

From a historical perspective, when considered together, both films do indeed constitute a "cinematic whole," one that contains a similar reflection on the exercise of democracy in two very significant and in part almost parallel historical moments: Spain's first political transition after Franco's long dictatorship with the emergence of the new democratic state in 1976, and the current moment, seen by many as a potential second political transition brought about by another emergence, in this case, that of a new civil society that has rebelled against the compromised existence and the structural rigidity of that formally democratic Spanish state. If we think about it from a historical perspective, Portabella's "cinematic whole" may be framed by the symbolic import created by the very beginning of the 1976 *Informe* and the ending of its 2016 sequel. Let us revisit for a moment those two extended sequences. The first one becomes an iconic instance of cinematic spectrality where the viewer is required to accompany Portabella in his critical visit to

Franco's tomb inside the Valle de los Caídos chapel.[7] Thus, after a series of aerial shots that circle around the huge stone cross that presides over the fascist monument, Portabella's camera pans its way into the dark walls of the chapel until finally zooming in to place its silent gaze on Franco's funerary urn.[8] At the end of *Informe General II*, Portabella's camera will also enter into a closed space; this time, however, it will be a workshop where voting urns or ballot boxes are being made.[9] From the monument to death, from Franco's funerary urn, we move to the place where the most crucial object in a democracy is created. Thus, Portabella ends his last film by stressing the materiality of the physical object, the urn (ballot box), which clearly symbolizes the historical need for a real and direct democracy that may resist the upheavals of the system's inner corruption and the attacks of an antidemocratic and globalizing neo-liberalism.[10]

---

7 In this sense, Portabella remains faithful to the spectral aesthetics shown in his two previous short films *Vampir-Cuadecuc* (1970) and *Umbracle* (1972). The importance of spectrality in the context of Catalan and Spanish film has been studied by Steven Marsh, who also contributes to this volume. See his "Editor's Introduction" and his recent volume *Spanish Cinema against Itself*, which he describes as "A spectral historiography, a subterranean history, and a history of interruptions written in the spirit of Walter Benjamin" (3).

8 Portabella's spectral criticism of the Valle de los Caídos is doubly resonant today given the significance of that monument as the largest mass grave in Europe. In recent years, moreover, Catalan documentary cinema has followed on the steps of Portabella's trailblazing films in its portrayal of the fight for the recovery of the country's historical memory. See, in this sense, my essay entitled "Historical Memory and Family Metaphor in Catalonia's New Documentary School." Also, concerning the struggle of many families to achieve the dignified return of the remains of their relatives who sided with the Republic during Spain's Civil War, see Montserrat Armengou's and Ricard Belis's *Les fosses del silenci* (*The Spanish Holocaust*, 2003), or their *Avi, et treuré d'aquí* (*I'll Get You out of Here, Grandad!*, 2013), which specifically deals with those Republican soldiers anonymously buried at the Valle de los Caídos, after, in many cases, having been exhumed and transported there from their original resting places. Such a struggle did not yield any results until 2018, as Sílvia Marimon's chronicle in *ARA* attests. The exhumation of Franco's remains from the Valle de los Caídos, carried out on 24 October 2019 after a series of legal obstacles, only reinforces the symbolic significance of this monument in Spain's collective imaginary.

9 I am implying the double meaning of the Catalan and/or Spanish word *urna*, which means either a funerary urn or the ballot box employed in most democratic elections.

10 Portabella's symbolic forewarning resonates with special force if one thinks of the fall of Mariano Rajoy's Popular Party government due to the sentences of the Gurtel corruption case and after the vote of no confidence presented by Pedro Sánchez (PSOE's president) in the Spanish Parliament. The significance of the materiality of

From an aesthetic perspective, the commonality of the cinematic whole formed by Portabella's two *Informes* may be seen in their aforementioned radical theatricality. In this case, in a parallel gesture to that passage from the tomb/urn to the voting/urn, the second *Informe* will renounce the spectral dramatization of the 1976 film in order to engage in a direct political performance. Indeed, in his early film, Portabella included a series of dramatized sequences interpreted by Francesc Luchetti, the Catalan actor who played several characters and who became an essential tool in the director's ability to introduce an uncanny sense of fictional (un)familiarity that disrupted the narrative structure of a traditional documentary film. Among these multiple acting embodiments, the viewer is invited to keep (re)encountering Luchetti, first as a young political activist who is arrested and tortured by the police in the film's most direct denunciation of the basic human rights violation. Then, as the impersonator of the cultural guide who silently interpellates the viewer during his spectral visit through the big halls of Franco's official residence, now a completely empty Palacio del Pardo. Finally, Luchetti will also become the solemn and sullen visitor whom we accompany in his dramatic promenade through the remaining ruins of several towns destroyed in the battles of the Teruel front during the Spanish Civil War. Instead of these phantasmatic dramatizations, in his 2016 film, Portabella will alternate between theoretical, political, and scientific testimonies using a series of "appropriate/appropriated" sequences, both in the sense of being pertinent and, in some cases, of being filmed by others. Many of these sequences will portray ludic popular demonstrations where the public space becomes an open stage for the "performances" of the new political subject that the film chronicles. As seen in this passage from the film's pressbook, the director was very conscious of his aesthetic and political gesture: "In terms of expression, the artistic work with languages and forms has its correlate in the way the film shows how the walks, demonstrations, and sit-ins constitute big performances whose expressive forms are the ways in which a political activity is being transmitted" (*Informe general II* pressbook).

It is precisely the aesthetic and expressive significance of this new political performativity that will be analysed in the second part of this essay.

---

the urn (voting box) has also received a new historical dimension after the long and failed police chase to find the actual urns or voting boxes in order to prevent the "illegal" Referendum for Independence carried out in Catalonia on 1 October 2017. As it turned out, most of them were hidden in thousands of people's homes and were made of plastic foldable components.

2. *Informe general II: El nuevo rapto de Europa*: Chronicle of a Dissension and/or the Birth of a New Political Subject

To fully understand the ideological scope of Pere Portabella's last film, it seems appropriate to follow Angel Quintana's suggestion in order to recall Jacques Rancière's political and philosophical work. In Quintana's own words:

> Tal como vaticinó Jacques Rancière en un texto mítico de principios de los años noventa, el paso clave consiste en cómo la crisis de la política entendida como deseo de conquista del poder, puede ser reemplazada por la emergencia de lo política visto como deseo de implicación en la construcción de comunidades. *Informe general II* documenta esta transición.
>
> (As Jacques Rancière anticipated in a mythical text from the early nineties, the crucial step consists in how the crisis of politics, understood as the desire to conquer power, may be replaced by the emergence of politics conceived as the desire to get involved in the construction of communities. It is this transition, precisely, that *Informe general II* documents.) (Quintana 45)

Indeed, at the very heart of Rancière's thought one finds the dichotomy of politics understood as the will to power or as the desire to articulate a community. And, at the very middle of these dialectics, there appears the concept of dissension or the idea of a "dissensus" opposed to the normative "consensus" as the basis of the traditional parliamentary system. In this sense, when the dissident subject ceases to be marginal or invisible and occupies the public space, such as has clearly been the case in Catalonia and in Spain in the last few years, one is faced with the emergence of a new political subject. That is precisely David W. Hill's understanding when he summarizes Rancière's volume *Dissensus: On Politics and Aesthetics*. Hill writes:

> For Rancière, politics is not the exercise of power but, rather, the rationally motivated action of a subject. Democracy is not one form of this amongst others: democracy *is* politics. Crucially, democracy is made up of not only the members of a given community but by those that it excludes also, making democracy "the count of the uncounted." [...] As such, the role of politics is to create a space in which the two worlds – of the included and of the excluded – become one. Or, put otherwise: "*The essence of politics is dissensus*" (38). This notion of dissensus should not be understood as mere conflict of interest, of opinions, or of values. Rather, it is "a dispute

over what is given and about the frame within which we sense something is given" (69). Consensus, on the other hand, shrinks the political space, reducing politics to the police. (Hill np; emphasis mine)

Therefore, if in his 1976 *Informe general* Portabella was reproducing, while contributing to its creation, the political space that allowed the emergence of a democratic consensus to overcome the Francoist dictatorship, now, in his 2016 *Informe general II*, the Catalan film-maker gives us another chronicle that again reproduces and recreates the new political space where Rancière's dissensus is being articulated, where the dissidence of those excluded takes centre stage against the passivity and, according to many, the complicity shown by our conventional politicians in the face of' a new "abduction of Europe" that is threatening to undo most of the social and political gains so painfully achieved by the citizens of the old continent.

Indeed, Portabella is very conscious that our historical time is defined by the emergence of a new political subject created by dissident popular movements which have already positioned themselves in the public space. The director himself was pointing that out in the emphasis placed on two groups that had been normally excluded from the political discourse and that now would be the basis of his film's structure and mise en scène. In Portabella's own words:

> Lo que justifica la estructura del film es que el Arte y la Ciencia se dejan aparte, como un mero añadido superficial. Por eso lo hago al revés: la película se abre con la puesta en cuestión de un modelo institucional, aquí el Reina Sofía, ese objeto urbano situado en el centro de Madrid, pero eso tenía que estar íntimamente relacionado con lo que pasaba en la calle, porque los movimientos sociales en aquel momento habían cogido una dimensión brutal. Estábamos en 2014 y desde 2011, desde el 15M, habían crecido; además, un mes antes del 15M se había constituido la Asamblea Nacional Catalana. Son dos movimientos que se convierten en sujeto político. […] Ya no son los partidos los que toman la iniciativa política, sino que es la presión de los ciudadanos la que arrastra, como en una especie de *performance*, de una forma muy distinta a las tradicionales confrontaciones corporativas.

> (What justifies the film's structure is that Art and Science have always been left aside, as something superficially added. That is why I turn it upside down: the film starts with the questioning of an institutional model, here the Reina Sofía museum, that urban object located in the centre of Madrid, but that fact had to be intimately connected with what was going on in

the streets because the social movements at the moment had achieved an enormous dimension. We were in 2014, and since 2011 and the 15-Movements , those movements had significantly grown. In fact, just one month before the 15-M we saw the formation of the Catalan National Assembly. These are two movements that become a political subject. […] It is no longer the parties that have the political initiative but the pressure from the citizenship that is taking over and is creating a new kind of *performance*, one that is very different from the traditional corporative confrontations.) (Monterde 44)[11]

In fact, as I have already mentioned, the entire film has to be understood from the perspective of its political performativity, both in the strict sense of documenting the political performances carried out by the aforementioned popular movements and, also, in its capacity to become a performative action inasmuch as its diegesis (re)produces the same dissident gesture that the film is actually chronicling. Or, to put it differently, just like many of the theoreticians and activists interviewed in the film declare the need to "take over the institutions,"
Portabella will articulate his critical gaze from within a specific institution, in this case the Museo Nacional Centro de Arte Reina Sofía in Madrid, not only to reflect on its function but to use it as an ideal mise en scène to stage his questioning of the entire system that this very institution emblematizes. Jordi Amat, in his study of Portabella's film, reaches a similar conclusion:

Molts anys després, Portabella, al·lèrgic a la nostàlgia, hi ha tornat. Primer de tot valdria la pena preguntar-se per què, camí dels noranta, reincideix. I la resposta encaixa amb el propòsit que va motivar la primera entrega: la convicció que som després de tot en un moment urgent i esperançat de canvi polític (ara a Catalunya i a Espanya però també a Europa) i l'afany de reforçar l'onada progressista que pretén transformar un sistema en fase de caducitat. Aquesta aposta sintonitza, i

---

11 The 15-M Movement was the final convergence of what came to be known as the "indignados" popular movement that would lead into the creation of Podemos (We Can), the recently renamed Unidas Podemas party that is currently governing Spain in coalition with the PSOE (Partido Socialista Obrero Español). The same movement resulted in the election of progressive mayors in several large cities throughout Spain, including those of Madrid and Barcelona. The ANC (Catalan National Assembly) has been one of the strongest expressions of the new civil society to emerge in recent years in Catalonia. It has had a central role in organizing the large pro-independence demonstrations that Portabella's film also documents.

així arrenca la pel.lícula, amb la reflexió sobre l'emergència d'un nou subjecte civil conscient de com els poders han allunyat la ciutadania de l'acció política i que vol reinserir-s'hi a través d'una democràcia directa que li hauria de permetre pilotar la transformació des del cor de les institucions. Es la qüestió que l'hivern del 2014 es va plantejar a l'encontre "El nou rapte d'Europa: deute, guerra i revolucions democràtiques" celebrat precisament al Reina Sofía i que ocupa els primers minuts del film. Aquell cicle, igual que la pel·lícula i l'aposta ideològica de fons que planteja, reflexiona sobre com es pot articular una crítica del sistema des de dins del sistema.

(After many years, Portabella, who seems to be allergic to any kind of nostalgia, has done it again. First of all, it might be worth asking why, so close to his ninetieth birthday, he has tried again. And the answer fits the purpose that motivated the first film; the conviction that we are, after all, in an urgent and hopeful moment of political change (now in Catalonia and Spain, but also in Europe), and the desire to support the progressive wave that is trying to transform a system about to expire. This goal harmonizes with, and that explains the beginning of the film, the reflection on the emergence of a new civil subject fully conscious of the ways in which the powers that be have removed the citizens from any political action. This new subject is now willing to reinsert itself in politics through a direct democracy that makes possible its leading role in this transformation from the very heart of the institutions. This was precisely the topic of the 2014 winter symposium "El nuevo rapto de Europa: deuda, guerra y revoluciones democráticas" ("The New Abduction of Europe: Debt, War, and Democratic Revolutions") held at the time at the Reina Sofía. The first part of the film will focus on this symposium, which shares Portabella's ultimate ideological goal and central reflection on the possible ways to articulate a criticism of the system within the system itself.) (Amat 24)

This is, indeed, what Portabella achieves in his 2016 *Informe general II: El nuevo rapto de Europa*: to focus his unflinching political gaze on the question(ing) of a democratic system that appears to have lost its connection with the citizenship that it purports to represent. This profound gap between the street and the institutions, both cultural and political, is what Portabella visualizes and thematizes throughout his film. And he does it, as Jordi Amat suggests, by repeating some of the strategies and, in some cases, some specific images from his 1976 *Informe general* in a clear statement of the inner continuities of his cinema and also of that rebellious and avant-garde spirit that characterized the Barcelona School, whose "invisible tradition" Portabella epitomizes.[12]

The Two *Informes*: A Reflection on Portabella's Contrastive Continuities

In what remains of this essay, I would like to explore further some of the continuities between the two *Informes* since they constitute a clear illustration of the cinematic whole already mentioned while also inscribing the profound difference between the political subjects of the two films. The first strategy shared by the two *Informes* is condensed by Jordi Amat in the word "diàlegs" (dialogues). Indeed, just like he did in his first *Informe*, Portabella will structure his film dialectically by staging and reproducing a series of theoretical and critical dialogues that constitute the basic discursive centre of the film.[13] This time, however, the protagonism of those dialogues will not be male but female. Instead of the omnipresence of masculine voices throughout the first *Informe*, we are now invited, almost from the very beginning, to witness the critical exchanges between different intellectual women activists, whose thoughts are foregrounded as one of the leading engines behind the configuration of the new political subject that Portabella's second *Informe* documents. In this way, as Amat recalls, instead of the endless coffees and the tobacco smoke filling the rooms, flats, and offices where we saw the dialogues of many key politicians of the first transition to democracy, such as Felipe González, Enrique Tierno Galván, Marcelino

---

12 As mentioned in the introduction to this volume, the concept of an invisible tradition was first adopted in the special issue on the Barcelona School published by the *Hispanic Review* and developed by Sara Nadal-Melsió, another of the contributors to our volume, whose editorial preface to that monographic issue on the Barcelona School was entitled "The Invisible Tradition: Avant-Garde Catalan Cinema under Late Francoism."
13 Another example of Portabella's inner consistency may be seen in the fact that he already employed it in his film *El sopar* (*The Dinner*, 1974), which was a clear precursor to his 1976 *Informe General* by staging the gathering of five former political prisoners who candidly discuss their experiences inside Franco's jails. Portabella's film acquires a special dramatic condition given the fact that, on that same day, Salvador Puig Antich, the notorious young Catalan political activist sentenced to death by a Francoist court, was executed despite the number of national and international pardon pleas sent to Franco himself. The historical significance of *El sopar* in the current political climate in Catalonia is well documented in the piece written by Xavi Antich on the occasion of the return of Portabella's film to a brief commercial run in Ventura Pons's own Texas cinema in Barcelona during February 2018 (see Antich).

Camacho, Santiago Carrillo, and Jordi Pujol, here we are presented with a series of public spaces where the female voice is directly articulated, and, quite frequently, in front of a glass of water or a cup of tea. Instances include the meaningful conversation between the architect and dissident political activist Itziar González and the philosopher Marina Garcés, which I will analyse in a moment, and the intervention from Ada Colau, the newly elected Barcelona mayor at the time, who speaks from the podium in one of the central presentations during the symposium entitled "The New Abduction of Europe," which is being held inside the Reina Sofía, and, as we have already mentioned, gives Portabella's film its subtitle while becoming its most direct political correlate. In both cases, following his usual style, the mise en scène will directly contribute to underline the facts that the social actors are verbalizing. A perfect illustration of this new articulation is the first conversation between Marina Garcés and Itzíar González, which Portabella stages within a small cafeteria just across the square presided over by the Sabatini palace where the Reina Sofía museum is located. In so doing, Portabella immediately visualizes (and thematizes) the inside/outside dialectics while emphasizing the importance of that square as part of a public space or "àmbit comú" (common ground) that already separates it from the institutional space represented by the large museum.[14] This visual frame certainly strengthens the critical vision of the two female thinkers who are, at the same time, participants in different workshops within the Reina Sofía symposium. That is why their dialogue becomes especially relevant when they question the validity of the museum as both the physical and the symbolic location of that very symposium. Here are some of their own words on the topic:

> Itzíar González: "Clar, et desmonten la veu, és a dir, ets una persona que vas a fer una cosa, entres dins d'aquella institució i et desconnecten, perds la connexió amb el flux de la vida i la seva transformació. Arribes a un lloc on tot es fa estàtic. Es llavors quan t'adones que tota la política, la capacitat de conciliar creativament. [...] Doncs, entres dintre i quedes

---

14 Benjamin Fraser, commenting on Manuel Delgado's work on the topic, writes: "Public space is seen as movement itself – rightly as a *process* instead of a stable location that has somehow disappeared" (Fraser 70; emphasis in original). Fraser and Delgado's notion of the public space as movement/process will be central in understanding the visual and symbolic tension created by Portabella between the open square and the museum in his film (see Delgado, *El animal público* and *Memoria y lugar*; see also Benjamin Fraser, "Manuel Delgado's Urban Anthropology").

160   Jaume Martí-Olivella

desconnectada, d'entrada, la institució et separa del 'fora.' Això és clar. Llavors, jo em pregunto, ¿no seran aquests fòrums un sistema de situació extractiva de la nostra creativitat? Pregunto, vull dir, ¿no hauríem d'estar fent el fòrum aquí a la plaça?"

("It's clear. They disrupt your voice. That is, you're somebody that is going to do something, you enter inside that institution and they disconnect you. You lose the connection with the flux of life and its transformation. You reach a place where everything becomes static. It is at that moment that you realize that all politics, all the capacity to creatively reconcile, [...] Well, you get inside and you're disconnected right away. The institution separates you from the 'outside.' That is quite clear. Then, I ask myself, are these forums not a situation that systematically extract from our creativity? I ask myself, well, shouldn't we be having the forum here on the square?")

Marina Garcés: "La plaça és el lloc, clar. La dialèctica dintre/fora, absolutament binària tampoc no serveix. Es a dir, també es pot caure en l'autosatisfacció dels moviments de pensar que només des la intempèrie es pot regenerar la vida social i llavors ..."

("The square is the place, clearly. But an absolute binary dialectics between inside/outside is not useful. That is, one can also incur in the self-satisfying notion of some movements when they think that social life can only be regenerated from without and then ...") (*Informe general II. Script*)[15]

Thus, the attempt to overcome the traditional binary structures, suggested here by Marina Garcés, will be considered in the context of bourgeois Western society's most recurrent polarity, namely, the public/private divide whose limits have become extremely porous given the incredible number and scope of the surveillance systems we face today, which not even Foucault's brilliant prescription could have foreseen.[16] And yet, in between the public and the private, as argued by González and Garcés, there appears the "àmbit comú," or the common space, here symbolized by the square that is revindicated anew both in terms of its contemporary value as a ludic meeting point, and also in its classical value as the agora, or space for the political forum. That is why

---

15 All the following quotes come from the film's script.
16 I am referring to Foucault's well-known volume *Surveiller et punir: Naissamce de la prison*, where he follows the history of Western prisons and the growing importance of surveillance as an essential state apparatus.

Marina Garcés criticizes the new and false disjunctive created in the workshop she is participating in as part of the symposium on "El nuevo rapto de Europa." Again, in her own words:

> El primer punt que ens vàrem plantejar com a eix de reflexió va ser "del públic al comú." Això es va plantejar en termes lineals i quasi com una disjuntiva, com si un model s'hagués acabat, que és el de la institució pública, el del servei públic, el de la relació entre l'Estat i la societat, ... I el comú com si fos allò que ve ara i que dibuixa tota una nova coherència. De fet, el que està passant és que des les pràctiques d'allò comú estem donant un altre sentit a allò públic i hi ha una possibilitat de reapropiar-nos i de donar un nou significat a allò que el domini públic hauria pogut ser ... El que no té cap sentit és pensar que ens tirarem al mar i que allà, en la pura intempèrie, seguirem cuidant-nos, educant-nos i articulant-nos. *El que hem de fer és assaltar les institucions, assaltar-les perquè són nostres.*
>
> (The first question we asked ourselves to articulate the whole of our reflection was the passage "from the public to the common." This issue was brought up in literal terms and almost like a disjunctive, as if a model had finished, that of the public institution, of the public service, of the relationship between the State and society, [...] and the common as something that is happening now and that contains a new kind of coherence. In fact, what is happening is that from the current practices of the common we're giving a new sense to the public and there is a possibility for us to take over and give a new meaning to what the public sphere could have been. [...] What makes no sense is to think that we'll jump into the sea and out there, in the naked outdoors, we'll continue taking care of ourselves, getting an education or getting articulated. *What we need to do is to take over the institutions. To take them over because they belong to us.*) (*Informe general II*, Script; emphasis mine)

After this brief "manifesto," both thinkers will continue their critique of the invisibility of the symposium workshops where they take part while Portabella's camera takes us into the now nearly dark and empty rooms of the conference. The director's visual underlining of the words uttered by Marina Garcés and Itzíar González will be expanded at the end of the sequence when his camera seems to be literally responding to the interpellation we have just witnessed. Thus, at the end of their conversation, Itziar González exclaims: "Clar, assisteixo aquí a aquest fòrum i observo que tots els activistes s'estan reunint i que no els podem veure!!" ("Of course, I'm attending this forum here while noticing that all the activists are getting together and we can't see them"; *Informe general II*). To this, in an almost banal tone, Marina Garcés adds: "Apa, anem, és una mica tardi I ara plou. ¿no?"

("Come on, let's go. It's a bit late and now it's raining"; *Informe general II*). To which, and with her usual irony, Itzíar González responds: "Tenim la fràgil institució d'un paraigües!" ("We have the fragile institution of an umbrella!"; *Informe general II*). Despite the humour and the apparent triviality of her remarks, Itzíar González manages to succinctly convey the central idea of the fragility and permeability needed by the institutions if they want to truly serve a common sphere that is now being forcefully vindicated by a dissident citizenship turned into a new political subject. It is precisely at this moment that Portabella's camera intervenes again directly with a new visual underlining. This time, the viewers will see the two women leaving the small cafeteria after they have gotten up from the table by the window where they were sitting. The director's camera, like us, will linger on this shot of the now empty table by a window that literally frames the Reina Sofía museum, symmetrically located at the other side of the square. Almost in real time, Portabella is holding his camera and our gaze on the empty teacups until we see the hands of the waiter who removes them and cleans the table carefully. This quasi-hypnotic travelling shot ends in a brief dissolve that returns our gaze to the view from the window. This time, however, the square appears packed with demonstrators who have gathered there precisely to protest against that very "abduction of Europe" that the Reina Sofía symposium wants to denounce. Thus, with this brief and effective ellipsis, Portabella reinforces the idea that Marina Garcés and Itzíar González have just articulated: that the "forum" has to take place at the same time in the square and inside the institutions. It is no surprise, therefore, that when the camera finally leaves the cafeteria and gazes onto the square and the demonstrators, we are faced with a placard bearing the slogan "Por una Europa social," which is a clear reminder of the need to achieve the kind of direct democracy that is now playing out in front of our eyes despite the massive police presence. Here, moreover, we can also hear some of the demonstrators' speeches, among which, I would emphasize the following words that yet again seem to summarize the theoretical debate we have just witnessed inside the small cafeteria: "Que lo importante es que los dignos y las dignas nos hemos hecho visibles!" ("What is important is that we, as the dignified ones, have

---

17 The use of the word "digno/a" relates obviously to the fact that this popular movement came to be known as that of the "indignados." The wordplay here stresses the fact that the only dignified position is to be rendered indignant by the corrupt political status quo.

become visible!"; *Informe general II*).[17] Indeed, the ultimate goal of Portabella's extended sequence is to document the visibility of these "indignados" and of all the other popular movements that form the new dissident political subject in Catalonia and in Spain today. In showing us the large staircase leading up to the Reina Sofía entrance completely taken by the police, moreover, the director gives us an irrefutable visual metaphor of the dramatic distance that still exists between the square and the institutions. And, as if in passing, he establishes a direct connection with the political situation described in his 1976 *Informe general* when the decaying institutions of late Francoism could only be protected by means of a constant policing of the streets. In fact, this street surveillance and its denunciation takes centre stage in Portabella's 1976 *Informe general* from the very beginning of the film. Let us recall here, in some detail, the centrality of the director's critical gaze on the subject and his technical ability to create meaning in the editing room. Thus, the juxtaposition of images from the cafeteria to the dark rooms of the museum and the demonstration at the Reina Sofía square, which I have just described, may be read as an expansion of a technique which was already essential in the 1976 film. Indeed, the initial sequences of the first *Informe general* already give us a perfect illustration of Portabella's use of a counterpoint that forces meaning by juxtaposition. Here, as is usually the case, the juxtaposition is linked via an extended visual metaphor that acquires a life of its own. In this case, it will be the age-old metaphor of the tunnel as time travelling that will represent the dangerous passage from a political clandestine situation into the still uncertain light of a nascent democracy. Previously, in the credit sequence of the film, we will have crossed another tunnel, the one leading to the streets of Barcelona that we reach after the first fade in, which follows the already mentioned initial visit to Franco's tomb at the Valle de los Caídos. Thus, the passage from the historical darkness of Francoism and its imposed silence over the lives of its citizens is also marked by the movement across the tunnel that leads us to the streets of a Barcelona that we soon learn is about to break that silence. The title of the film will appear, precisely, at the end of that first tunnel crossing. Portabella will truly take us for the ride this time. Indeed, after having crossed the first tunnel, the credit sequence continues with travelling shots that include some of the city's most recognizable landmarks, such as Gaudí's Casa Batlló at the Passeig de Grâcia or Puig i Cadafalch's Casa Terrades, the popularly called Casa de les Punxes at Avinguda Diagonal. This reference to the Catalan cultural patrimony will soon be juxtaposed with an entrance into yet another tunnel, which takes us into an apparent underground parking lot at the end of which we see a huge helicopter rising into the open skies above the city. We are right at the end of the credit sequence. Then, just when Portabella's own name as director appears on screen, we join the helicopter ride and his bird's-eye shots of the square-like structures of the streets of the Barcelona Eixample. Soon these aerial shots get juxtaposed with other down-to-earth travelling shots of the Barcelona centre. Then, the camera literally reaches the ground while Carles Santos's minimalist musical score suddenly changes to include audible interferences of police radios saying "hace falta personal" ("Help needed"). At this moment, we see the sign "Barcelona 1976" superimposed on the screen. Santos's music starts a restless crescendo until we see the first human figures of the demonstrators and their placards where the word "Amnistia" ("Amnesty") takes clear precedence. The clash between the police radio messages and Santos's own high-pitch, almost strident score becomes hard to bear and anticipates the real clash as we are about to enter into the midst of the political demonstration itself, where we can now read another placard stating "Todos por la Amnistía y la Libertad" ("All for Amnesty and Freedom"). Next, we see how the policemen are closing streets and preparing to charge against the demonstrators. Just then, the camera takes a dramatic low-angle shot to show us again the same helicopter, which we now know is not a marker of the flight of freedom at the end of the tunnel, as Portabella had made us believe, but the carrier of the police eye that is surveilling the demonstrators' movements from above in yet another modern expression of the Foucaldian *panoptikon*. Portabella's use of this counterpoint even in the middle of what appears to be archival images constitutes another of his personal signatures, as Domènec Font has noted:

> The presentation of documentary images that had been forbidden until now such as the fights for amnesty and autonomy and the popular demonstrations, despite not being able to completely abandon the spectacular gaze, appear constantly counterpointed by the film's soundtrack. Also, the presence of the actor Francesc Luchetti establishes a link between the different blocks of the film while traversing the author's viewpoint, and the falsely objective coldness of a documentary together with the arbitrariness of the different sequences that is used to break any notion of a traditional narrative continuum. (38)

Portabella's editorial "arbitrariness" is another expression of his radical theatricality, of his post-Brechtian wish to make us co-responsible for the meaning of his film. Thus, as suggested by Font, it makes perfect sense, besides being a great asset to the film's inner narrative, to include the figure of Francesc Luchetti as a fictional actor amidst the real social actors that the film represents. Perhaps the most extreme example of this technique may be seen in the fact that Luchetti's first appearance on screen happens anonymously and in the middle of this initial montage of the huge street demonstrations of February 1976 in Madrid and Barcelona. It happens right after the first sequences of police shooting tear gas and charging to break the first lines of the demonstration. These images are seen in colour and appear to be shot from an apartment overlooking the street. After them, we cut to a middle close-up of a young man with a moustache who is trying to escape the police charge. It is a quick montage but, in retrospect, we can identify this man as Francesc Luchetti. At this point, Portabella includes another dramatic low-angle shot that shows the helicopter hovering above and a series of eye-level shots showing cars trapped in between police jeeps while we feel the chaos, violence, and confusion. Once more, quite briefly, we see Luchetti running from the scene. Then, this fictional directorial intervention is made clearer in a sequence where we see a group of *sociales* (undercover policemen) intercepting another young man, whom they will beat and arrest. Portabella's goal here is a double one. With the introduction of a real actor in the middle of the historical demonstrations he pushes the envelope of his distancing technique and breaks, albeit for a short moment, the cinéma-vérité effect of those until now forbidden images. At the same time, he manages to inscribe his viewpoint, a sense of directness, of being there, a kind of narrative agency that, as Font suggested, is ultimately used to break any traditional sense of spectatorial identification or narrative closure. And yet, Luchetti's anonymous introduction also obeys a clear narrative principle since it foreshadows the film's most notorious fictional reconstruction: the nocturnal police intrusion into the flat of a group of young activists in the human rights sequence where Luchetti's and his girlfriend's naked bodies will mark the citizens' utmost sense of vulnerability in front of the State's repressive forces. This sequence becomes a narrative culmination of sorts also in the sense that it stages in no uncertain terms the haunting presence of Francoism, whose dark forces are still fully functioning. Ultimately, it offers a condensation of Portabella's distancing and metafictional approach while rehashing some of his fundamental cinematic strategies.

The final convergence between the two *Informes* that I would like to highlight here is the one Jordi Amat describes with the term "Parlament"

(Parliament). Thus, in both films, we will find the repetition of a very similar sequence, once again in front of a very significant staircase, this time leading into the main hall of Catalonia's Parliament in Barcelona. When comparing them, Amat writes:

> Escenes calcades. Però en el primer *Informe* el Parlament, *sepultat per la pols*, semblava una càpsula en el temps la recuperació de la qual podia determinar l'evolució de la democràcia a Espanya per al present. Allà continua, encarnada pels tres diputats de la CUP, la seva potencialitat com a àmbit capaç des del qual fonamentar la transformació de l'Estat.

> (Copied scenes. And yet, in the first *Informe*, the Parliament, *buried in dust*, looked like a time capsule whose recovery could determine the evolution of Spanish democracy onto the present. Embodied now in the three representatives from CUP, we can still see the potential of that institutional site to set the foundations for the transformation of the entire State.) (25; emphasis mine)

From Amat's description, I would like to underline the sentence "buried in dust" since it contains the most important aesthetic and historical key that separates the two *Informes*. In aesthethic terms, as previously mentioned, the first *Informe general* was characterized by a critical spectrality used by Portabella to make visible the absent presence of Franco's spectre haunting all the political debates that the film documents and also makes possible. In historical terms, this spectrality is dramatically performed in the figure of Francesc Luchetti, the same actor who, as we have just seen, embodies the political activist chased and tortured by Franco's police while also being the film's narrator, who guides the viewer through the series of spectral visits to both the literal and the metaphoric ruins of Francoism. Thus, when we see Luchetti and his two anonymous companions climbing the staircase leading into Catalonia's Parliament and walking through their dark and empty halls, the images remind us of a mausoleum, of a monument to democracy's death. And yet, the very endurance of these halls through time, as Amat suggests, allows us to conceive the hope of their being brought back to political life in the future, an idea that fits perfectly well with the critical discourse of Portabella's first *Informe* and its phantasmatic mise en scène. Now, when the sequence is echoed in the 2016 *Informe*, we can see a huge red carpet covering the same staircase, while the big hanging lights again show us an empty hall. This time, however, the three social actors we have accompanied since their arrival at the noble building are David Fernández, Isabel Vallet, and Quim Arrufat, the three CUP representatives elected to the

Catalan Parliament.[18] In the context of the film, moreover, the political significance of the CUP is akin to the one achieved by the "indignados" as yet another political group emerging as a result of the anti-system popular movements that Portabella both chronicles and celebrates. In terms of the pro-independence movement in Catalonia, on the other hand, the role of the CUP was and continues to be an important one. In this sense, Portabella's emphasis on the simple presence of these politicians inside the most important legislative institution in Catalonia becomes a strong reminder of the political need to bring new life, to "animate," or "to take over" the institutions, the claim first uttered by Marina Garcés in her aforementioned "manifesto," and later echoed many times throughout the film. Ultimately, what Portabella also reminds us is the fact that the *dissensus* called for by Jacques Rancière is no longer taking place only in the streets. This new reality will be punctuated by David Fernández when he refers to the pressure and the critiques raised by the status quo as a way of resisting any institutional takeover that could lead to a truly direct democracy. These are Fernández's own words: "Jo insisitiria contra la 'plutocràcia,' és a dir, que no ho decidiran ni el uns ni els altres, ho decidirà la gent" ("I would insist against any 'plutocracy." I mean this will not be decided by this group or that group. It will be decided by the people"; *Informe general II*).

In the final analysis, therefore, both Fernández and Portabella coincide: the last word will be uttered by the people in the streets since their active dissidence has constituted them into a new political subject that is not limited by any parliamentary representation and whose voice is capable of going beyond all the institutional boundaries. That is why the director invites us once more to witness one of his meaningful and recurring juxtapositions. This time not as a narrative and visual counterpoint but as a logical expansion. Thus, from the fade in at the end of the images portraying the Catalan Parliament, now full of light, Portabella's camera fades out into the spectacular images from the Via Catalana on 11 September 2013, the human chain of people raising *senyeres* and *estelades* that stretched more than 400 kilometres and carpeted in colour the entire length of the country.[19] These images inscribe Portabella's political commitment in an almost unprecedented manner since

---

18 CUP stands for Candidatura d'Unitat Popular (Popular Unity Candidacy), the anti-system political formation that sprang from the social movements described at the beginning and throughout this essay as expressions of the new "dissensus" of a civil society largely disappointed by the political status quo.

19 The *senyera* is the official flag of Catalonia and the *estelada* is the same flag with a blue star in it. The *estelada* has become the symbol of the pro-independence movement in Catalonia.

they include the moment when we see the director himself hand in hand with Lluis Llach,[20] both (con)fused in this collective body whose ludic dissidence becomes the fundamental historical and political correlate to the film *Informe general II: El nuevo rapto de Europa*, doubtlessly the most detailed chronicle of the second transition and the latest great document of Pere Portabella's unflinching political gaze.

WORKS CITED

Amat, Jordi. "Els dos informes de Portabella." *Culturals/La Vanguardia*. 13 February 2016, pp. 24–5.
Antich, Xavier. "El carceller darrera la porta." *ARA*. Barcelona. 31 January 2018. https://www.ara.cat/opinio/xavier-antich-carceller-darrera-la-porta_0_1953404684.html. Accessed 28 December 2020.
Cox, Anna. "A New "Cinema of Attractions"? The Barcelona School's Exhibionist Loops." *Hispanic Review*, vol. 78, no 4, pp. 529–49.
Delgado, Manuel. *El animal público*. Anagrama, 1999.
— *Memoria y lugar: El espacio público como crisis del significado*. Ediciones Generales de la Construcción, 2001.
Fanés, Fèlix. *Pere Portabella: Avantguarda, cinema, política*. Filmoteca de Catalunya/Ediorial Pòrtic, 2008.
Font, Domènec. "La Filmoteca se despide con el cine de Portabella." *El Correo Catalán*. 25 June 1977, pp. 38.
Foucault, Michel. *Surveiller et punir: Naissance de la prison*. Gallimard, 1975.
Fouz Hernández, Santiago: *Cuerpos de cine: Masculinidades carnales en el cine y la cultura popular contemporáneas*. Ediciones Bellaterra, 2013.
Fraser, Benjamin. "Manuel Delgado's Urban Anthropology: From Multidimensional Space to Interdisciplinary Spatial Theory." *Arizona Journal of Hispanic Cultural Studies*, vol. 11, 2007, pp. 57–75. *JSTOR*, www.jstor.org/stable/20641848. Accessed 28 December 2020.
Gianetti, Louis. *Understanding Movies (10th Edition)*. Pearson, 2005.
González, Chus. *Informe general II: El nuevo rapto de Europa. Pressbook*. Films 59, Barcelona, 2016.
Hill, David W. "A Review of Jacques Rancière's *Dissensus. On Politics and Aesthetics*." *Marx and Philosophy. A Review of Books*. 16 July 2010. https://

---

20 Lluis Llach is one of Catalonia's most popular singers and a member of the *nova cançó* (new song) movement that put music to the social and political protests since late Francoism to the present. He was elected to Parliament running for the Junts pel Sí (Together for Yes) alliance that brought the first pro-independence majority government into the Generalitat of Catalonia in 2015.

marxandphilosophy.org.uk/reviews/7588_dissensus-review-by-david-w-hill/. Accessed 28 December 2020.

Jamón, jamón. Directed by Bigas Luna, performances by Javier Bardem, Penélope Cruz, Juan Diego, Anna Galiena, Jordi Mollà, and Stefania Sandrelli, Lola Films, Ovideo and Sogepaq, 1992.

Llanos, Héctor, and Jaime Rubio. "El toro de Osborne de Santa Pola, convertido en lienzo para un Guernica antitaurino." *El país*, 22 May 2017. https://verne.elpais.com/verne/2017/05/22/articulo/1495445786_207917.html. Accessed 28 December 2020.

Marimon, Sílvia. "L'exhumació de dos republicans enterrats al Valle de los Caídos començarà el 23 d'abril: Fa més de sis anys que els familiars dels dos afusellats batallen per treure'ls del mausoleum." *ARA*. 19 April 2018. Article not found online.

Marsh, Steven. "Editor's Introduction. Untimely Materialities: Spanish Film and Spectrality." *Journal of Spanish Cultural Studies*, vol. 15, no.3, 2014, pp. 293–8.

– *Spanish Cinema Against Itself: Cosmopolitanism, Experimentation, Militancy*. Indiana University Press, 2020.

Martí-Olivella, Jaume. "Historical Memory and Family Metaphor in Catalonia's New Documentary School." *Journal of Catalan Studies*, 2014, pp. 53–71. http://anglo-catalan.org/oldjocs/16/Articles%20&%20Reviews/Versio%20pdf/04%20MartiOlivella.pdf. Accessed 28 December 2020.

Möller, Olaf. "Informe general II; El nuevo rapto de Europa." Program Catalogue, 45th Rotterdam International Film Festival, 2016.

Monterde, José Enrique. "Pere Portabella habla de su película." *Caimán*, vol. 46, February 2016, pp. 44–5.

Nadal-Melsió, Sara. "Editor's Preface. The Invisible Tradition: Avant-Garde Catalan Cinema under Late Francoism." *Hispanic Review*, vol 78, no. 4, pp. 465–8. doi: www.jstor.org/stable/25790597. Accessed 9 September 2018.

Nicholas, Lynn H. *The Rape of Europa*. Knopf, 1994.

Portabella, Pere, director. http://www.pereportabella.com.

– *Die Stille vor Bach*. Performances by Alex Brendemühl, Feodor Atkine, Christian Brembeck, and Daniel Ligorio et al., Films 59. 2007.

– *Informe general sobre algunas cuestiones de interés para una proyección pública*. Films 59, 1976.

– *Informe general II: El nuevo rapto de Europa*. Films 59, 2016.

– *Miró, l'altre*. Films 59, 1969.

– *Miró-Tapís*. Fundació Maeght, 1973.

– *Pont de Varsòvia*. Performances by Paco Guijar, Jordi Dauder, Carme Elias, Ona Planas, Josep M. Pou et al., Films 59, 1989.

– *El sopar*. Films 59, 1974.

– *Umbracle*. Performances by Christopher Lee, Jeannine Mestre, Films 59, 1972.

– *Vampir.Cuadecuc*. Performances by Christopher Lee, Herbert Lom, Soledad Miranda, Jack Taylor et al., Films 59, 1970.

Quintana, Angel. "Levantar acta. *Informe general II: El nuevo rapto de Europa* de Pere Portabella." *Caimán*, vol. 46, February 2016, pp. 44–5.
Rancière, Jacques: *Dissensus. On Politics and Aesthetics*. Translated by Steven Corcoran, Continuum, 2010.
Riambau, Esteve, and Casimiro Torreiro. *La escuela de Barcelona: El cine de la "gauche divine."* Anagrama, 1999.
Serra, Xavi. "Pere Portabella, cineasta total." *ARA*, 13 February 2018. https://www.ara.cat/cultura/Pere-Portabella-cineasta-total_0_1960603970.html. Accessed 28 December 2020.

7 Traversing the Real with the Reel: Infrapolitical Spectrality in Pere Portabella's *Vampir.Cuadecuc* and Albert Serra's *Història de la meva mort*

TERESA M. VILARÓS

I. Traversing the Reel with (Franco) and (Marx): Pere Portabella's *Vampir.Cuadecuc* (1970/2017)

There is no more "reality of desire," we would say, than it would be correct to say "the back of the front": there is one and the same fabric that has a front and a back.

Jacques Lacan, "The Logic of Phantasy"

During the sixties, it seemed that the harsh rules imposed by the Francoist dictatorship in Spain were beginning to loosen up, if only partially. However, at the end of the decade, and after two years of increasing social turmoil, in January 1969 General Franco imposed a "state of exception," followed up a year later by a drumhead court martial set against sixteen alleged members of the Basque organization ETA. The trial was staged in the city of Burgos in January 1970 and came to be known as *el proceso de Burgos*, or, simply, *El proceso*. It was during this time of extensive political unrest in Spain that Pere Portabella began filming *Vampir.Cuadecuc* in Catalonia, a movie hailed by many as one of the best experimental films of the last century.[1]

---

1 *Vampir.Cuadecuc* was finished in 1970, but Francoist censorship deemed it unacceptable for public viewing. It did premiere in 1972 at the MoMA in New York City. Although Portabella was originally scheduled to be present for the event, the Francoist regime denied him a passport. Before the presentation of the film, the organizers read the document Portabella sent them, denouncing the rampant political repression in Spain. The document is available on the director's web portal at http://pereportabella .com/en/documents/2009/03/screening-of-vampir-cuadecuc-in-moma-1972-en. The film, mostly unavailable for decades since that first run at the MoMA, was neither released in Spain nor abroad until 2017. Portabella's film, in my view, has not lost any of its excellence but in fact has gained even more poignancy.

Portabella embraced in his own way the avant-garde praxis characteristic of the so-called Escola, or Escuela, de Barcelona (EdB). Using the theme of the vampire – a motif not actually alien to other members of the school[2] – with *Vampir.Cuadecuc* he broke away from the conventional cinematographic language of vampire movies "by [providing] a precise analysis in order to overcome it and go on to the evocative powers of the images" (Portabella quoted by Expósito). Confirming the director's conviction that "the main political dimension of [his] films lies in attacking [cinematic] linguistic codes" (Expósito), *Vampir.Cuadecuc* is able to open an unexpected relation: it offers itself as a sort of spectral cinematic portal barely resting on its hinges, uncannily swinging between and across the medium of cinema (the reel) and the harsh political life under the dictatorship (the real).

On the side of the reel, *Vampir.Cuadecuc* is a reimagining of Jesús Franco's *Count Dracula* (heretofore J. Franco).[3] It pays homage to classic vampire-themed movies, "drawing sustenance from the vital juices of another movie" (Hoberman). Relentlessly, the film breathes down J. Franco's neck in *Count Dracula*, also pulling from F.W. Murnau's *Nosferatu*, Carl Theodor's *Vampyr*, and, of course, Bram Stoker's original novel. On the side of the real, the film's vampiric undertaking addresses the ongoing Francoist politics of the period. Rosalind Galt and others have already noted how the figure of Dracula will always already have "a whiff of political violence about it," mentioning that in Portabella's film, "Dracula is self-evidently a figuration of General Franco ... we can read the imbrication of political and cinematic language in each layer of

---

[2] Rosalind Galt points out the importance of the Transylvania theme for members of the school: "There was one place in which Spanish cinema was Europeanising in the mid-1960s, albeit in an area that failed to give the cultural prestige that [General] Franco desired. Genre films, and particularly B-movies, were flourishing, and were increasingly co-produced with partners in Italy, France, and West Germany. Like the Barcelona School, these low-budget horror and exploitation films engaged with contemporary European cinematic trends – in this case, Britain's Hammer horror cycle and the Italian *giallo* ... It is thus not surprising that the Barcelona School should have engaged with popular horror, as [Vicente] Aranda did with *La Novia ensangrentada* (*The Blood-Spattered Bride*, 1972), and [Pere] Portabella with *Cuadecuc, vampir.*"

[3] *Count Dracula* (1970) was not produced by J. Franco's usual Hammer house, but by Harry Alan Towers's company. It starred his usual actors, Christopher Lee, also a friend of Portabella, and Soledad Miranda, J. Franco's wife. Portabella engaged with the theme of the vampire film when he learned that while J. Franco was living in the UK at the time and filming low-budget horror movies for the Hammer Film Production Company, he arrived in Barcelona ready to shoot parts of a new Dracula movie in December 1970.

the film's fictions ... *Cuadecuc* mobilizes all of these resonances in creating an uncanny image of the Count" ("Mapping Catalonia"). It is then within this real-to-reel interaction that *Vampir.Cuadecuc* actually unfolds a spectral, extended image of the dictatorship using a particular point in history that involves December 1970 and the unfolding of the Burgos trial (*el proceso de Burgos*): real events and a real context that set forward a radically unhinged cinematic exercise.

The spectral cinematic quality of *Vampir.Cuadecuc* shows up in a variety of material ways: with Portabella's decision to shoot handheld on a 16 mm camera; his working with negative sound on variable raw densities; his making the frames reverberate through adjusting exposure (over or under, or even infra-exposing the film stock); his provocative use of high-contrast black and white film stock, which would render the original colour found in J. Franco's *Count Dracula* void; or his singular use of diegetic sound at the end of the movie, when Christopher Lee – a remnant of himself, as Steven Marsh wittily tells us ("Legacies") – recounts Mina Harker's description of the death of the vampire, reading directly from Bram Stoker's novel.[4]

Overall, *Vampir.Cuadecuc* uncannily echoes a series of discarded photographic negatives. As Marsh points out, "rather than being a film within a film [the movie] is more akin to a photo negative of the original."[5] Or, as I posit, it is akin to a series of discarded X-ray images that are able to bring a timeless reel-to-real spectral quality to an otherwise very specific contemporaneity: one referring to a particular time and place (Spain, 1970), a political context (Francoism, the Burgos trial, ETA, the Basque Country, Catalonia), and, last but not least, to a certain cinematic genre (vampire-themed cinema).[6] The film

---

4 In *Vampir.Cuadecuc*, Christopher Lee is, Marsh tells us, "a representation of the 'truly' undead among the apparently undead, a Dracula among stuffed, life-like, animals. Furthermore, however, Lee is an actor who is also not an actor (in this film he plays a person called Christopher Lee), a shadow of his own character. Unsettlingly, his being himself is less real than the character he habitually plays. He is what Jacques Derrida might call, in a rather different context, a 'copy of a copy' (*Dissemination* 219)" (553).
5 From Pere Portabella's website (http://www.pereportabella.com/en/features/features/vampir-cuadecuc-en). An original sound negative is "negative sound track recorded 'live' by an optical sound camera." Also referred to as OSN, "the original sound negative is the sound negative that is exposed in a film recorder and, after processing, is a negative sound image on the film. Can be variable density or variable area" (National Film and Sound Archive).
6 The seventies in Spain saw a surge in the making of, and taste for, vampire movies: a social phenomenon closely related to the symbolic appropriation of the figure of the vampire as a stand-in for General Franco and Francoism. The decade opens with

therefore cannot be classified as a *political* film (not even as one working undercover as vampire entertainment), and even less so as a militant (or Marxist) one.[7] It could perhaps be described as "impolitical" if we understand the term, following Mario Cacciari's conceptualization, as "what refuse[s] to engage in the representation of the political as a totality ... working to deconstruct that totality."[8] But even this descriptive measure falls short with regards to Portabella's film. I propose that *Vampir. Cuadecuc* is, at least partially, an uncanny example of cinematic, infrapolitical practice. It is an infrapolitical film *avant la lettre* if, in agreement with Alberto Moreiras, we understand the infrapolitical as "primarily a thinking of the step back ... a step back that ... moves away from the obvious light to take a better look at the clearing" ("Infrapolitical").

Vampir.Cuadecuc certainly takes a step back from the political state of affairs of the time so as to take a better, broader look at the bloody, cruel helio-political light of Francoism in general, and to *el proceso de Burgos* in particular. And, perhaps surprisingly, it does so by engaging humorously with such a serious state of affairs. Engaging with the vampire-themed history of cinema, *Vampir.Cuadecuc* gives a spectrally cold, seemingly apathetic, and also very funny look at the state of things in Spain circa 1970.

Humour is quite paramount here and cannot be dismissed; it is one way in which the film is able to traverse the distance from the reel to the real. Portabella's comically unattached cinematic consideration of a particular time, place, and set of correlating (political) emotions, while unhinged and deconstructed, is also precisely, almost mathematically set. Portabella's infrapolitical exercise actually lines up with Baruch Spinoza's detached proposition to study emotions with apathetic, mathematical precision.[9] That is, in applying our interest not only to

---

Portabella's and J. Franco's 1970 Dracula movies; Iván Zulueta's phenomenal *Arrebato* closes it in 1979. For a follow-up discussion on Zulueta's work on materiality and disappearance, see Brad Epps's "The Space of the Vampire: Materiality and Disappearance in the Films of Iván Zulueta." Portabella makes *Umbracle* in 1971, a fascinating follow-up to *Vampir.Cuadecuc*. J. Franco will continue to make vampire and gore-like movies throughout his career.

7 Portabella, although never a militant, was what was called a "fellow traveller" (a "compañero de viaje") of the PSUC, the underground communist political party in Catalonia (Partit Socialista Unificat de Catalunya).

8 For Mario Cacciari, "lo impolítico es aquello que resiste la representación de lo político como totalidad ... [es] el trabajo de deconstrucción de esta totalidad" ("Lo impolítico nietzschiano" 64) . I have already used Mario Cacciari's conceptualization of the term "impolitical" in my analysis of *Dante no es únicamente severo* (Joaquim Jordà and Jacinto Esteva, 1967), in my article "Barcelona come piedras."

9 See book 3 of Baruch Spinoza's *Ethics*.

Figure 7.1 Screenshot (39:33) from *Vampir.Cuadecuc* (1970).

emotional somatic symptoms, but to the "passion of the mind" (*pathema*), which he also describes as joyous and humorous.

But humour, nevertheless, can be quite dark. Camera in hand, Portabella takes a step back from the bright, helio-political staging and emotions of the Burgos trial and studies the case mathematically, even geometrically (Carles Santos's punctuation-precise musical score should be fully noted in this regard). As such, allusions to the unfolding military trial in Burgos are made elliptically. They are infrapolitically dark, barely noticeable, deeply hidden between the shadows and flashes that reverberate on screen. They emerge almost without being seen, ever so briefly appearing in two scenes showcasing a clapperboard with the words "El proceso" written in chalk (see figure 7.1).

The clapperboard's appearance is unexpected, seemingly coming twice out of nowhere, out of context, out of time, out of joint. Set back and away from whatever act of narrativization and synchronization we might have been hoping for or willing to adhere to, the image of the clapperboard jumps out at us, biting us in vampiric fashion. They are images that infrapolitically replicate themselves, appearing and disappearing in Portabella's Reel as though they were intrusions of the Lacanian Real.

In offering with the clapperboard an elliptical, infrapolitical visualization of "El proceso," Portabella makes at least three counter-uses of related vampire genre strategies that were very common to the B-rated movies of the time: 1) denarrativization countering narrativization; 2) humour and apatheia countering fear and terror; and 3) anachronism countering time. As per the first one, Portabella does not impose a political narrative, or narrative-like structure, onto the real experience of the Burgos trial. The film does not overtly speak about Francoism. There are no interpretations. No direct storyline: only the apparition of these two sudden images of the clapperboard, a nearly invisible infra-allusion to the reality of the ETA trial.

With regards to the second, the movie works by keeping one strategy often used in B-movies intact: humour – unabashedly present throughout the movie. Even the biting photograms hinting at "El proceso" provide a dark comedic commentary on the final and bloody years of General Francisco Franco's dictatorship in Spain: The clapperboard we (hardly) see seems to be hinting at a movie whose title is *El proceso*, a film presumably directed by Jesús Franco with Manuel Merino, one of Franco's real collaborators, listed as the director of photography (on the clapperboard, written as M. Merino). Due to this play of images, the fiction/non-fiction technical data presented as a film within a film makes it so that the Burgos trial, or *El proceso* as it appears in *Vampir.Cuadecuc*, can be satirically inferred as a B-rated, bloody movie in the making directed by Jesús Franco.[10]

But, at the same time, B-rated movies, particularly vampire-themed ones, while they can be eerily and creepily funny, are never indifferent to their political context; and, moreover, neither Jesús Franco nor Manuel Merino were exactly low-key, neutral figures in cinema.[11] Jesús Franco, Galt reminds us, "began his career as an assistant to Juan Antonio Bardem ... [and] was no stranger to the avant-garde himself." Portabella's movies, including of course this one, likewise relate to their contexts: in the director's own words, they do so "through the complexity – rather than the complication – of language, and through the subversion of the dominant codes" (Expósito).

---

10 Jonathan Rosenbaum writes that cinema "is a kind of fraud, and Portabella's project from the outset is both to expose and to play with its fraudulence, much of it founded on various forms of apparent continuity." While Rosenbaum's comment is specific to Portabella's 1968 *No compteu amb els dits (Don't Count with Your Fingers)*, his remarks can and should be extended to all of Portabella's cinema production. See Jonathan Rosembaum, "Introducing Pere Portabella."
11 Jesús Franco, Rosalind Galt reminds us, "ran into constant problems with censorship. In 1971, the Vatican named Franco and Buñuel as the two most dangerous film-makers in Spain."

It is with this in mind that the third counter-strategy at work in the film, anachronism, quickly follows. Within *Vampir.Cuadecuc* the gravity of the 1970 Burgos trial, and by implication the whole scene of the Francoist regime, is made to echo within a timeless vampiric stage. Distorting any expected chronological time-image synchronization – implicitly addressed by the appearance of the clapperboard in this movie – *Vampir.Cuadecuc* instead moves anachronically in a time out of joint, becoming at one and the same time that other (infrapolitical) movie, *El proceso*. Clocks, pocket watches, dead time, and dead hours tend to punctuate all vampire movies, and *Vampir.Cuadecuc* is no exception. But unlike other vampire-themed films, which tend to make use of time as a mode of chronological representation, *Vampir.Cuadecuc* flows anachronically, simultaneously flying back and forth from the contemporary time of the Burgos trial and Jesús Franco's filming of *Dracula* to the romantic times of the "real" literary Dracula. It folds, reverses, extends, and collapses time; and, in doing so, it moves away from representation into spectral incorporation. Time bending out of joint, using Jacques Derrida's conceptualization, in the film dates also "become unhinged"; time, "like deconstruction ... like a door on its hinges ... [is] *folding* back on itself" ("Time" 15).

Anachronism is always "essential to spectrality" (87), as Ernesto Laclau notes in his discussion on Jacques Derrida's notion of a time out of joint. And, as such, in Portabella's movie that *thing*, which is so difficult to name, that anachronical *thing* that also appears and disappears in a time out of joint, is the spectre. It is the vampire: moving un-dead within extended time. Movement embedded upon the wings of a bat, if we echo Rudolph Minkowski's conceptualization of extended time as butterfly nebulae: a mathematical concept of physics allowing for the present and past "to be temporally extended, as it is in human consciousness, rather than point like" (Savitt). As though it were like a bat traversing the window of extended time, Portabella's images in motion are also methodically supported by the punctuation offered by the extended-time nebulae where present and past simultaneously share their frame – that is, where our past and our present cohabitate.[12]

---

12 Portabella's work must always be considered in dialogue with avant-garde artistic experimentation of all kinds, especially painting (e.g., his works on Joan Brossa and Joan Miró), and music (e.g., his long-time collaboration with Carles Santos, who has worked on most of Portabella's musical soundtracks, and with whom Portabella collaborated on the short film *Playback* [1970] and *Acció Santos* [1973]). See, for instance, Santos Zunzunegui's "Pere Portabella: The Politics and Esthetics of Auteurism."

Within the given parameters of the extended-time nebula and its correlating vampire-cinema prompt – fog, of which *Vampir.Cuadecuc* offers plenty – Portabella opens a cinematic (infrapolitical) portal for us. It is no wonder that Portabella's last name in Catalan literally and appropriately means a beautiful (-bella) gate (Porta). The movie opens a door from where we can, on one hand, glimpse and attempt to make sense of the beautiful though darkly humorous quality of vampire cinema, and, on the other hand, take a quick though stark glance at the spooky, non-laughable political reality of Francoism during the Burgos trial. Enacting a series of eerie transpositions, a mirroring between his own name and the surname of both Jesús Franco and the Spanish dictator, General Francisco Franco, Portabella opens the door and unhinges time so that the two "Francos" can consistently traverse time in an extended nebula.[13]

Portabella's movie is a house of mirrors, and one that displays the constant intertwining between real and reel, mixing the past, the present, and even the future: jazzy music and atonal sounds; noise seemingly of planes cruising the skyline during a supposedly nineteenth-century gothic burial; contemporary street drilling set against the visualization of a "gothic" castle that does not hide the fact that it's a structure from the El Poble Espanyol theme park of Barcelona, built in the sixties. And, among other apparent incongruences – other than the two images of the clapperboard already mentioned – there are two time-lag interventions, now on the Catalan high culture of industrial modernism, both of which concern death, burials, and violence, and both of which also pop up quite unexpectedly.

The first: burial scenes of a figurative Transylvania are transported to a mausoleum in Arenys de Mar – a hypogeum built circa 1922 in the *indiano*-modernist style, which is guarded by a delicate marble sculpture of a young girl created by Josep Llimona.[14] The visualization of the hypogeum is disconcerting. Why is it there? With the inclusion of this scene, it is possible that Portabella is hinting that it is amidst the modernist *indiano* legacy of the early twentieth-century industrial bourgeoisie where the Francoist-like vampire (embodied by Christopher Lee) is able to find a suitable niche within the Catalan bourgeoisie, right after, or even during, the Spanish Civil War. Or, alternatively, even

---

13 To complicate the mirror-effect, let's note that the real Jesús Franco plays a part in Portabella's movie.
14 The pantheon, well known for the sculpture of Josep Llimona, was dedicated to the remains of D. Francesc Massaguer i Campins and family in 1922.

Figure 7.2 The 1970 production of *Ronda de mort a Sinera*. Photograph by Pau Barceló, 22 September 1970, at the Teatre Romea, Barcelona. Fuente: CDiMAE.

contingently: since the specific cemetery of Arenys de Mar cannot be disassociated from the cemetery imagined in the twentieth century by the quintessential writer of the Marrano register, the Catalan poet Salvador Espriu, perhaps there is a subtle infrapolitical, Marrano-like nod to "Sinera" (Arenys spelled backwards, albeit with the y – also known as the Greek i – replaced with an i).[15]

The Marrano and the infrapolitical register are indeed well related, since, as Moreiras states, the characteristic "Marrano's a-positionality is always already infrapolitical, which is its condition of freedom ... never defined, only invoked" ("Cabezas's A-Positional Freedom").[16] A play based on Espriu's Arenys/Sinera, *Ronda de mort a Sinera*, had performed in Barcelona in 1965 under the direction of Ricard Salvat.[17] In September 1970, the play underwent another successful run, now coinciding with the Burgos trial, and the pre-production and shoot of Portabella's film (see figure 7.2).

Portabella was of course well aware of Espriu, Sinera, and Salvat. And isn't Portabella's film, an a-positional movie shot during late Francoism, working in a quintessentially undercover, Marrano register? It is after all a text on masks and spectres where references to "Franco" (both the

---

15 For more information on Salvador Espriu's *Marrano* register, see my "Salvador Espriu and the Marrano Home of Language."
16 For the relation between infrapolitics and marranismo, see, among other essays, Moreiras's "Cabeza's A-Positional Freedom."
17 "*Ronda de mort a Sinera*, de la Escola d'Art Dramàtic Adrià Gual." Teatro Independiente-MCU, http://teatro-independiente.mcu.es/espectaculos/ronda-de-mort-a-sinera.php. Pau Barceló's picture also taken from the site.

cineaste and the dictator) work as an always-to-be-empty signifier. A vampire film echoing past bodies and ghosts – those of the Spanish Civil War, symbolically buried in Sinera;[18] of the present – the death penalties demanded in the Burgos trial; and even those of the future – those executed in the final Francoist years, and beyond.

The second time-lag intervention is another intriguing infrapolitical reference to the legacy of Catalan modernist industrialization. Here Portabella exercises a visual transportation of one of the most beloved characters in the bourgeois Catalan imaginary: Mariona Rebull, the eponymous heroine of Ignacio Agustí's 1943 novel fictionalizing the family saga of a quintessential *indiano* industrialist, Joaquin Rius – her husband.[19] In the final pages of the novel, in a scene reminiscent of one of Ramon Casas's paintings, Agustí evokes the figure of a young and beautiful Mariona sitting at Barcelona's Liceu opera house on the evening of 7 November 1893. The very night the anarchist Santiago Salvador threw two Orsini bombs at the theatre's stalls. One did not detonate, but the other did, causing fourteen deaths with thirty-five others wounded (see figure 7.3).

In Agustí's novel, Mariona will be one of the dead. In the book's final pages, the author closely narrates Mariona's death as the death described by the survivor's testimony. Before dying, Mariona sits listening to Gioachino Rossini's opera *Guglielmo Tell*, and we "see" her gorgeous mousseline dress delicately marking her long neck enhanced by a string of pearls (see figure 7.4). An imaginary visualization, Pere Portabella remakes this for his own *Vampir.Cuadecuc*, wherein Rossini's opera is likewise included. But unlike Agustí's horror scene, Portabella lets the young woman live – and even has Mariona mockingly wink at the spectator.

---

18 The Sinera-cemetery theme is extensively present in Salvador Espriu's work, and so is the presence of his alter ego, Salom. See, for instance, *Cementiri de Sinera*, or Espriu's third book, *Les hores*, dedicated to Salom, the dead on the day of the military coup that started the Spanish Civil War: "Recordant allunyadament Salom, (18-VII-1936)" ("Remembering Salom from a Distance, 18 July 1936"). "Salom," the inverted name taken from Espriu's mother's surname, Molas, is the name Savador Espriu i Molas gives to his alter ego. See also from Espriu, *Ronda de mort a Sinera* and *Llibre de Sinera*.
19 Ignacio (Ignasi) Agustí wrote the novel in 1943. A study of the economic rise of Catalonia at the dawn of the textile industrial boom, the novel is the first of a tetralogy, "La ceniza fue árbol." It follows the saga of a fictional family, the Rius's, from their humble origin (*Mariona Rebull*) to the Spanish Civil War. Written in Spanish.

Figure 7.3 The explosion caused by the Orsini bomb thrown at the stalls of the opera theatre El Liceu, Barcelona, by the anarchist Santiago Salvador Franch, on the cover of the newspaper *Le Petit Journal*, 25 Nov. 1893.

In the film, the bourgeoisie, the anarchists, and the Francoist-like vampires simultaneously are and are not laughing matters. Death and violence are and are not deeply serious *things*. Bombs of all kinds may or may not detonate. Curiously, as archived in the December 1897 issue of *La Vanguardia*, a photograph of the unexploded Orsini bomb thrown at the Liceu is shown above a signed letter of admission of guilt, by Salvador (see figure 7.5). A spectral image Portabella could very well have included in the film.

It is with his film, with that foggy house of extended time and mirrors that is *Vampir.Cuadecuc*, that Portabella detonates an (infrapolitical) bomb of his own against the cinematographic establishment of the time

Figure 7.4 Portabella's evocation of Mariona Rebull in *Vampir.Cuadecuc*. Screenshot (52:29).

Figure 7.5 Archival photo of Santiago Salvador's autographed letter confessing to the Liceu attack, with the second Orsini bomb thrown at the Liceu by Salvador, which did not explode.

of Francoism.[20] We know, of course, that Portabella is not a historical anarchist. If anything, and taking into consideration his political sympathies during the making of the film, he was and maybe still is a spectral Marxist. But even if Portabella were not a spectral Marxist, his work surely would be – particularly *Vampir.Cuadecuc* and *Umbracle*. And his work is so in a very infrapolitical way.

Ghosts, spirits, spectres, and spooks crowd Marx's texts. "Spectre" is the first noun one reads in the *Communist Manifesto*, Derrida reminds us in his classic text, *Spectres of Marx*: "There was a ghost waiting there, and from the opening, from the raising of the curtain … 'a spectre is haunting Europe, the spectre of Communism' … this, the thing ('this thing') will end up coming. The *revenant* is going to come" (4).

Vampir.Cuadecuc likewise opens its play with a spectre and revenant. But of what? Of Marxism, in part – the movie is imbued with phantasmic materialism, Portabella tells us. But also of a phantasmic materialism of another kind, one supplied by General Franco and Francoism. What distinguishes the spectre, or the revenant, from a spirit, says Derrida, is the spectre's potential for intrinsic material exchangeability: "the tangible intangibility of a proper body without flesh, but still [able to be] the body of some*one* as some*one other*" (*Spectres of Marx* 4, original emphasis). This is an active form of exchangeability, actually, that works against one of the most precious axioms of capitalism: the chain of equivalence. A Marrano form of exchangeability, we could add, which, with its constant appearing and disappearing and its refusal to position itself, is capable of utter destruction. *Vampir.Cuadecuc* is, in that sense, the ultimate destroyer, playing with its own (Marrano) phantasmic materiality. A spectral cinematic material body without flesh that both appears and disappears as some*one* as well as someone *else*, *Vampir.Cuadecuc* flaps its wings over everything and everybody. In Spain circa 1970, and even also in the Spain of today, revenants of Francoism continue to appear and disappear.[21]

---

20 Portabella's movie exercises "dos tipus de violència sobre la narrativa estàndard: elimina totalment el color i substitueix la banda sonora per un paisatge de col·lisions imatge-so a càrrec de Carles Santos" ("two types of violence on the narrative standard: it completely eliminates colour and substitutes the soundtrack with a landscape by Carles Santos made of sound and music colliding among themselves").

21 Jonathan Holland writes of *Vampir.Cuadecuc*: "Thus is that the materiality of Gothic, the diaries, notebooks, newspaper examples of say, Dracula – allows the work to become, as a whole, a questioning of the authoritarian, manipulatory nature of classical narrative. When we consider the material conditions under which Portabella's work was made, in which the Franco regime controlled the narratives which were

It is important to retain the materiality of the spectre here, wittily and beautifully composed by the poet and artist Joan Brossa, Portabella's frequent collaborator and co-scriptwriter with him. The film is a composite of material objects – Stoker's book, Jesús Franco's film, Portabella's own film-within-a-film, the cameras, the lights, the technicians, and the actors, as well as the real politics of the Burgos trial. It exposes, overexposes, and infra-exposes anachronically all things and matters in a *phantasmic* way: props, lights, cameras; plasterboard sets, or the actors' faces being made up; dust, fog, and thunderstorms; fake spiders and spider webs that are even more fake; fake bodies, and fake blood. All things moving both in unison and in isolation, as though all were floating through a collapsed history. As such, there is one thing we must not overlook: The film's *"phantasmic* materialism," its spectral, infrapolitical Marxism, always already expressed by the quintessential cinematic materiality itself – celluloid.

The celluloid *thing* that makes the simultaneous unleashing of the spectre (Marxist and otherwise) in real and material terms possible, also turns the movie into an ominous Lacanian *dispositif*, allowing the traversing from "reel" to "real." Rolling its translucent body from time to time, movement to movement, and image to image, the *thing* that implicitly allows both the veiling and unveiling of the movie, which gives it its peculiar *phantasmic* material quality, is not celluloid in general but the specific piece of celluloid that sits at both ends of a reel: the Cuadecuc. *Cuadecuc* as the precise, unequivocal material that attaches itself both to *Vampir* (the reel), as well as to the modernist industrial history of Catalonia up to the Spanish Civil War and the legacies and revenants of Francoism (the real).

In Catalan, "cuadecuc" literally means a worm's (*cuc*) tail (*cua*), which is mostly indistinguishable from its head. In Catalan cinematic parlance however, it indicates the part of unexposed celluloid left at the beginning and at the end of the canned film roll, or in any case, what is left over in the making of a film. As it is used in Portabella's film title, the term *cuadecuc* seemingly refers to – one could logically assume – celluloid that was left unexposed during the making of Jesús Franco's Dracula movie, and then (re-)used, or reappropriated, by the director for the making of his own film. A spectrally made film then,

---

permitted for publication, it does not seem farfetched to assume that this deconstruction of the narrative by Portabella and his co-scriptwriter, Joan Brossa, should be using counter-cinema to question the Francoist use of narrative in constructing the myth of the dictator himself" (251).

that, having sucked the blood of the last roll of unexposed celluloid left over in Jesús Franco's *Count Dracula*, unleashes the spectre that becomes *Vampir.Cuadecuc*. The movie is "a ghostly film as well as the ghost of a film, and perhaps the ghost of cinema itself" (Hoberman); or, in Portabella's own words, "*Vampir*, no a pesar de todo, sino como resultado de todo" ("*Vampir*, not despite everything, but as a result of anything").[22] It is an example of a totally spectral cinema at its most uncanny: boldly playing with time and its folds, *Cuadecuc* is also a reminder or a remainder of a "wormhole" dangerously establishing contacts through shortcuts and folds in time.[23]

Cuadecuc, the spectral celluloid, is that wormhole. It collapses time and space into the present of the visualization, constantly moving towards exposure and away from it; a move that marks the movie as that X-ray imaging of the materiality of Francoism circa 1970, and, even most uncannily, of contemporary Spain at the end of the second decade of the twenty-first century. By way of having inserted a worm's tail (and wormhole) into the title, *Cuadecuc* inevitably casts a ghostly material shadow onto Portabella's whole exercise. Worms, maggots, tails, fangs, and spider webs; the decrepit, the decaying and the spectral, left over in that worm's tail of Jesús Franco's unexposed film, all re-emerge now in Portabella's movie, not only as a remaking of *Count Dracula*, but also as an infrapolitical exercise where General Franco, Francoism, and the Burgos trial are felt as vampire-like bites; not only in 1970 but also today.

From reel to real and from real to reel, film-maker(s), vampires, films, and politics traverse through each other, and in their paths, they come to touch one another, if only fleetingly. This touching happens at a precise point. On the dot, the period, the point that both joins and separates the one from the other: *Vampir* dot *Cuadecuc*. This dot simultaneously comes into being as an evocation of those other little dots, those two small punctures so notoriously left behind by the fangs of a vampire. The *punctum*. A black hole. In *Vampir* dot *Cuadecuc*, the dot, or point, simultaneously reveals and veils itself as the site par excellence

---

22 Portabella, presentation of *Vampir-Cuadecuc* at MoMa, 1972 (Holland). Quote and pictures (Christopher Lee as Dracula in Jesús Franco's *Count Dracula*; photo of Francisco Franco, unknown origin) taken from Jonathan Peter Holland's doctoral thesis, "Frankenstein in Castile."

23 A wormhole is the theoretical passage through space-time predicted by the theory of general relativity "able to create shortcuts … bringing with it the dangers of sudden collapse, high radiation and dangerous contact with exotic matter." A wormhole "is not really a means of going back in time, it's a short cut, so that something that was far away is much closer"; "Wormholes may not only connect two separate regions within the universe, they could also connect two different universes" (Redd).

from and within where the Reel spectrally engages with the Real. It is the spectral site, away from the limelight, and out of the symbolic order; from where the sudden veiling/unveiling of the "El proceso" clapperboard emerges both as a reference to the Burgos trial and to the title of Kafka's book, *The Trial*. It is within and because of the dot that the vampire becomes that spectral "Thing that thinks," as Slavoj Žižek shrewdly notes in his now classic reading of the Gothic novel.[24] A thing that in Portabella's movie thinks infrapolitically.

Vampir.Cuadecuc offers an infrapolitical proposition: Vampires can "think" only because they can take a step back, and, as "things," they live undead in a speck of dust – or, in our case, a dot – encroached upon a sort of folded "present" time. A time that is folded, deferred, extended, and out of joint. A time where the present, past, and future are undecidable propositions. Traversing genres, locations, people, and characters, the film, Jonathan Rosenbaum writes, "creates a ravishing netherworld that seems to exist in neither the nineteenth century nor the twentieth but in a unique zone oscillating between these eras, just as it seems to occupy a realm of its own that is neither fiction nor non-fiction" ("Review"). This would be the riddle in Portabella's *Vampir.Cuadecuc* (or one of them): to clearly make telling heads from tails impossible, dissolving the ability to assuredly discern the master of light from the master of night, film-maker from film, both from the vampire, and the vampire from dictator. To make it impossible also to sharply discern old dusty Transylvania from old Francoist Spain – and even, we could add, from the Spain of today. Graves, spectres, vampires, peoples, cities, and cemeteries trade places, transform, and move in extended time. Past plagues or future or present revolutions cannot be told apart, nor can the reel from the real, and the front from the back. As Lacan once told us: "There is no more 'reality of desire,' we would say, than it would be correct to say 'the back of the front': there is one and the same fabric that has a front and a back."

And yet, all of it is so very real. From genre to genre, from one register to another, from one movie to the next, Portabella's *Vampir.Cuadecuc* opens up as an alternate version of Jesús Franco's *Count Dracula*, as well

---

24 "The catastrophic consequences of the encroachment upon the forbidden impossible domain of the [Kantian] Thing are spelled out in the Gothic novel: it is by no means accidental that the Gothic novel, obsessed as it is with the motive of the Thing in its different embodiments (the "living dead" and so on), is contemporary to Kant's transcendental turn ... What are the spectres that appear if not apparitions of the Thing? ... The apparitions in the Gothic novels are precisely this: *Things that think*" (Žižek 220; original emphasis).

as an alternate real-present of General Franco's miserable and decaying Spain. "Cuadecuc" and the vampire are separated only, if so, by a speck of dust, a dot. *Vampir* dot *Cuadecuc*. The dot that enables Portabella to simultaneously be a porter and a "porta," in order to carry and traverse fantasy, that is, Lacan's *fantome*, since, as he has said,"*Pour faire la fantasme il faut du pret à le porter*" ("The Logic of Phantasy" 6). Likewise, from *Vampir.Cuadecuc* to *Cuadecuc.Vampir*, and from Reel to Real, and vice versa, Portabella the film-maker turns out to be both the gate *and* the porter, that according to Lacan, is needed in order to *make* fantasy (and carry it and traverse it). From 1970 to, at least, 2017.[25]

II. Traversing the Real with Kant, Lacan, and Sade: Albert Serra's *Història de la meva mort* (2013)

"Retouching the real with the real."
Robert Bresson, *Notes on the Cinematograph*

If in the first part of this essay I have discussed Pere Portabella's *Vampir. Cuadecuc* as a cinematic infrapolitical *dispositif* working out its spectral quality within a mathematical, out-of-joint, extended time framing, in the second half of the essay I present another cinematic *dispositif* that is also infrapolititcal: Serra's uncanny film *Història de la meva mort* (*Story of My Death*).[26] While these two films are wholly distinct – even in the ways in which they can be read as infrapolitical films – I believe it is important to present them side by side. Of course, the analysis of the two films could have been independently done, but when understood through a time out of joint, through still or extended time, their conversation with one another makes itself heard. As I hope to have shown with Portabella's film, Serra's film is also implicated through a Marrano spectrality, or an infrapolitical exercise wherein someone and/ or something (the figure of Giacomo Casanova and his memoirs, in this case) repeatedly becomes, echoes, someone or something other to itself (Dracula and Casanova).

In *Història de la meva mort*, time (and time-out-of-joint), humour and infrapolitics likewise play important roles. In Serra's case, the role

---

25 *Vampir.Cuadecuc* was first given the name *Cuadecuc.Vampir* in its 1972 original presentation at the MoMA, New York. It was not again released until 2017.
26 For a discussion on Serra's singular cinema, and his emphasis on "what is in front," see my article "Albert Serra's Digital Singularity," where many bibliographic references on Serra's work can be found.

of time is more closely aligned with the Lacanian relation between *fantome* (fantasy), desire, and reality – other tropes Serra's film reinforces through its study of the sexual and perverted nature of the f/phantom(e), making the phantom/spectre the ultimate "pret-à-porter" for reality: a cinematic montage, as it were, for the real, the symbolic, the imaginary ... and the phantom.[27] *Història*, like *Vampir*, plays with a vampire. A phantom. Unlike Portabella though, who works the phantom/vampire fantasy through the structure of extended time and its correlating figure of the nebula with batwings, Serra cinematically engages its own vampire through *still* time: a move corresponding therefore not with a nebula, but with a bubble. A Lacanian bubble, we could say, and its primordial surface:

> [I]n order to make phantasy something ready-to-wear-it is necessary. What carries (*porte*) the phantasy? It has two names, which concern one and the same substance ... [a] surface ... [that is, two] shapes of a primordial surface ... [which are required] to make our logical articulation function ... this surface which I call *bubble* has properly speaking two names, *desire* and *reality* ... It is quite useless to exhaust oneself in articulating the *reality* of *desire* because, primordially, desire and reality are related in a *seamless texture*. They have no need of needle work, they have no need to be sewn together." ("The Logic of Phantasy")

With exquisite and perverse detail, Serra renders the film fantasmatic, creating a spectral relation between Casanova and Dracula that unfolds on the primordial surface of the screen. Spectrality and the f/phantom(e) bubble. In *Història*, Casanova and Dracula are the porters for the f/phantom(e), the former operating mostly under the urges of desire, the latter doing so under the pull of reality. While Portabella was mostly letting *cuadecuc* spectrally open up from within the f/phantom(e) reality of a political time and age working in extended time, Serra digitally emphasizes the closing-in of time and space through cinematic push-ins and pull-outs (also known as travelling or tracking shots); the almost microscopic, punctilious, and parsimonious shrinking of the cinematic gaze so that it can "focus" unabashedly upon the real. A series of digital "closing-ins" and close-up shots that allow for

---

27 Jacques Lacan specifies that phantasm is of sexual nature, and its main function is to "veil" castration anxiety. It is for this reason this phantasm will always be of a perverse nature. Lacan ends up calling the phantom (the *phantasme*, the *fantome*) the "treasure of sexuality": "a flower in the branch of guilt."

the transporting of the real. These techniques allow the film to traverse the Real, actually Retouching the real with the Real, as Robert Bresson would perhaps say. *Història* works as f/phantom(e) and porter for all that once was present in front of the camera. The camera is their agent, the spectre quietly and relentlessly informing its digital primordial surface of all the real fantasmatic materiality it has to offer, of which image and sound, carnality and desire, infuse.

Desire plays a large part in all Serra's work. I will argue below that the exploration of pleasure, and its sense of perverse pleasure in Lacanian terminology, is indeed explicitly and overly present in *Història de la meva mort* as well as in Serra's cinematic take on Giacomo Casanova's memoir, *Histoire de ma vie*.[28] But it is through Serra's cinematic exercise that the literal and literary figure of the famous libertine (Casanova) is able to transport himself at the beginning of the movie to another time, as a spectre that has always already been. An always already aging and aged Casanova, a character brilliantly played by Vicenç Altaiò, is shown living a solitary life in a palace reminiscent of the Dux Castle in Bohemia – a place where the real Casanova lived from 1785 till his death in 1798 – working as a librarian for Count Waldstein, the owner of the castle. For all its uncanny literality to Casanova's text – let's think how this is also true for Pere Portabella's *Vampir.Cuadecuc* in reference to both Bram Stoker's text and J. Franco's *Count Dracula* – Serra's film is not, or not totally, a cinematic interpretation of Giacomo Casanova's real memoirs. Instead, it offers itself as an intervention; a travelling – a transposition; a moving of sorts (it is, after all, cinema) – where Casanova meets Dracula, and vice versa, the latter played by a phenomenal Eliseu Huertas.

The movie, and its movement, however, does not take us from one point (Casanova) to another (Dracula); or, from a particular time period (let's say the time of the European revolutions circa 1789) to another (let's say, the Romantic period, or even to today) – in fact, all are present,

---

28 Giacomo Casanova was born in Venice in 1675. His parents were actors, most likely with ancestry going back to Sephardic Jews. Casanova, a freethinking libertine, led the travelling life of an adventurer: a spy, a lover, and a bon vivant, always short of money. He was suspected by the Inquisition of being a freemason (he was) and a magician (he was attracted by magic), and he spent time in prison for debts owed. Always on the go, and an avid reader and writer, he is best known for his memoir, *Histoire de ma vie*, a monumental work he wrote during his stay at the Dux Castle in Switzerland six years before dying of a urinary infection in 1798. His last words are reputed to be, "I have lived as a philosopher, and I die as a Christian" (Puppa and Somigli).

and all coexist fantasmatically. There is no linear arc of time in this film. As indicated by its very title, this is the story of Casanova's *death*, not of his life; and we therefore have to assume that what the movie shows, from beginning to end, is always already spectral. Serra, similarly to what Pere Portabella did with *Vampir.Cuadecuc*, gives a fantasmatic materiality to two of the most immaterial concepts, death and pleasure. *Història* does so by spectrally decoupling the figure of the gayest of lovers, Casanova, to the saddest of all figures, Dracula. That is, through the presentation of Casanova, the ultimate embodiment of living pleasure, not as one figure, but two (always already dead ones): Casanova as himself, and Dracula as Casanova (and vice versa). Both doomed to bear, as Richard Brody once stated, the "quiet weight of world-historical conflict." Both being one and the same, both inhabiting the heart of the movie; both sharing by blood their own unworldly relating to and communicating with the world, and with the real: the two men "don't have much to say to each other. Rather, they seem to communicate by way of blood, as when the traces of Casanova's sexual curiosity lure Dracula to one of his victims" (Brody).

From the very beginning, Serra's film spectrally traces Casanova's becoming Dracula. Casanova's actual exiting or vanishing, from his specific time and history, toward the next wand of time, inhabited as Dracula. Very much like Paul Klee's angel of history, which Walter Benjamin froze in flight forever, it brings with it the static and destructive experience of the traversing of modernity. From the age of the enlightenment to the dark side of Romanticism; from the French ancien régime to the new Age of Revolutions, Serra's *static* cinematic transposition – or a transposition in cinematic stasis – as opposed to Portabella's traversing in *movement*, is able to energize a brilliant and quite unexpected monstrance of life, pleasure, and death at the dawn of secular modernization.

No longer a memoir, but an intervention then, *Història de la meva mort* is a deconstructive, minimalistic reassemblage/deassemblage of *Histoire de ma vie*. Serra's film unfolds as Giacomo Casanova's story in reverse – an uncanny companion. Moving statically in sync to Marc Veragués's and Ferran Font's score, expressly composed for the film, and to pieces by Fauré and Bach,[29] *Història de la meva mort* traces some of what *Histoire de ma vie* left unsaid, untouched, and unseen.

---

29 Marc Verdagués, a designer and musician, wrote "Burn," "Trill," and "Brass Lament" for *Història de la meva mort* at Serra's request. Ferran Font is the composer of "Carretera," Ball," and "Duetta" (*Història de la meva mort*). He also composed for Serra's *Cuba Libre* (*Free Cuba*, 2013), *Els noms de Crist* (*Christ's Names*, 2010), and *Quixòtic/Honor de cavalleria* (*Honour of the Knights*, 2006).

Serra stays close to the spirit of Casanova's original text, transporting the literary qualities of the latter (its period modes, thinking, scenery, and events, all evocative) to a correspondent cinematic visual imaginary. Filmed in sombre milky and ochre tones, and shot with three digital cameras in a 4:3 ratio later converted to 35 mm, 2.35:1 CinemaScope view ratio, the movie takes on a strong, eerie, painterly tonality that echoes the time and spirit of Casanova's memoirs.[30] The late and decadent rococo period setting of the Swiss Castle in the first half of the film, delivered by Serra in fabulous Rubenesque and Vermeerian tones and accompanied by period music played at the clavichord, gives way, in the second half, to a much darker setting in the Carpathian Mountains. Beautifully shot by Jimmy Gimferrer, *Història de la meva mort* slowly darkens its sequences with images going from the milky-light tones of a Vermeer to the night scenes texturized in tones reminiscent of the tenebrist paintings of the Spanish baroque.

Most likely, Giacomo Casanova's *Histoire de ma vie* was born with a therapeutic aim in mind. At the Dux Castle, mocked by the servants and ignored by his host, Count Waldstein, Casanova suffers from melancholia and isolation. The writing of his memoirs allows him "to live life again, recalling happy experiences with retrospective pleasure. From this premise, his decision to end his account in the year 1774 seems clear: After the age of 40, all he would have to record would be a tale of declining vigour and increasing melancholy" (Puppa and Somigli 401). Serra's cinematic story, however, does not offer itself as therapy. On the contrary, the film, "a total magma of despair and crazy ideas," as the director himself describes it, takes off where and when the real memoir ends, and shows us an already old, decrepit, and very mortal Casanova happily engaging in infant developmental pleasures of the

---

30 Albert Serra explains the aspect ratio of *Història de la meva mort*: "The cameramen shot the film for 4:3, and in the middle of the shooting I realized it was better in 2.35. But I didn't tell them. So they composed the whole film for 4:3, which is exactly the opposite of 2.35. But then you get an image that is very strange, sometimes, because there is a lot of empty space, an absurd composition, because in editing I had to choose the upper part or the lower part, and this creates a completely new compositional style. So I think my main contribution was simply that, not telling the cinematographer during the shooting. But I'm rarely focussed on the composition of the shot, because I'm shooting with two or three cameras, depending on the scene, on the place, and I give the cinematographers a lot of freedom. I check the frame very rarely, only in a few cases. Here the idea was brilliant ... it's new. It never looks like it was composed because it was not composed! It was composed for 4:3, and it's absolutely the opposite of 2.35" (https://m.imdb.com/name/nm2247200/?ref_=m_nmqu_qu.).

Figure 7.6 Vicenç Altaió as Casanova in Albert Serra's *Història de la meva mort*.

body: oral, anal, and haptic (Cronk). The film takes the figure of the libertine from or beyond the physicality of life and pleasure, and into the domain of the spectral but no less pleasurable materiality of that which is left undead – to age and to die (see figure 7.6).

Echoing Casanova's depiction of his time travelling through the Swiss and the Carpathian Mountains, Serra's Casanova leaves the palace and travels through the country towards an unnamed Transylvania, taking with him a servant/companion, Pompeu, a gambler who will serve as his ear, played by Lluís Serrat in a role reminiscent of his Sancho Panza in Serra's *Quixòtic/Honor de cavalleria* (*Honour of the Knights*, 2006). In the mountains, Serra's Casanova stays with Pompeu at the inn described by Casanova in his memoirs: a rural hostel kept by the innkeeper and his three daughters. A hostel that in Serra's film reminds us of Immanuel Kant's joke of the satirical inscription he found on a sign at a Dutch inn, "Inn of the Perpetual Peace," a sign that the innkeeper had taken from a churchyard cemetery.[31] It is in this sort of sepulchral Kantian Inn of the Perpetual Peace where Casanova will be made to encounter his alter ego, Dracula, and where he will turn into the latter.

From northern European lights to central darkness, Serra casts a long shadow on the years before (and then after) the French Revolution.

---

31 Immanuel Kant opens his 1795 philosophical sketch, *Perpetual Peace*, with this note: "Whether this satirical inscription on a Dutch innkeeper's sign upon which a burial ground was painted had for its object mankind in general, or the rulers of states in particular, who are insatiable of war, or merely the philosophers who dream this sweet dream, it is not for us to decide."

Those years echoed in the film (1774 to 1798) are precisely when the drums of war and revolution were making noise in Europe. At the inn, and addressing his servant Pompeu on love, women, history, desire, and pleasure, Serra's Casanova is often seen ruminating over the state of things in Europe, and the state of nature. And yet, expecting neither a reply nor addressing any one person in particular, Casanova then offers his musings over the encyclopaedic illustration and his already (pre-) Romantic times: on the age of absolutist monarchy and the republic, on political theology and secularization, on Christianity and atheism – the relations between church and state sit at the heart of the movie in a very particular way. But it would be a mistake to call *Història de la meva mort* a militant or political film. Instead, it twists these political relations with those already present in Casanova's original text, which are also set in a Marrano register. There is an infrapolitical twist at play here. By interpolating the manner he does a fictitious morphing/encounter between Casanova and his very unusual Dracula, Serra's cinematic text ultimately takes a step back from the helio-politics of a modernization to come – its technologies, and its discontents ready to erupt and emerge with the Revolution. Similar, though all too different, to the way Portabella does in *Vampir.Cuadecuc*, Serra steps back from the helio-politics of the time.

By way of infrapolitically stepping back and of looking awry, by placing his Casanova-turned-Dracula in and around the unnamed inn of perpetually spectral peace, *Història de la meva mort* takes a long, paused, quiet, and very deep look at the storm and impetus of the period. In the film, the images feel almost frozen and the scenes are never arranged in sequential time. Light, sound, and movement speak to one other, they echo one another, they let each other be. Each are felt in a sort of Heideggerian existential way – all and everything steps back and out of sequential time. It is not *in*, *within*, *on*, or *about* time; the film *is* (frozen) time. It engages with temporality in a Heideggerian letting-it-be manner, through an ecstatic interpretation of original, or primordial, temporality.[32] As such, the movie always takes its time, always takes its still, ecstatic, and eerie time. It conjures the union of sound and image, letting them be until consumption (see figure 7.7). Letting for example the crackling of a fire, or the eating of a pomegranate, or the sound of defecation be one with their visualization until their own end.

---

32 See Heidegger, *Being and Time*, Section 65; see also Krell, *Ecstasy, Catastrophe: Heidegger from "Being and Time" to the "Black Notebooks."*

Figure 7.7 Vicenç Altaió as Casanova in Albert Serra's *Història de la meva mort*.

Ecstatic, still time is related to death and to the spectral. In forcing the encounter between a creepy-laughing Casanova and a stiff Kantian-like Dracula touched by a whiff of existential anguish, *Història de la meva mort* shines a surprising light onto the fate of modern (and contemporary) history. The dream/sleep of reason foreseen by Goya just a few years after Casanova's death indeed generated monsters. Dracula itself is one of them.

But with its understanding of the f/phantom(e) as that pret-à-porter "thing" articulating desire and phantasy Lacan was pointing to, and by fiercely letting the perverse sexual logic of the phantom be, Serra's eerily happy Casanova, in his pursuit of pleasure, twists the horrors of Goya and history without giving into the conditionals of a Kantian perpetual peace; or for that matter, the sad, cold, dry conditions of a Marquis de Sade one. True, from the illustrated philosophies of the eighteenth century on, from Voltaire to Kant to Sade and beyond, "El sueño de la razón" will produce monsters such as the horrors of the Napoleonic wars, the Holocaust, and now, our techno-wars. And the libertine's focus on the pursuit of sexual and bodily pleasures will not be able to escape that fate. But unlike Sade, Casanova does not subscribe to the dictum, "in order to know virtue, we must first acquaint ourselves with vice"; or the banal, "'sex' is as important as eating or drinking and we ought to allow the one appetite to be satisfied with as little restraint or false modesty as the other." Serra's Casanova, very much in line with his historical persona, while a necessary pervert, does not share the sort of malevolent libertine qualities attributable to Sade's characters. He is not, however, either a benevolent libertine such as the one portrayed in Lydia Flem's book, *Casanova: The Man Who Really*

Figure 7.8 Eliseu Huertas as Dracula in Albert Serra's *Història de la meva mort*.

Loved Women. Flem, a psychoanalyst, is, like Serra, very sympathetic towards her character. She, like Serra, presents him already from the very beginning as an exiled old man writing the history of his life in the Bohemian Dux Castle where he, at peace with himself and having given everything up, has "no possessions, no woman, no fortune, no house, no homeland. He gave and received freely, without calculation" (3) In his youth, Casanova enjoyed life "as few men – an even fewer women – have dared enjoyed it. He threw himself into life and required nothing in return except that most insolent, most scandalous of rewards: pleasure." Now at the end of his life, Casanova is "surrounded by death." And yet, writes Flem, today as yesterday, "he has a taste for happiness ... Whether worthy or unworthy, his life is his material and his material is his life. He has no other and he cherishes it."

Serra's beloved libertine is also pure pleasure. Except that Serra's Casanova, unlike Flem's, is working through the story of his death, not his life. Using life as cinematic material, and cinematic material as life, Serra's story unexpectedly leads us not to the open safe skies that Dante wanted to see while in Hell (*"E quindi uscimmo a riveder le stelle,"* Inferno XXXIV 139), but the sort of dark non-time, non-space where life and death are made indistinct, purely spectral materials. The stars Serra's Casanova/Dracula contemplates at the end of his life are shining a black light on a black sky (see figure 7.8).

And it is in Casanova's moment of perfect, ecstatic writing while at the Inn of the Perpetual Peace, "suspended between yesterday and tomorrow," where he unreservedly surrenders "to the pure present, pure loss," and where Serra, with his daring, and knowing no bounds, inserts the figure of Dracula.

Uncannily, and unlike the libertines portrayed by the Marquis de Sade, an almost contemporaneous historical figure with Casanova, Serra's singular libertine ethics emanates from the spectral non-site the film gives us: a painterly visualization of an infra-world. With *Història de la meva mort*, Serra forces Casanova to depart from the word of the living and morph into Dracula – the spectre living on the other side of the river, in the world of the undead. And in doing so, Serra forces us to enter into what Jacques Derrida called "another world, another source of phenomenality, another degree zero of an appearing ... a singularity on the basis of which a world is opened" (*Spectographies* 123). It is within the spectral quality of Serra's text that his libertine will morph into a Dracula – just as Bela Lugosi moved from playing Casanova in Alfréd Deésy's 1918 movie, to playing Dracula in Tod Browning's 1931 movie. Serra's depiction of Dracula pays homage to all the cinematic Draculas that come before his, from F.W. Murnaus's 1922 *Nosferatu* to Herzog's, Coppola's, and of course to J. Franco's and Pere Portabella's Dracula played by Christopher Lee. *Història* pays tribute to all previous depictions of Casanova, from Deésy's to Federico Fellini's. Serra's humorous cinematic quote on Lugosi's path involves, however, way more than a pun, since it is precisely Casanova's plunge into the spectral, his move from Reason to other than Evil – that is, Dracula – which lands him into the infrapolitical space; away, far away, from the "happiness in evil" theme already insinuating itself at the dawn of the nineteenth century. As Jacques Lacan says in "Kant with Sade":

> If Freud was able to enunciate his pleasure principle without even having to worry about marking what distinguishes it from its function in traditional ethics ... we can only credit this to the insinuating rise across the nineteenth century of the theme of "happiness in evil." / Here Sade is the inaugural step of a subversion, of which, however amusing it might seem with respect to the coldness of the man, Kant is the turning point, and never noted, to our knowledge, as such.

It is the infrapolitical, spectral-Marrano singularity present in Serra's film that actually frees his movie of having to make Sade Kant's "turning point." *Història*'s mode and tone, and by extension, all of Serra's texts to date, are far removed from Sade's texts, far removed from their humourless and strictly anti-Catholic perversions. On the contrary, with Serra, even noting his constant play with Catholic iconography in all his work, Casanova's and Dracula's pains and desires burst with humour and infrapolitical Marranity – a register also present actually in Casanova's real memoirs, but not often noted. Serra's Casanova-turned-Dracula is not the bearer of any anti-Christian ethics, nor of Christian ones – a role, the latter, that Lacan attributes to Sade: "Sadian fantasy situates itself better in the bearers of Christian ethics than elsewhere" ("Kant with Sade"). Casanova's cinematic memoirs are alien to Sade's purposes if not for all reasons, then for one: Serra's Dracula is Casanova's own figment of his imagination, made by his own fantasmatic, and cinematic, materiality. Casanova and Dracula are one and the same, as shown at the very end of the movie when Casanova dies, and when his last image is replaced by Dracula's, howling in the dark. Born out of the fire set by the Revolution, the end of the movie shows Dracula as Casanova's flesh-morphing future.

Serra's Casanova-turned-Dracula is not a monster coming out of Goya's dream (or sleep) of Reason. *Història de la meva mort*, set just a few years before the start of the French Revolution, has been described by critics as depicting a clash of two philosophical trains, a frontal collision between the old world and the new: a time when Revolution sweeps across Europe, Kantian reason gives way to progress and to the republic, and the Enlightenment gives way to Romanticism. A time when the real Casanova, then in the Dux Castle, was occupied with his memoirs. A time, writes Flem, when "the French Revolution is rumbling beyond the mountain, and his best friends are dying, and the women he loved are departing from this life"; a time "when the old world, to which he feels he still belongs, is being mocked, insulted, guillotined"; a time when "the new values he holds dear – individual freedom, the power of the Enlightenment and Reason, atheism – are not yet widely accepted" (3). But in Serra's Casanova, the good historical libertine portrayed by Flem safely (or unsafely) seated on the train that holds dear the power of Enlightenment and Reason, does not hold. Sure, Serra's Casanova, just like the historical figure, is a freethinker, a mason: an eighteenth-century libertine philosopher in pursuit of sexual pleasure, and usually in debt. He is a wanderer, always on the move, trying to escape revenge, death, and prison, and seemingly unrestrained and/or unconcerned by the laws of church and state, by morality and convention. But he is not a benevolent figure, just as he is not a malevolent one either – the latter qualification is usually given to Sade's libertine characters, not to Casanova.

Serra's Casanova-tuned-Dracula is an undead libertine in pursuit of sexual pleasure: a phantom, a ghost, a spectre. He is never a Supreme Being-turned-Maleficence as Sade's figures can be; neither he nor Dracula are evil, nor are the times in the film. Neither are the three girls – the innkeeper's daughters – Serra's Three Graces who gave themselves to Dracula, and who are muses of fertility no more; nor are their father and mother, nor are the peasants, who are all living under Dracula's spell. Serra's *Història* flows close to history and politics, morals, and ethics, close to the law, the church, the police, and the state. But, like Portabella's *Vampir.Cuadecuc*, it flows through their shadows, and casts a shadow onto them in return. Touching life, it reveals the infra-world of the undead. And as such, neither Serra's Casanova nor his Dracula are guilty of any crime (not even sexual ones). In fact, they are "saints," giving the term a Gracianesque undertone; that is, of being secular saints in the sense upheld by the three qualities necessary to achieve sanctity, such as Baltasar Gracián, the minimalist baroque Jesuit-marranesque thinker underlined in *The Art of Prudence*: Silence (oracular laconism); Absence (to eclipse in order to let presence be); and Showing or "Presencing;" "el parecer" (to seem), "el mostrar" (to show), "la muestra" (the showing). For if Gracián says that (spectral) presencing is precisely that which offers itself as food for thought, the nourishment capable of arousing in us the desire to know – or, simply, desire – then we can add that it is precisely that kind of spectral desire that Serra, in *Història*, is able to arouse in us. A (visual) passion of the mind. A Spinozian pathema similar to but altogether different in its exercise to that one Portabella exercises in *Vampir.Cuadecuc*. A cinematic nourishment, a visualization that allows an alternate opening into the history of the world: one that does not necessarily lead from Kant to Sade in the pursuit of pleasure, but, unexpectedly, from Kant, via Casanova, to a Dracula left to forever live at the Inn of the Perpetual Peace.

Serra's libertine-turned-Dracula is a practical man who dreams not of the sweet dream of perpetual peace but of another kind of enlightenment. Lacan noted how, in *La philosophie dans le boudoir*, for Sade "The apology for crime only pushes him to the indirect avowal of the Law. The supreme Being is restored in Maleficence. ... Of a treatise truly about desire, there is thus little here, even nothing. What of it is announced in this crossing taken from an Encounter, is at most a tone of reason" ("Kant With Sade" 74–5). In *Història*, Casanova and Dracula's libertine encounters are of another kind. A Marrano, the infrapolitical kind, cinematically achieved by Serra, by quietly engaging his Casanova/Dracula character not with Sade's characters but with the figure of the baroque libertine. The kind of libertine that, according to Michel Onfray, in following the dictate of "a bodily, or corporeal, reason" and "an imminent, material logic" establishes a direct affiliation with Montaigne.[33] A thinker of the Marrano register, that Montaigne. A thinker who Albert Serra, perhaps our ultimate, contemporary vampire, from real to real may have also touched in passing. Or will.

WORKS CITED

Agustí, Ignacio. *Mariona Rebull*. Castalia, 2006.
"Anarcoefemèrides." *Anarcoefemèrides*, anarcoefemerides.balearweb.net/post/42002. Accessed 29 Dec. 2020.
Arrebato. Directed by Ivan Zulueta, performances by Eusebio Poncela, Cecilia Roth, Will More, Nicolás Astariaga, P.C., 1979.
Bishop, Karen Lynn. *Documenting Institutional Identity: Strategic Writing in the IUPUI Comprehensive Campaign*. 2002. Purdue University, PhD dissertation.
Bresson, Robert. *Notes on the Cinematograph*. Translated by Jonathan Griffin, Urizen Books, 1977.
Brody, Richard. "Albert Serra's Story of My Death." *The New Yorker*, 20 Nov. 2014, https://www.newyorker.com/culture/richard-brody/casanova-meets-dracula.
Cacciari, Mario. "Lo impolitico nietzschiano." *Desde Nietzsche: Tiempo, arte y política*. Translated by Mónica B. Cragnolini and Ana Paternostro, Biblos, 1994, pp. 61–79.

---

33 Onfray points out that the baroque libertine "knows Montaignes's *Essays*." He goes on to affirm that we can barely find one libertine idea that is not already addressed implicitly or explicitly in the *Essays*. His list of baroque libertine thinkers amounts to six, all of them French, except for Spinoza, whom Onfray finds necessary to include. All coming of age at the time of the brutal religious wars in France, and all taking "a Montaignesque, sceptic stand towards morality and reason, directing, like Montaigne did, the sceptical arguments over how we can never have knowledge over what is universally right and wrong towards the fact that we can find within ourselves 'some firm convictions about the rights or wrongs of actions'" (Wee 209).

Casanova, Giacomo. *Histoire de ma vie*. 1789–98, edited by Jean-Christophe Igalens and Erik Leborgne, Bouquins, 2013–18.
Casas, Ramón. *El Liceu*. 1901–2, Cercle del Liceu, Barcelona.
El cochecito. Directed by Marco Ferreri, performances by José Isbert, Jose Luis López Vazquez, Films 59, 1960.
Count Dracula. Directed by Jesús Franco, performances by Christopher Lee, Herbert Lom, Filmar Compagnia Cinematografica, 1970.
Cronk, Jordan. "Cannes Interview: Albert Serra." *Film Comment*, 23 May 2016, www.filmcomment.com/blog/cannes-interview-albert-serra. Accessed 28 Dec. 2020.
Dante Alighieri. "The Project Gutenberg E-Text of *La Divina Commedia* de Dante, by Dante Alighieri." *Project Gutenberg*, 1327, www.gutenberg.org/files/1012/1012-h/1012-h.htm. Accessed 28 Dec. 2020.
Derrida, Jacques. *Spectres of Marx*. Translated by Peggy Kamuf, Routledge, 2006.
– "Spectographies." Jacques Derrida and Bernard Stiegler, *Echographies of Televison: Filmed Interviews*, Polity, 2002 (last edition, 2018), pp. 113–34.
– "Time Is Out of Joint." In *Deconstruction Is/In America*, edited by Anselm Haverkamp, New York University Press, 1995, pp. 14–38.
Epps, Brad. "The Space of the Vampire: Materiality and Disappearance in the Films of Iván Zulueta." *A Companion of Spanish Cinema*, edited by Jo Labanyi, and Tatjana Pavlovic, Wiley-Blackwell, pp. 581–96.
Espriu, Salvador. *Cementiri de Sinera*. *Obres Completes*. Vol. 10, Edicions 62, 2006.
– *Llibre de Sinera*. *Obres Completes*. Vol. 13, Edicions 62, 2006.
– *Ronda de mort a Sinera*. *Obres Completes*. Vol. 14, Edicions 62, 2006.
Expósito, Marcelo. "Pere Portabella: Pondering Complexity Through Cinema. In Conversation with Marcelo Expósito." *Catalogue of the Exhibition Experiments with Truth*, edited by Mark Nash for The Fabric Workshop and Museum, Philadelphia, 2005. https://marceloexposito.net/pdf/exposito_portabellaentrevista_en.pdf. Accessed 29 Dec. 2020.
Krell, David Farrell. *Ecstasy, Catastrophe: Heidegger from "Being and Time" to the "Black Notebooks"*. SUNY P, 2015.
Flem, Lydia. *Casanova: The Man Who Really Loved Women*. Translated by Catherine Temerson. Farrar, Straus & Girous, 1997.
Galt, Rosalind. "Mapping Catalonia in 1967: The Barcelona School in Global Context." *Senses of Cinema*, November 2006, www.sensesofcinema.com/2006/feature-articles/barcelona-school. Accessed 29 Dec. 2020.
Los golfos. Directed by Carlos Saura, performances by Manuel Zarzo and Luis Marín, Films 59, 1960.
Heidegger, Martin. *Being and Time*. Harper Perennial Modern Thought. Reprint, Harper Perennial Modern Classics, 2008.

Hoberman, J. "Elusive Vampire Film Steps Out of the Shadows." *The New York Times*, 22 Dec. 2017. https://www.nytimes.com/2017/12/22/movies/elusive-vampire-film-steps-out-of-the-shadows.html. Accessed 29 Dec. 2020.

Holland, Jonathan Peter. *Frankenstein in Castile: The Uses of the British Literary Gothic in Spanish Cinema after Franco*. 2013. Universidad Complutense de Madrid. PhD dissertation.

Kant, Immanuel. "*Perpetual Peace*, by Immanuel Kant – A Project Gutenberg EBook." *Project Gutenberg*, 1795, www.gutenberg.org/files/50922/50922-h/50922-h.htm. Accessed 29 Dec. 2020.

Karothy, Rolando. "Puntuación de escritos, II: Kant con Sade." *Seminario en la Escuela Freudiana de Buenos Aires* (17-9-1996). http://www.efbaires.com.ar/files/texts/TextoOnline_1216.pdf. Accessed 29 Dec. 2020.

Lacan, Jacques. "The Logic of Phantasy." *The Seminar of Jacques Lacan 1966–1967 Book XIV*. Translated by Cormac Gallagher, http://www.lacaninireland.com/web/wp-content/uploads/2010/06/THE-SEMINAR-OF-JACQUES-LACAN-XIV.pdf. Accessed 29 Dec. 2020.

Lacan, Jacques, and James B. Swenson. "Kant with Sade." *October*, vol. 51, 1989, pp. 55–75. *JSTOR*, https://doi.org/10.2307/778891. Accessed 19 Nov. 2023.

Laclau, Ernesto. "'The Time Is out of Joint.'" *Diacritics*, vol. 25, no. 2, 1995, pp. 86–96. *JSTOR*, www.jstor.org/stable/465146. Accessed 29 Dec. 2020.

Marsh, Steven. "The Legacies of Pere Portabella: Between Heritage and Inheritance." *Hispanic Review*, vol. 78, no. 4, 2010, pp. 551–67. *JSTOR*, www.jstor.org/stable/25790602. Accessed 29 Dec. 2020.

Marti-Olivella, Jaume. "Catalan Cinema. An Uncanny Transnational Performance." *A Companion to Catalan Culture*, edited by Dominic Kewon, Tamesis, 2011, pp. 185–206.

Moreiras, Alberto. "Cabeza's A-Positional Freedom." *Infrapolitical Deconstruction (and Other Issues Related and Unrelated.)*, 6 Oct. 2014, infrapolitica.com/category/marrano/page/2. Accessed 20 Dec. 2020.

– "On the Infrapolitical Image. Prep Notes for Conversation with Tarek Elhaik (U of California-Davis, April 24, 2017)." *Infrapolitical Deconstruction (and Other Issues Related and Unrelated.)*, 26 Apr. 2017, infrapolitica.com/2017/04/26/on-the-infrapolitical-image-prep-notes-for-conversation-with-tarek-elhaik-u-of-california-davis-april-24-2017. Accessed 20 Dec. 2020.

National Film and Sound Archive. "Original Sound Negative | NFSA." *National Film and Sound Archive*, www.nfsa.gov.au/preservation/preservation-glossary/original-sound-negative. Accessed 29 Dec. 2020.

Nobus, Dany. *The Law of Desire: On "Lacan with Sade."* Palgrave, 2017.

La novia ensangrentada. Vicente Aranda, director, performances by Simón Andreu, Maribel Marín, Morgana Films, 1972.

Onfray, Michel. "Les libertines baroques." *Contre-Histoire de la Philosphie.*, vol. 3. Grasset, 2007.

Permanyer, Lluis. "Un día en la memoria de Barcelona: Una bomba y una carta del asesino cierran la historia del atentado en el Liceo de Barcelona," *La Vanguardia*. 6 Nov. 1990, pp. 2–3. https://tertulieshistoria.files.wordpress.com/2011/04/vanguardia_06_11_19902.pdf. Accessed 20 Dec. 2020.

Portabella, Pere, Director. http://www.pereportabella.com.

– *Acció Santos*. Performances by Carles Santos, Films 59, 1973.

– *No compteu amb els dits*. Performances by Mario Cabré, Josep Centelles, Natacha Gounkevich, Films 59, 1968.

– *Playback*. Performances by Carles Santos, Films 59, 1970.

– *Umbracle*. Performances by Christopher Lee, Jeanine Mestre, Films 59, 1971.

– *Vampir.Cuadecuc*. Performances by Christopher Lee, Herbert Lom, Soledad Miranda, Films 59, 1970. http://www.pereportabella.com/en/features/features/vampir-cuadecuc-en; http://pereportabella.com/en/documents/2009/03/screening-of-vampir-cuadecuc-in-moma-1972-en.

Puppa, Paolo, and Luca Somigli, editors. *Encyclopaedia of Italian Literary Studies*. Gaetana Marrone, general editor. Vol. 1, (A-J). Routledge/Taylor & Francis, 2007.

Redd, Nola Taylor. "What Is Wormhole Theory?" *Space.Com*, 21 Oct. 2017, www.space.com/20881-wormholes.html. Accessed 28 December 2020.

Riambau, Esteve, and Casimiro Torreiro, *La Escuela de Barcelona: El cine de la "gauche divine."* Anagrama, 2006.

Rosenbaum, Jonathan. "Review Excerpt" *Vampir.Cuadecuc*. Second Run, 2017.

– "Introducing Pere Portabella." *Goodbye Cinema, Hello Cinephilia: Film Culture in Translation*. U of Chicago P, 2010.

– "Trying to Compute *Don't Count on Your Fingers*." *Jonathan Rosenbaum*, 2 Mar. 2009, www.jonathanrosenbaum.net/2009/03/trying-to-compute-dont-count-on-your-fingers. Accessed 20 Dec. 2020.

Sade, Marquis de. *Philosophy in the Boudoir: Or, The Immoral Mentors (Penguin Classics Deluxe Edition)*. Penguin Classics Deluxe ed., Penguin Classics, 2006.

Salvat, Ricard. *Ronda de mort a Sinera*. Catalan/Castilian edition. Barcelona: Barri gòtic, 1966.

Savitt, Steven. "Being and Becoming in Modern Physics." *The Stanford Encyclopaedia of Philosophy* (Fall 2017 Edition), edited by Edward N. Zalta, https://plato.stanford.edu/archives/fall2017/entries/spacetime-bebecome. Accessed 20 Dec. 2020.

Serra, Albert, director. *Cuba Libre*. Performances by Albert Serra, Lluís Carbó, and Lluís Serrat, producer Montse Triola, 2013.

– *Els noms de Crist*. Performances by Albert Serra, Lluís Serrat, and Montse Triola, producer Abert Serra, 2010.

– *Història de la meva mort*. Performances by Vicenç Alataió, Luís Serrat, Eliseu Huertas, Andergraun Films, 2013.

- *Quixotic/Honour de cavalleria*. Performances by Lluís Serrat, Lluís Carbó, and Jimmy Gimferrer, producers Albert Serra and Montse Triola, 2006.
Spinoza, Benedict. *Ethics*. Translated by Edwin Curley, Penguin Classics, 2005.
Verdagués, Marc. "Cartell 'Història de la meva mort' d'Albert Serra." 2013. http://cargocollective.com/marcverdaguer/Cartell-Historia-de-la-meva-mort-d-Albert-Serra. Accessed 20 Dec. 2020.
Vilarós, Teresa M. "Albert Serra's Digital Singularity." *Revista de Estudios Hispánicos*, vol. 52, no. 2, 2018, pp. 375–405. Doi:10.1353/rvs.2018.0060.
- "Barcelona come piedras: la impolítica mirada de Jacinto Esteva y Joaquim Jordà en *Dante no es únicamente severo*." *Hispanic Review*, vol. 78, no. 4, 2010, pp. 513–28.
- "Salvador Espriu and the Marrano Home of Language." *Writers in Between Languages. Minority Literatures in the Global Scene*, edited by Mari Jose Olaregi, Center of Basque Studies, University of Nevada, 2009, pp. 267–90.
Viridiana. Directed by Luis Buñuel, performances by Silvia Pinal, Francisco Rabal, Fernando Rey, Films 59, 1961.
Wee, Cecilia. "Montaigne on Reason, Morality and Faith." *History of Philosophy Quarterly*, vol. 28, no. 3, 2011, pp. 209–26. JSTOR, www.jstor.org/stable/23032338. Accessed 29 Dec. 2020.
Žižek, Slavoj. *For They Know Not What They Do: Enjoyment as a Political Factor*. Verso, 1991.
Zunzunegui, Santos. "Strategic Auteurism. Pere Portabella: The Politics and Esthetics of Auteurism." *A Companion of Spanish Cinema*, edited by Jo Labanyi, and Tatjana Pavlovic, Wiley-Blackwell, 2012, pp. 171–5.

PART FOUR

The New (Post) Avant-Garde

8 Beyond Melancholy: The Post-Avant-Garde Cinema of José Luis Guerín

JOSEP MARIA CATALÀ DOMÈNECH

Dante lived in a time when men still had visions.

T.S. Eliot

Melancholy is the joy of being sad.

Víctor Hugo

The documentary film, or better yet, what we perceive to be a documentary film, is based on some bizarre myth that accepts that its images are just direct and immediate takes of reality. No matter how much we discuss it or consider it, there is always an element, whether anthropologically or genetically inserted, that makes us unconsciously believe that an image has real value, even though we might even be convinced that this value is a cultural or subjective construction. That is why we believe that in the documentary genre the director's role is that of a witness – at least, that is what it should be. Marshall McLuhan argued that the camera is an extension of the eye. Then, we could argue that the eye is a mere extension of the camera: if this were the case, film directors would just watch or, in the best of circumstances, they would just look from behind the lens. This means that documentary images, along with photographs, are the simplest of all images. It is not so much that we think about it this way, but rather we feel this way. However, such an attitude is bound to create confusion and, most importantly, it prevents us from comprehending the true nature of documentary images.

If we are to understand the complex works of film-makers such as José Luis Guerín, then the above apriorism must be ignored. Guerín's works are far from observational, regardless of how they seem. For documentarists, there is a space that might not always be considered, but one that is both creative and conceptual and both dramatic and cerebral. This particular space stands between the two hegemonic modes of observing and intervening. It is indeed a space of the mind because it places the film-maker's subjective disposition in front of the reality to be filmed, and it is composed of a dramatic or technical space because it determines the characteristics of the filmed images. Throughout this essay I will examine how this dual space functions because, in my opinion, it is the origin of Guerín's cinema.

Elsewhere I have written about Guerín's films considering not the gaze but, rather, the act of gazing (Català, *El hombre que mira*). It was a way to deconstruct the virtual axis where reality, the camera, and its subject come together. This is because each of these elements tends to disappear under the weight of the structure that unites them, an entelechy of sorts, so that now only what is real is seen. For this article, instead of the gaze or the act of gazing, I focus on the entity of the images that emerge from the two operations when the subject becomes complicit with the camera in order to observe reality. It is no longer a virtual and hidden axis but a connection that works in unison and thus must be revealed each and every time. Seeing is not as easy as it seems. To see through the camera even less so. Few film-makers delve so deeply into the process of seeing as does Guerín. And I mean seeing with vision, in other words, in a transcendental sense.

The first time T.S. Eliot read Dante's *Inferno*, he wrote that it is better not to worry about the identities of the Italian poet's doomed characters. "What we should consider is not so much the meaning of the images, but the reverse process, that which led a man having an idea to express it in images." Eliot refers to Dante's time as a moment in which *"men still saw visions."* He wrote: "It was a psychological habit, the trick we have forgotten, but one that is as good as any of our own. We have nothing but dreams, and we have forgotten that seeing visions – a practice now relegated to the aberrant and uneducated – was once a more significant, interesting, and disciplined kind of dreaming" (Eliot 243).

Maybe Eliot forgot about watching films when he recalled medieval visions, which for him were a way to dream while being awake, of seeing dreams instead of dreaming them. The British poet might not have thought that a machine could fabricate images that could be equated to the subjective intimacy involved in the making of a poem such as Dante's. And he was half right because not all cinematic images can express both an interior and a personal world; not all images can meet Eliot's definition of being visionary. Cinema actually produces visions, but they do not "spring from below," as Eliot mourned, "We take it for granted that our dreams spring from below: possibly the quality of our dreams suffers in consequence." Instead, for the audience, and even myself, they spring from above, from the outside, as hallucinations. For some they spring from the screen while, for others, they spring from reality itself. The main question, though, is how they are produced. Given all the mechanics and money that it takes to produce an image, they are far from resembling an epiphany.

Eliot does not imply that in the thirteenth and fourteenth century people did not hallucinate naturally or that they did not see ghosts constantly. Instead, he is suggesting that ideas actually took the form of images. Eliot also talks about allegories, but it was a special kind of allegory since the process did not involve looking for an image to express an idea but rather the idea would present itself visually, spontaneously. *The Divine Comedy* would be a sort of historical and moral treaty constructed through intricate figurations that stem from reality, but a reality that had been transformed by ideas.

The characteristics of the contemporary documentary, its hybridity between digital technology and subjectivity, make it possible for us to imagine a return to that visionary capacity of the Middle Ages that Eliot deemed critical. Yet it is not an immediate return nor a return under the same conditions. Practically nothing connects us to the Middle Ages, except that the failure of modernity has made us susceptible to premodern soul states. *Los motivos de Berta* (*Berta's Motives*, 1985), Guerín's first film, is precisely structured across modernity and premodernity. Its melancholic style, a constant in his films, translates into a state of emotional indeterminacy between past and present. A state that postmodernity has, unsuccessfully, tried to resolve by settling into a present that only cares about the future and wants to get there as fast as possible.

Nowadays, cinema allows us to return to a visionary way of contemplating reality due to technological advances. Digitalization has reduced the presence of technology and, because it is more subtle, it assimilates the body and acts in rhythm with the same reality and thought process. It has also augmented the expressive potential of that same technology by permitting it to more directly formulate the film-maker's subjectivity. A documentary film-maker is now closer than ever to doing the work of a writer, fulfilling that old prophecy by Alexander Astruc about the *caméra stylo*.

New technologies are rapidly changing our way of seeing. Likewise, contemporary documentaries benefit from such innovation. But they are more effective than other equally pioneering experimental genres and, because of this, disregard subjectivity, dedicating themselves to a task that is purely aesthetic.

To See Again

What is this new way of seeing? And how is it different from or similar to medieval visions? If we look back at the history of cinema, we might see images that we could name as passive allegorical images in order to differentiate them from active traditional allegories. The latter seeks an image to better express an idea, while in the former the image is perceived spontaneously through images that have never before been allegorized. In this category, we could find images created by Jean Vigo, Tarkovsky, or Sokurov, to name but a few. Without a doubt, images produced by the great directors, from Dreyer to Hitchcock, from Antonioni, Ozu, or Fellini, connect directly to a visual way of thinking and feeling. But, if we want to be faithful to what Eliot says, the trajectory must be significantly reduced because in cinema the distance between the idea and the image is usually excessive for these tasks, and there are too many filters along the path that separate them so as to allow us to talk about visions in the strict sense of the word. They are visual constructions, not visions, no matter how powerful and significant they might be. The immediacy required to produce a true vision is easily found in drawing, a field in which technology is drastically reduced and where only the artist's imagination separates image and reality. In film-making, very few film-makers *draw* reality in that way. Maybe Mekas or Hanoun can frame what they see, but that does not make them visionaries. William Kentridge, an intense film-maker known for his animated drawings, might be a visionary. His technique is based on filming the drawings that he is constantly modifying. Documentary film-makers have yearned to resemble painters because their ideal is to match the rhythm of reality, a feat made possible in the 60s when a first technological wave made cameras smaller and more portable. However, the truth is that documentaries are the best place to find true visions where reality appears in the form of ideas and mental states can be accommodated.

We could address the problem of visions and ideas by bringing up poetic cinema, but that would be too simple because poetic cinema connects images to formalized emotions rather than ideas. It is not about how to present ideas to the audience, but how to induce them to the audience. Technology is a calculation. They are, therefore, shocking images; should they generate ideas and feelings it would be a second-degree order. But my focus is those images that correspond to an author's particular emotional state upon contemplating reality, but in a way that the emotional state is already embedded in reality itself through its perception. It is an emotional state made up of an indiscernible mixture of emotions and concepts that come from contemplating reality in a new way. The film-maker seeks to convey this vision, strives to preserve it in images. The director conforms to reality, apparently like any other documentalist, but in his case he conforms to a transfigured reality. This is not the same as making images so that they themselves become the event, so that they are only to be seen, because they could not have been seen before they were made.

We already have several characteristics that allow us to identify those passive allegories, those new visionary ways. First, emotion and intellect feed off each other in these images created to express the author's particular state of mind, which stems from a specific situation that has been presented as an epiphany. Thus, the images are subjective visualizations, and they highlight the effect on the film-makers themselves. The audience that subsequently sees those images in the film is not forced to feel the same as the author felt while seeing them, but in any case, the audience is urged to understand the subject that produced those feelings, and based on this knowledge is able to experience their own emotions.

In summary, they are intimate images that film makes public, and they resemble their production process; it is as if the camera decided to spontaneously film whatever was happening. Spontaneously would mean that the camera itself makes the decision; yet it is not the camera but the film-maker who has decided to start filming. In principle, the camera sees something different from what the film-maker sees. The problem lies in the mixing of these two contradictory visions. Upon watching those images, the audience believes it is perceiving what the director intended for it to perceive. However, it is not the same. What were once the director's visions are now just a performance. This does not mean that there lacks a direct relationship between these two moments, that of the visionary and that of the spectator's vision. Indeed, they are related, but the experience of one is radically different from the experience of the other. It is the same process as reading Dante or any other great poet. We are never encouraged to feel or see something concrete; instead, we are invited to confront a mystery even though we will only partially understand all of its dimensions. For example, when Dante pondered about Treachery in the Ninth Circle of Hell, the mythical figures who personified Dante's ideas, Cain, Judas, and Brutus, appeared in the last hell. Similarly, the Ninth Circle's tenebrous landscape is where three-faced Lucifer appears devouring the traitors. This landscape can be read through its visual components as a sort of moral discourse. However, the experience is very different for the reader. The reader visually visits the story and draws his own conclusions from the journey, while the author, in this case Dante, sees hell in reality itself, read reality through the images of hell.

The concept of passive allegory that I coined earlier might not be sufficient to delimit the event that we are discussing. It is akin to Gilbert Durand's symbolic formations and his distinction between symbol and allegory: "The allegory starts from the (abstract) idea to arrive at a representation, while the symbol is first and foremost itself a representation, and, as such, a source of ideas, among other things" (Durand 14). I was reluctant to use the symbol as a concept because its meaning is highly ambiguous and depends very much on the discipline that employs it. Regardless of the concept, whether it be that of passive allegories or symbols, visionary images transfigure reality.

José Luis Guerín's cinema is made up of such images that are rare in the history of cinema. In any case, the situation has now changed, since film-makers have at their disposal a technology that allows them to forgo the innumerable mediations that previously separated them from the creative process itself. Nowadays, the process of film has become as intimate and essential as that of a writer or a poet: to create intimate cinema, what was once the exception becomes easily achievable depending only on the film-maker's disposition. This, however, does not mean that all documentary film-makers can now be considered visionaries.

In the 1960s, a first technological revolution caused a cinematic transformation allowing for films that would break traditional structures. It would create films that were more direct, more subjective, and less dependent on industry rules. And this technology certainly impacted documentaries. In the sixties, new technologies caused a formal revolution still attached to the vanguards' momentum. But now, digitalization triggers a repositioning of the subject in front of the instruments and reality, so that new cinematic forms that are essentially subjective emerge in all possible meanings of the concept. It is from this subjectivity that new cinematographic forms emerge, different from what happened before, when the first results of technological innovation were directly formal, a formalism from which a repositioning of the subject could be derived.

To Be Victor Hugo

Concepts, which are born to give meaning to concrete phenomena, tend to get rid of this association and to float autonomously in the imaginary, so that they exist, or so it seems, beyond the persistence of their contents. This process is what happened to the vanguard concept. Born as an essential expression of modernity, the vanguard movement was quickly assimilated by all artistic forms, cinema included. By creating a radically new aesthetic, it offered a new artistic state of mind for artists whose belief in realist figuration had collapsed. Almost immediately, the vanguard movement started to slowly separate from the masses, an intrinsic part of the movement, and finally left behind its own aesthetic essence. First, an avant-garde characteristic died with abstract expressionism and its filmic correlations, such as in the works of Mekas or Stan Brakhage, where they are already close to painters of that same movement. And then, another characteristic survived thanks to conceptual art but, after a strong first impulse, it crashed, ethically and aesthetically, because of market expectations. This is not the most convenient place to sketch a history of the avant-garde from Duchamp onwards through this double movement that make up the positive and negative side of its fundamental characteristics. It suffices to add that, regardless of the opinions of curators working in contemporary art museums or academics, the aesthetic concept of the avant-garde is completely exhausted. It does not mean that avant-garde art is not being produced or that some valuable exponent does not still appear once in a while. It is not the artistic impulse that has been exhausted, nor the innovative spirit that is its main characteristic. What no longer works is the avant-garde imaginary.

When the avant-garde was in its zenith, the adjective justified the work's aesthetic goal. When a work was deemed avant-garde, all its components were already judged and its function did not need to be explained. This is no longer possible, and the impossibility of using the term causes many misnomers. Avant-garde used to mean that the absence of meaning was not up for discussion. Now the term can erroneously justify an inane work of art by appealing to its allegorical or symbolic reading. When the work itself is aesthetically inane, it is excused by appealing to the ideas it represents allegorically or symbolically, but the original aesthetic and emotional link between image and concept has been lost. It is a dead-end street that forces us to look for new solutions. We must accept that we are in a post avant-garde epoch, both in cinema as well as other arts. Old characteristics are no longer valid, although many critics are still using them as if they still retained their original meanings.

In this new artistic period, which started in the 1990s, the old equivalence in film studies between the new Catalan avant-garde and the Barcelona School of Cinema from the 1970s can no longer be sustained. If we keep using the empty term, devoid of any hints of the original avant-garde, we are bound to lose the specificity of each historic moment and the films that each produced. We usually make the historicist mistake of believing that the development of events in general, particularly in art, occurs unitarily so the different cases naturally succeed one another as if it were one unique body that produces different gestures over time.

This is just a mirage, and in the case of the avant-garde, makes us believe that there is a link between them just because we use the same term for both movements.

In 1967 at the Mostra Internazionale of New Cinema in Pesaro, Joaquín Jordá said the now famous line "If we are not allowed to be Victor Hugo, we will be Mallarmé," which nowadays we interpret less as an artistic manifesto and more as a matter-of-fact statement. The Barcelona School chose Mallarmé not because they could not choose Victor Hugo, but rather because they were the heirs of the last members of the early avant-garde. It was not a real option for them, not because of the lack of industry resources or a disregard to classic narratives, but because they decided to be Mallarmé without ever considering if they could actually be Victor Hugo.

Arguably, the new wave of Catalan film-makers with its post-vanguard characteristics is closer to Victor Hugo than Mallarmé, even if the distinction still retains some of the transcendental sense that Jordá implied back then. The new film-makers, if indeed they are a group, adopted Mallarmé and dressed themselves in Victor Hugo's inherited heavy gear and what he represented: romantic and visionary realism, leaving aside naturalism and more traditional realistic approaches.

It is significant that the Barcelona School chose Mallarmé over Rimbaud. However, their attempt to penetrate Mallarmé's world without any preambles, regardless of how metaphoric their attempt was, was complete foolishness. That is the only way to effectively consider Jordá's manifesto, even though it was baseless, because in order to arrive at Mallarmé one has to go through Victor Hugo. I do not know if film-makers from the Nouvelle Vague knew that it was indeed the road, but they acted as if they had assumed it. They attacked *daddy's cinema* from its roots, carefully deconstructing it as an intrinsic part of their credo. Those who rushed in search of toys, remained locked in the game for quite some time.

The Barcelona School was basically a formal movement with political implications that stemmed out of an historic context. However, the new film-makers that belong to a not very cohesive version of the School of Barcelona do start from a subjective transformation that make them break traditional structures that are almost impossible to assimilate as a group. Their new style is far more incisive and lasting because it is not bound to rules or styles, but emerges from personal queries. Its consequences are also political and are related to a less strict, albeit far more complex, context. The most paradigmatic of this new movement is Guerín's films. But if we should analyse other important film-makers such as Albert Serra,

Marc Recha, and Isaki Lacuesta we would conclude that their formalism is not the essence but a consequence.

Happenstance, a recurring motif in Guerín's work, comes from necessity. If we are to follow Jordà's metaphor, Guerín's cinema is closer to Hugo's aesthetic than to Mallarmé's. Or maybe it is the time to correct the old mistake and appeal to Rimbaud? But we will soon realize that Rimbaud would also be wrong.

My intention is not to address the reach of the Barcelona Film School but to establish the differences with contemporary Catalan cinema, and, in particular Guerín's cinema, which constitutes a very special case among the new film-makers who have long abandoned avant-garde splendour.

The Aesthetic of the Signifier

Guerín is not an avant-garde artist. He cannot be because his cinema is far more intimate and subtle than that of the avant-garde, and it does not contain any of the fanfare that usually accompanies avant-garde works. He is not interested in the future but, instead, only wants to look at how the past always comes back through open wounds. In *Los motivos de Berta* (1985), Friedrich Hölderlin's verses and his spirit come back in a liminal space. John Ford returns in/to *Innisfree* (1990); and in *Tren de sombras* (*Train of Shadows*, 1997), a love story comes back amid forgotten film strips. In a gentrification project, the vestiges of an old cemetery reappear in *En construcción* (*Work in Progress*, 2001), while the sordid story about a suicide is central to *Recuerdos de una mañana* (*Memories of a Morning*, 2011). Pliny the Elder and the birth of painting are central to *La dama de Corinto. Un esbozo cinematográfico* (*The Lady of Corinth: A Film Study*, 2011), and the love of Dante and Petrarch are brought forth in *Unas fotos en la ciudad de Sylvia* (*Some Pictures in the City of Sylvia*, 2007) and in its homologue, *En la ciudad de Sylvia* (*In the City of Sylvia*, 2007), a labyrinth of gazes pulls the audience into a present represented by dreamt and impossible women. The old muses are personified in La academia de las Musas (The Academy of the Muses, 2015) to revisit old Provençal courtly love. And lastly, are not all epistolary forms a return to the past? Letters are not sent to the future but to a past that awaits them and that permeates the writer. When a message is written or filmed, the answer is not as important as the letter from the past or its sender. *En construcción* is so powerful because it obliterates the modernist discourse on progress and it focuses on the uncertain terrain between past and future. A past that is disappearing fast and an uncertain future. Guerín's gaze is more interested in a past that is about to disappear than in the future splendour of the neighbourhood. Like the women in *Some Pictures in the City of Sylvia* and *In the City of Sylvia*, the Raval neighbourhood is moving towards the past, not the future.

The avant-garde movements intended to create a new way of looking by eliminating its basic tenets. They were paradoxically iconoclastic. Gilbert Durand wonders "how can a civilization that is full of images, that invented photography, cinema and many other ways for iconographic reproduction be considered inconoclastic?" (25). In order to answer his own question, he divides iconoclasm into two types. The first one is related to orthodoxy, but "the second type of iconoclasm, because of excess, because the senses evaporated, was the founding and constant trait of Western Culture" (25). If Durand is right, avant-garde movements would present an unexpected profile: instead of breaking tradition, they would have fully endorsed it. Through its drastic aesthetic recomposition, they would have installed in art the symbolic extinction process so characteristic of positivism. Here, the imaginary agrees with that of the classic documentary, markedly objectivist, and therefore contrary to the symbol. The spirit of the time is not always correctly interpreted by its actors. Yet although it may be true, we cannot forget the visionary tendency of the avant-garde that has its origins in Rimbaud and ends with surrealism. That is the reason why Benjamin would define surrealism "as the last snapshot of European intelligentsia" (301).

The spirit of the time has changed and the surrealist way is no longer valid. According to Benjamin, "They bring the immense forces of 'atmosphere' concealed in these things to the point of explosion" (306). Benjamin's use of *Stimmung* can be translated as *climate, atmosphere*, but also as *state of mind*. The latter would be the best transcription to describe the relationship between visionary film-makers and the world that surrounds them. Surrealism aside, the avant-gardes acted as if someone did not trust the image that a puzzle has built and they would rather break it all up to admire the meaningless chaos that the pieces make up. Thus, it does so without a true vision, assuming that this is a way of returning to the origin, of sticking to the basics. To the contrary, the most contemporary of the aesthetic currents return to what is real, and do so through the image. The new artistic movements welcome documentary film-making and its trust in the epistemological vision, in its capacity to examine things through images empowered by the mixture of subjectivity and technology that is paramount to many contemporary film-makers, Guerín included. Hal Foster wrote that

> the avant-garde work is never historically effective or fully significant in its initial moments. It cannot be because it is traumatic – a hole in the

symbolic order of its time that is not prepared for it, that cannot receive it, at least not immediately, at least not without structural change. (This is the other art scene that critics and historians need to consider: not only its symbolic disconnections but the *failures to signify*). (29; emphasis in original)

At the end, after more than a century of postponing the long-awaited encounter between trauma and the structures that can heal it, the conclusion is that the constant failure of signifying is no longer tenable. Thus, post-avant-garde or neo-avant-garde, as Foster calls them, intends to boost vision through a process of refiguration.

This is why I have no doubt in qualifying Guerín as a visionary and bringing back the idea of vision that Eliot mentioned upon writing about Dante and his time. However, I will expand the concept to make it more pragmatic, because visions are produced nowadays with technology.

My two objectives from now until the end are first, to delimit this new way of seeing appearing in documentaries, and of which Guerín is a prime example, and second, to investigate these visions and the emotion that triggers them.

To Be Rimbaud?

I would like to discuss the aforementioned Victor Hugo since he was a well-known visionary and his experiences allows us to specifically understand the visionary processes that are now taking place. Thanks to technology, some individuals have regained a visionary capacity, in very specific fields such as the documentary, which before was only reserved for a select few. Such disposition is clearly existential in its direct relation to technology and image.

Few people know that Hugo was also a painter, and this facet received almost no attention. However, his unsettling images allow discussion of his visionary capacity and how it would materialize directly in his paintings. At a particular time in his life, Victor Hugo's imagination, usually expressed in poems and novels, escapes first through tenebrous images in paintings and then through clearly allegorical photographic images. His change from imagination to vision, from an interior to an external ability, is one of the first modern examples of current modes of visualization. A fundamental characteristic of this phenomenon is that visualization, technology, and subjectivity, elements that together form an ecology, are thus capable of generating, in some exceptional cases, visionary images.

218   Josep Maria Català Domènech

While in exile on the islands of Jersey and Guernsey, Hugo took an interest in photography. It is important to know how his interest is born and what it resulted in:

> Hugo pasea por la playa, con marea baja, en la isla de Jersey, cuando le llama la atención un grupo de troncos de altos árboles trasplantados, cuyo número, forma y disposición -casi podríamos decir su actitud- producen en él la impresión de un encuentro. Hugo proscrito, físicamente trasplantado de su entorno social, de su *habitus* parisino, había tenido que exilarse a Jersey [...]. Estos troncos de árboles arrancados, como él, de su medio natural, suscitan en su mente referencias anatómicas, convocan fantasmas de desmembramientos, de cuerpos troceados, de restos humanos [...]. Este *Rompeolas* de imponentes dimensiones Hugo lo percibe como una "presencia spectral," y de ahí la clásica "impresión de inquietante extrañeza" que siente. Surge una sensación de empatía que desencadena un proceso de identificación del Proscrito con esos árboles-tibias. ¿Acaso se habrá producido algo así como un proceso de transubstanciación? En todo caso, en aquel instante, en la playa, Hugo se sintió árbol. A cualquiera que conozca la propensión a la percepción alucinatoria de este hombre habitado no le constará entender que se identificara con los troncos trasplantados [...]. La segunda fase del proceso consistió en materializar y encarnar de modo visible la imagen mental mediante un procedimiento fotográfico que les resultaba familiar a los Hugo, padre e hijo.

(Hugo is walking along the beach, at low tide, on the island of Jersey, when his attention is caught by a group of trunks from tall-transplanted trees. Their number, shape, and arrangement – we could almost say their attitude – gave him the impression of a meeting. Hugo, outcast, physically transplanted from his social environment, from his Parisian *habitus*, had to go into exile in Jersey [...]. These trunks of trees, uprooted, like him, from their natural environment, aroused anatomical references in his mind, summon ghosts of dismemberment, of chopped up bodies, of human remains [...]. This breakwater of imposing dimensions is perceived by Hugo as a "spectral presence," and hence the classic "impression of disturbing strangeness" he feels. A feeling of empathy arises that triggers a process of identification of the outcast with those limb-like trees. Could something like a transubstantiation process have taken place? In any case, at that moment, on the beach, Hugo felt like a tree. Anyone who knows the propensity for hallucinatory perception of this inhabited man will understand how easily he could identify himself with the transplanted trunks [...]. The second phase of the process consisted of materializing and visibly embodying the mental image through a photographic procedure that was familiar to the Hugos, father and son.) (Lebel 32)

Similar to medieval visionaries, Hugo interprets reality allegorically and, within it, he discerns his interior life, his subjectivity. He now converts that particular vision into photographic images. He does not reconstruct reality by creating allegories to accommodate them to his visions, such as he did in his paintings. He photographs what he sees, but what he sees is more than what can be seen objectively. Allegory is then imbedded in reality because his observing reality triggers an allegorical vision. This is the difference between a passive and an active allegorization. One transforms ideas into things while the other, which is the basis for modern allegory, transforms instinctively things into ideas, into emotions, into feelings. Thus, reality ends up revealing hidden forms both from its own plot and the characters' inner plots, which is what Lebel called transubstantiation.

This possibility reveals how complex documentary images can be even when film-makers do not expect them to be so. There is always some subjective slippage in documentaries because it is a reality-based cinema and it expresses more than any other medium the subjectivation process, whether intended or not. However, the director's will and the understanding of the process are fundamental in allowing a true visionary transformation, so an epiphany can turn into an image. Guerín's cinema fits this phenomenology, and it adds its power to connect with reality through different emotions that affect both the film-maker and the things being observed.

Both José Luis Guerín's and Mekas's oeuvre is a perfect example of the visionary framing of reality. To write a letter is always an intimate and subjective process, but when it is filmed the images are saturated with subjectivity even more than are words because they are closer to the emotions: words are abstract but images are concrete. At the beginning of letter number 3, for instance, Guerín mentions the windows of his apartment and what he sees through them. In his voice-over, he informs us that it is an interior and an exterior window that the film-maker relates to spring and winter. What do the spring images show? Through tree leaves we can see the house across the street. The camera zooms to a sign that shows the building's construction year – 1900 – which makes the film-maker remember the cinema of that particular time, Méliès, for example. In front of that house was another that was built in 1922, which he relates to Fitz Lang and F.W. Murnau. What might seem just an observation is actually the embodiment of a state of mind, which in turn generates ideas, and the combination of intellect and emotion transforms reality. For an ordinary person these buildings would be situated in the present, regardless of the age of the buildings, age being only a date. But for Guerín they are doors to the past. Instead of looking at them as classic time, the one that goes linear from past towards the future caught in a present without qualities, Guerín breaks the temporal inertia and digs deep in the architecture to imagine their origins. Through this process, the buildings become emotional objects to be studied. As Benjamin wrote, "It is not that what is past casts light on what is present, or what is present its light on what is past; rather, image is that wherein what has been comes together, in a flash with the now to form a constellation" (Benjamin, *Arcades*, 462).

If we compare the attitude towards reality that Jonas Mekas adopts in his letters, we will soon see the difference between someone who only observes and someone who sees in a transcendental manner. Mekas is the film-maker of the gaze. He is happy with what he sees. However, his vision does not return anything, unlike Guerín's. Mekas seems to say that this is all he has seen, that his images prove it. However, Guerín's images are particularly disturbing because there is an intellect that can transport ideas and emotions to those who can read them through the forms that make up its visuality and that the voice-over corroborates. But even if they were silent, they contain a particular brightness that characterizes them because they are intrinsically melancholic.

Madame de Staël wrote that rarely could words express what the heart feels. We should add that it is also rare to express through a camera lens what the heart feels, through images that, at the beginning, seem to exactly correspond with a reality that should exist regardless of who is looking at it. In a conversation held at "La casa encendida de Madrid" with Guerín and Mekas, the latter happily confesses that he never thinks when he is filming, he just films. However, he tells Guerín that he is always talking about cinema ... and that is beautiful, he adds. In one of his letters to Guerín, Mekas had already confessed that the necessity to film was for him compulsive and inexplicable. For Guerín, though, the filming process is a combination of happenstance and necessity, or as he says, calculating and chance. However, it is not compulsive but an answer to a way of seeing because between calculation and randomness and randomness and necessity is where vision resides. The visionary, through an eventful, impromptu reality, sees a kernel of thought or the making of an idea that is literally moving. And he pursues that intuition, joins that thought that is transported by the image because, little by little, in it he discovers the profiles of his intimacy, as well as those of the world that surrounds him.

If we move beyond the purely optical notion of seeing, we must distinguish between the gaze (and its phenomenological theory on the *act of gazing*) and the vision. Among documentary film-makers, there are those who gaze and others who see. We could even go as far as to say that there is a documentary cinema of the gaze and another of seeing. Adam Sitney called visionary all the US avant-garde film-makers from Maya Deren on. Deren might have been the only one who was truly a visionary (Sitney, *Visionary Film*). He was not satisfied with the terms "experimental" or "poetic cinema" and he also did not agree with calling them avant-garde artists. He chose "visionary" because the films from the New American Cinema or underground cinema came out of a basic, and more precisely ethereal romanticism that culminated, according to Sitney, in a direct relation with Emerson and Whitman. "Most of the films discussed in the previous pages present us with peaks of perfect exhilaration, often extended passages in which the film-maker succeeds in conveying his or her rapture with the moment of taking a shot, the ecstasy of camera or vehicular movement, or the perfection of a sequence of shots falling together in a figure of montage" (Sitney, *Eyes Upside Down* 392). Sitney clearly refers to a lyric conception of cinema despite his reservations about the concept of poetic cinema. The underground film-maker, as a good romantic would be, is in ecstasy in front of nature, or, as M.H. Abrams argued in his seminal work,[1] in front of the universe. These film-makers inherit from the classic documentary an allegedly innocent way of looking at reality that returns it to the foreground, but they do not notice that in those moments it is irremediably sinister. Instead, they chop and manipulate reality. They want to make it look abstract and, finally, they serve it cold like vengeance. The film-makers' catalogue that Sitney discusses in his two books is so large that it is almost impossible that they all fit into one category or one state of mind. However, the number of film-makers that makes us think and not only feel is very limited, and even more limited are those that makes us feel and think at the same time.

The Melancholy Science

According to Slavoj Žižek, "The fundamental paradox of symbolic fictions is therefore that, in one and the same move, they bring about 'the

---

[1] See Abrams, *The Mirror and the Lamp*. In this classic treatise on aesthetic criticism, Abrams points out that all theories relate to four elements: the universe, the work, the artist, and the audience, each one of them being well distinguished. This needs to be taken into account for further research.

loss of reality' and provide the only access to reality: true, fictions are a semblance which occludes reality, but if we renounce fictions, reality itself dissolves" (91). Žižek's reflections on symbolic fictions demonstrate one of the fundamental aspects of contemporary documentary: an understanding about what they can reveal that he calls *symbolic functions* where the procedures of fiction and subjective movements are included. The classic documentary did not know this but acted otherwise. The modernity-related documentary clearly rejected the possibility of symbolization except in an introspective aspect, which declared speculation to be more important than the need to symbolize.

Unlike Dante's educated contemporaries, we are not able to have an immediate link to a mythical tradition as rich as Dante's. That it came to life before his eyes was powerful. But in the best cases we maintain a moral inventory that allows us to be in an effective relationship with the world. The new vision and the new visionaries feed on this moral substratum that might just prove to be as important as the mythical archetypes, although it lacks sufficient figuration. This new "direct cinema" of certain film-makers, among whom Guerín is perhaps the most influential, finds in reality the figures of an emotional-intellectual grouping, and that vision is what the camera alone confirms and formalizes in all its dimensions: film-makers find in reality the necessary shapes that they need in order to convey the moral depth that so interests them. Gilbert Durand states that "a myth [...] is the repetition of certain logical and linguistic relations between ideas or images expressed verbally" (18). Thus, in some documentaries the visionary expression is presented only by avoiding verbal expression: namely, this image is an expression of a *myth* formulated through certain relationships that are not merely logical or linguistic, but also visual because they are discovered in reality itself. Guerín himself may have been expressing this when he said: "I really like those films in which you can see aspects of the film-maker, even intimate ones, but from materials that do not directly concern him. It is in that territory that I have placed myself."[2] Not an image that mirrors the world, but the world as a mirror of the film-maker who contemplates that world.

Within *Unas fotos en la ciudad de Sylvia* there is a section dedicated to two famous poetic couples, Dante-Beatríz and Petrarca-Laura. For numerous transcendental reasons this part is prototypical of the visionary quality now under discussion. In fact, the entire film, if we can classify it as such, is visionary in its mythical construction. However, this

---

2 Interview for "Días de cine," La 2 de TVE, 31 March 2014.

vision becomes a kind of facade behind which there are many other meanings. Guerín's work is made up of a series of diverse layers, but not layers that must be peeled back one by one in order to reach the nucleus where essence or the *truth* is found, but rather the opposite. Layers must be added instead of removed because the ultimate meaning is found on the surface and not within. For example, when layers of voyeurism, gazing, and feeling are applied, a view appears which joins these layers together in a common meaning.

On the internet we can find a copy of the extract just mentioned. More so than the film, it shows Guerín's visual reflection regarding what the philosopher Walter Benjamin called esoteric love, a type of love in which "the lady matters least" ("Surrealism" 210). In this segment more emotions are revealed, if that is possible, than those behind the shifting of the director's gaze, as much in reality as on screen, thereby confirming those feelings experienced during the filming. This extract shows that the director's viewpoint is visionary; that it is possible to confirm how the filming of places, of the traces left by Dante's and Petrarch's stories respectively, have turned the director's eyes towards profound and particular visions. Benjamin was right: in these cases the lady matters least. I say this without the slightest bit of criticism and only with the intention of continuing to define an emotional character, the basis of a feeling that defines the vision of reality.

What is this feeling? Or perhaps it would be better to ask ourselves that of the various emotions that run through the aforementioned extract, which is the most powerful? This is regardless of whether such emotion might be the most abstruse: what state of mind is behind the author's feeling in those places where history's presence is almost violent? The answer is clear: melancholy is the feeling.

Melancholy implies, among many other things, a subversion of temporality. Existence is no longer the apparent passing of time. An imbalance exists between temporality and the subject that brings the past to light where it is superimposed over the present. This traumatic unhinged time, a phenomenon witnessed by the twentieth century on numerous occasions, first occurs as an internal recomposition of the subject, one that intensely lives that uprooting: "Binswanger [...] highlights an uprooting of the 'pure self' which fails to redirect an existence in which transcendental constitutive acts come together inextricably, until the possibility of all movement is destroyed, the retention of the past and the propensity towards a future mortgaged by grief [...]. With melancholy, life's course can no longer be experienced 'naturally,' that is, without problems and without reflection" (Starobinski 182). If Rimbaud hoped to become a visionary through a systematic disorganization of the senses, the current visionary capacity appears when the inner world has already been altered: it is not the forced disorder of the senses that provokes such visionary capacity, but rather the vision arising from within and disrupting the senses.

Perhaps too insistently melancholy is associated with depression, but the truth is that the melancholic state is not necessarily pathological. At best, it is a mental state, and although it cannot be described as euphoric without being contradictory, it continues to be a source of enthusiasm, a lyrical and profound enthusiasm that colours the vision of things and reconciles those things in a conversation long ago ended. In the well-known treatise on the relationship between Saturn and melancholy, Klibansky, Panofsky, and Saxl point out that beginning in the fifteenth century this relationship was conceived as an intensified consciousness of self: it was the author Jacques Legrand from the first half of that century who turned the focus to "the nexus that unites the ideas of death, melancholy and self-consciousness" (Klibansky, Panofsky, and Saxl 230). And they go on to say that "some one hundred years later this consciousness was already so inseparable from self-esteem that there is hardly a refined man who is not genuinely melancholic, or at least not a man who does not consider himself melancholic or seen by others as so" (230).

Vision and Death

Some might believe that relating melancholy to death is sufficient for diagnosing depression, but there are innumerable voices that say otherwise. Freud, for example, said that during a conversation with a certain poet friend, this friend tried to devalue beauty on the basis of it being ephemeral, to which the psychoanalyst replied that it was just the opposite, that such transience only added to beauty's value (quoted in Kristeva 110). It is in this *Freudian* way that melancholy becomes visionary epistemology, a way of awareness. But death seems inescapable at the moment when time becomes visible.

The women who escape Guerín's gaze and that of his camera in *Unas fotos en la ciudad de Sylvia*, or those who are surreptitiously gazed at from afar in *En la ciudad de Sylvia*, form perhaps the best allegory presenting loss as death. These images are required to be melancholic. They have turned into visions through the allegorical projection of feeling – a feeling that arises prior to this incessant disappearance. The gaze struggles against the fleetingness of the simultaneous occurrence of time and events, and comes to an end because a gaze can only be retained as a memory and therefore dies at the precise moment in which it is seen. It is true that memories live on as images, but these images, ones which seemingly defy expiration, become eminent signs of the same in an unavoidable testimony to the cessation of being. They are visionary precisely because of this, because they are not limited to expressing feelings, rather they are proponents of paying attention to the feelings that are found within. It is about a visual and emotional configuration that also characterizes installations such as the eloquently titled *Las mujeres que no conocemos*, a grouping of images of women who are turned into a gaze, that is, subjectivized through a feeling provoked by distance. They are feminine figures, presented as symbols of an impossible love and through the constant loss of that love's object.

Death, in its many aspects and meanings, is present throughout Guerín's work, from a cinephile's attempt at an impossible reclaiming of time lost in *Innisfree*, to the fictional salvaging of a love story hidden in a collection of damaged and scattered frames in *Tren de sombras* (*Train of Shadows*, 1997). One needs to remember that a large part of Guerín's work takes place between two suicides, the first being a fictional one, that of Demetrio in the author's first film, *Los motivos de Berta*, and a real one, the suicide of the Caspe Street musician in one of Guerín's last productions, *Recuerdos de una mañana* (*Memories of a Morning*, 2011). But where Guerín faces death most directly is in the previously mentioned letter number 3 to Mekas. In it he tells his American correspondent about meeting in Lisbon with a young cinephile who died shortly afterwards.

Guerín says that he met the girl during an interview he was giving at the film festival taking place in Portugal's capital. She was the spokesperson for a team of reporters and the director confesses that her gaze captured his attention – "one of those gazes that helps us make films." That is why he decided to reverse the roles. He himself began to ask the questions even though it made the rest of the team impatient. It is at that moment that the visionary act occurs, that epiphany in which Guerín discovers something peculiar that moves him and impels him to film her. In this instance he films the woman as an idea – an idea of love, beauty, chance ... who knows? But it is by tragic chance that she dies shortly thereafter, such that the images allegorized for the first time in Guerín's gaze are then allegorized again, this time with an added layer of melancholy. Love, melancholy, and death merge in that small segment, just as they do in a tale by Poe. But these characteristics are found in the images, characteristics that imply and demonstrate a synthesis that occurs when the subject is linked to reality.

On the one hand, Guerín's visionary melancholy embraces death, and on the other, the courtly love of the troubadour who eternally idealizes the object of his desire. It is not easy to unravel the limits of those factors that make Guerín's melancholic gaze extend beyond melancholy proper, thus constructing an equation that is not entirely novel, one found in the Romantics and the Symbolists, and one used in Edgar Allan Poe's great models. However, what makes it novel in this case is that the images created in literature become visible in cinema through reality itself. Reality is dressed in the archetypes' clothing, where it acquires a differentiated visibility. We do not witness the evocation of some fantastic story, but rather true drama taking on a spiritual form.

As much as the classic documentary's imaginary structure is organized through the reality-camera-observer axis, and the subsequent contemporary documentary's arrangement is established through image, technique, and subjectivity, which together form its ecology, both are surpassed by the equation composed of melancholy, love, and death. This highly subjective arrangement is superimposed upon its predecessors, thus supporting a new type of vision. It deals with a process that becomes ever more complex through an increased conceptualization of the apparatus, being that abstract forms from the last apparatus, forms which Guerín clearly reveals in his cinema, are only maintained through the profound acknowledgment of previous frameworks.

These elements' alchemy transpires in Guerín's previously referenced video letter to Mekas. The Barcelona director explains towards the end of the letter that the girl died in the Philippines, murdered along with her partner, apparent victims of a common crime. After offering these explanations, Guerín goes silent while images are shown of the young woman captured in Lisbon, of a highly intense close-up that he connects with tree leaves previously shown at the beginning of the letter: two ascending pan shots, the first culminating in the number 1900, which had allowed him to imagine different cinematographic figures. The letter ends with a short written message: "Good health and long life to you, comrade Jonas. José Luis." A conceptual veil has been placed on the images of the dead girl, a veil which at other times is represented by the windows and reflections that separate Guerín's gaze from the women he will never know.

The dead and their romance are resurrected when the remains of a film strip are found in the fictional work *Tren de sombras*, much like when in reality bones appear in the skeletons of an old cemetery uncovered in the Raval neighbourhood during *En construcción*, a tribute, almost a parody, to Rossellini's *Te querré siempre*, which shows bodies that are found mummified by lava in Pompeii. It is impossible to view that scene in Guerín's film as a genuine parody precisely because of its reference to the neorealist film-maker's work, a reference itself buried. Superficial comments, some even amusing, made by a variety of characters around the archaeological discovery stand in contrast to the anguish revealed in Rossellini's exhumation scene. Guerín views the event as a desecration that underscores the moment's melancholy, since not only does the past reappear in the present, but the present is incapable of relating to the past. Guerín does not directly show us the tombs; he does not direct his gaze at them just to reveal an unexpected finding, but rather to focus on those who take the unexpected epiphany for a joke. The confusion around time is especially disturbing at this point because it shows to what extent modernity's blind drive devastates not only the past itself, but also feelings that might connect us with the past. It is through an inverted vision, meaning disrupting the importance of what is shown, that a void is created, thus revealing melancholy as the most genuine emotion suitable for understanding the drastic transformations that push reality towards an uncertain future.

Most likely it is Guerín's least known film that is most directly related to death, *Recuerdos de una mañana*, the title coming from a posthumous work by Proust. In this documentary Guerín attempts to reconstruct the suicide victim environment. As if lava gave shape to the bodies of the Pompeians and moved them to posterity as empty forms, as outlines of absence, the Barcelona director attempts to use setting as a means to recover the character's shape, the character who one morning jumped from the fourth floor.

Recuerdos de una mañana is one of Guerín's most melancholic pieces, and one in which the voyeuristic drive is emphasized. And similar to Hitchcock's *Rear Window*, the point of view, the place where the gazing occurs, is the director's own home. His camera captures his neighbour doing chores through the window, and it is from this drastic positioning that the director's presence is revealed as the outline of a hole. It is from this voyeuristic focal point that the suicide is investigated. This leads to an exploration of the grim terrain of an intersection to the right side of the Eixample district in Barcelona and its rich anthropology.

In one of the most controversial images of the documentary, the deceased, a musician, appears playing the violin half-naked next to the balcony in his house. This is the only time we see the character; all the other times are an evocation of his life and his way of being. The point is that this image was captured before the documentary was conceived and this demonstrates two things: first, the effectiveness of the director's voyeuristic drive, and second, that this basic voyeurism is driven by visionary intuition. It is not the voyeur's typical curiosity that moves him to film intimate situations like this, but the epiphanic condition that allows him to perceive, in this specific and real scene, the potential discovery of a symbol that only later will acquire full meaning.

Elsewhere I included Guerín's cinema in the supposed, and certainly controversial, melodramatic documentary genre (Català, "Melodramatic Thought" 61–74). I did it before I was familiar with this film, and this only corroborates the accuracy of my classification. The basic vocabulary used in melodrama and in other films by the director is present, but in this film its presence is more palpable: death, house (as home), identity, reality, and the sinister. If in his previous melodramatic outings Guerín avoided music, now in *Recuerdos de una mañana* it appears in full force. Not only is the main character a musician, but Guerín surrounds him with musicians, some of whom actually lived near his home. Music, in the origins of melodrama, was at first consubstantial and eventually secondary. An example of this is in the cinematic melodrama, where in some documentaries music eventually took on an emotional form (see Català, *Pasión y conocimiento*). In this case there are two underlying facets. First there is the musical itself, largely personified, and then there is the visual, which is silently shown through a certain form of the image or a cadence provided by a set of them.

I already mentioned that drawing to a close an interpretation of Guerín's cinema is no easy task. It is like a hermeneutic operation but in reverse. Layers are slowly added and the pieces, once scattered, are reunited in meaning. Seldom does a work that at first appears so minimalistic develop into one as complex as this one after being examined in depth. So what materializes, in addition to the various profiles of voyeurism, is the gaze and the act of gazing, each having multiple roles, the signs of a melancholic emotion revealing what are seemingly invisible secrets. This feeling can become melodramatic when those secrets accumulate and visually appear as emotions. Melancholy disrupts reality and turns the familiar into the unfamiliar, which can then become sinister, as in *Tren de sombras*, *Recuerdos de una mañana*, or *En construcción*. But at other times the melancholic gaze is eroticized and is able to express vanishing ideals in an operation that is nevertheless always disrupted. Ruined above all by death, life's tenacious organizer takes on the form of time or, just the same, under Kronos, related to Saturn, hence belonging to melancholy's wise ways. Endeavours are frustrated by the cruel yet epistemologically powerful forms of a time, about which Shakespeare said *is out of joint*.

This intricate architecture can only be organized through a visionary way of seeing, by a gaze that is able to detect in reality those deep currents of its own subjectivity, currents that are at the same time models of the world's subjectivity. It is this visionary and melancholic gazing that moves the film-maker away from the epic forms of classical avant-garde, destined to change the world through a frontal attack on what the world represents. But was it not Rimbaud who said that in order to change the world it is necessary first to change life? In other words, to change oneself?

Translated by Anton Pujol

WORKS CITED

Abrams, M.H. *The Mirror and the Lamp: Romantic Theory and the Critical Tradition*. Oxford UP, 1953.
Benjamin, Walter. *The Arcades Project*. Translated by Howard Eiland and Kevin McLaughlin. Harvard UP, 2003.
– "Surrealism: The Last Snapshot of the European Intelligentsia." Translated by Edmund Jephcott. *Walter Benjamin: Selected Writing*, Vol. 2, Part 1, 1927–1930, edited by Michael W. Jennings, et al. Harvard UP, 1999.
Català, Josep M. *El hombre que mira. Alegorías del espíritu: imagen, ensayo y subjetividad*. Shangrila, 2017.
– "Melodramatic Thought in Contemporary Spanish Documentaries." *Hispanic Research Journal*, vol. 15, no.1, February 2014, pp. 61–74.
– *Pasión y conocimiento: El nuevo realismo melodramático*. Cátedra, 2009.
Durand, Gilbert. *La imaginación simbólica*. Translated by Marta Rojzman. Amorrortu editores, 1968.
Eliot, T.S. *Selected Essays*. Faber and Faber Limited, 1934.
Foster, Hal. *The Return of the Real: The Avant-Garde at the End of the Century*. MIT Press, 1996.
Guerín, José Luis, director. *La Dama de Corinto. Un esbozo cinematográfico*. Museo de Arte Contemporáneo Esteban Vicente, 2011.
– *Dans la ville de Sylvia/En la ciudad de Sylvia*, performances by Pilar López de Ayala and Xavier Lafitte, Eddie Saeta, S.A., 2007.
– *En construcción*, performances by Juana Rodríguez Molina and Iván Guzmán Jiménez, Ovídeo, S.A., 2001.
– *Innesfree*, Le Sept Cinéma, 1990.
– *Los motivos de Berta*, performances by Silvia Gracia and Iñaki Aierra, P.C. Guerín, 1984.
– *Recuerdos de una mañana*. Seoul: JIFF, 2011.
– *Tren de sombras*, performances by Ivan Orvain, Juliette Gautier, and Carlos Romagosa. Producers Pere Portabella, Héctor Fáver, Joan Antoni González and José Luis Guerín, 1997.
– *Unas fotos en la ciudad de Sylvia*, performances by Pilar López de Ayala and Xavier Lafitte, Eddie Saeta, S.A., 2007.
Klibansky, Raymond, Edwin Panofsky, and Fritz Saxl. *Saturno y la melancolía*. Translated by María Luisa Balseiro, Alianza Editorial, 1991.

Kristeva, Julia. *Soleil noir: Dépresion et mélancolie*. Gallimard, 1987.
Lebel, Jean-Jacques. "El Rizoma Hugo." *Víctor Hugo "caos en el pincel ..."* Museo Thyssen-Bornemisza, 2000.
Sitney, P. Adams. *Eyes Upside Down: Visionary Filmmakers and the Heritage of Emerson*. Oxford University Press, 2008.
– *Visionary Film: The American Avant-Garde 1943–2000*. Oxford University Press, 2002.
Starobinski, Jean. *L'encre de la mélancolie*. Éditions du Seuil, 2012.
Žižek, Slavoj. *Tarrying with the Negative: Kant, Hegel, and the Critique of Ideology*. Duke University Press, 2004.

9 On the Threshold of the Diegetic World: Optical and Haptic Visuality in *Elisa K*

EVA BRU-DOMINGUEZ

In the course of the last two decades, visual culture scholarship has gradually turned to the study of physical and multisensory responses to film and new media. This shift in focus can no doubt be traced back to the publication in 1992 of Vivian Sobchack's groundbreaking book *The Address of the Eye: A Phenomenology of Film Experience*, where the film theorist explains audience identification as a sensate encounter rather than an exclusively visual affair. Sobchack's critique to cinema studies' privileging of sight and her understanding of film as material surface paved the way for a growing theoretical corpus of work which is more attentive to sensorial stimulation, notions of embodiment, and the social, historical, and cultural specificity of the subject's viewer body. Laura U. Marks has termed this favouring of proximity and contact in visual imagery "haptic visuality," which she describes as "a form of representation based on getting close enough to the other thing to become it" (*Touch* xiii). Whilst Marks is fully aware that this form of viewing is contingent on individual predisposition and/or cultural awareness (*Skin* 170), she notes that most films often fluctuate between optical and haptic modalities, the former asserting definition by means of distance and the latter closeness and abstraction. According to Marks, the shifts between these two modes of representation mimic our need for sensuous closeness as well as symbolic understanding. In the words of the film critic, "[l]ife is served by the ability to come close, pull away, come close again" (*Touch* xvi).

This chapter examines optical and haptic cinematic techniques in *Elisa K* (2010), an adaptation of the novella *Elisa Kiseljak* (2005) by Lolita Bosch co-directed by husband-and-wife team Judith Colell and Jordi Cadena. Drawing on Marks's exploration of sensuous perception and the work of Thomas Elsaesser and Malte Hagener on spectatorship and the senses, it discusses formal and aesthetic aspects of the film and considers how *Elisa K* engages visually with questions of memory loss and psychological trauma. These stylistic elements of the film are situated in a continuum with the post-war European avant-garde movements – including painting and conceptual art – and the work of the Escola de Barcelona (Barcelona School) in particular, all of which are key referents in the cinema of Cadena (Vidal 18, 26, 46).

Elisa K tells the story of the rape of a ten-year-old girl by a family friend, and explores traumatic amnesia and the later and unexpected recovery of memory. Moved by Bosch's approach to child abuse, the couple saw in this text an opportunity to work jointly on a project "sobre el record, i sobre la memòria, i sobre la fragilitat de l'ésser humà" ("about remembrance, memory and the fragility of humankind"; Filmoteca 2011). Its focus on memory echoes the widespread concern with historical and cultural discontinuities in the Catalan cinema of the noughties and the recovery of the collective's fractured and unwritten past. As noted by Jaume Martí-Olivella, many film-makers of this generation have chosen the documentary genre to address the historical voids in two different, albeit consecutive, periods: Franco's dictatorship and the Spanish Transition ("Tradició" 52). In the same vein, Montserrat Lunati explains that under the influence of postmodernist and post-colonial thought, the endeavour to restore the voids in the nation's historical past has prioritized private and personal narratives, which are in turn inscribed in specific social and political contexts (80). Many of the documentary films produced in the course of this decade centre on narratives of illness and, more specifically, on the degeneration of the brain. In *Nedar* (*To Swim*, 2008), director Carla Subirana affectionately documents the downturn in her mother and grandmother's mental health. As the only child in a line of single mothers, Subirana strives to salvage the memories of these women to put together a narrative of her family history and recreate the identity of her grandfather. Similarly, journalist Albert Solé's search for his own origins in the documentary film *Bucarest, la memòria perduda* (*Bucharest, Memory Lost*, 2008) is framed by the gradual mental deterioration of his father, Jordi Solé Tura, a key political figure of the Spanish Transition. According to Martí-Olivella, the family unit in these films acts as the custodian of a personal history that speaks of a national claim ("Tradició" 53).[1] Abigail Loxham, on the other hand, has noted these two

---

[1] Other films produced in the course of the 2000s that deal with questions of memory include *La casita blanca: La ciudad oculta* (*The White House: The Hidden City*, 2002) by Carles Balagué, *Dies d'agost* (*August Days*, 2006) by Marc Recha, and *Bicicleta, cullera, poma* (*Bicycle, Spoon, Apple*, 2010) by Carles Bosch.

films' emphasis on trace and the material object, which she reads as a means to represent the "tangible nature of memory" (131). Here, I argue that the exploration of memory and trauma in *Elisa K* is firmly embedded in the mechanics of the medium of the cinema as well as its history and, as such, the film engages in an interrogation of modes of viewing and representing. The co-direction perspective in the film, or more specifically, the visual dialogue that is established by the different viewpoints presented by Cadena and Colell, challenges the idea of the single auteurist perspective. Furthermore, I show that this metafictional aspect of the film is in line with the interests of the film-makers of the Barcelona School, whose aesthetic and stylistic approaches not only sought to move away from the types of films that were being made in Spain at the time but also to engage with the artistic practices of the European avant-garde (Martí-Olivella, "Tradició" 4). This group of film directors, to whom Sara Nadal-Melsió refers as the "invisible tradition" (465), developed a new aesthetics and cinematic language, which operated at the very margins of late Francoism's cultural production. This invisibility and lack of historicity of Catalan avant-garde cinema (465) becomes an undercurrent in a film that engages with the topic of memory loss.

The films of Cadena have been informed by visual and conceptual art and are in overt dialogue with the work of the directors associated with the Barcelona School. In the course of the 1970s, Cadena produced a series of documentaries about artists such as Joan Miró and Joan Vila Casas, and documented the 1974 Granollers' *happening*, successfully integrating painting and the theoretical premises of conceptual art into the cinematic code (Vidal, 13–14). His most experimental piece, *Es quan dormo que hi veig clar* (*It Is When I Sleep That I See Clearly*, 1988), establishes a relationship between the poetry of J.V. Foix and the medium of cinema and features the visual artist and playwright Joan Brossa, one of the founding members of the avant-garde group *Dau al Set* (Martí-Olivella, "Tradició" 14). In the words of the film director:

> És cert que m'inspiro en l'esperit i les troballes formals de l'Escola de Barcelona, però els condicionaments sociològics i polítics dels anys vuitanta són uns altres. La presència de Joan Brossa a la pel·lícula és un reconeixement explícit d'aquesta devoció, però el plantejament és d'ara'.
>
> (It's true that I take inspiration from the spirit and the formal discoveries of the Barcelona School, but the sociological and political conditioners of the eighties are different. The presence of Joan Brossa in the film is an explicit acknowledgment of this devotion, but the idea is of the moment.) ("Tradició" 64)

In *Elisa K*, a film that deals with spectrality, traces of the Barcelona School can be found in its abundant references to painting, composition, and film-making – movement, light, and montage. Elisa's sister attentively uses a kaleidoscope while peacefully swinging on a hammock next to an absent-minded Elisa, and their mother is an artist who manipulates images, cutting and editing them to create new means of narrating. The numerous references to viewing contraptions hark back to the popular optical toys that emerged in the 1830s, which simulated movement, rotation, and repetition. As Anna Cox reminds us, these early devices, alongside Eadweard Muybridge's photographic series, have been regarded as primitive means of filmic narration (534). Cox draws on Tom Gunning's concept of the "cinema of attractions," an early form of film that "directly solicits spectator attention, inciting visual curiosity, and supplying pleasure through an exciting spectacle" (384), to explore the cinematic techniques that informed the work of the members of the Barcelona School. Gunning's term underscores the notion of exhibition, the interaction that the film establishes with the spectator, its roots in the fairground attractions, and its influence on the avant-garde movements (384–5). Cox argues that the directors of the School incorporated these early cinema practices, which "had a potentially disrupted eye-opening effect on the spectator who has been conditioned by mind-numbing homogeneous displays encroaching on all areas of everyday life" (536–7). *Elisa K*'s references to these early visual apparatuses and the relationship that the film establishes with the Barcelona School will be explored alongside its recurrent use of doors, windows, and mirrors. Shots of the first two architectural structures often result in the division of the frame into smaller units of representation, whereas the mirror-effect of the recurrent glass panes continuously reflects the lights and movement associated with the outside world. These formal aspects of the film coupled with its focus on memory are highly suggestive of a text that has a concern with the medium itself, that is, with the processes of film-making.

Elisa K is divided into two distinct sections, and each one engages with different spaces and periods of time, a structure which also signals a divide in the character's personality. The first and considerably longer part, directed by Cadena, is filmed in black and white and is distinctive for its use of reflective surfaces, long shots, and voice-over narration. This section mostly centres on Elisa's childhood years and recounts the traumatic sexual attack that young Elisa will almost immediately blank out. The use of voice-over narration here could be read as the character's inability to experience life at first hand, that is, the realization of her life as the psychological effect that trauma can have. Colell takes over the direction of the second part, which is set fourteen years later and follows Elisa's departure to study abroad. It is in this new and unspecified place where the sudden memory of the long-forgotten assault brings about a psychotic bout. Whilst Colell shoots in colour, she opts for muted and subdued tones creating a more intimate and naturalistic atmosphere, which is in turn intensified by her frequent use of close-up and jerky camera movements. Commenting on the structure of the film and its discrete styles, the cinema critic Olga Pereda has referred to *Elisa K* as "una pel·lícula dividida en dues" ("a film split in two"; 2010). Indeed, the directors' strikingly different formal choices might be seen to be in conflict with one another and/or to function as distinct units of representation. In response to this, Colell and Cadena have always maintained that *Elisa K* is a film directed "a quatre mans" ("in concert"; Filmoteca 2011), which asserts the commitment of both parties to the overall integrity of the project. With regards to the structure of the film, Martí-Olivella asserts that the directors' choice emulates in cinematic language the literary text's stylistic split ("Tradició" 63) and in his analysis, he identifies a number of points of contact between the two parts.

In line with Martí-Olivella's argument and attention to questions of image composition and form, this chapter explores the many ways in which these two seemingly disparate cinematic languages complement one another. Whilst each part of the film is discussed in terms of optical and haptic modes of visuality, I will also draw on more recent approaches to tactile visuality, in particular, the work of Jennifer Barker, who argues that sensuous spectatorship is not only felt at skin level but also involves the viewer's musculature and viscera. The chapter suggests that the unity and coherence of *Elisa K* lies in its ability to mimic the viewer's need – to paraphrase Marks – to come close and pull away (*Skin* xvi). Moreover, it shows how visual imagery in this film not only encodes society's attitudes and responses to memory and trauma but also the director's careful attention to geometry and form – as well as colour, texture and gesture – can stimulate, or in some cases manipulate, the public's physical as well as intellectual engagement with this subject matter. This interest in form remains at the basis of contemporary auterish cinematic practices in Catalonia and is rooted in the aesthetic and conceptual concerns of the historic avant-garde – introduced into Catalonia at the end of the 1940s by the collective of artists and writers *Dau al Set* – as well as the 1960s and early 1970s film productions of the Barcelona School. Rosalind Galt has noted the School's engagement with the theoretical approaches of the European avant-gardes, its "aesthetic and political impurity" (491), and its varied combination of forms (498), including painting, pop art, and audiovisual technology. Galt draws on Peter Bürger's understanding of the avant-garde as a rejection of the bourgeois status and location of art and stresses the political stance of the members of the School who believed that "the institution of art was entirely associated with the Francoist state" (493). In line with the praxis of these film directors, the aesthetics of *Elisa K* have been informed by extraneous materials, in particular painting and narrative. Engagement with painting and sculpture as well as theatre and literature is also present in the cinematic practice of other Catalan film directors, most notably, the experimental Albert Serra. With regards to Serra's *Honor de Cavalleria* (*The Honour of the Knights*, 2006), Horacio Muñoz Fernández has noted that the film successfully evokes Don Quixote's nostalgia for the Golden Age and his yearning to be one with God by integrating aesthetic elements from Romantic painting (97).

In cinema studies, "mise-en-scène is bound up with a criticism which is sensitive to the way film works as a medium" (Gibbs 60). In their composition of the interior scenes in the first part of *Elisa K*, the directors found inspiration in the work of the Danish painter Vilhelm Hammershøi (Filmoteca). Indeed, the treatment of light and the recurrence of doors, windows, and framed images hark back to the quiet mood and stillness so characteristic of Hammershøi's paintings of his Copenhagen home. While, in this way, the mise en scène conjures up timeless and impenetrable physical and mental spaces, these are also elements that have a long tradition in the history of the cinema as they are metaphorically related to the process of film-making and viewing. As Sobchack reminds us, picture frames, windows, and mirrors are the three most prevalent metaphors in contemporary film theory and "relate directly to the screen rectangle and to the film as a static *viewed object*, and only indirectly to the dynamic activity of viewing that is engaged in by both the film and the spectator, each *as viewing subjects*" (15). Generally read as signifiers of the cinematic medium, Sobchack notes that these metaphors stand for the idea of the screen as a separate viewed object and as such, they are representative of the hegemony of the gaze in present-day visual culture (15). The querying of the importance and meaning granted to these metaphors is not exclusive to phenomenological approaches to film but has recently been echoed in other research areas in the field of visual culture. The trope of the window in cinema has also been studied by Elsaesser and Hagener, who have described it as "ocular-specular, transitive (one looks at something) and disembodied (the spectator maintains a safe distance)" (14). With regards to the spatial distribution between viewer and object seen, the film theorists note that the window refers to a way of seeing that favours the moral and the emotional detachment from the spectator (14). This ethical dimension is of particular relevance to *Elisa K*, a film that draws frequently on the window and the frame metaphor to address issues of child molestation and psychological trauma. Additionally, the use of the window and frame trope is also suggestive of how Elisa sees her life from the outside – she has become a spectator as a consequence of the trauma she suffers from. Elsaesser and Hagener distinguish between the invisibility of the glass pane, which gives the impression of realism and transparency, and the contouring frame, which delimits the scene and "shifts the attention to the organisation of the material" (18), in other words, it draws attention to the artificiality of the image seen as well as to spectatorship and the more voyeuristic act of seeing in itself.

Elisa K opens with a long take of a building, a simple and rectangular structure with several glass doors and windows of different sizes and variant degrees of opacity, transparency, and reflectiveness (see figure 9.1). Its rectangular shape is replicated in the doors, windows, and dividing panes, creating a mise en abyme that is suggestive of the several ways in which a story can be framed and seen. The symmetry and angularity of the architectural features as seen on the screen are evocative of regularity and order, yet the image could also be read as an imaginary cabinet of curiosities that contains the diegetic worlds that the spectator is about to enter. Shot from the garden outside, the brick structure appears to be unoccupied, and this seeming lack of human activity coupled with the endless references to the screen foretells the experience of being at the cinema at the time when the curtains are about to be drawn. The voice-over narrator explains that the building is the rural village school and gives precise information about the location of the classrooms and the teaching that is taking place inside. The following sequence situates the spectator at the back of a room and facing a large and rectangular blackboard that takes up most of the front wall. The pupils are seated at their individual desks, which are perfectly aligned in rows, and on the left-hand side of the room, a range of vertical glass panes allows natural light into the space. The camera has been placed just behind one student with long hair, and because of the shallow depth of field, the rest of the class appear slightly out of focus. The teacher announces that he is to talk about something very important and makes some illegible annotations on the blackboard, although only the year 1929, written in large numbers, can be discerned: "avui us explicaré qui va ser Martin Luther King" ("Today, I'm going to tell you about Martin Luther King"). In this spatial arrangement, Elisa is placed as a viewing subject, and the somewhat unfocused writing on the blackboard is suggestive of her imminent loss of memory. The relevance of the

238 Eva Bru-Dominguez

Figure 9.1 Screenshot from *Elisa K.* showing rectangular shapes – glass windows and doors. © Jordi Cadena.

teacher's reference to Martin Luther King will not become evident until the end of the film, when Elisa confronts her father and calls into question his courage and failure to protect her when she was abused by recalling the name of the leader of the American civil rights movement.

In the next scene, a brief close-up of a smiling young girl with long hair situates the narrative in a more relaxed and festive environment. Again, the scene insists on the notion of viewing, as the girl is part of a group of children who are watching a private indoor puppet show. Here, the emphasis on architectural structures and geometric figures continues as the focus on the girl is immediately followed by an image of a small theatre stage where a cartoon house gradually appears (see figure 9.2). The constant references to the multiple modalities of the screen (frame, transparency, permeability, and opacity) and to filmic means (montage, light, and camera placement) situate the narrative in overt dialogue with the processes of film-making. In so doing, Cadena calls into question the relationship between the spectator and the image on the screen, and this self-awareness of the nature and history of the cinematic medium in the first part of *Elisa K* allows the director to interrogate the way in which child abuse is both (represented and perceived in a wider social context.

Elsaesser and Hagener note that "screens hide and protect, but they also open up and reflect. Screens are (semi-permeable) membranes through which something might pass, but they can also keep something out: they act as sieve and filter" (39). Like memory, which alters our perception of reality, the references to the screen in *Elisa K* are evocative of the suppression of a traumatic memory. In the film, the transparency

On the Threshold of the Diegetic World 239

Figure 9.2 Architectural structures used at the indoor puppet show. © Jordi Cadena.

Figure 9.3 Elisa's reflection on the train window. © Jordi Cadena.

of the screen is often rendered problematic as windows and large glass panes are used as surfaces where two (or more) levels of reality converge. Elisa looks pensively out the train window as she travels back to her mother's home with her siblings after having spent the weekend at her father's place in Barcelona. Her face is turned towards the window and her downcast gaze is reflected onto the windowpane, imbuing the scene with a sense of profound melancholy. Elisa's spectral image appears against a rapidly changing cityscape that has been set in motion by the movement of train (see figure 9.3). Spectrality has been explored widely by experimental Catalan film directors, most notably Pere Portabella, José Luis Guerín, and Isaki Lacuesta. However, as Steven

Marsh, another of the contributors to this volume, has noted, studies of the representation of the ghostly in the wider context of Spanish cinema have traditionally been framed in historiographical accounts of a nation that is still haunted by its traumatic past. Marsh proposes forms of analyses that move beyond the boundaries of historical memory for "[c]inema's components ... confuse and confound the status of presence and absence, they turn on the translucent and the opaque" (293), and this spectral quality "directly concerns the constitutive properties distinctive of the medium of film itself" (293). This level of engagement with cinematic technology is particularly relevant to the study of *Elisa K*, for the question of memory in this film is embedded in the mechanics of filmic production and its history.

Elisa has been sexually assaulted at her father's house and, despite having repressed the memory of this traumatic event, she appears slumped in deep dejection as she aimlessly looks out the window unable to connect with a world that is passing her by. In this scene, the feeling of physical and mental dissociation is conveyed visually in the overlapping of Elisa's ghostly reflection on the windowpane with the shifting background scenery. At the same time, here, the window frame may be read as a metaphor for both the mechanics of the cinema and the materiality of the celluloid. Elsaesser and Hagener remind us that "[t]he cinema developed at the end of the nineteenth century from advances in photography, mechanics, optics and the scientific production of serialised images (chronophotography)" (1). Activated by the motion of the train, the sequence of images that is seen through the window is evocative of the early studies of movement, such as the pioneering work with photography undertaken by Eadweard Muybridge in the late nineteenth century. This reference to the medium, that is, to the light-sensitive strip where "a trace, something directly stencilled off the real" (Sontag 154) is imprinted, may also be read in connection to the fragility and tangibility of memory.

With regard to cinema, Giuliana Bruno writes that it "incarnates [the] ability to 'animate'; it is a machine that activates lifelike (e)motion" (147) and associates the machine-led image in movement with the mechanical doll or automaton:

> Film work emerged from waxwork by way of automata. From the very beginning there were wax figures mobilized by wind-up clockwork, which created a spectacle of simulated life in motion. Automata made in wax or other media were featured in a form of mechanical theatrical spectacle known as a "moving picture" or "mechanical picture." Such moving

mechanical picture shows foregrounded the spectacle of motion pictures, born in the age of the mechanical reproduction of (body) images. (150)

Bruno's assertion is in accord with Gunning's notion of the 'cinema of attractions," which informs Cox's analysis of the Barcelona School aesthetics. Cox argues that these film directors' insistence on repetition and interpellation is rooted in this type of proto-cinematic optical and mechanical devices (533), which elicit a more active response in the part of the spectator. She terms these dynamics the "exhibitionist cinematic loop" (536) and suggests that whereas Francoist film enchanted and tamed the viewer, the visual and mechanical strategies deployed in the cinema of the members of the Barcelona School "[align] the spectator with the transgressive behaviour he experiences through the peephole or on the screen" (536). The correspondence that is established between *Elisa K* and the aims of the 1960s film-makers operates not only at a stylistic level but also in terms of the relationship between the spectator and the viewed subject/object.

In the first part of the film, Cadena draws on the association between the apparatus for representation and the domain of human perception and affect to articulate the emotional withdrawal of Elisa. In her analysis of the connection between the human body and the cinema, Barker notes that "the fact that moving pictures grew up in such close proximity to the roller coaster and other physical attractions suggests that it offered a similar kinetic thrill" (132). This film theorist is interested in exploring early cinema's allure for musculature and motion as well as the physical involvement of the spectator, which was made manifest "most literally by the act of dropping one's coin into the machines' coin slot" (133–4). In the scene at Tibidabo, Barcelona's oldest amusement park, *Elisa K* alludes to the physical participation and emotional response of the spectator in primitive forms of cinema viewing. Elisa's brother and the children of his father's friend visit the museum of automata where a collection of mechanical theatre toys and other small-scale fairground artefacts are exhibited. The children operate the motors and bring about movement into the lifeless toys located behind the glass panes. Their incredulous reaction to the violent acts performed by the dispassionate clockwork-driven figures and their delight in the robotic movements of the harlequin and other circus creatures is reflected onto the glass (see figure 9.4). The brutality enacted by these mechanical figures anticipates both the sexual abuse that Elisa will be subject to and the visual dynamics that are later to be established. As the group moves to the next object, the youngest of the three sets into motion a miniature Ferris wheel and uses a toy camera to take a photograph of the rotating device

242   Eva Bru-Dominguez

Figure 9.4   Reflections of the children against the mechanical circus characters. © Jordi Cadena.

Figure 9.5   Elisa's young brother takes a photo of the miniature ferris wheel with a toy camera. © Jordi Cadena.

to the amusement of Elisa's older brother (see figure 9.5). At this point, the scene is intercut by an image of Elisa enjoying a ride on the large Tibidabo Ferris wheel, which towers over the expansive views of the city. A pause in the mechanical system causes Elisa to become trapped in the swinging basket and to remain momentarily suspended high above the ground. For Martí-Olivella, the cup-like capsule "esdevindrà una mena d'anti-madalena proustiana que propiciarà el moment del record" ("will become a kind of Proustian anti-madeleine, which will trigger her memory"; "Tradició" 15). In this instance, Elisa not only sees the world from afar – as an observer – but she has also been symbolically incorporated in the mechanisms of film-making, whereas the rest of the children are constructed solely as viewers and operators of the medium. In so doing, the story of Elisa is rendered the object of the spectator's gaze.

Several sequences in the film are set against the background of a noisy and shifting Barcelona, which is being constantly mirrored on the large glazed facades of the restaurants and cafes regularly visited by the family. In his study of the construction of myth in cinema, Irving Singer notes that mirrors "increase the spatial properties of almost any cinematic setting [...] Being instruments of refraction, mirrors *enlarge* our field of perception, backward in depth as well as forward and sometimes to a simulacrum of infinity" (31). The exterior shots of the neighbourhood's eateries and cafes endlessly reflect a city that is in constant movement, whereas the framed mirrors and paintings inside the restaurants remind us of the screen's function to demarcate and delimit. Here, the use of reflective surfaces results in the convergence of inner and outer spaces onto the same plane and situates the story of Elisa in between a continuous mise en abyme that beckons to the spectator. Singer has pointed at the psychological dimension of the mirror in the narrative of a film, which serves as a means to explore unconscious mental and emotional forces (31). The symbolism ascribed to the mirror in film studies has also been studied by Elsaesser and Hagener, who note how it challenges the notion of the window and the door as the threshold between diegetic realms and, in line with Singer, problematizes the relationship between spectator and screen for "[a] look into the mirror necessitates a confrontation with one's own face as the window to one's own interior self" (56). More than this, as a metaphor for the silver screen, the window-cum-mirror in *Elisa K* is also indicative of "an arrangement that hides something or someone by dividing a space" (Elsaesser and Hagener 38). In the city scenes, the reflections on the glass panes slightly glaze over the main action and prevent the spectator from achieving any level of intimacy with the family (see figure 9.6). The audience's feeling of inaccessibility and detachment is intensified by the noise emerging from the ongoing traffic, which muffles the conversation between the family members and often forces the spectator to rely exclusively on the account of the voice-over narrator. Actually, it is this matter-of-fact and extradiegetic voice that at one point in the course of the narrative will announce impassively: "El pare, que ha begut més del compte durant el dinar, s'adormirà d'aquí poc i uns minuts més tard, l'Elisa serà violada. Després perdrà la memòria" ("The father had a bit too much to drink at lunch and will soon fall asleep, and a few minutes later Elisa will be raped. Then she'll lose her memory"). The

Figure 9.6 City scenes reflected on the café's window panes © Jordi Cadena.

narrator alerts the audience of the attack that is to come, and the assault on Elisa takes place off screen, sparing the audience the horror of witnessing child abuse.

The scene that precedes the rape is shot at a zenith angle and focuses on two coffee cups – symmetrically arranged on a tray – a cafetière, and a milk jug. As the coffee and milk are being poured into the cups, the voice-over narrator describes with precision the location in the room of a range of off-screen objects and pieces of furniture. An image of the living room soon follows showing Elisa's drowsy and semi-drunken father slouching on one of the sofas while his sober-suited and stiff-looking friend – a jeweller – sits by a very quiet Elisa on the other one. A film is on TV and its strident soundtrack fills the room with a sense of fatality. The mise en scène is framed by the glass-panelled door and windows, which fill the room with a subdued light. Elisa's brother asks for permission to go out into the terrace and disappears outside the frame, and Elisa's father is soon fast asleep. Sipping at his coffee, the jeweller begins to eye his victim up. In the meantime, the rhythm of the music rapidly accelerates as if it were a warning of the danger that is to come. Fourteen years later, the sound of a very similar tune on TV and the smell of fresh coffee will jog Elisa's memory of the abuse and prompt a psychotic bout. The camera averts the violent attack that takes place in the father's living room and focuses, by contrast, on the swaying motion of the children's swing situated on the terrace outside. The metaphor of the swing is self-explanatory: the back-and-forth movement of Elisa's brother, the screeching sound of the metal, and the eventual rupture of the chain, which causes him to fall. In the future, when Elisa moves to Barcelona to go to university, she will try to avoid

Figure 9.7 The swing's broken chain. © Jordi Cadena.

living at her father's flat on the grounds that she is afraid of the swing (see figure 9.7). Despite Cadena's concern with optical visuality, when dealing with the scene of the sexual attack the director avoids visual mastery over the subject of vision and fosters instead a more context-sensitive means of looking. Moreover, the visual dynamics employed in this sequence can be read as a commentary on the invisibility of sexual violence and its traumatic psychological effects in a sociocultural landscape where visual perception reigns supreme. The main problem in this scene is the presence of her father in the room at the time of the assault. Allegedly fast asleep, his awareness of the violation remains in doubt throughout the film. Elisa's memory of the aggression is immediately repressed at the jeweller's promise of a bracelet, and the uncertainty about the father's knowledge is only revisited in the closing sequence, when Elisa confronts him at one of their habitual neighbourhood cafes: "Pare. Tu te'n recordaves?" ("Dad. Did you remember?"). As he weeps and affirms having no recollection of the abuse, Elisa slowly turns round towards the camera and probingly gazes at the spectator as well as the technical apparatus that has thus far framed her own story, acknowledging her trauma and dismantling the mechanisms of objectification (see figure 9.8). The scene is shot in colour, because this part of the film has been directed by Colell, who reinscribes one of Cadena's usual sets with her use of extreme close-ups and subdued palette. Significantly, with this final episode she revisits the place and some of the techniques used in the first part of the film, locating both image and audience in the same spatial organization. Initially, Elisa's conversation with her father at the cafe is shot from the outside in a manner reminiscent of the episodes at the cafes previously discussed. By contrast, in this rather long

246   Eva Bru-Dominguez

Figure 9.8 Elisa gazes at the camera. © Jordi Cadena.

scene, the sparse dialogue between Elisa and her father is completely deadened by the sounds of car engines, continuous beeps, and ambulance sirens. This outside traffic noise functions as a filter which is suggestive of the difficulties to communicate, to remember, or to talk about trauma. In fact, it is only through the physical proximity of the close-up that Elisa's words are eventually clearly heard: "Alguna vegada penses en persones com el Martin Luter King?" ("Do you ever think about someone like Martin Luther King?"). Elisa's question harks back to the opening scene in the film, when her teacher introduces the name of the civil rights activist at the school's classroom, and where she is located as passive spectator. In this occasion, however, Elisa has taken control of the situation and is the enabler of dialogue not only with her father but also with the audience.

Despite the range of visual and aural strategies utilized by Cadena in the first part of the film, the relationship between audience and image is seldom altered, allowing the public to maintain a certain level of distance and perspective with respect to the image and the storyline. Even the frequent long silences provide the viewer with some needed respite from Elisa's suffering. In addition to this, the voice-over narrator anticipates the events and, in so doing, protects the spectator and prevents his/her full emotional involvement emulating the same detachment from reality that Elisa might suffer from after the rape. In fact, there is only one instance in this section of the film where this sense of regularity and contained order is disrupted, and that is when Elisa dreams that she is in a forest and is being persecuted by her abuser. However, this scene – reminiscent of the "Little Red Riding Hood" fairy tale – maintains a sense of uniformity, made manifest by the strong breathing and the rhythmic background sounds, which are evocative of the rocking movement of the swing used in the rape sequence.

This recurrent sensation of order and the safe distance with the film's subject matter is reversed in the second part of the film, where the viewer is often brought to close proximity to Elisa, in particular, during the long scene when she suffers from a psychosis and the spectator is compelled to respond emotionally as well as physically to her profound distress, prompting an awakening in both the character and the audience. This stylistic and atmospheric shift can also be explained in terms of the differences between optical and haptic perception, as formulated by Marks:

> Optical visuality requires distance and a center, the viewer acting like a pinhole camera. In a haptic relationship our self rushes up to the surface to interact with another surface. When this happens there is a concomitant loss of depth – we become amoeba-like, lacking a center, changing as the surface to which we cling changes. We cannot help but be changed in the process of interacting. (*Touch* xvi)

The body, in this episode in particular, becomes the focus of attention and here both the director and the actor convey visually as well as through performance the unexpected eruption of a traumatic memory that had long been lodged in Elisa's unconscious.

In order to do so, Colell and Cadena took inspiration from the portraits of Egon Schiele (1890–1918) and Lucian Freud (1922–2011). While in terms of aesthetics, these are, indeed, very different artists, they both addressed the human form as a means to depict their sitter's inner self. Schiele – a key figure of Austrian expressionism – radicalized his approach to the nude genre and unflinchingly sought to capture humankind's most painful secrets. He was a master of line and colouring, and his frequently contorted, vulnerable, and highly sculptural nudes appear to have been cut through the epidermis to reveal the rawness of the musculature underneath. Freud also had an interest in bodily shape and structure and was famous for his intense and mercilessly explicit nude paintings of alienated individuals, always executed in a mute palette. While Schiele's austere line contrasts with the richly textured canvasses of Freud, their work unquestionably is a statement on the fragility of the human condition. This awareness of corporeal structure – skin, flesh, and musculature – and its links with the mind and the unconscious are evoked in Colell's use of jarring camera movements in her depiction of Elisa's abrupt recollection of the assault. The director has described the over-the-shoulder shot used in this episode as a form of harassment that emulates the way in which the memory of abuse assails Elisa (Filmoteca). In turn, the frenzied camera movements induce a physical and/or emotional reaction in the spectator, whereas the intrusive motions of the camera as well as the sometimes excessive proximity to Elisa may also be seen either to mimic our desire to help bring out the traumatic memories that have so suddenly started to besiege her or our impulse to get close to Elisa and comfort her. Here, I argue that the potential to induce corporeal or sensuous responses from the audience is relevant to the analysis of the representation of memory and trauma. Etymologically speaking, trauma is a wound consequence of a sudden physical impact that tears and damages the body. Yet trauma also refers to the psychological symptoms that follow a deeply distressing experience, which might eventually lead to somatization disorder. Indeed, as Diana Taylor reminds us, "[t]rauma, by nature, is performatic. Before it can be talked about, trauma manifests itself as an acting out in both the individual and the social body" (1674). In order to account for the physical relationship that Taylor establishes between the personal and the social in representations of trauma, I draw on Marks's notion of reversibility in haptic viewing, which entails "making oneself vulnerable to the image" (185) and read this episode in terms of empathy, mimesis, and, ultimately, affect.

The term "haptic" originates from the Greek *haptikos*, meaning to come in contact with, and *haptein*, to fasten (37), and indicates tactility and/or pressure. In art, film, and new media, haptic visuality refers to a manner of seeing that draws upon multiple forms of sensorial experience. It is a corporeal affair mostly determined by the way in which we inhabit our own bodies and is attentive to the sociocultural context in which these are located. Haptic representation avoids visual mastery and involves out-of-focus, distorted, or grainy shots and detailed, intimate images that pull the spectator "away from a symbolic understanding and toward a shared physical existence" (Marks, *Touch* xii). Its emphasis on palpation, contact, and sensation is certainly redolent of the writings of Luce Irigaray and has led many scholars to associate the haptic with the feminine (Marks, *Touch* 7), and for the reasons stated above, it is also considered an erotic form of representation (16). Given the associations of this sensorial form of representing with femininity it is relevant to note Colell's contribution to the film *El domini dels sentits* (*The Realm of the Senses*, 1996), where five female Catalan film-makers co-directed an exploration of each one of the senses from the perspective of the female experience. Interestingly, in this film, Colell focuses on sight and relies on the metaphor of the window to examine the experience of the protagonist as an observed spectator.[2]

In *The Tactile Eye*, Barker takes this physical mode of viewing deeper into the body. Drawing on the notion of mimesis as a form of perception that elicits the representation of that which is perceived back to itself, she explores the muscular encounters particular to the handshake and the chase in a range of films. Barker argues that we feel certain camera movements, such as whip pan, slow motion, long takes, or tracking shots, with our own muscles because we have previous and corporeal knowledge of these actions (75). Moreover, for Barker, watching a film can make us aware, often quite unexpectedly or even violently, of our inside organs. The horror genre is particularly effective when it comes to bringing our innards into relief. In her seminal work on the horror film genre, Barbara Creed draws on Julia Kristeva's notion of the abject as that which "disturbs identity, system, order" (Kristeva 4) and notes that the experience of viewing a horror film signifies "to throw up, throw out, eject the abject (from the safety of the spectator's seat)" (Creed 10). Indeed, as Baker reminds us, in the act of viewing the physical connections may be activated and, as corporeal beings, we might hold our breath, gasp in terror, feel butterflies in our stomach, or sickness and repugnance (124). In *Elisa K*, the soundtrack of a film causes the adult Elisa to feel unwell and, unaware of the repressed memories that the music is about to revive, she lays down on the sofa and gently presses her hands onto her seemingly upset stomach in the same way she did the day after the rape. At this point, it is useful to return to Creed's understanding of the abject in the cinema and of the "biological bodily functions" (9) in which it might be experienced. This is certainly true of Elisa, whose first memories of an abject experience are solely felt in the form of stomach ache. Shortly after, when Elisa unhurriedly prepares a coffee and brings the cup to her lips, the smell and taste of the fresh brew will trigger a series of spasms and leave her gasping for breath (see figure 9.9). The sensorial experience has brought back the memory of abuse in the form of physical pain and provokes a psychotic bout and temporary loss of her sense of identity. Kristeva has spoken of "the shameless rapist" (4) as a cause of abjection, and in a desperate attempt to expel the abject memory, Elisa sobs, vomits, cuts her flesh open, and eventually initiates a cleansing ritual. During this excruciatingly painful episode, the jolting motion of the camera and extreme proximity to

---

2 Teresa de Pelegrí explored taste, Núria Olivé-Bellés touch, Maria Ripoll hearing, and Isabel Gardela smell.

Figure 9.9 Elisa drinking a cup of coffee. © Jordi Cadena.

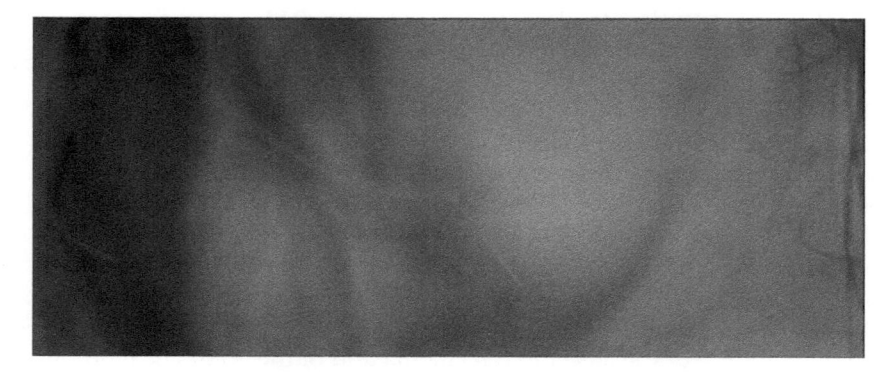

Figure 9.10 Elisa's heavy breathing. © Jordi Cadena.

Elisa appeals to our senses, muscles, and viscera, and as active viewers, we mimetically respond to her feeling of nausea, her pain, the breathlessness, her spasms and convulsions. The camera focuses on the base of her neck, where the panting and heavy breathing is most noticeable, and it turns to her trembling limps and watery eyes (see figure 9.10). This fragmentation of the body is replicated in Elisa's next action, as she shatters the mirror – that powerful symbol of both identity and the silver screen – into small pieces and walks over the shards, allowing the razor-sharp edges to dig into her bare feet (see figure 9.11). The pain Elisa feels when she sees herself reflected in the mirror has prompted her to turn this instrument of reflection into an object of torture.

Back at her mother's house and willing to accept help, Elisa initiates a healing process that will in due course lead her to come face

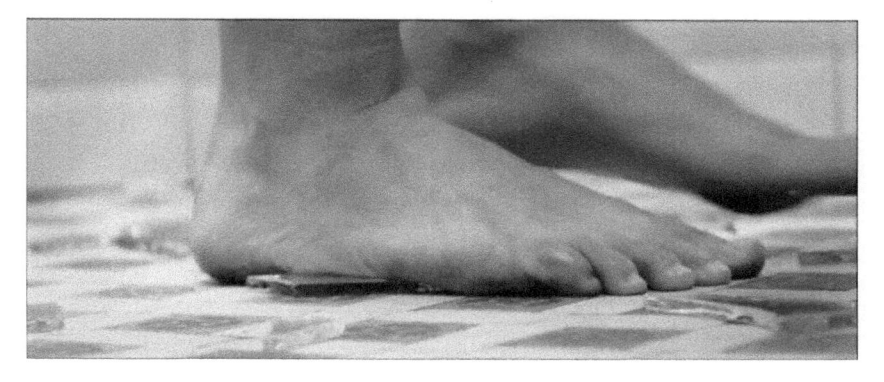

Figure 9.11 Elisa walking over the shards of the broken mirror. © Jordi Cadena.

to face with her own father. Before this, however, the attempt to rid herself of the symbolic dirt that still haunts her returns in the form of a dream, which is reminiscent of an act of cleansing and rebirth. In this scene, Colell uses slow motion to show how Elisa dives deep into water and, after various forward rolls, manages to push herself vigorously back to the surface. Here, the water is ascribed with the same symbolic meaning that Loxham identifies in the swimming pool in Carla Subirana's documentary film *Nedar*, namely, as the repository of history or that "safe, secure pre-memorial uterine space" (135). The appeal to the sensory system in this scene and its association with the maternal (and abject) body must not be underestimated: the splash of the water as Elisa launches herself in, the extradiegetic sobs that echo the first tears that Elisa shed immediately after the abuse, her fetal position as she rolls forward, and the translucent oxygen bubbles that appear to multiply rapidly as she comes nearer the surface (see figure 12). This dream finally takes her back to her father, and in this scene Colell replicates the mise en scène that characterized the external shots of the restaurants and cafes previously discussed. Here, the director momentarily restores visual perspective for the spectator to the detriment of engaging the other senses. Seen through the cafe's glass pane, Elisa's voice is inaudible and has become entangled in the rhythms of a busy and uncaring urban context. However, and because of our previous proximity to her, our prior awareness of her pulsating body and our knowledge of her physical and psychological pain, we are drawn closer into her image and, in spite of the constant reflections of cars and pedestrians that hamper our clarity of vision, we

252 Eva Bru-Dominguez

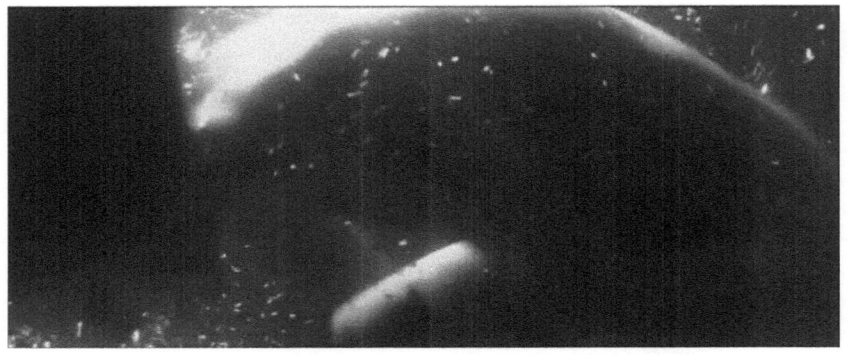

Figure 9.12 Elisa dreams that she is under water. © Jordi Cadena.

might even be able to identify some of the words she utters from the movement of her lips.

The directors have spoken of their interest in "la mirada final de l'espectador" ("the spectator's final gaze"; Filmoteca np), a concern that is echoed in Elisa's final penetrating look. The importance granted to the audience's response is in accord with the work of the members of the Barcelona School, who integrated elements of early cinema that beckoned the engagement of the spectator. By including proto-cinematic elements in the film, such as the automata or the Ferris wheel, Cadena not only draws a historical and aesthetic continuum with this group of film-makers and their roots in the historical avant-gardes, but he also subtly appeals to the senses of the viewer. Colell's visual strategies, her jarring camera movements and extreme close-ups, undoubtedly elicit a more direct form of physical engagement with the audience. All in all, as spectators, we might have finally rejected a means of looking that is vacuous and insentient, like that of the puppets and mechanical dolls that feature in the first part of the film. As haptic criticism would have it, we might have learned to look with our senses and with our culturally and historically specific bodies. Moreover, through empathy and mimesis, we might even have dug deep into our unconscious and unearthed some unpalatable memories on the way, for *Elisa K* primarily is a film about re-establishing continuities between past and present, and therein lies its relevance in our present-day context, where, urged by the primacy of making space for the enforced gaps in our history, culture, and society, the recovery of lost memory has become a crucial endeavour.

WORKS CITED

Balló, Jordi. "L'estratègia del desplaçament." *Comunicació: Revista de recerca i d'anàlisi*, vol. 29, no 1, 2012, pp. 10–23.
Barker, J. M. *The Tactile Eye: Touch and the Cinematic Experience*. University of California Press, 2009.
Bicicleta, cullera, poma. Directed by Carles Bosch, Cromosoma, 2010.
Bruno, Giuliana. *Atlas of Emotion: Journeys in Art, Architecture and Film*. Verso, 2007.
Bucarest, la memòria perduda. Directed by Albert Solé, Sagrera TV, 2008.
La casita blanca. La ciudad oculta. Directed by Carles Balagué, Diafragma Producciones Cinematográficas, 2002.
Cox, Anna. "'Cinema of Attractions'? The Barcelona School's Exhibitionist Loops." *Hispanic Review*, vol. 78, no. 4, 2010, pp. 529–49.
Creed, Barbara. *The Monstrous-Feminine. Film, Feminism, Psychoanalysis*. Routledge, 1993.
Dies d'agost. Directed by Marc Recha. Lauren Films, 2006.
El domini dels sentits. Directed by Teresa de Pelegrí, Judith Colell, Maria Ripoll, Núria Olivé-Bellés, and Isabel Gardela, performaces by Núria Prims, Silvia Munt, and Gustavo Salmerón, Filmax, 1996.
Elisa K. Directed by Jordi Cadena and Judith Colell, performances by Aina Clotet, Hans Richter, and Lydia Zimmermann, Obreron Cinematogràfica, 2010.
Elsaesser, Thomas, and Hagener, Malte. *Film Theory: An Introduction through the Senses*. Routledge, 2010.
Es quan dormo que hi veig clar. Directed by Jordi Cadena, performances by Joan Brossa, Núria Cano, Hermann Bonnín, and Ona Planas, Septimània Films, 1988.
Filmoteca de Catalunya. "Els directors d'*Elisa K* comenten una escena del film." *Cicle Catalunya Cinema*, Feb. 2015. https://www.youtube.com/watch?v=M50F1VEUIDO, 2011.
Galt, Rosalind. "Impossible Narratives: The Barcelona School and the European Avant-Gardes." *Hispanic Review*, vol. 78, no. 4, 2010, pp. 491–511.
Gibbs, John. *Mise-en-scene: Film Style and Interpretation*. Wallflower, 2001.
Gunning, Tom. "The Cinema of Attraction[s]: Early Film, Its Spectator and the Avant-Garde." *The Cinema Of Attractions Reloaded*, edited by Wanda Strauven, Amsterdam UP, 2006.
Kristeva, Julia. *Powers of Horror: An Essay on Abjection*. Translated by Leon Roudiez, Columbia University Press, 1982.
Loxham, A. "Subjective Pasts and the Imaginative Power of the Image in *Bucarest, La memòria perduda* and *Nedar*." *The Noughties in the Hispanic and Lusophone World*, edited by K. Bacon and N. Thornton, Cambridge Scholars Publishing, 2012, pp. 130–41.

Lunati, Montserrat. "Recordar per oblidar? Trauma i gènere a *Elisa Kiseljak* (2005), de Lolita Bosch." *Els Marges*, vol. 98, 2013, pp. 76–101.
Marks, Laura U. *The Skin of the Film: Intercultural Cinema, Embodiment, and the Senses*. Duke University Press, 2000.
– *Touch: Sensous Theory and Multisensory Media*. University of Minnesota Press, 2002.
Marsh, Steven. "Editor's Introduction. Untimely Materialities: Spanish Film and Spectrality." *Journal of Spanish Cultural Studies*, 15, no. 3, 2014, pp. 293–8.
Martí-Olivella, Jaume. "Catalan Cinema: An Uncanny Transnational Performance." *A Companion to Catalan Culture*, edited by D. Keown,Tamesis, 2011, pp. 185–206.
– "Historical Memory and Family Metaphor: New Catalan Documentaries." *Journal of Catalan Studies*, 2014, pp. 53–71.
– "Tradició i modernitat al nou cinema català: El cas d'*Elisa K*". *Ciutat de l'amor: scrivere la città, raccontare i sentimenti*, edited by Maria Carreras, Núria Pugdevall, Patrizio Rigobon, and Valentina Ripa. *Rivista Italiana di Studi Catalani*, vol 3, 2013, pp. 53–74.
Muñoz Fernández, H. "Paisajes románticos y estéticas sublimes: El cine de Albert Serra." *Archivos de la Filmoteca*, vol. 72, 2013, pp. 91–105.
Nadal-Melsió, Sara. "Editor's Preface. The Invisible Tradition: Avant-Garde Catalan Cinema under Late Francoism." *Hispanic Review*, vol 78, no 4, pp. 465–8, doi: www.jstor.org/stable/25790597. Accessed 9 September 2018.
Nedar. Directed by Carla Subirana, Barton Films, 2008.
Pereda, Olga. "*Elisa K*, de Judith Colell i Jordi Cadena impacta a Sant Sebastià." *El Periódico*. 22 September 2010. http://www.elperiodico.cat/ca/noticias/cultura-i-esp ectacles /20100922/elisa-judith-colell-jordi-cadena-impacta-sant-sebastia /491370.shtml. Accessed 28 December 2020.
Singer, Irving. *Cinematic Mythmaking: Philosophy in Film*. MIT Press, 2008.
Sobchack, Vivian. *The Address of the Eye*. Princeton University Press, 1992.
Sontag, Susan. *On Photography*. Doubleday, 1990.
Taylor, Diana. "Trauma and Performance. Lessons from Latin America." *Modern Language Association of America*, vol. 121, no. 5, 2006, pp. 1674–7.
Vidal, Núria. *Jordi Cadena: Entre l'experiment i la indústria*. Enciclopèdia Catalana, 2006.

10 Watching Novels and Reading Films: Deleuzian Affects in Catalan Cinema

ANTON PUJOL

"Anything becomes interesting if you look at it long enough." This quote from Gustave Flaubert (1821–80) appears on screen at the beginning of Marc Recha's *El cielo sube* (*Heaven Rises*, 1991), an adaptation of *Oceanografia del tedi* (*Oceanography of Tedium*) by Eugeni d'Ors (1881–1954), first published in 1916. D'Ors does not cite it, but it perfectly prepares the audience to embrace the young Catalan director's first feature film in which time will literally stand still and meaning avoid figuration. D'Ors's fragmented and ambiguous text is avant-garde, constantly forcing readers to adapt to a narrative of "affects" in the Spinozan sense. Although Recha never said what he saw in *Tedi*, it might be precisely the structure that d'Ors frames to elicit shifting responses to the work of art.

Here, I want to foreground three encounters: first, the encounter of affects in d'Ors's *Tedium*; second, the encounter between d'Ors and Recha; third, the encounter between Recha's film and the Barcelona School of the late 1960s and early 1970s. I will look at Deleuze and Guattari's concept of affect to show how it elucidates d'Ors's text, Recha's cinematic adaptation, and the Barcelona School's artistic endeavours beyond their disruptive approach to generic conventions.

Oceanography of Tedium

A brief overview of the short text is essential to fully comprehend why *El cielo sube* represents a radical change in Spanish cinema. D'Ors wrote *Tedium* under the pseudonym Xènius. It was first published in the newspaper *La Veu de Catalunya* between 10 August and 17 October 1916. In an introduction, three parts consisting of one-to-two page "chapters," or scribblings on sensations, and an epilogue, d'Ors employs a highly sophisticated, sometimes jarring language to describe a strange situation. The introduction plunges readers into a scenario that comes into focus word by word. The plot, for lack of a better word, of *Tedium* starts with a character named "Author" repeating his doctor's prescription: "No conversa, silenci. No lectura, letargi … Tant com sia possible, ni un moviment, ni un pensament!" ("No talking, silence. No reading, lethargy … as much as possible, not even one movement, not even one thought"; *Tedium* 5). Author is following the doctor's orders, and we find him resting in a quiet garden, sinking into tedium exactly as a shipwreck victim sinks into the sea (10). The introduction ends with the narrator announcing that Author will create an oceanography by discovering things that would seem monotonous only if you were not paying close attention, echoing the quote from Flaubert with which Recha opens his film.

In part 1, Author describes every tick of his physical experience while lounging in the garden from subtle changes in temperature to imperceptible vibrations to delicate smells, or what I will later refer to as affects. Author's senses become hyperfocused; he describes in painstaking detail the many sensations that go through his body when someone is watering the grass: the sun, sky, clouds, the white wall he faces, the shades of green. Chapter 14 exhaustively depicts the "delicacies" of a muscular cramp, which can only be savoured once the more mundane "plaers hermètics del rogall incipient" ("hermetic pleasures that stem from a cough's early symptoms"; 41) have been mastered. The narration oscillates between phenomenological digressions on the effect of a particular sound or various ailments to literary and cultural opinions on Dante, Wagner, Horace, and Nietzsche. Part 1 ends when a young "Woman" dressed in white appears, reading a French novel in a nearby chaise longue.

Part 2 welcomes "dramatis personae" (51) in the form of two goddesses: one is the "Will to Change" and the other the "Will to Order." The former is audacious and tempts Author to engage with Woman. The latter cautions him to avoid risks and fleeting adventures, advice he will ultimately follow. A sudden storm interrupts his three "tedious" August hours in the park, and he runs away. The epilogue finds him abruptly checking out of his hotel just one day after his arrival, although the languid narration has implied he has been there for days. He returns to Barcelona and, that same night, writes that it is impossible to escape from oneself, and "ja no sent més la fadiga, d'ençà que sap que ell no pot conèixer el descans" ("He is no longer fatigued since he discovered that he cannot experience restfulness"; 102). The work ends with a quote from Horace's *Odes* (2.16): "Quid brevi fortes iaculamur aevo / multa? Quid terras alioi calentis / sole mutamus? Patriae quis exsul / se quoque fugit?" ("Why do we strive for so much in such a short time?

Why do we yearn for new lands with different suns? Can exile flee from itself?"; 104).

D'Ors's *Tedi* is emblematic of the Catalan cultural movement he termed Noucentisme in his 1906 *Glosas*, brief writings on the arts and politics. It was "founded on concepts such as structure, rhythm, harmony, and order, and presented as an exercise in organization, as opposed to the emotionalism and spontaneity of modernista art" (Suàrez and Vidal 227), which explains why the "Will to Order" wins in the end. Joan Cuscó i Clarasó summarizes d'Ors's style:

[A]n orchestral symphony that must be able to capture simultaneity in language, because simultaneity also occurs in reality and, at the same time, in order to generate a non-dogmatic viewpoint. To this end, the philosopher creates a double distancing, or estrangement in his work: the first is the writer's regarding what he writes and the second concerns the ideas in relation to the ideas themselves. That is, in relation to reality and in relation to what is said on the basis on reality. (94)

Tedi was part of the *Glosari*. Its extremely brief episodes are dense, moving from hyperrealism to a profound abstraction that keeps readers at bay. The style is humorous and always ambiguous, both techniques of distancing. Jaume Vallcorba describes the mixture of irony and philosophical debate throughout the text as a "boutade," "a playful textual impertinence." D'Ors wrote: "Yo no sé narrar. Mi natural inclinación, cuando encuentro narraciones bajo mi mirada, es dejarlas quietas. Lo cual no significa, en modo alguno, dejarlas inertes" ("I do not know how to narrate. Whenever I find narrations under my nose, my usual inclination is not to disturb them. But that does not mean to leave them inert, far from it"; Vallcorba ix). Again, this remark resonates with Flaubert's. It might be superfluous to note that a highly abstract text parsing uneventfulness seems a poor choice for a first film, but Marc Recha thought it perfect for his big screen debut.

El cielo sube

Writer/director Joaquín Ojeda recommended the project, and Recha thought it would be easy: "a black and white movie [that] could be made without direct sound" (Vidal 14). He added that "era una necesidad imperiosa de demostrar que desde la periferia, desde el margen, se podía hacer una película" ("it was of the utmost necessity to prove that a film could be made from the periphery, from the margin"; Vidal 16). He did not spell out which margin, but it could be geographical

(Barcelona vs. Madrid), historical (a contemporary adaptation of an early twentieth-century text), and artistic, taking a formalist approach at odds with the realistic proposals of Spanish cinema. Like *Tedi*, *El cielo sube* defies categories. It is a hybrid that recalls such cryptic works of the Barcelona School as Esteva and Jordà's *Dante no es únicamente severo* (*Dante Is Not Only Harsh*, 1967) and Pere Portabella's *No compteu amb els dits* (*Don't Count with Your Fingers*, 1967) and *Nocturno 29* (1968), to name a few. With a budget of approximately $150,000, the film was shot in 240 takes over three days at Ojeda's family farmhouse in Turre (Almería); finished with five more takes in Barcelona, like the novel; and edited in just two weeks (Angulo 33).

Recha and Ojeda closely followed the structure of d'Ors's text, even inserting the chapter titles on screen to force the disoriented spectators to reckon with watching a novel and reading a film. For example, "S'acosta una tempestat" ("A Storm Approaches"), chapter 5 in part 3, consists of eleven segments, each with a different title. In the film, the titles appear on the screen while the voice-over (Luis Porcar) reads their few sentences. Similarly, the title of the next chapter, "El tro" ("The Thunder"), remains on screen, while the text is replaced by a loud thunderclap.

There are two major differences between the novel and the film. First, the protagonist, Author, is renamed Juan de Dios (played by Salvador Dolz), and the two goddesses (Will and Order are replaced by a "chapter" titled "La Binovia" ("The Bi-bride"), in which a blonde woman, dressed in white, faces a woman with black hair dressed in black. The woman in black grabs the blonde by the neck and starts smelling her. When their lips get close, the blonde blows air into her face. They seem about to kiss but never do. The woman in black then blows air into the blonde's face. The only sound is heavy breathing (Juan de Dios or the women?) and the soft whistle of the wind. Then they are gone, and we never hear or see them again. Apart from these two changes, the voice-over faithfully reads all the humorous, nonsensical, elitist language of the Noucentista author.

While adapting *Tedi* as a film and reading directly from it, even screening its chapter titles, are already daring moves, Recha's visual style is extraordinary and anything but casual. He put a greenish scratch on the right side of the squared frame, so the film would look old and worn, like a film from the twenties, technically primitive with shaky camerawork and sound that seems tacked on. Angulo wrote that "Una fotografía en blanco y negro, conscientemente manipulada para darle un aspecto un tanto amateur" ("[b]lack and white photography has been heavily manipulated to give it an amateurish look"; 33). Thus, the spectators are always conscious of the film's fragility and its artificiality and its substantive reality.

After the Flaubert quote, the opening sequence is a series of indecipherable flashes, like brushstrokes. A shot of grass, and the voice-over softly whispers the doctor's instructions: "Don't move, don't think!" The photography by Miguel Llorens accentuates visual contrasts – shady and sinuous shapes, ambiguous and stark – every image is an inconclusive guessing game. The camera may also dwell on an object or nothing at all for a long time, sometimes without any sound. The many close-ups of both Juan de Dios and the blonde woman may linger on a specific body part. In the early chapter "Concert," Juan de Dios's body is compared to a harp played by the breeze; close-ups of different elements (a shoe, his nose, eye, brow) are briefly shown in a circle across the screen. Recha presents his visual dismemberment, while the voice-over provides little textual coherence.

Throughout, the film lays bare the artistic enterprise behind the scenes, embracing and retrieving the avant-garde techniques that were crucial to the cinema of the Barcelona School. In the same way that d'Ors's mischievous style disconcerts readers, Recha and his team shatter spectators' expectations and ask them to create their own paths to understanding, accomplishing one of the main goals of the Barcelona School: to open "a radical alternative to realist film practices" (Ledesma 272). The school was not creating "art for art's sake" as is sometimes argued but "an opening onto a different organization of aesthetics" (Galt 494). *El cielo sube* challenges us to re-evaluate the passive process of watching a movie from its first scratched frame right up to the closing credits.

Chapter 7, "Cenestèsia" ("Coenaesthesia"), is a turning point in the text and the film. *Webster's Dictionary* defines cenesthesia as "the general feeling of inhabiting one's body that arises from multiple stimuli from various bodily organs." Medical dictionaries explain it as a "general sense of existing, derived as the aggregate of all the various stimuli and reactions throughout the body at any specific moment to produce a feeling of health or of illness." Johann Christian Reil coined the term in 1794 to denote "the global experience in which all the single bodily sensations are synthesized, the crossroads of all sensibility on which consciousness is grounded, including the feeling of existing, of being a self and of being separated from the external world" (Stanghellini 57). Its basic symptoms are somatic depersonalization, sensations of motor weakness, and a variety of migrating, electric, thermic, or pain sensations. If patients become too hyperaware of all the sensations that surround them, they are diagnosed with cenesthetic schizophrenia. When Author/Juan first experiences the intermingling of physical and emotional sensations, he feels happy and exhilarated, but, in the end, strange and disembodied. I consider the sensations he experiences and painstakingly describes affects since they are immediate and yet alter him. They are both material and method for D'Ors and Recha.

Affect

Philosopher Gilles Deleuze (1925–95) and psychoanalyst Félix Guattari (1930–92) collaborated on several works of cultural criticism. Affect is the core of their philosophy. Derived from Spinoza's concepts of *affectus* and *affectio*, Deleuze argues that *affectus* is the capacity to both affect and be affected, while *affectio* is merely the reaction to the mixing of two bodies. For Spinoza (1632–77), he argues, "Affects are becomings ... Bodies are not defined by their genus or species, by their organs and functions, but by what they can do, by the affects of which they are capable" (Deleuze and Parnet, "Superiority" 60). They "can compel systems of knowledge, history, memory and circuits of power" (Colman 12) because they are immediate, adaptive, and need not rely on old practices. Not surprisingly, in *What Is Philosophy?* Deleuze and Guattari place affects as an integral part of art:

> What is preserved – the thing or the work of art – is *a bloc of sensations, that is to say, a compound of percepts and affects*. Percepts are no longer perceptions; they are independent of a state of those who experience them. Affects are no longer feelings or affections; they go beyond the strength of those who undergo them. Sensations, percepts, and affects are *beings* whose validity lies in themselves and exceeds any lived. They could be said to exist in the absence of man because man, as he is caught in stone, on the canvas, or by words, is himself a compound of percepts and affects. The work of art is a being of sensation and nothing else: it exists in itself. (164; emphasis in original)

Spinoza's anti-Cartesian philosophy allows Deleuze and Guattari to see works of art as a compendium of affects; their intensities and variations are specific in time yet indefinite, impossible to comprehend. Colman writes that, in its largest sense, affect "is part of the Deleuzian project of trying-to-understand, and comprehend, and express all of the incredible, wondrous, tragic, painful and destructive configurations of things and bodies as temporally mediated, continuous events" (11). Thus, affect produces art that forces us to move beyond old patterns of thinking, figuration, and narration. Affect in art disrupts, challenges, and complicates our relation to the world. True art creates a dialogue, an encounter where solutions are never provided.

In "I Feel, Therefore I Am," Emily Eakin writes: "In the middle of the 17th century, Spinoza took on Descartes and lost." Spinoza argued that body and mind are a continuum, not two separate entities. and that the famous Cartesian Cogito was untenable. For Spinoza, reason "is shot through with emotion," and "thoughts and feelings are not primarily reactions to external events but first and foremost about the body. In fact, [Spinoza] suggested, the mind exists purely for the body's sake, to ensure its survival" (Eakin). While Spinoza was shunned in his time, his theories have been validated by neuroscience; emotions, cognition, and physiology are inextricably intertwined. In Deleuze's reading of Spinoza, a body is constituted, like a work of art, by its capacity to be affected. In his lecture on Spinoza, he underlined the connection: "a body must be defined by the ensemble of relations which compose it, or, what amounts to exactly the same thing, by its power of being affected. As long as you don't know what power a body has to be affected, as long as you learn like that, in chance encounters, you will not have the wise life, you will not have wisdom" ("Lecture"). Coenaesthesia, short of psychotic distress, is the ideal state since the body is open to receive affects. The doctor's orders that open d'Ors text and Recha's film announce a Cartesian denial: "Don't think."

Since d'Ors read both Descartes and Spinoza, his *Ethics* in particular, the opening of "Cenesthesia" cannot be considered unrelated. The chapter starts with a resounding reversal of the Cartesian principle: "Jo no penso. Doncs, jo existeixo. Si jo pensés, ja mon existir no fóra tan segur" ("I do not think. Therefore, I exist. If I were to think, my existence would not be so certain"; 27). The doctor's instructions – "Don't move! Don't think!" – are the coordinates for a sensorial experiment that Author does not know he can accomplish. In one of the few chapters narrated in first person, Author delimits his body as a territory that extends from the tops of his shoes to below his eyebrows; what his eyes perceive is his only reality. Deluze and Guattari would call this frame the body's *longitude*: "the sum total of the material elements belonging to it under given relations of movement and rest speed and slowness" (*A Thousand Plateaus* [henceforth *ATP*] 260). From now on, every chapter revolves around how Author is experiencing the sensible world in what seems an eternity, or Deleuzoguattarian *latitude*, which is where the body registers the affects it can "at a given degree of power, or rather within the limits of that degree" (*ATP* 256). The minutiae of Author's existence comprise everything he is feeling, the many shades of green in the garden, the various thermal sensations, the incipient ailments of his quasi-hypochondriac existence – any colours, smells, sounds, and phosphenes (stimulation of the visual system other than by light), no matter how small or almost imperceptible, rate a paragraph. The narrator describes Author's Spinozan state: "Autor es sent voltat de possibilitats sensibles ... Es sap mestre i artista de les seves sensacions, organista d'una orga màgica ... Cinc sentits, o sis, o set, I els altres sentits de què no es coneix el nom" ("Author feels surrounded by sensible possibilities ... He knows he is the master and artist of his feelings, the organist of a magic pipe organ ... Five senses, or six, or seven, and all the other senses that the world is still to name"; *Tedium* 17). This surplus of senses that Author cannot recognize awakens self-awareness; he need not relate them to previous modes of knowledge or signification. Bruce Baugh's explanation of bodies and affects clarifies Deleuze and Guattari's concepts:

> Bodies are affected by different things, and in different ways, each type of body being characterized by minimum and maximum thresholds for being affected by other bodies: what can and what cannot affect it, and to what degree ... If an external body is combined or "composed" with a body in a way that increases the affected body's power of being affected, this transition to a higher state of activity is experienced as joy ... It is impossible to know in advance which bodies will compose with others in a way that is consonant with a body's characteristic relation or ratio to its parts, or which bodies will decompose a body by causing its parts to enter into experimental relations. (31)

Author's response to his new sensorial experience of the world will be, however temporarily, joyous. He demarcates his body as the longitude where the affects – latitude and cenesthesia – are invited to wreak havoc with thought, organizing systems, and any previously experienced or recognized sensation.

In both the text and the film, the protagonist becomes like Spinoza; he will experience everything that happens around him, no matter how small or trivial, as affects, which Claire Colebrook defines as "just a sensible or sensibility not organized into meaning" (34). Author becomes a hypersensitive, reactive organism welcoming and describing the new experiences. For example, someone watering the garden with a hose sparks each of the five (or six, or seven) senses and a shower of adjectives and nouns:

> Delícia de veure regar! Delícia de sentir regar! Delícia d'olorar com reguen! Delícia de respirar com reguen! I delícia inconfessable de les voladores

gotetes perdudes que han caigut a tocar aquesta pell ardent, aquesta mà balba!

I, vet aquí, l'espectacle es fa encara més meravellós. El raig d'aigua dansa. Ara violentament s'escurça. Ara es projecta al lluny del lluny. De dreta a esquerra, de lluny a prop, dansa. Sembla ubriac. I de veure'l ubriac així, ubriaga. Ubriaga de joia infantívola i violenta.

(What a pleasure it is to watch how they water the plants! What a pleasure it is to hear how they water the plants! What a pleasure it is to smell how they water the plants! What a pleasure it is to breathe in how they water the plants!

And what an ineffable pleasure it is to feel how a few lost, flying drops have fallen to touch my burning skin, my tired hand!

And, look at this, the spectacle turns even more wonderful. The water stream dances. Now, violently, retreats. Now it shoots far, far away. From right to left, from far to near, it dances. As if it were drunk. And just by observing, in its drunken state, it gets you drunk. It gets you drunk with childish and violent joy.) (33)

The doctor's orders forbidding thinking or articulating a thought allow Author to concentrate on affects, to experience and explore the sensible world without the old codes and regimes. Sensation takes precedence over any other mental process, and his few random ramblings are not organized into a construct readers can categorize. Whether a smell, a sound, a muscle cramp, or an incipient migraine, Author welcomes and allows its repercussion through his body. "For Deleuze," Simon O'Sullivan writes, "such an encounter is always with an object of sense that in itself involves the short-circuiting of sorts of our cognitive and conceptual capacities" ("Aesthetics" 197). In first or third person, d'Ors's writing reflects Author's aimless scrolling through affects. The result falls into what Deleuze and Guattari understood as true art because, as Colebrook argues, "Art works by taking us back from composites of experience to the affects from which those synthesized wholes emerge" (35), and true artistic endeavours always encompass "singular affects and percepts, freed from organizing and purposive viewpoints" (36), which is what Author and later Juan de Dios are trying to accomplish.

In the second part of the book, everything changes. The two goddesses appear and explain why Author should follow their respective dicta. The "Will to Order" compares Author's current state of sensible extasis to being drunk. "Allà on el sentits s'ennuvolen … allà és el mal … Fes la teva vida, com l'elegant demostració d'un teorema matemàtic"

("Right there, where the senses become cloudy... right there, evil lives ... Live your life as if it were an elegant proof of a theorem"; 55). The exact world of mathematics, a closed regime of signification where problems have perfect solutions, sharply contrasts with the Author's submerged explorations. Throughout their oeuvre, Deleuze and Guattari conceive the "Body without Organs" (usually denoted BwO), inspired by the writings of Antonin Artaud, to describe a state similar to the one engulfing Author. In *A Thousand Plateaus*, they write, "After all, is not Spinoza's *Ethics* the great book of the BwO?" (153) because for them, the BwO is not opposed to the organs but to the "organic organization of the organs" (158). To become a BwO, you must

> [l]odge yourself on a stratum, experiment with the opportunities it offers, find an advantageous place on it, find potential movements of deterritorialization, possible lines of flight, experience them, produce flow conjunctions here and there, try out continuums of intensities segment by segment ... Connect, conjugate, continue: a whole "diagram" as opposed to still signifying and subjective programmes. (161)

Throughout the first part of *Tedi*, the full experience from the chaise longue in the corner of the park is a stratum described as "aula meravellosa per l'oceonagrafia del tedi" ("a wonderful classroom for the oceanography of tedium"; 46), which is why "Autor es sent voltat de possibilitats sensibles" ("Author feels surrounded by sensible possibilities"; 45). The sensible possibilities, or the continuum of intensities, will turn into lines of flight. Author will connect and conjugate affects, reporting each without explanation. Readers just receive the sensible world as experienced by Author.

However, the entrance of "Will to Order" terminates the affective encounters. The Author's *jouissance* is immediately censored. Regardless of the justifying discourse, society always seeks to repress the sensible state. Deleuze and Guattari were against discourses imposing conformity:

> Where psychoanalysis says, "Stop, find yourself again," we should say instead, "Let's go further still, we haven't found our BwO yet, we haven't sufficiently dismantled our self." Substitute forgetting for anamnesis, experimentation for interpretation. Find your body without organs. Find out how to make it. It's a question of life and death, youth and old age, sadness and joy. It is where everything is played out. (*ATP* 151)

At the end of the second part, Author caves in; he swims to the surface. To make matters worse, his hand signs the Cross – "el gest the l'eficaç exorcisme" ("the gesture of the efficient exorcism") – over his body, still "reeling from some contrary forces" ("combatut encara de forces contraries"; 71). The contrary forces, the affects, are stripped off. They cannot be reasoned into traditional and religious discourse; they cannot be controlled; they just happen and produce various, complex, surprising reactions. When Author opens his eyes, the woman, the chaise, the book are gone. The prosaic scenario, an ordinary garden, returns. The pleasures, pain, experiences, and fantasies produced before reason and order entered his mind have evaporated.

The third part opens with Author quoting Catholic verses in Spanish to indict himself as an old man. He is perhaps also signalling two discourses (Spanish and Catholic/religious) that have been notorious in Catalonia at certain moments in history for their reterritorializing impulses. He wonders if his exhaustion is the result of experiencing all the wonders of his tedium or living through the battle of reason versus adventure. He claims that the victories of the "Will to Order" are cold, like the feeling of melancholy (75). A cloud appears over the garden; the wind blows, and the chill he experiences is "precisament localitzat" ("precisely located") behind his ear. Instead of flowing with playful affects, with the coarse pain, "[o]bligades nocions d'osteologia tornen a la seva memòria" ("required osteological concepts return to his memory"; 89). He dutifully substitutes cause-and-effect medical discourse for his exuberant reactions to random affects. Another signifying discourse finishes off Author's adventures in the realm of the sensible.

As a storm approaches, Author wonders what would have happened if the Pope had commissioned Raphael to paint a room completely devoid of historic episodes or allegory, and readers may wonder if that has been d'Ors's goal. Instead of the old and tried, Raphael would have painted "hermetically, a hieroglyphic riddle" (89) that might force a contemporary art lover to abandon all ideological signification ("la ideològica signifcació del tot," 89) and symbolic meanings ("la significança del symbol"). Syllogistically, Author is asking readers to abandon regimes of signification that no longer apply. Now, every artistic element must be experienced freshly and only then considered in a new paradigm not chained to some fixed significance. The narrator informs us that, exactly like the art lover in front of the indecipherable painting, Author is standing "davant els signes que van mostrant l'acostament de la tempesta" ("in front of all the signs that indicate that a storm is approaching"; 89). "Es delecta en les formes i no en confegeix el significant" ("He is mesmerized by the shapes but fails to comprehend the meaning"; 89) before an "infernal thunder detonates" over his head and shakes him, once and for all, out of his reveries. He will be drenched in no time.

Although the plunge into affect pleased him, the thunder and the storm are his enemy; they expel him from his chaise and garden. He complains: "I jo, que he estat celant un orga admirable de sensacions, una a manera de pura estàtua marmòria, sense moviment ni pensament; jo, que del perfecte compliment de la rigorosa sentència me n'havia fet un orgull, per tal que aquest compliment esdevingués com una obra d'art i fruita singular de l'albir" ("And I who took care of an incredible organ of sensations, as if I were a pure marble statue, without a single movement, without a single thought; I, who was extremely proud of having obeyed my strict sentence, so my obeying would turn into a work of art and an exceptional fruit of my free will"; 91), now he is passive before nature's power. Losing the battle to Order humiliates him, but he knows that during his stay in the garden, he lived more and experienced more sensations than if he had travelled to the Orient. His feelings of "[v]ergonya, fadiga i buidor i enyor de cosa perduda" ("shame, fatigue, and emptiness and a longing for something lost") vanish as he realizes they are his punishment for having dared to "transgredir una llei" ("break a law"; 95). He is who he is; he cannot change, nor he should try. Returning to Barcelona the next day, he meets a friend just back from a clinic in Switzerland, who says he is still not cured because you cannot change who you truly are. The Horace verses that end the text – "what fugitive from his homeland can flee from himself?" – are tainted with sadness.

D'Ors's ambiguous, inscrutable, riotous, and melancholic text frames the story of Author. Although he feels as if he is drowning when he first dives into sensation, he immediately realizes that this different paradigm has awoken his "conscience/mind." He is swimming among "[e]ssers singulars" ("strange beings"), privileged to "navigate" a "rich and multiple" universe interpreted as monotonous by those who do not pay attention (12). He tries to submerge completely in this world that few can or will experience. According to Daniel Smith, the body without organs "[]an be defined as the becoming-machine of the organism; it is what happens when one part of the body enters into combination with some other machine in a way which allows it to escape from the organism's regularizing, normalizing processes. Seen in this way, the body previously considered an organism is opened up to a whole host of new connections, each of which may lead to the production of an event" (109).

Author opens up affective possibilities by submerging himself, becoming a perceiving body, a vessel. By obeying his doctor's prescription, he is going against his own will, his frenetic life. He immobilizes himself at a new abstract threshold where conscious reason cannot enter.

D'Ors's text stands at the threshold of genres and disciplines, presenting a multitude of intertexts that leave the reader uncertain what to think. Its equivocality must be a central reason Recha chose to adapt it for the big screen. His films have always challenged spectators. Elsewhere, I summarized his "unconventional aesthetic," combining "narrative obscurities and precious visuals," to create "a jarring effect" in which

> [u]nhurried narratives meander, confusing and seemingly confused. Pascale Thibaudeau attributes these longueurs to Recha's ultimate objective: to show spectators how much they rely on overly codified messages and to disturb their usual way of receiving information (2009, 108). Thus, minimal plots walk a problematic line between narrative and documentary; fiction, verisimilitude, and reality; past and present. In the Rechian universe, cinema's classical concepts and expectations are challenged and obliterated in an unresolvable chaos of sophisticated styles, media, and references. (Pujol 178)

Joaquim Jordà, a key member of the Barcelona School, sees in Recha's films echoes of Jean Renoir (1894–1979), Roberto Rossellini (1906–77), Otar Iosseliani (1934), and especially Marcel Hanoun (1929–2012). For Jordà, Recha "inventa día a día su propio itinerario cultural. Esto supone riesgos y vacíos, pero permite ... la euforia creativa del descubridor, sin mapas previos, de un territorio virgen, subjetivamente virgen" ("invents every single day his own cultural itinerary, which implies risks and silences but allows ... the creative euphoria of the discoverer, without previous maps, of a virgin territory, subjectively virgin"; 5).

You can see this style emerging in his rather dark, cryptic, and disturbing short films, like *El zelador* (1989), *La por d'abocar-se* (1990) and *La Maglana* (1991). Carlos F. Heredero summarizes their characteristics thus: "[l]a exploración contemplativa de estados de ánimo, emociones, y pensamientos mediante unas imágenes entrecortadas, despojadas al máximo de toda referencialidad y llevadas casi hasta la frontera de la abstracción que pugnan por captar lo esencial desde el registro de lo físico, de la luz y de los sonidos" ("the contemplative exploration of moods, emotions, and thoughts through choppy images, completely stripped of referentiality, is taken to the border of abstraction while trying to encompass what's essential in the surroundings, in the light, in the sounds"; 300). He concludes that Recha's short films penetrate a sensory universe that the camera tries to personify ("adentrarse en un universo sensorial al que la cámara intenta dar cuerpo"; 298). Note, however, that the dramatic short film welcomes experimentation and open and ambiguous narratives more than feature films, where Recha continues to defy expectations. His kinship with d'Ors's text should not be surprising.

Angulo writes that Recha saw cinematic possibilities from the first moment he read *Tedi*. He claims that Recha's obsessions have always been embedded in the text: "la voz en *off* como elemento narrativo, su constante reflexión sobre el tiempo, el gusto por los detalles y las imágenes fragmentadas" ("the voiceover as the narrative element, its constant reflection on time, the attention to details and fragmented images"; 35). He also comments on Recha's detailed use of light and shadows and how the careless-looking frames and shots aim to reflect the protagonist's inner state. Angulo summarizes *El cielo sube* as a quest for abstraction and "an orgy of the senses" (38) since the protagonist's quiet tedium "multiplies the power of the senses" (39). Heredero found it to be "un ensayo audiovisual más que una propuesta narrative" ("an audiovisual essay more than a narrative film"; 299) and concludes that it wants "en dar consistencia visual a lo meramente sensitive, en buscar textura y densidad para la materia del pensamiento" ("to make the senses visually tangible by lending thinking a texture and density"; 300).

Heredero's attempts to define the film's style suggest Deleuze's distinction between movement image and time image. In *Cinema 1: L'image-mouvement* (1983) and *Cinema 2: L'image-temps* (1985), he characterized the two modalities, which were separated by the collapse of the sensory-motor schema, or the crisis of the action-image. The Deleuzian time-image responded to the new cinema that appeared after the Second World War, namely, neo-realism in Italy and, later, the French Nouvelle Vague. Amy Herzog traces this change: "The emphasis shifts from the logical progression of images to the experience of the image-in-itself. What we find here are pure optical and sound situations (opsigns and sonsigns), unfettered by narrative progression, and empty, disconnected any-space-whatevers. This move from 'acting' to 'perceiving' carries over to the characters in the film, who cease to be 'agents' and become, instead, 'seers'" (20). An important concept in Deleuze's taxonomy is the "espace quelconque" ("any space whatsoever"), which, he argued, results from the broken link between time and movement in cinema. These virtual conjunctions (*Cinema 2* (C2) 109), shaped by shadows, lyrical abstractions, and colour, depict "urban cancer, an indifferent surface, a wasteland" (C2 258) through images of a "marshalling yard, disused warehouse, the undifferentiated fabric of the city"

(*Cinema 1* (*C1*) 208). Deleuze linked the last neorealist cinema, particularly the works of Michelangelo Antonioni (1912–2007), to these spaces since they became "dispersive, elliptical, errant or wavering, working in blocs, with deliberately weak connections and floating events" (*C1* 1) and added that "the real was no longer represented or reproduced but 'aimed at.' Instead of representing an already deciphered real, neorealism aimed at an always ambiguous, to be deciphered real" (1). In d'Ors's text, Recha found a way to assemble a "dispersive and lacunary reality ... a series of fragmentary, chopped up encounters" (*C1* 212) into not a traditionally coherent structure, but a visualization of affects that Author, now Juan de Dios, experiences while trying not to think. Heredero writes that "Los objetos y las imágenes que rodean a Juan de Dios aparecen desgajados de sus raíces espaciales, la cámara siempre en equilibrio inestable" ("All the objects and images that surround Juan de Dios are free from their spatial roots, the camera always in an unstable balance"; 301). Again, Deleuze distinguishes an affection-image, which is the close-up: "Affective framing proceeds by *cutting close-ups* [*gros plans coupants*]. Sometimes howling lips or toothless sneers are cut into the mass of the face. Sometimes the frame cuts a face horizontally, vertically or aslant, obliquely. And movements are cut in their course, the continuity shots systematically false, as if it was necessary to break over-real or over-logical connections" (*C1* 107). Recha turns Author's canvas-like immersion in affects into Juan de Dios, a composite of the narrator's voice and images that may or may not imply a subjective or an objective point of view. The spectator is never sure about the origin of the images; they might be a dream, a comment, an accident, real or imagined; they might present the narrator's or the somnolent Juan de Dios's point of view.

Deleuze uses Henri Bergson's definition of affect as "a kind of motor tendency in a sensory nerve" (Bergson 110). Similarly, in d'Ors's text and Recha's film, Author/Juan de Dios is a receptacle of ambient sensations/affects. For Deleuze, when "[t]he moving body has lost its movement of extension, and movement has become movement of expression ... this combination of a reflecting, immobile unity and of intensive expressive movements ... constitutes the affect" (*C1* 88). He adds: "The affection-image, for its part, is abstracted from the spatio-temporal co-ordinates which would relate it to a state of things, and abstracts the face from the person to which it belongs in the state of things" (*C1* 99). From the beginning, Recha's "oceanography" will be composed of non-narrative images and sounds only. His images are blurred and rarely show the whole object. The camera movements are unstable, translating Author's disorientation for spectators. Recha then edits these amorphous shots into a strangely detached, dismembered, and incomplete narrative. Affect resides in the space between the sensory effect and its reception. According to Deleuze: "Affection is what occupies the interval, what occupies it without filling it in or filling it up. It surges in the centre of indetermination, that is to say in the subject, between a perception which is troubling in certain respects and a hesitant action. It is a coincidence of subject and object, or the way in which the subject perceives itself, or rather experiences itself or feels itself 'from the inside'" (C1 65).

Recha creates in the spectators' experience the affective equivalent of what transpires between Author and his own experience. Author and spectators are motionless subjects experiencing intensive expressive movements. The decentred interval occupied by words in d'Ors's text is now occupied by Recha's hazy shots, fragmentary editing, and the seemingly scratched film.

Recha also exploits the concept of "espace quelconque," which, for Deleuze, is "the genetic element of the affection-image" (C1 100):

> It is a perfectly singular space, which has merely lost its homogeneity, that is, the principle of its metric relations or the connection of its own parts, so that the linkages can be made in an infinite number of ways. It is a space of virtual conjunction, grasped as pure locus of the possible. What in fact manifests the instability, the heterogeneity, the absence of link of such a space, is a richness in potentials or singularities which are, as it were, prior conditions of all actualization, all determination. (109)

The garden where Author/Juan de Dios rests is an "espace quelconque" not because of its function or spatial coordinates but because of the way it is presented. In Recha's film, the garden is a space to encounter affects, bereft of bucolic conceits. After we see the body of Juan de Dios and hear the doctor's prescription, the camera frames the white wall almost accidentally; shadows are intercepted with angled views of balconies and coffee cups, body parts, closeups of grass, among other objects. The framings thwart narrative coherence, they isolate and extract but never explain or establish an equivalence with any established meaning. Once Juan de Dios sinks into tedium, the images turn even more expressionistic. The camera lingers for long periods of time on the white wall, branches, shadows. In "Photosphenes," for instance, Recha uses an extreme close-up to frame Juan de Dios's closed eyes as he rubs them, while the images that accompany "Coenaesthesia" are almost inscrutable: white sheets, maybe just shades of white, slowly blowing in the wind? At times, the garden looks as if it exists on another planet. Except for the brief appearance of the two phantasmagorical women, it is desolate, empty. Thanks to this highly formalistic visual approach, it becomes an abstract space. Deleuze asks, "How can any-space-whatever be extracted from a given state of things, from a determinate space?" (*C1* 111) and answers shadows and the creation of shadows: "The shadow extends to infinity. In this way it determines the virtual conjunctions which do not coincide with the state of things or the position of characters which produce it" (112), and "It is therefore shadows, whites and colours which are capable of producing and constituting any-space-whatevers, deconnected or emptied spaces" (120). Once the rain starts, Juan de Dios will escape the garden, but until that moment he has been immobilized, the receiver of all sorts of affects.

The moment exposes another significant difference between Author and Juan de Dios. Once Author leaves the garden and later the hotel, he seems to return to a regular state where he is in control of his actions. His arrival in Barcelona is described with rather ordinary adjectives in sharp contrast to the exultant, precise, erudite language he used in trying to convey his sensations. His migraine is no longer "libinidosa" ("libidinous"), and even the clouds "that used to be so interesting" have lost their remarkable shape and are no longer black or white, just "llis i de color de fum" ("flat and of smoky colour"; 86). The intensities that impregnated sounds and sights have disappeared. O'Sullivan writes: "This world of affects, this universe of forces, is our own world seen without the spectacles of habitual subjectivity" (*Art* 50) in a process similar to Author's. He is going back to his old self. The experiment has ended and with it, the dynamic subject who entered the depths of mental and sensorial oceans. Paradoxically, now that Author believes it is not in his nature to relax, we find him more relaxed, sadder, and less curious. He reasons, he deduces, he understands the medical and religious discourses that escaped him before, but he is silent. He has returned to a world where signifiers rigidly follow signifieds.

Recha takes a different approach. Before the thunder explodes, he places the chapter's eleven (sub)titles on screen, and the voice-over reads the brief paragraphs that constitute each. We then see Juan de Dios awakened by the rain, the chaise longues under the rain, and various shots of rain. However, this straightforward visual narrative is short-lived. When Juan de Dios arrives in Barcelona, the images turn chaotic. The unblemished Barcelona of the text is inscrutable, dark, fuzzy; the reflections of hectic lights or maybe marquees on the wet pavement could be on the moon. The last part of the film is filled with pure sound optical situations. Without any transition, the final credits roll. Since Recha dispenses with the signifying figure of the "will to order," Juan de Dios never organizes his thoughts, forms conclusions, follows codes and meanings. Even in Barcelona, he translates words producing affect in d'Ors's text into the upheaval of affect-images. Felicity Colman explains how the affect-image enhances intensities:

> In these terms of the affect-image, the camera is as much a body of interactivity as an actor's body, or the body of a landscape, or the body of a director's work, or as we say, the body of a film genre. Affect is what will cause the movement from one state to another. The movement and subsequent mixing between any animate or inanimate bodies produces affects: on screen it could be an entity like rain, or the sound of an animal, a computer-generated monster or a particular space or colour. The affect is an intensity that will produce a dynamic expression in a body causing it to alter its composition and its potential trajectories. This is different to a screen effect, which concerns the technicalities (stylistic and technical) of how to render that affect. Technicalities in themselves can produce further affects. (84)

In the first part of the film, Recha uses affect-images to convey Juan de Dios's sensory perceptions; toward the end, he combines affection-images with quick edits to sever the film and the text from any known discourse, iconography, or figuration. While the voice-over continues narrating Juan de Dios's arrival and early days in Barcelona, visually, the city has lost its coordinates and seems depleted of humans. Recha has fully embraced the will to chaos and robs the spectator of any signifying relation in a stark departure from d'Ors's text.

In his first long feature film, Recha uses a written text to challenge (deterritorialize) cinema. He creates a new, hybrid narrative that the spectators must piece together, but the irrational cuts and affection-images they see on the screen cannot be made coherent. The sensory-motor schema that we expect from films is broken from the first frame. While Recha had already explored some of these techniques in his short films, a genre that allows more "time-images," ambiguity, and mischief, his iconoclastic approach in his first feature anticipates the kind of director he would be. For him, cinema-making is about breaking free from norms, meanings, and concepts. In the same way that Author/Juan problematize their being, their subjectivity each step of the way, Recha questions his role as a film-maker. In the garden, Author/Juan encounters affects in a continuous present that seems to last an eternity. The affect and lack of movement open new, creative avenues of thought for the characters and, for Recha, new ways to challenge old ways of seeing and understanding. O'Sullivan summarizes the purpose of art:

> Another way of saying this is that art is a deterritorialisation, a creative deterritorialisation into the realm of affects. Art then might be understood as the name for a function, a magical and aesthetic function of transformation, less involved in a making sense of the world and more involved in exploring the possibilities of being in – and becoming with – the world. Art is less involved in knowledge and more involved in experience – in pushing forward the boundaries of what can be experienced. (*Art* 52)

Quim Casas correctly argued that *El cielo sube* is imbued with a "tono desafiante de cada encuadre" ("a challenging attitude in each frame"; Vidal 40). He asserts that although approaching Recha's work is daunting for spectators, the director seems fully conscious of what he wants his cinema to convey. Nick Davis writes that, for Deleuze, if cinema is to inspire reflection and resist "the medium's anaesthetizing potentials," it must eschew rigid narratives and "systematized relations among shots" (108). The affection-images, taken from d'Ors's text, complicate our tried ways of understanding stories. The affect is always independent of space and time; in our case, it drifts in an oceanography of boredom that has its own particular coordinates. Recha frames the intensities of chained sensorial experiences that span a deserted space, bypassing any kind of story-telling and frustrating spectators. In *Gilles Deleuze*, Colebrook summarizes the effect that such a procedure entails: "The proliferation of intensities in art destroys the image of a unifying viewing subject who recognizes a meaningful world that is there for us all. Intensities skew or scramble the faculties; the eye may desire while memory or judgement recoils in horror" (39).

Deleuze and Guattari believed that artists create affects to challenge our tried modes of understanding, or, as O'Sullivan summarizes, affects "operate to rupture certain circuits of reception and consumption and other habits of 'spectatorship' (those that reinforce a certain 'knowledge' of art, or even a given subjectivity) whilst opening us up to other perhaps more unfamiliar but more productive economies" ("Aesthetics" 157). Not surprisingly, Deleuze raves about the "French Wave" because those films created a rupture between old and new ways of seeing: they "broke shots open, obliterated their distinct spatial determination in favour of a non-totalizable space: for example, Godard's unfinished apartments permitted discordances and variations, like all the ways of passing through a door with a missing panel, which takes on an almost musical value and serves as accompaniment to the affect" (*C1* 121).

He might also be talking about the Barcelona School and the similar rupture that its films caused in Spanish cinema. As Rosalind Galt argues:

> Certainly, the stylistic and thematic overlaps are profuse. The use of natural lighting and non-professional actors, the lack of complete scripts and oblique narrational strategies all figure prominently across the Barcelona films. Critics have compared the films to those of Michelangelo Antonioni, Vera Chytilova and Jean-Luc Godard, and, in case we miss the connection, both *Dante* and *Cada vez que...* feature references to *Pierrot le fou* (Godard, 1965). (9)

Jean-Paul Aubert, in his seminal *Seremos Mallarmé: La escuela de Barcelona, una apuesta modernista*, traces a direct line between the Catalan and French film-makers of the two groups. He uses Deleuze's definition of time-image to unite them since they adopted similar sound and visual options to create a new language that questioned old tenets of classic cinematic storytelling. Heredero likens Recha to a "francotirador" ("sniper") because his cinema breaks all possible moulds, while declaring him "el único heredero de los cineastas radicales de los años setenta" ("the only heir to the radical film-makers of the 70s"; 299).

Even if Recha never read Spinoza, d'Ors had; that's why I link both to the affects of their respective works. In *Expressionism in Philosophy: Spinoza*, Deleuze wrote that

> If we have a knowledge of external bodies, of our own body, of our soul itself, it is solely through these ideas of affections. They alone are given us: we perceive external bodies only insofar as they affect us, we perceive our own body only insofar as it is affected, we perceive our soul through the idea of an idea of an affection. What we call an "object" is only the effect an object has on our body; what we call "me" is only the idea we have of our own body and our soul insofar as they suffer an effect. The given here appears as the most intimate and vital as well as the most confused relation between our knowledge of bodies, our knowledge of our own body and our knowledge of ourself. (146)

D'Ors dramatizes the affects on Author's body, the novelty of their perception, and how they challenge his subjectivity. Two parts of the text relate how he is perceiving affects. His body maps where they take place. Recha visualizes those same affects, and the result is two-pronged: spectators are affected, but, more important, the way they watch cinema is challenged. Not only does Recha make them watch a text, divided by titles and often read aloud to them, but he also uses a battery of affection-images that precipitate thought, as Deleuze argued, to disorient them. He intensifies the sensorial experience that d'Ors's Author and narrator painstakingly describe by angular frames and incomprehensible shots through a camera that seems to wander; close-ups; the fragmentation of all elements of the composition. Last but not least, everything on screen is printed on scratched film that looks old and damaged. Recha does not conform to anything. His shots are incoherent, if we follow our old axioms, but intense and affecting. As Author experiences a series of sensorial encounters, spectators of Recha's film experience another, genuine encounter that expedites thought, as O'Sullivan writes: "Our typical ways of being in the world are challenged, our systems of knowledge disrupted. We are forced to thought. The encounter then operates as a rupture in our habitual modes of being and thus in our habitual subjectivities. It produces a cut, a crack" (*Art* 1). The true artistic encounter forces us to generate our own ideas, and we need not reconcile them with any other idea. Recha does what artists are supposed to do, according to Deleuze and Guattari: "artists are presenters of affects, the inventors and creators of affects. They not only create them in their work, they give them to us and make us become with them, they draw us into their compound. Van Gogh's sunflowers are becomings, like Durer's thistles or Bonnard's mimosas" (*What Is Philosophy?* 173). Recha's space is any-garden-whatsoever where his angles and shots present affects that spectators feel but must struggle to read.

Carlos Losilla wrote that in Recha's filmography, we uncover "propuestas figurativas que se disuelven en manchas de color. No hay conflicto entre ambos extremos, sino una fluctuación constante que en el fondo no se dirige a ninguna parte ... se trata de un cine de lo fugaz, lo pasajero, que busca sin encontrar" (seemingly figurative scenarios that melt into colour spots. There is no conflict between extremes, just a constant fluctuation that truly does not go anywhere ... it is a cinema about the ephemeral, the fleeting; a cinema that seeks without ever finding"; 58). These characteristics apply, not only to Recha, but to the Barcelona School and the work of many other contemporary Catalan film-makers, such as José Luis Guerín (Barcelona, 1960), Isaki Lacuesta (Girona, 1975), and Albert Serra (Banyoles, 1975). Their filmic language is an affective and intensive experience for spectators. As Author and Juan de Dios must invent a process of signification and enunciation, readers and spectators experience their own encounter with d'Ors and Recha's work. Affect is a way for us to understand the importance of *El cielo sube* as well as the extent to which any film manipulates our watching.

In "Is There a Deleuzian Aesthetics?" Jacques Rancière compares Deleuze's conception of the work of art with "the power of a pure, a-signifying sensible" and Deleuze's ideas on Francis Bacon and the process of defiguration to Flaubert's "clearing of the terrain" style. He also links Flaubert's writing style to Proust's through the power of affect, although he does not use the word:

> [Flaubert's clearing-of-the-terrain style] undoes, line after line, the grammatical conjunctions and semantic inferences that make up the ordinary substance of a story, thought or sentiment. This clearing of the terrain has the precise purpose of equating the power of the phrase with the power of a sensibility that is no longer the sensibility of the man of representation, but the sensibility of the contemplator become object of his own contemplation: foam, pebble or grain of sand ... In the same way, Proust links the power of the work of art to the experience of a sensible removed from its conditions, to that moment when two worlds reunite and all reference points shatter; the world of the pure sensible, of the sensible sensed by stones, trees, landscapes or the moment of the day. The ideal book dreamed of by the young Proust is familiar: the book made of the substance of a few instants arranged in time, the book made of "tastes of light," of the substance of our most beautiful moments. (12)

In *El cielo sube*, Recha's cinematic language also undoes "the grammatical conjunctions and semantic inferences that make up the ordinary substance of a story." The film is as surprising to audiences as d'Ors's text must have been to its original readers. From the start, Recha plunges spectators into a garden that doubles as a very foggy aquarium. Ironically, the doctor's prescription forbidding Juan de Dios to think prompts a sensorial chain of events. While he drowns in tedium, Recha drowns spectators in an unrelenting succession of anachronic, unexpected, and confusing images and sounds. We cannot rely on old, signifying codes to understand what Recha is putting on the screen. The minimal narrative element of the film – Juan de Dios seeking treatment for exhaustion – is presented in a puzzling barrage of visual and sound situations. Recha's filmic grammar is his own and responds to no one. It dares us to become the thinking-perceiving body that Author strives for in the original text. It challenges us to question not only the narrative elements, but, more important, the nature of film itself. The unceasing scratches and stubborn framing keep us aware of the artifice of the process and our participation in it. Recha throws out these affects and intensities to make us grapple with the consequences of watching a film. He makes (seemingly) nothing become interesting. (Seemingly) nothing becomes art, and (seemingly) nothing is art.

WORKS CITED

Angulo, Jesús. "El cielo sube." *Nosferatu: Revista de cine*, June 2004, pp. 32–9.
Aubert, Jean-Paul. *Seremos Mallarmé. La Escuela de Barcelona: una apuesta modernista*. Shangrila, 2016.
Baugh, Bruce. "Body." *The Deleuze Dictionary*, edited by Adrian Parr, Edinburgh UP, 2005, pp. 30–2.
Bergson, Henri. *Key Writings*. Edited and translated by Keith Ansell Pearson and John Mullarkey, Continuum, 2001.
Casas, Quim. "*L'arbre de les cireres*: El peso y el paso del tiempo." *Nosferatu: Revista de cine*, June 2004, pp. 40–5.
"Cenesthesia." Merriam-Webster, n.d. https://www.merriam-webster.com/medical/cenesthesia. Accessed 18 July 2017.
"Cenesthesia." *Mosby's Medical Dictionary*, 8th edition. Elsevier, 2009. https://medical-dictionary.thefreedictionary.com/cenesthesia. Accessed 9 September 2018.
El cielo sube. Directed by Marc Recha, performances by Salvador Dolç and Corinne Alba, NOMA films, 1991.
Colebrook, Claire. *Gilles Deleuze*. Routledge, 2002.
Colman, Felicity. *Deleuze and Cinema: The Film Concepts*. Berg Publishers, 2011.
Cuscó i Clarasó, Joan. "Eugeni d'Ors: Philosophy and Humanism in the Twentieth Century." *Journal of Catalan Intellectual History*, vol. 6, 2013, pp. 91–114. http://revistes.iec.cat/index.php/JOCIH. Accessed 9 September 2018.
Davis, Nick. *The Desiring-Image: Gilles Deleuze and Contemporary Queer Cinema*. Oxford UP, 2013.
Deleuze, Gilles. "Lecture Transcripts on Spinoza's Concept of Affect." *Les Cours de Gilles Deleuze*, 24 January 1978, http://www.webdeleuze.com/php/sommaire.html.
– *Cinema 1: The Movement-Image*. Translated by H. Tomlinson and B. Habberjam, University of Minnesota Press, 1986.
– *Cinema 2: The Time-Image*. Translated by. H. Tomlinson and B. Habberjam, University of Minnesota Press, 1989.
– *Expressionism in Philosophy: Spinoza*. Translated by Martin Joughin, Zone Books, 1990.
Deleuze, Gilles, and Claire Parnet. "On the Superiority of Anglo-American Literature." *Dialogues II*, translated by Hugh Tomlinson and Barbara Habberjam, Columbia UP, 1983, pp. 36–76.

Deleuze, Gilles, and Félix Guattari. *Anti-Oedipus: Capitalism and Schizophrenia*. Translated by Robert Hurley, Mark Seem, and Helen R. Lane, Athlone P, 1984.
– *Kafka: Toward a Minor Literature*. Translated by Dana Polan, U of Minnesota P, 1986.
– *A Thousand Plateaus: Capitalism and Schizophrenia*. Translated by Brian Massumi, Athlone P, 1988.
– *What Is Philosophy?* Translated by Hugh Tomlinson and Graham Burchill, Verso, 1994.
D'Ors, Eugeni. *Glosas: Páginas del Glosari de Xènius (1906–1917)*. Editorial Saturnino Calleja, 1920.
– *La Lliçó de tedi en el parc: Altrament dit Oceanografia del tedi*, edited by Jaume Vallcorba, Quaderns Crema, 1994.
Eakin, Emily. "I Feel, Therefore I Am." *New York Times*, 19 April 2003. https://www.nytimes.com/2003/04/19/books/i-feel-therefore-i-am.html. Accessed 9 September 2018.
Galt, Rosalind. "Impossible Narratives: The Barcelona School and the European Avant Gardes." *Hispanic Review*, vol. 78, no. 4, 2010, pp. 491–511. doi 10.1353/hir.2010.0011. Accessed 9 September 2018.
Heredero, Carlos F. *20 nuevos directores del cine español*. Alianza Editorial, 1999.
Hernández, Rubén. *Pere Portabella: Hacia una política del relato cinematográfico*. Ediciones Errata Naturae, 2008.
Herzog, Amy. "Images of Thought and Acts of Creation: Deleuze, Bergson, and the Question of Cinema." *Invisible Culture: An Electronic Journal for Visual Culture*, vol. 3, 2000. https://ivc.lib.rochester.edu/images-of-thought-and-acts-of-creation-deleuze-bergson-and-the-question-of-cinema/. Accessed 3 September 2018.
Jordà, Joaquim. "Acróstico incompleto dedicado a Marc Recha." *Nosferatu: Revista de cine*, June 2004, pp. 4–6.
Ledesma, Eduardo. "Intermediality and Spanish Experimental Cinema: Text and Image Interactions in the Lyrical Films of the Barcelona School." *Journal of Spanish Cultural Studies*, vol. 14, no. 3, 2013, pp. 254–74. doi: 10.1080/14636204.2013.888259. Accessed 9 September 2018.
Losilla, Carlos. "Carta abierta a Marc Recha a partir de algunos textos sobre sus películas(a modo de comentario bibliográfico)." *Nosferatu: Revista de cine*, June 2004, pp. 57–9.
Nadal-Melsió, Sara. "Editor's Preface. The Invisible Tradition: Avant-Garde Catalan Cinema under Late Francoism." *Hispanic Review*, vol. 78, no. 4, 2010, pp. 46–58. doi: www.jstor.org/stable/25790597. Accessed 9 September 2018.
O'Sullivan, Simon. "The Aesthetics of Affect: Thinking Art beyond Representation." *Angelaki: Journal of the Theoretical Humanities*, vol. 6, no. 3, 2001, pp. 125–35.
– *Art Encounters Deleuze and Guattari: Thought beyond Representation*. Palgrave Macmillan, 2006.

Pujol, Anton. "Ventura Pons's *Barcelona (un mapa)*: Trapped in the Crystal." *Studies in Hispanic Cinemas*, vol. 6, no.1, 2009, pp. 65–76. doi: 10.1386/shci.6.1.65/1. Accessed 9 September 2018.

Rancière, Jacques. "Is There a Deleuzian Aesthetics?" Translated by Radmila Djordjevic. *Qui Parle*, vol. 14, no. 2, 2004, pp. 1–14. https://www.jstor.org/stable/20686174. Accessed 9 September 2018.

Resina, Joan Ramon. "'Barcelona Ciutat' en la estética de Eugeni d'Ors." *Revista Hispánica Moderna*, vol. 43, no. 2, 1990, pp. 167–78. https://www.jstor.org/stable/30203264. Accessed 9 September 2018.

– "Las glosas de *La ben plantada*." *Oceonagrafía de Xènius: Estudios críticos a Eugenio d'Ors*, edited by Carlos X. Ardavín, Eloy E. Merino, and Xavier Pla, Reichenberger, 2005, pp. 149–64.

Rius, Mercè. *D'Ors, filòsofo*. Universitat de València, 2014.

Smith, Daniel. "What Is the Body without Organs? Machine and Organism in Deleuze and Guattari." *Continental Philosophy Review*, vol. 51, no. 1, 2017, pp. 95–110. http://doi.org/10.1007/s11007-016-9406-0. Accessed 9 September 2018.

Stanghellini, Giovanni. "Embodiment and Schizophrenia." *World Psychiatry*, vol. 8, no.1, 2009, pp. 56–9. https://www.ncbi.nlm.nih.gov/pmc/articles/PMC2652898/. Accessed 9 September 2018.

Suàrez, Alicia, and Mercè Vidal. "Catalan Noucentisme, the Mediterranean, and Tradition." *Barcelona and Modernity: Picasso, Gaudí, Miró, Dalí*, edited by William Robinson, Jordi Falgàs, and Carmen Belen Lord, Yale UP, 2006, pp. 226–33.

Vallcorba, Jaume, editor. Introduction. *La Lliçó de tedi en el parc. Altrament dit Oceanografia del tedi*. Quaderns Crema, 1994, pp. ix–xiii.

Vidal, Nuria. "Interview with Marc Recha." *Nosferatu: Revista de cine*, June 2004, pp. 7–26.

Vilaseca, David. *Queer Events: Post-deconstructive Subjectivities in Spanish Writing and Film 1960s–1990s*. Liverpool UP, 2010.

PART FIVE

Minimalism and Beyond

11 Formal Disruption, Minutiae, and Absence in the Films of Jaime Rosales

AGUSTÍN RICO-ALBERO

Since 2007, when the global financial crisis started in Spain, there has been a chaotic political, economic, and social context, which, combined with multiple cases of political corruption, have caused social unrest both in Catalonia and Spain. Within this challenging environment creators of independent cinema have needed to reinvent themselves using new and more affordable formats (e.g., mobile phone cameras) to survive in a local market that has struggled to subsist due to the downward trend in audience numbers in Europe and particularly in Spain, where the government raised VAT on cultural goods and services from 8 per cent to 21 per cent in 2012, which has negatively impacted public access to culture. Indicative of the problems faced in the cultural industries was the closure not only of independent production companies but also the collapse in 2013 of Spain's leading distributor, exhibitor, and producer, Alta Films, after forty-four years (Gómez).

However, despite the difficulties faced in the last few years, it has also been one of the most prolific periods in Catalan film-making history, producing a diverse body of works including political films like Ramon Térmens's *Catalunya über alles!* (2011) and Joel Joan and Sergi Lara's *Fènix 11*23* (2012), "new documentaries" such as Isaki Lakuesta's *El cuaderno de barro* (*The Clay Diaries*, 2011) and Neus Ballús's *La plaga* (*The Plague*, 2013), "new cine-lit" literary adaptations like Agustí Villaronga's *Pa negre* (*Black Bread*, 2010), the first ever Catalan-language film to be selected by the Spanish Academy to represent Spain at the Oscars, and Judith Colell and Jordi Cadena's *Elisa K* (2011), and finally, "new minimalist" films mainly represented by Jaime Rosales's works *La soledad* (*Solitary Fragments*, 2007), *Tiro en la cabeza* (*Bullet in the Head*, 2008), *Sueño y silencio* (*Dream and Silence*, 2012), *Hermosa juventud* (*Beautiful Youth*, 2014), *Petra* (2018) and *Girasoles silvestres* (*Wild Flowers*, 2022).

Within this context, and similar to their artistic antecedents of the Escola de Barcelona, the directors of this thematically and aesthetically diverse films rather than constituting a cohesive movement instead converge in their refusal to conform to the cinematic mainstream. Writing after the start of the financial crisis of 2008, Joseba Elola notes that this is "a movement that is diametrically opposed to the Hollywood canon, a movement with integrity, aesthetically dissident, of restless and daring filmmakers, more concerned with the tempo of the film than with the tempo of the box office" (46). The commonality between the Escola de Barcelona and these contemporary directors is precisely that both stand in opposition to the traditional aesthetic and narrative canon and the demands of the mainstream cinema industry, focussing instead on form and connecting with contemporary artistic expressions in a similar context of social conflict and crisis.

This chapter will explore the significance of this emphasis on stylistic emancipation and the rejection of homogeneity in the context of Catalonia's struggle for self-determination, and consider the implications of the fact that these Catalan film-makers have garnered more international than local recognition, as happened with the Escola de Barcelona. Against this backdrop, it will look at how Rosales's films subtly reflect the political and social situation without explicitly being political, again a trait typical of the Escola de Barcelona, and do this by focussing on small details (minutiae) cleverly combined with stylistic choices that make his work unique. It will focus in particular on Jaime Rosales's place on the Catalan and Spanish cinematic spectrum, and amongst his generation of film-makers who have forged a place for themselves at international forums and festivals as they search for renewed narratives and disruptive aesthetic and visual forms. Film historian Román Gubern suggests that this group of film-makers are the Escola de Barcelona reborn, as "what they have in common is their radicality, they share a sensibility and stand in opposition to a dominant canon" (qtd. in Elola 47). This chapter will also examine how Jaime Rosales's cinema intersects with a series of proposals, including the self-financing of productions, a focus on the formal features of the images and the structures of the narration, and using non-professional actors whenever possible (Elola 42), which were all championed by Joaquim Jordà, one of the pioneers of the Escola.

In addition, this chapter draws on film critic Carlos Losilla's notion that by allowing images to "speak for themselves" this is an "other model of quiet cinema" that stands in opposition to a more commercial, "chatty model of cinema" (Losilla 20). This concept of "quiet" can also be linked to what Jaume Martí-Olivella describes as the "forms of (in)visibility" that shape some of Rosales's films like *Bullet in the Head*, where he deals with the complex theme of terrorism (Martí-Olivella 1). In his portrayal of the minutiae of everyday life and transgression of formal and narrative conventions, Rosales's films could be said to render invisible subjects visible. Focussing on two of Rosales's quiet yet fiercely confrontational films, *Las horas del día* (*The Hours of the Day*, 2003) and *Hermosa juventud* (*Beautiful Youth*, 2014), I will examine how his subtle but all-pervading anti-establishment tone responds to his social and political context and connects to Catalonia's cinematic genealogy.

In contrast to the commercial cinema associated with directors like Alejandro Amenábar, one of the most popular Spanish film-makers, Jaime Rosales has sought to disassociate himself from mainstream genre cinema, choosing instead to try to create films that defy conventional expectations. In his own words:

> When I started to think of making the film, I just wanted to tell a different story ... I wanted to tell the story without giving the reason why Abel (the psychopath) kills ... in fact, this film cannot be included in any kind of genre since it is not a thriller or a melodrama ... I defend an auteur cinema and a cinema influenced by our culture but it seems that the authorities are not interested in this. (DVD audio commentary, *The Hours of the Day*)

He describes his stylistic choices as being based on "principles of austerity, realism and distancing" (DVD audio commentary), and recognizes how directors such as Bresson, Rossellini, Pasolini, and Godard – all associated with their own particular expressions of realism – have influenced him. The complex concept of realism in cinema has raised numerous academic debates over the years. The fact that so many "realist" trends or waves have existed in Europe has made it inevitable that realism has become one of European cinema's major traditions, and one that uses cinematic conventions to invite the spectator to reflect upon our societies' problems. Some of the Nuevo Cine Español films such as Carlos Saura's *La caza* (*The Hunt*, 1965) did just this. And although the group of Madrid-based directors has traditionally been perceived in opposition to the Escola de Barcelona, in fact, they both shared an interest in reflecting on the social issues of their time.

Released in 2003, *The Hours of the Day*, Rosales's first feature-length film, is not presented as "a social problem melodrama" or as a thriller; indeed, it eschews narrative and conventional generic features, focusing instead on the creative cinematography that defines his experimental style and a non-conformist reimagining of genre elements. Similarly, some Barcelona School directors like Pere Portabella with films like

Vampir.Cuadecuc (*Vampire,Cuadecuc* 1971) or Vicente Aranda's *Fata Morgana* (*Left-Handed Fate*, 1966) proposed new readings of the fantastic film, questioned traditional generic conventions, and established their own auteristic reinterpretation of this genre. In a similar vein, Rosales reinterprets some features of the psycho-killer film but with his own experimental twist.

In his later films, Rosales has continued to experiment with cinematic conventions such as the creative use of split screen and a static camera as in *Solitary Fragments* (2007), a film that won three Goya awards in 2008 including best picture. It is also worth mentioning how in other films such as *Bullet in the Head* (2008), which tells the story of the daily life of an ETA terrorist, Rosales experiments with the zoom lens, plays with long shots, and uses dialogue that the spectator cannot hear.

The Hours of the Day tells the story of Abel (Alex Brendemühl), a young man who lives an apparently normal life with his family and girlfriend in a working-class town near Barcelona. However, twenty-four minutes into the film Abel starts killing people without any apparent motivation or explanation. He is not depicted as a sadistic serial killer, but rather as a normal guy who just happens to commit acts of brutal violence. The film's poster, part of its "narrative image" (Ellis 31), does not show any evident violence either. Nevertheless, there is undoubtedly something menacing about the poster's fragmented close-ups of the protagonist's face and the abrupt horizontal cut at his brow line combined with the thick orange and red lines that follow the curve where the crown of his head should be and yet never meet, leaving the shape unresolved. The film's central themes are therefore eloquently captured in the poster's unsettlingly fragmented imagery: expressions of two profoundly differentiated worlds in the protagonist's mind – one perfectly ordinary, the other extremely violent.

Abel leads an unremarkable life working in a clothes shop, living with his mother, and spending time with his friend Marcos (Vicente Romero) and girlfriend Tere (Àgata Roca). He holds banal conversations with them, and on the face of it there is no indication that he is struggling with any kind of major internal or external conflict. Everything seems normal. Using lingering long takes filmed from a fixed point, Rosales focuses on Abel's mundane daily routine and interactions with other characters, yet this is punctuated by two sudden and brutal murders of random strangers with no explanation for his violent behaviour. As Esther Gimeno Ugalde suggests, the absence of any logical reasons forces the spectator to imagine possible psychological or sociological explanations (57).

The film is set in El Prat de Llobregat, a working-class city in the Barcelona metropolitan area, and the first scenes reflect the daily routine of the murderer and the other characters who live there. Rosales's use of this setting is not coincidental as this place is representative of other working-class areas in Catalonia and Spain, where the depressing consequences of the economic transformation of the last decades is inscribed into the urban landscape. His choice of locations and treatment of these urban spaces evokes that of the Escola de Barcelona, which was active during a previous period of economic transformation in Spain. Jean-Paul Aubert points out that this economic transformation of the 1960s resulted in "precarious jobs, a mass exodus towards the cities, and an increase in economic inequality" (23), and while the government wanted to portray Spain as positive and open this group of film-makers instead created images of a society that still had to confront an authoritarian regime, the discovery of consumerism, and the development of mass tourism. After decades of implementing the principles of a capitalist economy and urban speculation, Catalan and Spanish society fell victim to the excesses associated with these in the 2000s. It could be argued that *The Hours of the Day*, as it was released in 2003, anticipated frustration about a lived reality in which society is far from cohesive, stable, or equal as expressed through the weariness and exasperation that saturates the minutiae of the protagonist's daily life, and through the duality of the protagonist's characterization and his acts of violence. Yet rather than putting forward any kind of explanation for Abel's violent behaviour or explicitly criticizing the political environment at the time, the film, through its quietly dispassionate camerawork, instead takes on the role of a detached observer. This seemingly apolitical approach was also typical of the Escola de Barcelona (Vilarós 513). It has, however, later been recognized by some critics, such as Aubert (215), that the Escola de Barcelona directors' political commitment was expressed implicitly through formal choices that deviated from the mainstream. For example, the way Pere Portabella in his 1972 film *Umbracle* channels a scathing attack on an oppressive society and the harsh economic and political realities daily faced by many people in Spain into the way he portrays details like the deserted streets of a hostile city, a kidnapping, and the irritating buzz of a fly (Aubert 221). This is an approach that we can see echoed in Rosales's work, as an analysis of the first scenes of *The Hours of the Day* will demonstrate.

The film starts with an establishing shot, followed by long shots of different parts of the apparently tranquil city accompanied by direct sound capturing typical urban noises of cranes and cars. The director progressively brings the shots closer to the block of flats where Abel lives, then abruptly introduces him through an intimate head-and-shoulder shot as he shaves and looks at himself in the mirror. What strikes the spectator here is the length of the shot and the fact that it is a handheld shot that mimics a static shot. Using a technique that is usually contrary to the shot type makes for a subtle manipulation or disruption of conventional formal choices. According to the director, this sequence is one of the most important sequences in the film as it suggests what kind of film the spectator is going to see: a film with a completely different perspective (DVD audio commentary). This will not be a typical serial killer film, but rather an auteur's view of the topic. The length of this sequence, coupled with what seems like the exaggerated inaction of both the character and the camera, disrupts conventional expectations of cinematic narrative pace and in doing so transmits a certain suspense that forces the spectator to start to question what the film is about. The stillness of the sequence inexorably draws the spectator's attention towards Abel's intense eyes, the only outward manifestation of the real action – the disturbed personality that we have yet to discover – hidden behind his enigmatic, self-appraising gaze. The mirror also reflects this split in Abel's personality, two completely different sides, one of them filled with the potential for violence.

The following sequence, in which Abel has breakfast with his mother, also emphasizes this daily routine of the character and the slow pace of the film. It opens with a frame-within-frame shot, a technique used repeatedly throughout the film (and in most of Rosales's other films), which goes against the conventional ways characters are normally introduced in traditional narrative films. Then, the camera approaches the characters and again nothing seems to be happening, just a banal conversation which helps to maintain the tension over what is going to happen next, and, as the spectator continues to be given no clues, the storyline instead of developing becomes increasingly obscured. This fragmented mode of storytelling is reminiscent of Pere Portabella's work, of which Fèlix Fanés notes, "even though they tell stories, they are not narratives; there is a continuity, but they are made of fragments, isolated scenes" (31).

As mentioned earlier in this study, Rosales also reshapes the generic features of the film and reinterprets the way the psycho killer is portrayed. For example, with regard to the aggressor's personality, Abel is clearly portrayed as selfish and narcissistic. For instance, in the scene in which he tries to convince his employee to leave her job for a derisory pay-off, he accuses her of being selfish, when in fact he is the one who is being egotistical since he offers her a pittance in compensation for being made redundant. Another example occurs on his friend's wedding day when Abel tells him a story that implies the bride is willing to cheat on her husband. He does not care about his friend's reaction and shows no empathy towards him.

Although Rosales presents a psychopath, with the selfish and narcissistic traits typical of psycho killers (Garrido Lora 79), the violent scenes in which Abel is involved are portrayed in a different way. His victims, a female taxi driver and an old man, are seemingly chosen at random. Writing about the two murders, Tom Dawson notes:

> What proves so disconcerting is that the killing of strangers (of which there are two instances) is treated in exactly the same matter-of-fact tone as a quiet drink at a bar, or a discussion with an employee over severance pay, or the viewing with a partner of a flat. Moreover, the positioning of the first murder around the half-hour mark generates a degree of tension: Abel seems to make no substantial effort to cover his tracks and every individual he encounters thereafter appears to be a potential victim. ("Las horas del día")

There is certainly an effect of suspense, yet it differs completely from mainstream psycho-killer movies in which tension and suspense were probably the directors' main objectives. Here, in contrast, Rosales focuses on presenting to the spectator Abel's daily routine and uses completely different cinematic techniques for this purpose.

The first murder sequence starts with Abel in a taxi being driven along a motorway. Suddenly, Abel tells the female driver to take a turn off that leads to a deserted road in an uninhabited rural landscape, a kind of no-man's-land that provokes a certain tension for the spectator. However, this setting with its towering greenery would also be familiar to Spanish audiences as a typical Mediterranean landscape. The sudden eerie sense of isolation contrasted with this familiarity sets up an unsettling sense of the conflict to come, and yet does not prepare the spectator for the brutality of the violent act that resolves this tension. Abel is largely obscured from view until he starts to attack his victim. At this point, he abruptly moves into the centre of the frame and begins clumsily trying to strangle her, which takes him several attempts. Emphasizing the objectivity and realism the director is pursuing, the spectator becomes the witness of this criminal act from a third-person point of view. Here, as elsewhere in the film, non-diegetic sound is absent, as only diegetic sound is used. The sequence is completely devoid of the kind of orchestral soundtrack conventionally used to underscore mood and action, but which also serves as a reminder that what we are watching is fiction. The stark credibility of the diegetic sound makes the violence feel particularly brutal. Rosales confronts the spectator with the unadulterated sounds of violence – the victim's coughs and muffled desperation, ragged gasps for air, Abel's grunts of physical exertion, the flesh-against-flesh thump of repeated punches, and the dull thud of a stone against a skull. This unflinching concentration on the aural minutiae of violence, treated in the same way as everyday noises like brushing teeth in the preceding sequence or plates being cleared away in the following, makes this violent act uncomfortably accessible to the spectator. Using this violent act as an extreme resolution of the monotony of a protagonist's daily routine is reminiscent of some Escola de Barcelona films, like the documentary *Lejos de los árboles* (*Far from the Trees*, 1972), by Jacinto Esteva, which focussed on boredom as a means to challenge the disconnect between tough lived realities and the cheerful sheen of the regime's tourist propaganda. Against a backdrop of tedium Esteva uses rural festival traditions to represent a Spain where people experience release though violent traditions, such as bull running and religious processions that inspire blood-curdling cries of devotion, to counter this positive spin. Similarly, violent acts are cathartic for Rosales's protagonist (also representing the Other) in a Spain where hope still seems painfully elusive.

Alex Brendemühl's improvisation, something the director claims was a constant feature of the acting process throughout the film (DVD audio commentary), contributes to this unsettling sense of verisimilitude. Rosales wanted the actor to work on his character's personality, while he focussed on the pace of the film. Combining scripted and improvised acting creates a narrative friction that not only augments the realistic quality of the finished film but also intensifies the will-he-or-won't-he-kill-again tension that dominates after the first murder. It is significant that, in contrast to the overt presence of blood in mainstream films about serial killers, barely any blood is seen throughout *The Hours of the Day*. The conventional use of make-up to present graphic violence in a stylized way is absent. In fact, according to Rosales, this caused a dispute with his special effects team, who wanted to portray the violence in a spectacularly gruesome way, which conflicted with the distant objectivity that Rosales was aiming for (DVD audio commentary). Indeed, in the sequence where the taxi driver is murdered, the mise en scène is constructed in such a way that although we can see the victim while Abel tries to strangle her at the beginning of the attack, she is hidden from view whilst she is being beaten. The fatal violence is clumsy and enacted not with premeditated props typically used in psycho thrillers, but with his bare hands and an improvised weapon – a stone that he picks up to finally finish her off.

In terms of cinematography, close-ups are not used in this sequence, or anywhere else in the film. This formal choice emphasizes the sense of detached realistic objectivity that the director wanted to achieve. This objectivity is reinforced by the total absence of subjective point-of-view shots in this sequence, leaving the spectator with neither the victim's nor the aggressor's point of view. All these cinematic devices, which are crucial elements of the film's representation of violence, also create a distance or gap between the spectator and the characters of this film. The spectator's ability to read Abel's reaction to his crime is frustrated by his unchanged impassive face that shows neither remorse nor pleasure. It is significant how Brendemühl subtly uses facial expressions to portray the character as psychologically contained and indifferent as part of the mise en scène. And it is no coincidence that all the actors chosen for this film, including the protagonist, were unknown in Spain at the time. The choice further adds to the sense of objectivity and brings to mind Joaquim Jordà, who proposed not using professional actors as one of the principles for the Escola de Barcelona.

Hence, in contrast to the common portrayal of serial killers in either American or Spanish mainstream films such as Alejandro Amenábar's *Tesis* (*Thesis*, 1996), Rosales does not produce a genre film. Instead, he reshapes violence, reconstructing the figure of the psychopath using a combination of mise en scène, absence of non-diegetic sound, and stylistic choices taken directly from realistic conventions. Furthermore, he does not seem to seek the social or psychological reasons for the psychopath's actions, despite portraying the story in a hostile environment, but rather focuses on the daily routine of a psychopath who appears relatively "normal."

Rosales uses some of the same narrative and cinematic techniques in his *Beautiful Youth* (2014). However, by contrast this is a more accessible film likely to appeal to a wider audience; indeed, in some respects it is closer to a more commercial cinema as he himself seems to suggest in some interviews with the media (Peláez Barceló). Rosales once again portrays everyday life, this time the struggles of two young characters living in the midst of a now established economic and social crisis. Although social and economic difficulties were constantly present in the background in *The Hours of the Day*, in *Beautiful Youth* they move to the foreground. This shift is also present in Portabella's later films. Influenced by the Escola de Barcelona, films such as *Informe general para unas cuestiones de interés para una proyección pública* (*General Report on Certain Matters of Interest for a Public Screening*, 1977), and more recently in *Informe general II: El nou rapte d'Europa* (*General Report II: The New Abduction of Europe*, 2015), which were discussed in chapter 6, are stirring accounts of the post-financial crisis and how these difficulties shape the young characters, the "beautiful youth," who are presented as victims of that crisis and of a decadent political system.

Beautiful Youth tells the story of Natalia (Ingrid García Jonsoon) and Carlos (Carlos Rodríguez), Madrid-suburbs-dwelling twentysomethings, who are part of the so-called *generación ni-ni*, those young people who neither work nor study (Carlos works in the building industry but only earns 10 euros a day). They are representative of the consequences of the economic crisis and the Partido Popular's austerity measures in Spain. These measures have provoked indignation all over Spain and have fuelled the struggle for self-determination in Catalonia, where acute economic austerity has been imposed to reduce public expenditure (Fernández Manjón 34). It is against a backdrop of such economic hardship that Natalia finds out that she is pregnant. In their desperation to find a solution to their financial situation, Carlos asks Natalia to shoot a porn film, in which they will be the actors, so that they can earn some money. Once again Rosales plays out the characters' struggles and frustrations through the portrayal of their quotidian life and daily routine, but this time instead of violence pairs it with the controversial and widely neglected topic of pornography and sexual exploitation.

To portray these youngsters' reality, Rosales continues to experiment, combining a conventional narrative approach with popular digital communication formats like photographs shared via their mobile phones and WhatsApp conversations that fill the full screen for several minutes. He has noted that it was important to portray these digital platforms, as most young people use them, but also because they allowed him to "speed up the narrative" (Rosales, "Interview"). For example, the elliptical sequence where Rosales uses selfies that Natalia has taken on her mobile phone to fast forward through her pregnancy to the point where the baby is a few months old. The director also transgresses the boundaries of conventional images in/of the cinema with new formats, creating two different spaces on the same timeline. Like the sequence where a WhatsApp window is juxtaposed with a video game screen as Carlos chats and plays simultaneously. Rosales argues that he did this to emphasize how young people's continuous creation and sharing of images using their smartphone cameras and other technologies trivializes images, as if all images have got the same importance or relevance. He suggests that this symbolizes a "trivialization of human experience" (González and González) in an environment where what matters is the quantity of images, not what they portray. The Escola de Barcelona also engaged with the aesthetic, exploring different formats that came with modernity and referring to other European movements and directors as a means of making a radical statement. One example is Portabella's use of the montage in *Vampir.Cuadecuc* (1971), the film analysed in depth in chapter 7, with its multiple fails in the raccord (sound and visual) that make the editing more perceptible and ensure the film is, as Steven Marsh puts it, "marked by discontinuity" (554). In the case of *Beautiful Youth*, Rosales's use of new formats serves to firmly connect the film to a period increasingly defined by online platforms and the global technologies that have transformed contemporary youth.

In contrast to the detached objectivity in *The Hours of the Day*, there is an attempt to minimize the distance between the spectator and the characters. Indeed, in *Beautiful Youth* Rosales shifts away from his customary use of long shots towards a more dynamic and conventional style to approach his protagonists in a more intimate way. Long shots, together with his characteristic frame-within-frame shots, are still present but here they are juxtaposed with frequent close-ups, thereby giving the spectator a more subjective experience and emphasizing the characters' emotions, or lack thereof.

Rosales again avoids engaging directly with the causes of the situation his characters face, addressing them only obliquely through his portrayal of suburban Madrid as a hostile environment and the decisions the characters need to take. In *Beautiful Youth* the violence portrayed is mundane yet destructive in its own way; as the director suggests, "the most conspicuous violence is the social violence associated with not being able to find a job" (Esteban). This categorization of violence can be related to what sociologist Dorothy Van Soest calls structural and cultural violence (13). These types of violence are less visible and more difficult to recognize as they are embedded in political, social, and economic systems, to the point that they become widely ignored and accepted by societies. In Rosales's mind, however, this structural violence in the form of unemployment "is almost a form of social terrorism" (Esteban). In the scenes where violence is more explicitly portrayed, for example when Carlos is beaten after reporting someone for kicking a vending machine, Rosales again opts to use only diegetic sound, lending a verisimilitude to the incident and characters that is typical of all his films. If in the 1960s films like Vicente Aranda's *Fata Morgana* and Pere Portabella's *Nocturno 29* (*Nocturne 29*, 1968) reflected the period of significant political and economic change in Catalonia and Spain when neo-liberalism and capitalism were welcomed, then *Beautiful Youth* shows how this neo-liberalism has affected Spain's youth and in doing so arguably draws parallels with the institutional violence of the late Francoist period.

In *Beautiful Youth*, Rosales uses actors who are professional but likely to be unknown to the wider public, hence heightening not only a credible spontaneity and naturalness of the characters but also their vulnerability in a sombre environment. Rosales again admits that he allowed the actors to improvise dialogues so that the spectator is exposed to a portrayal closer to the reality of the crisis ("Interview"). This film could be included in what Dean Allbritton calls "crisis cinema" as it "functions as a shorthand for those Spanish films that engage with or confront what it means to live in crisis," and it also attempts "to organize the individual experience of precarity and vulnerability into a communal one" (103). In other words, the individual experiences of characters in *Beautiful Youth* exposes an endemic problem not only for Spanish youth but also a generation traumatized by growing unemployment and a widening global social divide. As was the case with the filmmakers of the Escola de Barcelona before him, Rosales wants to expose and confront the spectator with a portrayal of a reality while challenging them to interpret it in a different way (Belinchón).

However, as with *The Hours of the Day*, and following the (a)political principles of the Escola de Barcelona, the director does not explicitly question the current political climate in Spain. In an interview, Rosales points out,

> I met a lot of young people for several months. All of them lived in the suburbs of Madrid. One of the things that surprised me was the fact that they were completely detached from politics. They didn't have any interest for the current media news or the political parties ... I don't judge them. I don't think it's either good or bad, I'm not even interested in the politics of political parties so I wasn't trying to impose anything. (González and González)

This sentiment is clearly exemplified in the sequence that juxtaposes Carlos and his friends talking about trivial topics like mobile phones and shopping with a conversation between Natalia and her female friends about how difficult it is for young people in Spain to get a job.

In addition, whilst in *The Hours of the Day* Rosales changed the conventions of the cinematic genre with a psychopathic character, in *Beautiful Youth*, despite the detailed portrayal of the characters' quotidian lives, the absence of any melodramatic portrayal is predominant in the narration, mainly removed in quite a few scenes with a time-space ellipsis in which the spectator imagines what has happened. In this more recent film, Rosales concentrates only on portraying the difficulties and frustrations of their daily lives and on the fact that they do not seem to be able to change their destinies. Again, the director does not provide the spectator with any answers, and this encourages the audience to find an answer themselves. Once again, Rosales's subversion of genres with an auteristic point of view (with his focus still on aesthetic elements) echoes the Escola de Barcelona, the Nouvelle Vague and other avant-garde cinemas of the time.

It is worth mentioning that like most of the Escola de Barcelona's films, none of Rosales's films are in Catalan. Aubert points out that this may be linked to the Escola's idea that any manifestation of nationalism contradicted their commitment to being open to foreign influences from other cinemas (e.g., the Nouvelle Vague) (205). This is why Pere Portabella was also critical of the fact that the "movement" was so distant from its Catalan social, cultural, and historical context (Portabella, in Aubert 206).

One can easily conclude that Rosales's films are characterized by a focus on contexts in which frustration results in moments of physical, social, or institutional violence that affect the characters' lives. Rosales's cinematic texts shape an avant-garde cinema that although not part of a film movement follows on from the principles of the Escola de Barcelona. He focuses the spectator's attention on the minutiae of the protagonists' lives as a means to reflecting on their solitude and frustrations, disconcertingly presenting violence as a quotidian part of life. However, his disruptive approach to cinematic form in portraying this violence is far removed from conventional representations in mainstream films. By carefully combining violence and realist techniques, he distances himself from mainstream generic features and instead creates transgressive, stylistically emancipated films that interrogate the capitalist commercialization of Spanish cinema. His work embodies a trend towards keeping alive a cinema that rebels against a dominant capitalist film industry and against an endemic system in a subtle way and with an absence of an explicit reflection on the issues. As in the case of the cinema of the Escola de Barcelona, active during another transitional period of Catalan and Spanish history, Rosales's films become a parallel cinema to that of the mainstream Spanish cinema by being transgressive and innovative in their approach at a cinematic, generic, and formal level.

WORKS CITED

Allbritton, Dean. "Prime Risks: The Politics of Pain and Suffering in Spain's Crisis Cinema." *Journal of Spanish Cultural Studies*, vol. 15, no. 1–2, 2014, pp. 101–15.

Aubert, Jean-Paul. *Seremos Mallarmé. La Escuela de Barcelona: una apuesta modernista*. Shangrila, 2016.
Belinchón, Gregorio. "Quiero salir de la deriva que llevaba mi carrera hacia el cine de museos." *El País*, 18 May 2004. http://cultura.elpais.com/cultura/2014/05/17/actualidad/1400340094_415557.html. Accessed 3 Apr. 2017.
Catalunya über alles. Directed by Ramon Térmens, performances by Gonzalo Cunill, Paula Jiménez, and Assumpció Ortet, Segarra Films, 2011.
La caza. Directed by Carlos Saura, performances by Ismael Merlo, Alfredo Mayo, and José María Prada. Elías Querejeta Producciones Cinematográficas, 1966.
El cuaderno de barro. Directed by Isaki Lacuesta, performances by Miquel Barceló, Josef Nadj, and Alain Mahé, Tusitala Producciones, 2011.
Dawson, Tom. "*Las horas del día* (*The Hours of the Day*)."*BBC Films*, 2 Jun. 2004, http://www.bbc.co.uk/films/2004/06/02/the_hours_of_the_day_2004_review.shtml. Accessed 27 Jan. 2016.
Elisa K. Directed by Jordi Cadena and Judith Colell, performances by Aina Clotet, Clàudia Pons, and Lydia Zimmermann, Catalan Film & TV and Generalitat de Catalunya, 2010.
Ellis, John. *Visible Fictions*. Routledge, 1982.
Elola, Joseba. "Son pocos, son valientes." *El País*, 10 Feb. 2008, pp. 46–7.
Esteban, Ramón. "Jaime Rosales: El paro es casi una forma de terrorismo social." *Radiotelevisión Española*, 28 May 2014, http://www.rtve.es/noticias/20140528/jaime-rosales-paro-casi-forma-terrorismo-social/944340.shtml. Accessed 4 Apr. 2017.
Fanés, Fèlix. *Pere Portabella: Avantguarda, cinema, política*. Pòrtic, 2008.
Fata Morgana. Directed by Vicente Aranda, performances by Teresa Gimpera, Marianne Benet, and Marcos Martí, Films Internacionales, 1966.
*Fènix 11*23*. Directed by Joel Joan and Sergi Lara, performances by Nil Cardoner, Rosa Gàmiz, and Alex Casanovas, Arriska Films, 2012.
Fernández Manjón, Desiderio. *Cataluña y España: La Autodeterminación de Cataluña*. Liber Factory, 2013.
Garrido Lora, Manuel. *Violencia, televisión y publicidad: Análisis Narrativo de los spots publicitarios de contenido violento*. Alfar, 2004.
Gimeno Ugalde, Esther. "La narrativa del silencio y la 'desnudez' estética en el cine de Jaime Rosales." *Quo Vadis Romania*, no 34, 2009, pp. 45–63.
Gómez, Rosario G. "Is There an Audience Left for Independent Film in Spain?" *El País*, 23 Apr. 2013, http://elpais.com/elpais/2013/04/23/inenglish/1366722094_003838.html. Accessed 7 Apr. 2017.
Gónzalez, María, and César González. Entrevista a Jaime Rosales Director de Hermosa Juventud (2014). *Oficina Precaria*, 5 Aug. 2015, http://oficinaprecaria.org/2015/08/05/jaime-rosales-un-chico-me-dijo-no-es-una-pelicula-para-mi-nosotros-estamos-perdidos-es-para-chicos-de-15-y-para-padres-de-45/. Accessed 8 Jan. 2018.

Lejos de los árboles. Directed by Jacinto Esteva, performances by Manuel Cano, Marta Mejías, and Antonio Gades, Filmscontacto, 1972.

Losilla, Carlos. "Un impulso colectivo." *Caimán Cuadernos de Cine*, no 19, 2013, pp. 20–1.

Marsh, Steven. "The Legacies of Pere Portabella: Between Heritage and Inheritance." *Hispanic Review*, vol. 78, no 4, 2010, pp. 551–67.

Martí-Olivella, Jaume. "Forms of (In)visibility in Recent Spanish Films on Basque Terrorism." *Re-Visioning Terrorism Proceedings. An International and Interdisciplinary Conference*, Purdue U, 8–10 Sept. 2011, http://docs.lib.purdue.edu/revisioning/2011/909/29/ pp.1–14. Accessed 8 Jan. 2016.

Pa negre. Directed by Agustí Villaronga, performances by Franscesc Colomer, Marina Comas, and Nora Navas, Massa d'Or Produccions and Televisió de Catalunya, 2010.

Peláez Barceló, Antonio. Interview with Jaime Rosales about *Beautiful Youth*. Vimeo, 2014, https://vimeo.com/97035999. Accessed 9 March. 2017.

La plaga. Directed by Neus Ballús, performances by Raül Molist, Maria Ros, and Rosemarie Abella, El Kinògraf and Televisió de Catalunya, 2013.

Portabella, Pere, director: *Vampir. Cuadecuc*. Performances by Christopher Lee, Herbert Lom, and Soledad Miranda, Films 59, 1971.

– *Informe general sobre unas cuestiones de interés para una proyección pública*. Performances by Octavi Pellissa, Lourdes Barba, and Montserrat Caballé, Films 59, 1977.

– *Informe general II. El nou rapte d'Europa*. Performances by Jesús Carrillo, Zdenka Badovinac, and Ada Colau, Films 59, 2015.

– *Nocturno 29*. Performances by Lucia Bosé, Mario Cabré, and Ramón Julia, Films 59, 1969.

– *Umbracle*. Performances by Christopher Lee, Jeannine Mestre, and Miguel Bilbatúa, Films 59, 1972.

Rosales, Jaime. "Interview about *Beautiful Youth*," *Cineuropa*, 2014, http://cineuropa.org/vd.aspx?t=video&l=en&did=257746. Accessed 8 March 2017.

Rosales, Jaime, director: *Hermosa Juventud*. Performances by Ingrid García Jonsoon, Carlos Rodríguez, Inma Nieto, and Fernando Barona, Cameo Media, 2014.

– *Las horas del día*. Performances by Alex Brendemühl, Vicente Romero, María Antonia Martínez, and Àgata Roca, Cameo Media, 2004.

– *Petra*. Performances by Bárbara Lennie, Alex Brendemühl, and Joan Botey, Fresdeval Films, 2018.

– *La soledad*. Performances by Sonia Almarcha, Petra Martínez, and Miriam Correa, Fresdeval Films, 2007.

– *Sueño y silencio*. Performances by Oriol Rosselló, Yolanda Galocha, and Alba Ros, Fresdeval Films, 2012.

– *Tiro en la cabeza*. Performances by Asun Arretxe, Ion Arretxe, and Nerea Cobreros, Fresdeval Films, 2008.

Tesis. Directed by Alejandro Amenábar, performances by Ana Torrent, Fele Martínez, and Eduardo Noriega, Sogepaq, 1996.

Van Soest, Dorothy. *The Global Crisis of Violence: Common Problems, Universal Causes, Shared Solutions*. NASW Press, 1997.

Vilarós, Teresa M. "Barcelona come piedras: La impolítica mirada de Jacinto Esteva y Joaquim Jordà en *Dante no es únicamente severo*." *Hispanic Review*, vol. 78, no. 4, 2010, pp. 513–28.

12 Identity Kit: Where to Meet Isaki Lacuesta

JOSETXO CERDÁN AND MIGUEL
FERNÁNDEZ LABAYEN[1]

The final scene in Isaki Lacuesta's *Entre dos aguas* (*Between Two Waters*, 2018), the film that returns to the life of the brothers Isra and Cheíto, the two protagonists of one of the two parts that formed Lacuesta's *La leyenda del tiempo* (*The Legend of Time*, 2016), barely lasts one minute and a half and is composed of three takes: a first take of Isra looking up to stare at the right part of the frame; the counter-shot of what Isra is seeing, his three daughters playing in the marshes; and a return to Isra's take where, before a fade to black, he briefly returns his gaze to the camera. In these three shots, we can anticipate at least two cinematic allusions that cinephiles will promptly identify. First, Isra's final look into the camera is inspired by the mythical gaze performed by Antoine Doinel in François Truffaut's *Les quatre cents coups* (*The 400 Blows*, 1959), a seminal image from the cinema of modernity. The second one, perhaps less well known, is the shot of the three girls, which resonates with that of three other girls on a road in Iceland that marks the beginning of Chris Marker's *Sans Soleil* (*Sunless*, 1983). This figure, according to the narrator's voice-over in Marker's film, is "the image of happiness."

Lacuesta had already paid homage to the French film-maker in *Las variaciones Marker* (*The Marker Variations*, 2008), pointing to a stronger connection between this new quotation and its reference rather than the previous wink to Truffaut. The image of the girls on the Icelandic road is not only the first image in Marker's film, but it is also followed by a fade to black that lasts a few seconds. The voice-over narrator in *Sans Soleil* explains the possibility of uniting this image of happiness

---

1 The authors have written this chapter in the context of the research projects CSO2017–85290-P and PID2021-123567NB-I00, funded by the Ministry of Science and Innovation of Spain and the European Regional Development Fund.

with any other shot, even with a black screen: then, she argues, if the spectators do not see happiness in that first image of the girls, at least they will see the colour black. Lacuesta seems to find the solution to what Marker intends to present as an unsolvable problem: Isra's final gaze in *Entre dos aguas* is what gives sense to the image of happiness. In other words, there is no image that may stand for happiness; there is only a gaze that places its ideal of happiness upon an image. These cinephilic references are part of a wide film archive that Lacuesta has been able to mobilize throughout his career as a film-maker (Vidal). But these are not the only traces that one can find in the three closing takes of the film.

In 1904, Pío Baroja finished *La busca* (*The Quest*), the first of the three novels that formed his trilogy *La lucha por la vida*, with his main character, Manuel, having to make a decision that would condition the rest of his life:

Comprendía que eran las de los noctámbulos y las de los trabajadores vidas paralelas que no llegaban ni un momento a encontrarse. Para los unos, el placer, el vicio, y la noche; para los otros, el trabajo, la fatiga, el sol. Y pensaba también que él debía de ser de éstos, de los que trabajan al sol, no de los que buscan el placer en la sombra.

(He understood that the lives of the night lovers and those of the workers were parallel lives that never met each other. For ones, pleasure, vice, and night; for others, work, exhaustion, and sun. He thought that his must also be one of those who work under the sun, and not one of those who search pleasure in the shadows.) (Baroja 167)

In 2018, Isra finds himself confronted by a similar choice and, like Manuel, chooses the path of work and, in his case, also the path of taking care of his daughters, who return to him the image of happiness. It does not matter if this reference is a mere coincidence or if it constitutes a tribute to the Basque author by the screenwriters Lacuesta, Isa Campo, and Fran Araújo. In any event, it allows us to expand Lacuesta's universe beyond cinephilia. Our main goal in the pages that follow is not as much related to the cinematic or cultural references that Lacuesta mobilizes in his audiovisual works (not only films, as we shall see), but to understand, in the first place, his means of production from an anthropological perspective, after analysing them in relation to the contact zones of the historical cinematic cultures that coincide in Catalonia. Later, we will focus on Lacuesta's public persona in regard to a series of special events in Spain's recent history. Finally, we will try to explain how his cinema has evolved in tandem with his greater public projection towards a more experiential and sensitive orientation.

0. Perhaps Not the Right Distance

We have written extensively about Isaki Lacuesta's work for over a decade and, in a more or less direct way, we have been tied to the production of three of his short films: *Marte en la tierra* (*Mars on Earth*, 2007); *La repetición* (*The Repetition*, 2012); and *La matança del porc* (*The Pig Slaughter*, 2012). Hence, our closeness to the film-maker is impossible to hide or disguise. As academics researching the production of a cineaste, in this case we come closer to anthropology's participatory observation methods than to sociology's analytical work on data or to some of the evaluatory premises of film criticism. In fact, we have always analysed Lacuesta's career without establishing hierarchies between the formats, durations, or origins of his different projects. On the contrary, we have been and are still equally engaged with his entire production: short and feature films, installations and performances, fiction and documentary films, personal projects and commissioned work, writings, public interventions, speeches, web entries, and blogs.

At present, our goal is to revisit this wide range of sources in order to understand the continuity and coherence of his work in the context of all that he has had to confront to make his films: that of the post-cinema in a legal frame such as the Spanish and the Catalan (since the Generalitat also legislates in cinematographic/audiovisual matters), with big changes in the way of making and financing films; and, last but not least, in a very agitated context in social and political terms. It has become a commonplace over the years to define Isaki Lacuesta as a film-maker who has a chameleonic capacity of transformation, of reinventing himself in order to take on very different projects. In this chapter, we try to understand the logic behind all of these movements from a culturalist perspective: one that considers these apparent changes, not from the logic of authorship, but as a response to the identity conflicts that characterize many of the films produced in the twenty-first century. In order to do so, we have divided the present chapter into four sections. In the first one, we recover the notion of the *bricoleur* put forth by Claude Lévi-Strauss to consider in a pertinent way the coherence in Lacuesta's work. Next, we point towards a necessary historiography of film culture in Catalonia, which may be helpful in order to reconsider Lacuesta's output. The third section deals with the configuration of the film-maker's public persona. In it, beyond his works, we tackle some of the best-known, polemic, and possibly for many (perhaps himself included) unfortunate episodes of his interventions in the public sphere. Finally, we devote the last section to study some of Lacuesta's works in an attempt to identify how all our previous considerations reverberate in them and, more specifically, to see how this heterogeneous group of elements may connect to the evolution of those very works.

1. Lacuesta, the *Bricoleur*

In 2007, we pointed out how Lacuesta's then emerging work already showed two complementary trends: popular culture and primitivism (Cerdán). The thematic content of the two feature films produced until then had made it quite clear. In *Cravan vs. Cravan* (2002), the director was navigating the crossroads between avant-garde and popular culture that was embodied in the myth of the poet and boxer Arthur Cravan. In *La leyenda del tiempo* (2006), it was the figure of the flamenco singer Camarón de la Isla that connected *La voz de Isra* and *La voz de Makiko*, the two stories that shaped the film as an indirect and suggestive mirror game. The idea of the search for a first time, of authenticity, plus formal research and the quest for a genuine aesthetic experience were the poetic impulse that inspired both films. But their primitivism was not only a thematic concern, since it was also articulated through its relation with the films' background. To do so, Lacuesta teamed up in both films with a group of people that embodied such a spirit in one way or another: the poet Enric Casasses and musicians Pascal Comelade, Raimundo Amador, and Jesús Monje "Pijote," to name but a few. Through the mediation of these people, the production of these films became enriching vital experiences, setting out a mode of production wherein personal and collective encounters become a major part of what it means to make films.

From an aesthetic perspective, primitivism has always been a bit suspicious: "The more you prefer the primitive, the less you can become primitive" (Gombrich 297). And yet, the anthropological gaze and, more specifically, the one elaborated by Claude Lévi-Strauss in his seminal *La pensée sauvage* (*Wild Thought*, 1964) can help us situate Lacuesta's desire for primitivism and primitive culture in a more organic manner: by paying more attention to the creative processes and not so much to the formal results of his films. Lévi-Strauss opposes two ways of thinking, the mythical (primitive) and the scientific. One deals with the event, the contingent, whereas the other considers what is structural and strictly necessary. According to him, mythical thought develops "structured sets, not directly out of other structured sets, but from the residues and debris of events: 'odds and ends,' as English puts it, or, in French, bribes et morceaux, fossilized witnesses to the history of an individual or a society" (25). Next, the French anthropologist considers the question of artistic creation. He distinguishes three types of artistic creation: wise art (which would essentially mean Western art as it reaches the twentieth century), primitive art, and the applied arts. Western plastic arts, Lévi-Strauss points out, have as their goal art itself (*l'art pour l'art*), establishing a dialogue with previous models in the Western artistic tradition. On the contrary, primitive arts do not engage in any given tradition, and much less try to respond to its questions, since they emerge from a conversation that each creator establishes with the matter with which he or she is working. It is an art of the present that is generated at the moment of its execution and is, therefore, opposed to the wise art. And yet, as Lévi-Strauss writes, "Every form of art involves all three aspects and is distinguished from the others only by their relative proportion" (34). On a practical level, the anthropologist compares primitive thought to the work of the *bricoleur*, who is capable of carrying out a wide range of tasks with a very limited instrumental universe. The *bricoleur*'s fundamental rule "is always to make do with "whatever is at hand" – that is to say, a set of tools and materials that is finite at each moment, as well as heterogeneous, because the composition of the set is not related to the current project, nor indeed to any given project" (21). Therefore, if there is something that characterizes the ensemble of materials and instruments that constitutes its repertoire, it is precisely its instrumentality and not an (artistic) project that validates it from outside. There is no doubt that, seen in perspective, Lacuesta's unrelenting will to keep producing materials, creating random pieces from the instruments at hand at any given moment, clearly places him in the path of the *bricoleur*, that is to say, in the path of the primitive art of the present.

Our main goal in this chapter is to prove how his work, which has so often been claimed as an expression of wise art, which is usually identified with the film festival circuit, is in fact closer to primitive art. Needless to say, there is always a presence of the three elements at play, and, as we have already suggested, Lacuesta himself has activated a dialogue with film history and other artistic fields. And yet, throughout the years and perhaps more specifically after 2009, it has been without a doubt his work as a *bricoleur* that has taken off. That dialogue has been mainly established by working with all kind of available materials and has been done instrumentally. The year 2009 marks the release of his feature film *Los condenados* (*The Condemned*) and of his installation *Lugares que no existen. Goggle Earth 1.0* (*Places That Do Not Exist. Goggle Earth 1.0*). That same year he held his cinematic correspondence with Naomi Kawase, *In Between Days*, while helping to create the collective Cineastas Contra la Orden (CCO), a group of film-makers who, as we shall see, publicly opposed the turn taken by the director of the Institute of Cinema and Audiovisual Arts (ICAA), Ignasi Guardans. The three films mentioned above but also, and quite significantly, the series of events that happened between 2009 and 2011 in Spain, compelled Lacuesta to take a public stance, a positioning that starts precisely with his public rejection of the legal move taken by Guardans.

We cannot close this section without foregrounding the collaborative work between Isa Campo and Isaki Lacuesta. Both created the production company La Termita Films in 2011, but Campo's presence alongside Lacuesta's work has been constant since the very beginning. Lacuesta himself was conscious of their teamwork since their initial steps, when he decided to adopt the acronym Isaki (Isabel plus Iñaki) to sign all his/their works. A simple revision of the works produced in the past two decades clearly shows how Isa Campo's presence has been persistently growing, though she has always been an essential part of the creative and producing processes. Such a presence became more public than ever in 2016 when it reached a level of normalization by having both names appear as co-directors of *La propera pell* (*The Next Skin*, 2016). And, despite the fact that in Lacuesta's last feature film, *Entre dos aguas* (*Between Two Waters*, 2018), he assumes again the directorship on his own, Campo appears clearly integrated in the creative team both as co-producer and co-screenwriter. This is again a sign of the work of the *bricoleur*, located halfway between the domestic sphere and the industrial condition, something that defines what the couple does in their films and multiple projects.

We understand this process as part of the evolution that gender issues has had in Spain in the last fifteen years, but we also see it as the clear result of the way the couple have been reconfiguring their collaborative work beyond any outside labels. It shows a work spanning two decades composed of slow, subtle, and yet unrelenting changes, with little or no visibility, but which ultimately permit the establishment of new ethical and political positions. The way that the Campo/Lacuesta tandem has modulated their work throughout all this time becomes a perfect place from which to observe the changes that have taken place in our society.

2. Notes for a History of Catalonia's Cinematic Culture with Isaki Lacuesta in the Background

In recent years there has been a process of legitimization and institutional grounding of what, in general terms, could be defined as Catalan cinema made for the film festival circuit. The initiatives have been plenty in this respect. Let us focus, for instance, on the exhibition *Todas las cartas: Correspondencias fílmicas* (*All the Letters: Cinematic Correspondences*), which was sponsored by the CCCB (Centre for Contemporary Culture of Barcelona) in 2011 and in which Isaki Lacuesta participated. In this case the legitimization is generated through the epistolary and videographic relationship established between five new (and not so new) film-makers (all of Catalan origin except for the Mexican Fernando Eimbcke, who was included in the exhibition thanks to the participation of the Centro Universitario Tlatelolco from the Universidad Nacional Autónoma of México), each one with an international and prestigious colleague of his choice. The five invited film-makers were all men and the same happened with their invited interlocutors, the only exception being Lacuesta, who chose a woman for his epistolary exchange: the Japanese Naomi Kawase. It seems clear, therefore, that one side of the institutional process surrounding those Catalan film-makers has to do with their international prestige. The exhibition, also due to the support of Acción Cultural Española, travelled to France, Mexico, Turkey, and South Korea. The other side, of a diachronic nature, has been forged as a historical discourse that places these directors (and their works) as inheritors of the most popular (among connoisseurs) avant-garde movement in the history of Catalan cinema: L'Escola de Barcelona (the Barcelona School). It is on this construction as historical discourse that we want to focus for a moment. Our hypothesis in this case is that the relationship between these new film-makers with the Barcelona School has become a critical given, which, as it is often the case, needs only to be mentioned in order to be validated. There are very few occasions in which that connection has been taken beyond the fact of the presence of a figure like Joaquim Jordà in both movements. Jordà's dual presence, thus, propels a narrative, mostly originated in the Master in Creative Documentary program from Pompeu Fabra University (UPF) in Barcelona (Balló, 2010), according to which, Jordà would personify the link between those two periods (Villamediana; Riambau; Comella). It goes without saying that such a narrative hides Jordà's presence in Madrid in the context of the most traditional film industry working with (although not only with) Vicente Aranda, or his first attempt to return to Catalan cinema in the second half of the nineties with a crime comedy, a sort of Catalan *Twin Peaks*, as Jordà himself liked to refer to it, such as *Un cos al bosc* (*A Body in the Woods*, 1996), with Rossy de Palma in the leading role. Jordà's figure is especially relevant in Lacuesta's case since he became his mentor in the context of the master's program mentioned above and they developed a solid friendship. Even if Lacuesta has always acknowledged the importance of Jordà as a person in his development as a film-maker, he has, however, deliberately limited Jordà's formal influence on specific films (Lacuesta in Cerdán).

We would not like to fall here into any sort of reductionist statement. Indeed, it is certain that other figures in the Catalan cinema of the sixties and seventies have also lately received critical attention, as is the case of Pere Portabella (Expósito; Fanés, *Pere Portabella*) and Helena Lumbreras (Camí-Vela; Fernández Labayen and Prieto Souto, among others). In spite of this, the Barcelona School continues to occupy the central place in the institutional process of legitimation of contemporary Catalan cinema and of its historiography. It is from this vantage point, the one that connects the current Catalan cinema produced for the festival circuit with the work of the Barcelona School, that one perceives Lacuesta's work at best as chameleonic and mutant, or diffused and lacking direction in the worst case. Here, nevertheless, we would like to take a different approach. We do not want to reproduce a genealogy of Catalan cinema that legitimates its current festival output but open up a reflection on the diversity of the film cultures in Catalonia, which may, at the same time, help us understand the inner logic of a body of works like the one created by Isaki Lacuesta. It is not a matter of offering an itinerary through the uses of Lacuesta's cinematic archive but to provide an approximation to his work as echoing different expressions of the film cultures developed in the territory. In order to do so, we need to start with the identification and the writing of a history of Catalan cinema.

In an exercise as much political as historiographic, Miquel Porter i Moix set the basis for an identification of an object of study that went from being Catalan cinematography (1958) to a history of Catalan cinema (1969), and ended up as the history of cinema in Catalonia (1992). In all his work, Porter i Moix struggled to structure his approach to the history of cinema as a cultural industry. Given the clear political and national component of his project, he needed to pay attention to certain aspects of film culture, especially those based on policies for the promotion and support of cinema. In any event, the idea of cinema as an industry led Porter i Moix (and those who followed his historiographical efforts) to minimize other issues that, from a cultural and political viewpoint, might have been more fruitful. We are thinking of those horizontal web-like structures, film cultures, that set in motion not only ideas (symbolic capital), but also workforce (human capital), and, finally, goods (films). Critical attention to film cultures may offer a different view of the history of Catalan cinema from the traditional topdown structure that derives from an industrial perspective. For example, a horizontal look upon film cultures is important to understand 1930s European cinema: "to create a conceptualization of Europe not as a series of distinct national territories, but as a unified (even though highly heterogeneous) space in which energy flows stagnate and redistribute themselves regardless of national frontiers" (Hagener 241). Such a transnational film culture strongly attached to the avant-garde, which Hagener identifies, had at least two important expressions in the Spanish territory: the cine clubs culture, which has already been studied, among others, by Román Gubern (1999); and the essentially, although not exclusively, Catalan amateur film culture.

At the beginning of the 1930s, and with the arrival of the Second Republic, there were several relevant cinematographic developments in Catalonia. A fundamental one was the creation in 1931 of the amateur cinema section of the Centre Excursionista de Catalunya, which was not only a bourgeois society but also Catalan speaking and clearly in favour of political Catalanism. And yet, when Porter i Moix published what would be his final work in 1992, the history of Catalan cinema, this fact was relegated to the last paragraphs of the section immediately previous to the one devoted to the cinema of the Civil War. Such a downgrading of amateur cinema is even more telling given the fact that amateurism had been given important coverage in his 1969 volume. However, in 1992 the pioneer historiographer foregrounded three major events of the early 1930s, a time when, in his own words, "semblava ésser la gran ocasió, el moment per donar un impuls definitiu al que hauria pogut ser una indústria nacional, amb un vessant lingüístic i cultural" ("it felt like the great occasion, the right moment to give a final push in the direction of what would have been a national industry with a clear cultural and linguistic component"; Porter i Moix, *Història del cinema a Catalunya* 182). These three elements include the creation of a cinema committee by the Generalitat; the first academic film program offered by the Universitat de Barcelona (conceived and coordinated by Guillermo Díaz-Plaja); and the inauguration of the Orphea Studios. The first two undoubtedly respond to the permeable situation of film culture in Catalonia in those years, although both are top-down initiatives, and the third has a clear industrial character.

It was only later that Fèlix Fanés and Joan M. Minguet took on the task to analyse the phenomenon of the expansion of the cinematic culture in Catalonia during the first half of the twentieth century. Fanés and Minguet devoted part of their work to research the filiations and convergences between the intellectual elites and the art world (mainly plastic arts) with the world of cinema, or even with the world of mass culture (Fanés, *Salvador Dalí and Pintura*; Minguet, *Cinema and Salvador Dalí*). Both researchers opened up the field to some of the special forms employed in film culture in those early stages, and yet, the history of amateur cinema in Catalonia continued, and we might say it still continues today, being like a footnote or, at least, a separate, isolated, and ultimately minor chapter, with some exceptions (Fibla-Gutiérrez). It is also important to note, however, that this marginal position of the amateur cinema in Catalonia is also generated from within. To prove it, we need look no further than to *El cinema amateur a Catalunya*, the book that has been considered so far the main reference work on the subject. The authors, Jordi Tomàs i Freixa and Albert Beorlegui i Tous, state that "En els darrers temps, per exemple, la participació de films provinents d'escoles de cinematografia als concursos de cinema amateur, ha presentat seriosos dubtes sobre la legitimitat de la seva inscripció en aquest tipus de manifestacions" ("In recent years, for instance, the participation of films emerging from cinema schools in amateur cinema contests has shown serious doubts regarding the legitimacy of their inscription in these kind of venues"; *El cinema amateur* 23). Thus, on the one hand, we see how the official historiography marginalizes the expressions of amateur cinema while, on the other, one can also notice that such a marginal position becomes considered an inherent condition. These counterposed readings of amateur cinema neglect the evidence that points to the historical interconnection and overlapping of circuits between amateur cinema and industrial production in Catalonia. In fact, the trajectories of a wide group of Catalan film-makers, such as Miguel Iglesias, Pere Balañà, José Luis Comerón, and Jordi Feliu, and even that of Llorenç Llobet Gràcia, one of the most vindicated figures of the last decades, are clear proof of such an important connection. Thus, amateur film culture in Catalonia, from its very beginning, is not as separated from the industrial model as some of the most orthodox historical narratives invite us to think. And although we may accept that such a marginal position was more understandable a few decades ago, when the industrial value and the cinematographic policies occupied the entire field of vision of the historiographers, it is, nevertheless, quite obvious that the arrival of digital cinema has eroded those frontiers in very clear ways. In that sense, to think today about contemporary cinema's relationship with the past (its history, its genealogies), implies the capacity to be able to subvert the values that historiography has traditionally used. And that is the position where a cinematic corpus such as that created by Isaki Lacuesta may be a perfect platform wherefrom one can return the gaze to the past in search of a different configuration of the most relevant historical events. The benefit is double: to reinterpret history to understand the present (reconfiguring the relationships between centre and periphery) and to comprehend Isaki Lacuesta's work by considering it through a historical logic. In that sense, the use Isaki Lacuesta makes of cinema as a tool for the sensible, the fact of his work as *bricoleur* with the leftover of previous (de)constructions, and his privileging the dialogue with the materials over any other condition at the moment of developing his work are all elements born from a domestic or amateur conception of cinema, which he stubbornly develops in industrial contexts.

As we have discussed elsewhere (Cerdán and Fernández Labayen, "La quête"), this interconnection between avant-garde, amateur, militant, and commercial practices can be found in the seventies and afterwards. Take for instance the genealogy of (Catalan, but also transnational) film culture that finds its epicentre in the touristry town of Sitges. Home to the controversial First International Week of Cinema Schools in 1967, which brought together a part of the bourgeois film culture represented by the Barcelona School with the ever-growing militant cinema of the time (which, at least in some cases, had a more working-class origin), only a year later, in the symbolic year of 1968, the same town of Sitges inaugurated the International Week of the Fantastic Cinema (which after the following year, 1969, would add "and of Horror" to its title). It is interesting to note how the use of the fantastic and horror labels in order to erase the growing conflict of the presence of militant cinema was adopted in a quick way, and how later the festival finds a path to become the official platform for the diffusion of Catalan cinema. In 1973, in the late years of Francoism, the event becomes a competitive contest, which can be read as a clearly capitalist change. In 1981 (the fourteenth edition), the title appears in Catalan, Festival Internacional de Cinema Fantàstic i de Terror, or, at least, that is the language of the poster reproduced in the web page for that year (Archivos del Festival). It will be, however, in 1997, and coinciding with its thirtieth anniversary, that the most significant name change takes place. That year, in an obvious gesture of political and institutional legitimization of the festival, the Generalitat decided to turn it into the event of reference in Catalan cinema and labelled it as Sitges: Festival Internacional de Cinema de Catalunya. And yet, in 2009 its generic denomination was recovered (its contents had never ceased to be based on horror and fantasy) and was called Sitges: Festival Internacional de Cinema Fantàstic de Catalunya.

The Sitges festival has branched out into a series of other initiatives, such as the experience of the Fantastic Factory (2000–5), created by Julio Fernández from Filmax together with the American director Brian Yuzna, in what has been termed "the construction of a Spanish horror film culture" (Lázaro-Reboll, 231). At the same time, it has become one of the most salient identity markers of contemporary Catalan industrial cinema. Indeed, the Catalan directors who have the farthest reach in today's world cinema are not those devoted to the art film circuit but rather figures like Juan Antonio Bayona, Jaume Balagueró, and Paco Plaza (the latter, Valencian by birth, although his work started within the Catalan industry). All of them started their careers as horror filmmakers and owe a great deal to the Sitges festival, as they themselves have stated numerous times.

Having reached this point, it may seem clear that the different film cultures at work in Catalonia have been fighting throughout decades to occupy the same spaces of visibility and that this has generated all kinds of contact zones. It may not be without value to mention here that *Cravan vs Cravan*, Isaki Lacuesta's first feature film, was officially entered precisely in the Sitges Film Festival, where it received the main award in the Gran Angular section and also the *Citizen Kane* award to the best new director. If, in 2009, Carlos F. Heredero celebrated Lacuesta's presence as a "ciudadano de la galaxia audiovisual" ("citizen of the audiovisual galaxy"; Heredero 5), our goal here is to approach the director's heterogeneity through a diachronic lens that helps us understand the reasons behind his work from a series of crossovers that are more cultural, ethical, and political than technological, or even, industrial. In this way, the *bricolage* method suggested by Lévi-Strauss would not be anything else but the creative ways that allow Lacuesta to work with the materials at hand at any given time. Those materials, when referred to the different film cultures at work in Catalonia, would obviously include the Barcelona School, although they inscribe it historically within a genealogy that precedes it, and also within a much wider and multifaceted idea of avant-garde practices. From this perspective, Lacuesta does not renounce anything and configurates his work through a ludic experimentation that, in its own way, questions all the pre-established cinematic categories: amateur, militant, bourgeois, industrial. Thus, his *Ressonàncies Magnètiques*, a 2003 commissioned piece for the series Nuevas fronteras de la ciencia y el pensamiento (New Frontiers in Science and Thought), whose narrative dealt with a comically failed attempt to analyse the visual alterations produced by emotions in the brain (that of Isa Campo, who was identified in the credits precisely as "Cervell" [Brain]), ended with an "Epíleg per ara i aquí" (Epilogue for here and now). The epilogue appeared on screen just after the credits and contained a last cerebral image with this juxtaposed text: "Els destructors de cervells no accepten la raó ni la intel.ligència. Bush+Aznar+Blair= Sadam. Al tribunal de La Haya!!!" ("The destroyers of brains accept neither reason nor intelligence. Bush+Aznar+Blair= Sadam. Send them to The Hague Court!!!"). This is a clear example of an urgent political intervention done in a commissioned piece by a museum that directly leads us into our next section.

3. An Itinerary of Isaki Lacuesta's Life and Work during the Financial Crisis, the 15-M, and Its Aftermath

By mid-2009 Spanish cinema was shocked by the circulation of the original version of the Ministerial Order that developed the 55/2007 Law, better known as the Cinema Law. Though we are not going to confront the contents of that proposal, it is important to recall that more than two hundred cinema workers came together under the name of Cineastas Contra la Orden (CCO; Film-makers against the New Law, 2009) to try and stop the final publication of the law. Among the undersigned there were Isa Campo and Isaki Lacuesta. The latter, moreover, took a step ahead and played a leading role in the conflict generated by such an opposition. He was one of the best-known names at the time to sign the document, together with David Trueba and Javier Rebollo, and, as such, he received a lot of media coverage. Moreover, Lacuesta was a member of the group that led the direct negotiations with the ICAA (Cinema and Audiovisuals Arts Institute), alongside Ignacio Gutiérrez Solana, Manuel Martín Cuenca, Lola Mayo, Alberto Morais, Javier Rebollo, Pedro Pérez Rosado, and Felipe Vega, and his confrontations with Ignasi Guardans, the director of the ICAA and main supporter of the Ministerial Order, spread throughout social media. In general terms, these tensions resulted in everybody in the industry taking sides, which created a serious split in the Spanish film milieu among those defending each side of the issue. In the end, the original version, after a few minor changes, was published on Saturday, October 24, of that same year (Orden CUL/2834, 2009). But only one month later, after the legal protection sought by the CCO, the European Commission decided to suspend the law while requesting more information from the Spanish government to see if it fit the European legislation on the subject. The news contributed to a further radicalization of the positions, to the point that some referred to it as a civil war, a term still very charged semantically in Spain (Hermoso).

All of this forced Alex de la Iglesia, president of the Academy of Motion Picture Arts and Sciences of Spain at the time, to try to mediate and redirect the situation (De la Iglesia). Be as it may, the affair ended in the middle of the following year when a new order, slightly modifying the previous one, was published on June 30 (Orden CUL/1767, 2010). Despite all of this, CCO, far from dissolving, continued its collective work and kept open a discussion channel through its mailing lists, although the public statements stopped. Of particular importance in that discussion group was the debate surrounding the so-called Sinde Law (popularly named after the minister of culture, Ángeles González Sinde, but, in fact, officially termed the 2/2011 Law of Sustainable Economy from March 4), which called for the closing of websites that allowed illegal unloading of film materials from the Internet. This was another important conflict within Spanish cinema, which, among other things, was responsible for the resignation of Álex de la Iglesia as president of the Academy (Triana Toribio, 2016).

Only two months after the Sinde Law took effect, an event happened in Spain that nobody had predicted and that shook the entire country: the 15-M (or Indignados) Movement. Its origin was a concentration of citizens, mainly organized through social media, at Puerta del Sol in Madrid on 15 May 2011. This mobilization, which (in a very significant gesture) soon became a campout and sit-in the public square, spread through the entire country and even beyond its borders. Several squares in major cities in Spain were peacefully occupied and a series of campouts was organized to protest and carry out civic actions. At the time, Lacuesta was in Barcelona teaching a workshop and did not hesitate to put its infrastructure at the service of the movement, which, in Barcelona, was located at Plaça de Catalunya. During the month that the campout lasted, Lacuesta lived among the activists and recorded all kind of activities, letting the flow of events dictate the course of action. The filmed material would not become a proper film until almost a year later, when Lacuesta entered *La matança del porc* (*The Pig Slaughter*) as part of the Flaherty Film Seminar in 2012.

But even before that, and with the Indignados Movement still generating a lot of important activities, Lacuesta presented his *Los pasos dobles* (*Double Steps*, 2011) at the San Sebastián International Film Festival. The jury awarded the film the highest prize, the Golden Shell, in a decision that was met with an irritated reaction by film critics from some of the top Spanish dailies. A huge controversy broke out in the social media with accusations sent both ways, which neither the journalists nor the people responsible for the film avoided. Lacuesta kept his answer within the traditional media and did not make it public until the film was commercially released in early November that same year. He did so with a text titled "La crítica espectacular," published in the Barcelona daily *La Vanguardia*. In that piece, he named *El País*, *ABC*, and *El Mundo* as examples of media outlets that support bad professional practices by film critics in Spain. It may not be entirely irrelevant to recall that Isaki Lacuesta was himself a film critic before becoming a director and that, even today, he is a regular contributor to many print media outlets. *La crítica espectacular* would also be the name of the blog that the director created the same day his text was published. The controversy would spread throughout several publications. A month later, Lacuesta himself summarized it and considered it closed in another post of his blog entitled "Reacciones a la crítica espectacular."

Those unprofessional practices that Lacuesta confronted had already been denounced several times previously. Five years earlier, in 2006, *Tren de sombras*, one of Spain's first websites devoted to film criticism, which took its title from José Luis Guerín's well-known film, published a text titled "La catatonia nacional." In this column, the professional integrity of the same newspapers' film critics was already questioned, this time in the context of the Venice International Film Festival of that same year. Signed by José M. López Fernández, the article featured a compilation of those dailies' film reviews from the festival, put together by Raúl Pedraz, as a way of proving the main argument (López Fernández and Pedraz). Two years later, again with the exhibition in Venice as a background, the controversy sparked once more. This time thanks to a letter to the director published in *El País* and signed by a hundred names. Among them, in a prominent place, there were those of Miguel Marías, film critic and previous director of the Spanish Cinematheque, and Víctor Erice and José Luis Guerín. The letter railed against critic Carlos Boyero (then writing for *El País* and two years earlier for *El Mundo*), who, sent to cover the Venice Festival, showed a disrespectful attitude towards what he defined as "el llamado 'cine de autor' que hoy se hace en el mundo" ("the so-called 'auteur' cinema that is practised today in the world"; Erice et al., "*El País* y el cine"). Not even a year had passed when, in this case during the Cannes Film Festival and on the occasion of the presentation of his *Los abrazos rotos* (*Broken Embraces*), Pedro Almodóvar denounced, via a lengthy publication in his web page, the arbitrariness and lack of professionalism of, once more, Carlos Boyero's festival reviews (Cerdán and Fernández Labayen "Almodóvar"). Be as it may, these three examples serve to reflect how, already before the controversy in which Lacuesta took part, the situation between the film-maker and Spanish film criticism was convoluted. Although this is not the place to analyse this fact in some depth, we do believe that the creation of the CCO, together with the four public clashes that happened in this period (2006–11) between critics and directors of different generations, gives an idea of a more or less spontaneous attempt to question the relationships between the centre and the peripheries of Spanish film circuits (including the critics' circuit). It is not by chance that all of this happens during the first stages of the recession and the economic crisis, with the imposition of the harshest budget cuts, and the response of the Indignados Movement. The public and political engagement shown by Isaki Lacuesta in all of these causes is of particular relevance. Maybe the epilogue to this section was written in May 2014, when, after more than a year of meetings, an important part of the members of CCO established a cultural association under the name of Unión de Cineastas. Thus, a juridical shape was given to an initiative that, as suggested by its name, was a way of giving continuity to the CCO initiative, now no longer united urgently and with a specific goal, but with the idea "reivindicar el cine de nuestro país y resituarlo como un elemento cultural fundamental para la sociedad y su ciudadanía" ("to vindicate the cinema in our country and to place it again as a fundamental cultural element in our society and its citizenship"; Unión de Cineastas). Isaki Lacuesta was again among the supporters of the initiative, and he became one of the main proponents in the information sessions and the working meetings held in Catalonia. Only after Unión de Cineastas was set in motion, and after all these years of public intervention, did he step aside to a more discrete position.

Our specific survey of Lacuesta's public life during the years of the recession and the economic crisis has highlighted his engagement with and participation in some of the most important cultural debates regarding cinema in Spain in the 2000s and 2010s. We also must remark on Lacuesta's critical positions in the face of the 15-M's aftermath as they affect his own production.

In the last few years, we have witnessed a revisited vindication of the culture of the sixties and seventies, the *long sixties*, in general, and of some of its revolutionary movements in particular. If such a vindication has travelled throughout Europe and the United States, in the Spanish case it has received a special push after the 15-M Movement and the socio-cultural concerns of what came right after that historical period, that is to say, the public critique of what is known as *Cultura de la Transición* (Martínez). In 2008, Lacuesta released his short film co-directed with Pere Vilà, *Soldats anònims* (*Anonymous Soldiers*), where he questioned the empathic effect of what Angel Loureiro called "la retórica del patetismo" ("pathos rhetoric"; 22–5) regarding the films about mass graves being unearthed in Spain. That reflection would be extended the following year to the Latin American revolutionary context in his film *Los condenados* (*The Condemned*), in what becomes a frontal critique of the armed option (Cerdán and Fernández Labayen, "Memory"). We are going to close this section by paying attention to the way Lacuesta, who was implicated in the civil protests during those years we have just reviewed, has positioned himself regarding the discourses of vindication of the revolutionary fights during the long sixties. There are at least three examples, stemming from what may be called the 15-M spirit, that mark his distance from that vindication discourse. They are *La matança del porc* (*The Pig Slaughter*, 2012), *Murieron por encima de sus posibilidades* (*They Died beyond Their Means*, 2014), and *I Tupamaros ci parlano* (*The Tupamaros Speak*, 2016).

La matança del porc is almost a didactic film, given its basic and stark structure that follows Eisentein's, Pudovkin's, and Alexandrov's seminal idea of the sound counterpoint. The film is organized around a phone conversation between Lacuesta and Pep Armengol, a real estate consultant about to go bankrupt whom Lacuesta met during the 15-M mobilizations in Barcelona. In the film we can only hear Armengol's words, which take the shape of a hopeless critical discourse against Spanish democracy. The short film is presented from that very discourse as a paradox: it was the real estate managers and the bubble they created which was key to the Spanish economic crisis. At the beginning of the short, we can see images from the first democratic elections held in Spain after the dictator's death. Shot in Super 8, we soon find out that they were taken by the person whose voice-over we are hearing. And yet, his narrative begins with a more or less folkloric description of his memories of the traditional slaughtering of the pig, in which most of his family and even his neighbours took part. From that ritual, according to Armengol, "lo que salía era una necesidad de participación democrática" ("what emerged was a need for a democratic participation"). After hearing these words, while the voice-over narrator starts talking about the need he felt to record the first democratic elections, the images start showing the ritual slaughtering of the pig. The effect of the sound counterpoint becomes extreme at several points, as when the images showing the beheading of the pig coincide with a nostalgic moment in the voice-over: "en fin, aquellas horas tan bonitas, previas a lo que pensábamos podia ser una revolución, y que después fue una transición" ("Oh well! Those pretty moments, just before what we thought would be a revolution, and that later became a transition"). The images return then for a few seconds to show electoral mural paintings and posters (some with a content that, due to our bad collective memory, might appear rather surprising today): "El feminismo es internacional porque todo gobierno es patriarcal" ("Feminism is international because all governments are patriarchal"). The voice-over then concludes: "Eso resume estos cuarenta años. Ahora se da esta paradoja, lo que allí era ilusión para ir a votar, ahora es una desmitificación del voto" ("That summarizes these forty years. Now we have this paradox: what was there an illusion to vote is now a demystification of the vote"). Then we have a fade to black with a fast forward of almost forty years, at which point the digital images place us in the midst of a 15-M assembly during a vote taken by hand. From that moment on, while we keep seeing different images of the people mobilized in Plaça de Catalunya, the voice-over continues sharing thoughts about the way the system has frustrated the illusion of participation in political life.

Armengol finally reaches what he considers the two ways out from the situation. First is the utopian one that he defines vaguely as knowledge, which could be linked to the more or less popular idea, at least among some generations, that education makes us better. The second one, a bit more elaborated, and that is going to occupy the second half of the short, becomes an apology of violence against the representatives of the system (politicians, banking officials, business executives, etc.). The real estate promoter then shifts his discourse and spares their lives. At that moment, on screen we can see the juxtaposition of the digital images from the Plaça de Catalunya with those of the pig being slaughtered. The voice-over concludes summarily: "o se corrige el sistema democrático o hay que ir a la vía directa" ("either the democratic system is changed or we need to take the direct path"). The editing then plays with the gestures and faces of the people camped out at Plaça de Catalunya, which, one way or the other, seem to be approving the words from the real estate promoter. According to Armengol, however, the 15-M Movement would be a kind of a "political Greenpeace" and would not therefore follow the path to action. He nevertheless distances himself from that position. His final sentence, a Catalan saying, cannot be more explicit: "On no hi ha sang, no es poden fer botifarres" ("Where there is no blood, one cannot make any sausages"). That is not however Lacuesta's position, but Armengol's. Lacuesta leaves the discursive space of the film (the voice) to Armengol, but through the sound counter-point he establishes a reasonable distance. Whereas the interpellation to violent action might awaken a sympathetic reaction among some of the people camped out, and possibly among some audiences, the distance introduced by the montage reduces Armengol's comments (we cannot forget that he is a real estate agent, after all) to a humoristic game, most certainly a liberating one, but one that cannot ultimately be taken seriously. In this way, Lacuesta would place himself closer to the political

Greenpeace version of the 15-M Movement, and despite having given the word to the cause of violence, he has done so in order to undercut it through his humoristic montage. *La matança del porc* thus retakes the positions suggested by Lacuesta in *Los condenados*, while digging deep into the contradictions and simplifications generated by the search for univocal solutions.

Even though *Murieron por encima de sus posibilidades* was released two years later than *La matança del porc*, Lacuesta and Campo were already at work with the former when the latter was released. *Murieron por encima de sus posibilidades* is a film produced by all its participants, who worked under a cooperative model. Lacuesta and Campo decided to revisit this production system (relatively popular during the sixties) for a project that was truly peculiar in their trajectory: a choral comedy with popular undertones (a meta-hyper *españolada*, in their own words) that represents in its own way a kind of response to the confrontations held with the ICAA (something like *we won't stop making films, even if some people don't like it*), and also a unique effort within Spanish cinema to let oneself be moulded, at the time of making a film, by the influence of the 15-M Movement. But almost nothing was understood regarding this truly and harshly political project, which played against many structural aspects of the country and whose long production process (three years) clearly harmed.

If we look at the critics' response, we first find those who had been at the centre of the controversy with Lacuesta on the occasion of his having won the Golden Shell for *Los pasos dobles*. All of these were harbouring an obvious negative feeling towards the director and were waiting to dismantle his next film. It would have been the same no matter what kind of film, but the fact that Lacuesta came up with an ambitious and yet grotesque film (it could not have been any other way) made things pretty easy for them. The condescension with which, in the best cases, the film was received by those who had previously defended Lacuesta's work may have been even a worse reaction. In other areas, and we are thinking, for instance, about its distribution, the film did not have the slightest chance. Its blatant pamphlet-like quality and its will to recur to an abrupt and even gross idiom, taken from the terse surface of the contemporary Spanish audiovisual corpus, and quite popular at street level despite its lack of political correctness, blocked any possibility of a more or less acceptable commercial run. In that way, all venues to reach the wide audience for which the film was designed were closed even before it was released. The film was not even taken seriously within the political milieu surrounding the positions created around the post-15-M Movement that were taking shape at the time.

Murieron por encima de sus posibilidades fleshed out Armengol's fantasy in *La matança del porc*, a fantasy, on the other hand, that was shared by a substantial part of the population. In Lacuesta's own words: "En el futuro no querremos recordarlo, pero en 2011, el sueño del que más se hablaba en los bares españoles de la crisis era el maltrato físico a nuestros políticos y banqueros" ("In the future we will not want to remember it, but in 2011, the fantasy most shared in the bars during the economic crisis was that of doing physical harm to our bankers and politicians"). Even in 2017, a sizeable part of the Spanish population reacted to banker Miguel Blesa's suicide in terms of poetic justice. And yet, *Murieron por encima de sus posibilidades* may not be reduced to a simple illustration of that vertical idea of power and its abuses. Rather, in a much more Foucauldian way, the film spreads the responsibility among all social layers and denies a happy ending to their avenging protagonists. To take justice into one's hands, despite its appearance of achieving a kind of justice, does not become a valid way out for the film's protagonists since the inflicted violence ends up being turned against them.

The year after the release of *Murieron por encima de sus posibilidades*, in 2016, Lacuesta was invited to participate in the seminar "La toma de la palabra: Diálogos con el archivo del cine militante" ("Taking the Word: Dialogues with Militant Cinema's Archive"), held in San Sebastián's Tabakalera Centre for Contemporary Culture on November 25 and 26. The event was part of Pablo La Parra Pérez's research project *Europa, futuro anterior*, which was aimed to explore "the transferences between the militant film archive and the contemporary visual and artistic practices" (La Parra Pérez). The commission made to Lacuesta for that event was titled *I Tupamaro ci parlamo*. It consisted of a performance that re-enacted a supposed film screening led by Joaquim Jordà in 1969 at the festival of militant cinema held in Porretta Terme, Italy. Jordà, who was practically the only source to document that event, used to say that the program was based on the projection of Mario Handler's short film entitled *Liber Arce, liberarse* (1969), and that it was divided in two parts, with his hour-long monologue telling who the Tupamaros were from the cabin and with a pitch black screen in the middle. Lacuesta was probably invited by the organizers for two reasons: his well-known status as disciple and, more importantly, friend of Jordà, and for having been one of the few Spanish film-makers of his generation to have confronted the theme of the long and violent sixties.

We want to reproduce here a bit *in extenso*, given its relevance, some fragments of the text performed by Lacuesta, while walking around the seated audience, in a dark theatre, with a frontal light on his head illuminating the papers, on the night of November 26 in Hall 1 of Tabakalera:

> Si queremos sentarnos – o sentirnos- de verdad en aquella sala de cine de 1968 [*sic*], en Porreta Terme, lo primero que deberíamos hacer es olvidar.
> Empecemos por olvidar por el final, y vayamos avanzando hacia el pasado. Olvidemos que ha muerto Fidel Castro. Olvidemos el pacto de paz entre las FARC y el gobierno colombiano. Y ahora ya no sabemos que ETA renunció a usar las armas.
> Y ahora olvidemos que Pepe Mújica, tupamaro, pasó quince años preso, salió de la cárcel, se hizo parlamentario y ganó las elecciones presidenciales de Uruguay.
> Y ahora olvidemos que Joaquim Jordà murió.
> [...]
> Sigamos, pues, olvidando. Olvidemos ahora la masacre del Filtro en 1994.
> Y ahora olvidemos que los tupamaros abandonaron la lucha armada y desde finales de los 80 participan del sistema democrático.
> Y ahora olvidemos el dinero que ETA envió a los tupamaros, no porque ETA fuera más o menos importante en la historia tupamara, sino porque estamos en Donosti y hasta eso hay que olvidar.
> Y olvidemos que entre los guerrilleros siempre hay un traidor y que el delator de esta historia se llamó Amodio Pérez.Y olvidemos los ataques contra miembros de los Escuadrones de la muerte, los policías muertos, los civiles muertos, los guerrilleros muertos y a los hombres y mujeres que murieron porque pasaban por ahí. Y olvidemos sobre todo a Pascacio Báez, peón rural, hombre de campo, que tuvo la mala suerte de descubrir por azar un refugio de armas tupamaro y estos lo asesinaron.
> Y ya puestos, tenemos que olvidar que el autor de nuestro libro sobre los tupamaro, Antonio Mercader, abandonó sus simpatías hacia la lucha armada de los tupamaro y terminó siendo ministro de cultura de un gobierno llamémosle conversador.
> Olvidemos, olvidemos, olvidemos. Aprovechemos que en este país se nos da bien olvidar. Olvidemos todos estos años y ...
> 1969. Estamos en Porretta Terme.
> [...]
> Sigo recordando a Jordà, y nuestras conversaciones de bar. Le añoro mucho. Para quien no le conociera, hay que aclarar que Jordà tenía un carácter de la hostia. Si hacía falta imponer un argumento, no le costaba ser cruel. Por suerte, conmigo nunca se ensañó, solía ser más cómico. [...]
> Nunca olvidaré el único día que nos cabreamos en serio con Jordà. Hablábamos, precisamente, sobre la legitimidad o no de la lucha armada.

Joaquim defendió que era legítimo matar a políticos elegidos democráticamente. "¿Y a un concejal de pueblo, que solo hace política municipal?," le provoqué. "Por supuesto. Esos son los peores. Al fin y al cabo," dijo, "los concejales son unos arribistas." Enumeré a todos nuestros amigos y conocidos comunes que, sin duda, eran unos trepas y unos arribistas, en el cine, o aún peor, en la universidad. Los arribistas del sueldito fijo. ¿Los matamos también? Aquella noche discutimos y nos despedimos antes de lo habitual.

(If we want to sit – or to feel – truly in that cinema theatre in 1968 [sic] in Porretta Terme, the first thing we need to do is to forget.

Let us start forgetting from the end and let us keep moving towards the past. Let us forget that Fidel Castro has died. Let us also forget the peace agreement between the FARC and the Colombian government. And now we do not know that ETA renounced the use of violence. And now, let us forget that Pepe Mújica, a Tupamaro, spent fifteen years in jail, left the prison, became a parliamentary member, and won the presidential election in Uruguay. And now let us also forget that Joaquim Jordà died.

[...]

Let us continue forgetting. Let's forget the Filtro massacre in 1994.

And now, let's forget that the Tupamaros abandoned their armed struggle and since the end of the eighties participate in the democratic system.

And now, let's forget the money that ETA sent to the Tupamaros, not because ETA was more or less important in the history of the Tupamaros, but because we are in Donosti and even that we need to forget.

And let's also forget that there is always a traitor among the guerrilla fighters and that the betrayer in this history was called Amodio Pérez. And let's forget the attacks against the Death Squads members, the dead policemen, the dead civilians, the dead guerrilla fighters, and the men and women who died because they happened to be there. And let's forget, above all, Pascacio Báez, a rural worker, a countryman, who had the misfortune to run into a Tupamaro weapons hideout by chance and that the Tupamaros killed him because of it.

And, since we are at it, we have to forget also that the author of our book on the Tupamaros, Antonio Mercader, dropped his sympathies towards the armed struggle and ended up being the Secretary of Culture in the cabinet of a rather conservative government.

Let's forget, forget, forget. Let's take advantage that in our country we are good at forgetting. Let's forget all these years and ...

1969. We are back in Porretta Terme.

[...]

I continue to remember Joaquim Jordà and our bar conversations. I miss him a lot. To those who did not know him, one must clarify that Jordà had a very rough character. If an argument needed to be upheld, he didn't hesitate to be cruel. Luckily, he never fought with me, he used to be more comical [...]

I will never forget the only day we truly got mad at each other. We were precisely talking about the legitimacy or not of the armed struggle. Joaquim defended that it was legitimate to kill politicians that had been democratically elected. "And a town councilman, who only carries out municipal policies?" I provoked him. "Of course. These are the worse, since," he added, "the councilmen are always the upstarts." I enumerated all of our common friends and acquaintances, who doubtlessly were social climbers and upstarts in the world of cinema, or, even worse, in the university world. The upstarts of the fixed salary. Do we also kill them? That night we had an argument and left each other before the usual time.)

Always provocative, as a good follower of Jordà, Lacuesta underlines two things in his performance: first, we cannot forget all the consequences of the armed struggle and the cinema that defended it; and second, it is not the same to be born in 1935 as forty years later, in 1975. Between those two years, the birth dates of Jordà and Lacuesta respectively, there was a civil war and a dictatorship in Spain, and a world war, a cold war, and the long sixties in the world context at large. The translations and mirror games cannot leave aside all these painful questions. Isaki Lacuesta was engaged from the beginning or even before with the answers given from the civil society, or with the weaker positions within Spanish cinema, in the face of the recession and the economic crisis. His public stance got him involved in a series of public fights, some of which were not understood (neither by film professionals or cinema lovers nor by the critics who had supported him until that moment), others would charge him their price a posteriori. It is even possible that at the moment of writing these lines, in 2018, they continue to do so. It is a symptom that something is wrong when somebody who has recently won more than six awards at the Málaga Film Festival (the biggest venue for Spanish cinema in Spain) with his *La propera pell* has to recur to such a humble resource as Abycine Lanza, a talent development program organized by the Albacete film festival Abycine, in order to complete the budget of his next film, *Entre dos aguas*. A film, on the other hand, that has done a pirouette that deserves to be studied, by having been able not only to enter again the official competitive section of the San Sebastián International Film Festival but winning once more the Golden Shell award. Lacuesta's public engagement has influenced his work, but it has done so always with a critical gaze, even for those who travelled with him. Always far from any maximalist stance, Lacuesta continues to dig deep into those unstable, marginal, obscure, or even hidden life registers that are placed far away from the public eye, and he works through exploring the haptic and the link with the senses and the body. To study this connection will be the focus of our last section.

Biological Inscriptions: Maps, Bodies, History
(As a Kind of Conclusion)

Had it been written in the eighties, this section might have been called something like "representaciones del pueblo" ("representations of the people"). Today that is no longer possible. The term "pueblo" has not only ceased to be used but it is seen with distrust. In the cinematic field, it was Gilles Deleuze who, following an idea first formulated by Paul Klee, pointed out the absence of people as one of the defining characteristics of his time-image (that is, what is known as the cinema of modernity). Specifically, Deleuze mentions Alain Resnais and the couple Straub-Huillet as "probably the greatest political film-makers in the West, [...] because they know how to show how the people are what is missing, what is not there" (215–16). Since that faraway moment when Deleuze wrote those lines, the idea has been repeated plenty of times to keep showing how political cinema inhabited that absence, and still does. One has insisted so much on that disappearance that, finally, the term itself has been void from any content and its simple mention becomes suspicious. Gonzalo Aguilar has recently questioned the limits, or better, the actuality of Deleuze's work. Indeed, that is only a rhetorical question that he himself answers:

> Si los orígenes de la historia del cine son la construcción de un punto de vista de la no persona, y eso se ha mantenido con bastante integridad durante casi todo el siglo XX, el fenómeno al que asistimos hoy es el de la inscripción de la primera persona en la imagen [...] la cámara misma se transforma en un organismo, en una prótesis, porque ya no vivimos fuera de la imagen y todos somos hacedores de imágenes digitales.

> (If the origins of the history of cinema are to be found in the construction of a non-person viewpoint, and that has been kept with enough integrity throughout most of the twentieth century, the phenomenon we are facing today is that of the inscription of the first person in the image [...] the camera itself becomes an organism, a prosthesis, because we no longer live outside the image since we are all makers of digital images.) (78)

If the recovery of the "pueblo/people" (both in cinematic and theoretical terms) is still impossible, we may perhaps access through our living experiences of the sensible something less terminologically pretentious or easier to tackle without awakening so many suspicions, such as "personas/human beings." A survey of Lacuesta's production during the years of the economic crisis as the one we have outlined might give the false impression of a pessimistic gaze on the human condition. Nothing is further removed from reality. Beyond his hypothetical fugues, his multiple directions, and his skin changes, what seems to have always interested Lacuesta is precisely that – the people. If we cannot use the term "pueblo," or if even that of "cultura popular" might seem inadequate or out of context, when one considers that the differences between high and low culture have been practically erased, Lacuesta continues to work without any complex with and about the life experiences of people and characters. He is interested in people's daily lives, with their problems and joys, their dreams and their nightmares. In his approach, there is neither idealization (of the invisible, the marginal, the primitive) nor denial of its complex and many times contradictory condition. The bodies that inhabit his films (no matter if they are narrative or documentary ones) live in actuality, a here and now where even digital technologies may look like primitive tools for the *bricoleur*.

This happens in his *Besar-te com un home* (*To Kiss You Like a Man*, 2016), a short film produced for "Diversitat en curt" (an initiative promoted by the Feminisms and LGTBI Office of the Barcelona City Hall and coordinated by the Fundación La Casa y el Mundo) that includes five pieces by five different directors. These short films are planned out as pedagogical resources to work with sexual and gender diversity in classrooms and beyond. *Besar-te com un home* stages a dialogue between a series of homoerotic images, recorded by Lacuesta in U-matic in 1996 and based on a personal experience (when he was still a student), and a Skype conference between two of the protagonists of his film *La propera pell*, Àlex Monner and Igor Szpakowski. In their conversation, the two actors recall the shooting of a scene with homosexual content that both performed in the film. As Lacuesta himself unfolds throughout the images, homosexual relationships generated all kind of hesitations among young people of the nineties. Thus, his goal in returning with his actors to that scene was no other than "veure si al segle 21 tenen les idees més clares. O no" ("to see if in the twenty-first century they have clearer ideas on the subject. Or not"). In this short, which was commissioned with a pedagogical aim (two notions with a very bad press in the Spanish cinematic profession), the U-matic analogue recording shot by Lacuesta in 1996 precedes the digital ones of the Skype conversation. Twenty years and an ocean of technological changes separate both groups of images, but for Lacuesta, the *bricoleur*, that is only secondary. Both groups of images, moreover, end up achieving a strange kind of unity thanks to the clearly imperfect nature they share. An imperfection that gives a flair of something primitive, unstable, ethereal, of something about to vanish, and that becomes a bridge between the analogue video of the nineties and the digital sign of the second decade of the new millennium. It is precisely on that nature of the images as an imperfect and primitive surface where the fundamental elements that form the short are deposited, where the paradox that the film sustains (whether the new generations have overcome the social taboos surrounding homosexuality or not), acquires its full significance. Despite everything, we are not so far removed, and U-matic and Skype are reunited in their imperfection as surfaces whereon Lacuesta first, and Monner and Szpakowski later, will deposit their experiences. We are thus fully immersed in that biological character referred to by Aguilar in which "vivir y filmar o registrar se hace a menudo en un solo acto" ("living and filming or recording is often done at the same time"; 77).

As Thomas Elsaesser and Malte Hagener have reminded us, "The intercultural and phenomenological schools correspond to a fascination with the human body, its surface and vulnerability – all of which are important themes in the cinema of the past twenty years" (110). That surface is no other than the skin and the sense of touch with which it is associated. As early as 2007, Lacuesta already said:

> Creo que lo más interesante del cine es esa presencia de rastros de personas, de cuerpos. Es algo que yo trabajo en alguno de mis cortos. Yo creo que aunque sean conceptuales forman parte de un aprendizaje cada vez más centrado en la materia y en los cuerpos.
>
> (I think that the most interesting aspect of cinema is that presence of human traces, of human bodies. It is something that I work with in some of my shorts. I think that despite being conceptual they form part of a learning process that is more and more centred on the material and the human body.) (Cerdán 242–3).

In fact, we believe that in the long decade since he made that statement, Lacuesta's cinema has consistently moved from that idea of the evanescent, of the "rastros de las personas" ("traces of people"), the remnants, the ghostly images, to the rotundity of "los cuerpos" ("the bodies"), the presences, the skin and its sensitive dimension. Such a move has made Lacuesta's films steadily more physical and less ethereal. It is obvious, in this sense, the leap produced in the dyptic formed by *La leyenda del tiempo* and *Entre dos aguas*. Between the two films one can observe some of the most substantial changes that turn Lacuesta's cinema into an ever-expanding physical experience (for the audience, but also possibly for all of those who participate in the production of the film from both sides of the camera). From the film's mise en scène to the shooting choices (moving from a more cerebral and contained framing, with a preference for the tripod, to the use of a closer and more nervous handheld camera), to the editing process (with more abrupt cuts and more evident postproduction manipulations or digital alterations of images). It is doubtlessly a process to find, among the possible materials, the most adequate for each work, though the tactile temptation to treat the images as surfaces and its main formulation on the skin of the human body has been there for a long time. It was already present as a central theme in *Teoría de los cuerpos* (*Theory of the Bodies*, 2004), which, alongside the comical rotundity of Isa Campo's brain images in *Ressonàncies magnètiques*, seem in themselves already an answer to that fascination with the ghostly traces of the human body that he was already chasing in *Caras vs Caras* (*Faces vs. Faces*, 2000) and *Microscopías* (2003).

In this process, Lacuesta's work would have moved from what Vivian Sobchack considers an idealist ethics and aesthetics, and therefore a "top-down" process, to a "bottom-up" one that is generated through the carnal experience that crosses the bodies (of the film-maker and of the protagonists): "Our own lived bodies provide the material premises that enable us, from the first, to sense and respond to the world and the others – not only grounding the logical premises of aesthetics and ethics in 'carnal thoughts' but also charging our conscious awareness with the energies and obligations that animate our 'sensibility' and 'responsibility'" (*Carnal Thoughts* 3).

Thus, it is not only a matter of carnal thoughts, but the fact that the logic of sensibility and responsibility is the one that moves, ever more explicitly, Lacuesta's work. In a recent text dealing with the work of different Spanish film-makers that included Lacuesta's installation *Lugares que no existen. Goggle Earth 1.0* (*Places that do not exist. Goggle Earth 1.0*), we pointed out two ideas that we would like to recall here. On the one hand, we noted that "The differences between the subjects being filmed and the filmmakers blur and give birth to new forms of agency, empowerment, and affective relationships." Secondly, we also noted that those film-makers understand the maps as a result "of interactions between a social group, a technology and a geographical space" (Cerdán and Fernández Labayen, "Cartographic" 240–1). In *Lugares que no existen:*

Goggle Earth 1.0, through co-creation processes (not very removed from the *cinema verité* espoused by Jean Rouch) and transforming the God-like gaze, implicit in Google Earth into a ground level gaze, Campo and Lacuesta give a body and a visibility to those areas which the digital tools render invisible, those areas that for political, economic, or military reasons, remain hidden under a blurred pixel that appears as a cloud or a blot. That double impulse that organizes *Lugares que no existen. Goggle Earth 1.0*, the collaborative work, and the need to document those places that officially do not exist or are going to be removed (that is, to draw audiovisual maps with those who inhabit or have inhabited them), is present and has been the creative engine in Lacuesta's work from its very beginning. *Déjà vu 1: Paisatges que desapareixen (Déjà vu 1: Landscapes that Disappear*, 2003) is an exercise that consists in the recovery of images from *Cravan vs. Cravan* that were not used. In these images we see poet and performer Enric Casasses walking through the ruins of Las Arenas, the Barcelona bullfight arena, just before it was transformed into a commercial mall. In Lacuesta's own words:

> Cuando rodamos estas imágenes, el espacio de las Arenas ya hacía años que estaba abandonado, cada vez más lejos de los viejos espectáculos, de las corridas de toros y combates de boxeo (Casasses me contaba que allí mismo vio bailar a Nureyev, cruzando de sol a sombra el ruedo reconvertido en inmenso escenario) y cada vez más cerca de verse restaurado y convertido en un macrocentro comercial. Las formas de entender el ocio también cambian junto con los perfiles de los edificios. Cuando la filmamos, Las Arenas servían de refugio nocturno a los inmigrantes marroquíes sin techo. La plaza nunca fue ni será nunca tan bella como entonces: no hay otra razón que justifique esta pieza.
>
> (When we filmed those images, the space of Las Arenas had been abandoned many years before, it was more and more removed from the old spectacles, the bullfights and the boxing matches. (Casasses told me that he had seen Nureyev dancing there and crossing from sun to shadow the entire ring now turned into an enormous stage) and it was ever closer to being renovated and transformed into a big commercial mall. The ways of understanding leisure also change with the buildings profile. When we filmed it, Las Arenas was being used as a night refuge for homeless Moroccan migrants. The place was never and will never be more beautiful than at that time: there is no other reason that justifies this short). (Lacuesta, np)

Bodies and geographies (architectural structures, in this case), or their cartographies, also inscribe the history, embodying it even when it might be invisible. In 2012, *La desaparición* (*The Disappearance*) recovered a found little short shot in Super 8 in the catamaran boat that used to cross L'Estany de Banyoles, the Banyoles lake. In that place, the film-maker tells us, both he and his father spent some of the happiest hours of their adolescent and childhood years, and they also found their first love there. The recovery of the film is the way to activate the sentimental memory of the place (Cerdán and Fernández Labayen, "Memoria"), but going beyond the inane happy summer images (they include not only the anonymous Super 8 reel but also the film-maker's family pictures), the short recalls an accident involving a big boat that cost the life of twenty retired French workers in those waters in 1998. There is thus a clash between those happy memories and the historical event, but the conclusion is not a simple one. "History happens now in the public sphere where the search of a lost object has led […] to the quickening of a new historical sense and perhaps a more active and reflective historical subject" (Sobchack, "Introduction" 7). From that position of historical reflexivity, Lacuesta concludes in his short film *La repetición*: "Todas las familias felices se parecen ... pero cada familia desdichada es peculiar. El naufragio asusta menos que la repetición" ("All happy families look alike ... but every unhappy family is unhappy in its own way. The shipwreck is less scary than the repetition").

Entre dos aguas starts literally with a repetition if we consider the sequence that closes *La voz de Isra*, the first of the two parts that form *La leyenda del tiempo*. In this scene, Isra reiterates to Saray his decision to not sing again despite the fact that more than a year has already passed since his father's violent death. This is an event that we can only imagine in *La leyenda del tiempo* through the kids' conversations, since when the film starts it has already happened and is never explained. Instead, in *Entre dos aguas* this event is going to be represented, not only once but twice. The new film not only reintroduces the two brothers, Isra and Cheíto, but, more importantly, it renders their traumas visible. Isra's refusal to sing in 2005 is followed now by a series of silences as an adult since he is still trapped by the trauma of having witnessed his father's violent death. He also feels also trapped by a place and a time that do not seem to offer him any way out. Unlike in the previous film, however, now everything is more physical and material. As we have just said, for instance, the father's death is represented twice and in different ways. First, we are told about it in full detail in a dramatic conversation that the two brothers have at the beach near the film's end, in which both give up on the vengeance that looms like a threat during the entire film. Then, we also learn about it through a narrative element that articulates part of the story: Isra's desire to cover his entire back with a tattoo containing an allegorical representation of the moment of the killing. If in *La voz de Isra* tattoos were a way of growing up, or to believe that one was growing up, that is, of projecting oneself into the future, in *Entre dos aguas* tattoos, on the contrary, will assume the weight of the past. With the allegory of his father's death, Isra literally puts on his shoulders the trauma of the killing. Tattoos also abound on Cheíto's body and on the bodies of the two brothers' friends, mainly on that of El Pollo, and are maps of life, a way in which the body inscribes one's biography. Tattoos were also obsessively prominent on Gabriel/ Léo's skin in *La propera pell*, but in that case they appeared as mysterious symbols that the audience could only aspire to interpret: as keys of an uncertain and never fully revealed path. Here, on the contrary, the tattoos anchor the biographies and embody both traumas and happy moments (on the body of both brothers we see the name of the father but also of their wives and daughters). *Entre dos aguas* shows the rotundity of the bodies becoming present on screen and, as such, generating carnal thoughts that shake the spectators. However, that rotundity may also be found in the materiality of the places. If, in 2003, La Casería beach, where the characters live, might have seemed like a place in the margins of progress, but also as a kind of lost paradise where time has stopped, by 2018 it had become a much more aggressive place for the characters. Whereas before there were only small houses (almost like a shanty town), now there are bridges, military installations, storage areas for vehicles that have been confiscated from the drug traffickers, and tall apartment buildings. It may be interesting to recall here that one of the videos that form *Lugares que no existen: Goggle Earth 1.0*, entitled *San Fernando*, was precisely shot on that same La Casería beach in order to document the presence of three tall tourist apartment buildings that will reappear in *Entre dos aguas*. They are not only three huge blocks that break any possible horizontal harmony in the landscape seen in *La leyenda del tiempo*, but they also provide the rooftops wherefrom, in alternation (first ones and then the others), both policemen and drug traffickers control the circulation of goods throughout the bay. But they also control the life of the inhabitants of La Casería, whom they observe, with sharp high-angle shots, in their efforts to survive their daily lives. Even so, the two brothers are able to find their own happiness there. After picking up Isra when he leaves the prison, the first thing Cheíto and his brother do is go for a swim under a concrete bridge on which the freeway runs. The place is truly inhospitable and yet Isra refers to it as being in paradise and even momentarily starts to sing.

Almost two decades after Isaki Lacuesta started his cinematic career we can point out how his films and his ideas about cinema have grown, but they have done so from a series of potentialities that his cinema showed from the beginning. Carnality, geography, political commitment, and history become intertwined in these almost twenty years of work and public intervention. The *bricoleur*, who has always been there, has continued, and will probably still continue, to try out on all kinds of arts and combinations of traces and remains to compose his work and to give it a horizontal ethics, which places him on a carnal reverberation with the human beings that inhabit his works.

Translated by Jaume Martí-Olivella

WORKS CITED

Aguilar, Gonzalo. *Más allá del pueblo: Imágenes, indicios y políticas del cine*. Fondo de Cultura Económica, 2015.

Archivos del Festival. Sitges. 51 Festival Internacional de Cinema Fantàstic de Catalunya. http://sitgesfilmfestival.com/cas/arxiu. Last accessed 22 July 2018.

Balló, Jordi. "Cronología de una transmisión (El Máster de Documental de la UPF)." *Realidad y creación en el cine de no-ficción (El documental catalán contemporáneo, 1995–2010)*, edited by Casimiro Torreiro, Cátedra, 2010, pp. 105–22.

Baroja, Pío. *La lucha por la vida 1: La busca*. Biblioteca El Mundo, 2001.

Camí-Vela, María. "Entre la esperanza y el desencanto: El cine militante de Helena Lumbreras." *Plan Rosebud: Sobre imágenes, lugares y políticas de memoria*, edited by María Ruido, Xunta de Galicia, 2009, pp. 543–54.

CCCB. *Todas las cartas. Correspondencias fílmicas. Dossier itinerancia*. Barcelona, CCCB. http://www.cccb.org/rcs_gene/DossierTLC_ES_.pdf, 2011. Accessed 13 April 2018.

Cerdán, Josetxo. "Una nube es una nube." *Al otro lado de la ficción: Trece documentalistas españoles contemporáneos*, edited by Josetxo Cerdán and Casimiro Torreiro, Cátedra, 2007, pp. 211–39.

Cerdán, Josetxo, and Miguel Fernández Labayen. "Almodóvar and Spanish Patterns of Film Reception." *A Companion to Pedro Almodóvar*, edited by Marvin D'Lugo and Kathleen M. Vernon, Wiley-Blackwell, 2013, pp. 129–52.

– "The Cartographic Imagination in Spanish and Latin American Documentaries: Technological, Social, and Physical Mapping across the Hispanic Atlantic." *Screen*, vol. 59, no. 2, 2018, pp. 240–8.

– "Memoria y documental de la Guerra Civil española y el Franquismo: De la memoria patética a la memoria sentimental." *Pasajes: Revista del pensamiento contemporáneo*, vol. 51, 2016, pp. 58–73.

– "Memory and Mass Graves: Political Strategies of Independent Documentaries." *L'Atalante: Revista de estudios cinematográficos*, vol. 23, 2017, pp. 187–98.

- "La quête (bribes et morceaux)." *Le cinéma d'Isaki Lacuesta*, edited by Brice Castanon-Akrami and Sergi Ramos Alquezar, Éditions mare & martin, 2018, pp. 115–50.
Cineastas Contra la Orden. "Manifiesto." https://bit.ly/2VjpR9W. 2009. Accessed 5 April 2018.
Comella Dorda, Beatriz. *Filmar a pie de aula*. Publicacions URV, 2013.
De la Iglesia, Álex. "No podemos seguir así ..." *El País*, 29 November 2009. https://elpais.com/diario/2009/11/26/cultura/1259190003_850215.html. Last accessed 26 February 2018.
Deleuze, Gilles. *Cinema 2: The Time-Image*. Translated by H. Tomlinson and B. Habberjam, University of Minnesota Press, 1989.
Elsaesser, Thomas, and Malte Hagener. *Film Theory: An Introduction through the Senses*. Routledge, 2010.
Erice, Víctor, et al. "El País y el cine." *El País*, 13 September 2008. http://elpais.com/diario/2008/09/13/opinion/1221256808_850215.html. Accessed 1 March 2018.
Expósito, Marcelo, coordinator.: *Historias sin argumentos: El cine de Pere Portabella*. Valencia: Ediciones La Mirada and MACBA, 2001.
Fanés, Félix. *Pere Portabella: Avantguarda, cinema i politica*. Filmoteca de la Generalitat/Pòrtic, 2008.
- *Pintura, collage, cultura de masas: Joan Miro, 1919–1934*. Alianza, 2007.
- *Salvador Dalí: La construcción de la imagen, 1925–1930*. Electa, 1999.
Fernández Labayen, Miguel, and Xose Prieto Souto. "A Network of Affinities: Helena Lumbreras's Collective Films and Social Struggle in Spain." *Modern Language Review*, vol. 112, no. 2, 2017, pp. 397–412.
Fibla-Gutiérrez, Enrique. "A Vernacular National Cinema: Amateur Filmmaking in Catalonia (1932–1936)." *Film History*, vol. 30, no. 1, 2018, pp. 1–29.
Gombrich, Ernst H. *The Preference for the Primitive: Episodes in the History of Western Taste and Art*. Phaidon, 2002.
Gubern, Román. *Proyector de luna. La generación del 27 y el cine*. Anagrama, 1999.
Hagener, Malte. *Moving Forward, Looking Back. The European Avant-garde and the Invention of Film Culture, 1919–1939*. Amsterdam University Press, 2007.
Heredero, Carlos F. "Brumas del presente, esperanzas de futuro" *Cahiers du Cinema España*, vol 28, 2009, p. 5.
Hermoso, Borja. "Guerra Civil (en la cinematografía) Española," *El País*, 25 November 2009. https://elpais.com/cultura/2009/11/25/actualidad/1259103607_850215.html. Accessed 5 April 2018.
Lacuesta, Isaki. "La crítica espectacular." *La Vanguardia*, 6 November 2011. http://hemeroteca.lavanguardia.com/preview/2011/11/06/pagina57/88117311/pdf.html?search=Lacuesta. Accessed 28 February 2018.

- "Déjà vu 1. Paisatges que desapareixen," nd. http://www.latermitafilms.com /es/obras-isaki-lacuesta/cortometrajes/deja-vu-1-paisatges-que-desapareixen/. Accessed 3 April 2018.
- *Les films doubles*. 2018. Unpublished.
- "Los locos del manicomio." http://murieronporencima.blogspot.com.es /2015/02/los-locos-del-manicomio.html. 2015. Accessed 25 August 2017.
- "La termita atómica." http://murieronporencima.blogspot.com.es/2015/02 /isa-campo-la-termita-atomica.html. 2015. Accessed 25 August 2017.

Lacuesta, Isaki, director. *Caras vs Caras*, 2000.
- *Los Condenados*. Performances by Daniel Fanego, Arturo Goetz, Bárbara Lennie, Versus Entertainment, 2009.
- *Cravan vs Cravan*. Performances by Frank Nicotra, Enric Cassasses, Eduardo Arroyo, Benecé Produccions, 2002.
- *Dejà vu 1. Paisatges que desapareixen*, 2003.
- *Entre Dos Aguas*. Performances by Israel Gómez Romero, Francisco José Gómez Romero, Filmax, 2018.
- *La Leyenda del Tiempo*. Performances by Israel Gómez Romero, Makiko Matsumura, Francisco José Gómez Romero, Sagrera TV, 2006.
- *Lugares que no Existen: Goggle Earth 1.0*, 2009.
- *The Marker Variations*, 2008.
- *Marte en la Tierra*, 2007.
- *La Matança del Porc*, 2012.
- *Microscopías*, 2003.
- *Murieron por encima de sus posibilidades*. Performances by Raúl Arévalo, Julián Villagrán, Albert Pla, Versus Entertainment, 2014.
- *La Propera Pell*. Performances by Àlex Monner, Emma Suárez, Sergi López, BTeam Pictures, 2016.
- *La Repetición*, 2012.
- *Ressonàncies Magnètiques*, 2003.
- *Teoría de los Cuerpos*, 2004.

Lacuesta, Isaki, performer. *I Tupamaros ci parlano*, Tabakalera, 2016.
La Parra Pérez, Pablo. "Presentación." *Europa, futuro anterior*. Residencia de Investigación Artística, San Sebastián: Tabakalera / Donostia-San Sebastián 2016, Capital Europea de la Cultura. http://europafuturoanterior.com /presentacion/. Accessed 7 April 2018.
Lázaro-Reboll, Antonio. *Spanish Horror Film*. Edinburgh University Press, 2012.
Les Quatre Cents Coups. Directed by François Truffaut, performances by Jean-Pierre Léaud, Albert Rémy, Claire Maurier, Cocinor, 1959.
Lévi-Strauss, Claude. *Wild Thought*. Translated by Jeffrey Mehlman and John Leavitt. The University of Chicago Press, 2021.
López Fernández, José M., and Raúl Pedraz. "La catatonia nacional." *Tren de sombras*, 6–7, 13 September 2006. http://www.trendesombras.com/num6 /art_venecia2006.asp. Accessed 28 March 2018.

Los Abrazos Rotos. Directed by Pedro Almodóvar, performances by Lluís Homar, Penélope Cruz, Blanca Portillo, and José Luis Gómez, Sony Pictures, 2009.
Loureiro, Ángel G. "Argumentos patéticos. Historia y memoria de la guerra civil." *Claves de Razón Práctica*, vol. 186, 2008, pp. 18–25.
Martínez, Guillem. "El concepto CT." *CT o la Cultura de la Transición. Crítica a 35 años de cultura española*, coordinated by Guillem Martínez, Penguin Random House, 2012, pp. 13–23.
Minguet Batllori, Joan M. *Cinema, modernitat i avantguarda (1920–1936)*. Editorial 3 i 4, 2000.
– *Salvador Dalí, cine y surrealismo(s)*. Parsifal, 2003.
Porter i Moix, Miquel. *Història del cinema català*. Editorial Taber, 1969.
– *Història del cinema a Catalunya (1895–1990)*. Generalitat de Catalunya, 1992.
Porter i Moix, Miquel, and Guillemette Huerre. *Cinematografia catalana (1896–1925)*. Moll, 1958.
Riambau, Esteve. "Cuando los monos no eran como Becky." *Realidad y creación en el cine de no-ficción,* edited by Casimiro Torreiro, Cátedra, 2010, pp. 11–31.
Sans Soleil. Directed by Chris Marker, 1983.
Sobchack, Vivian. Carnal Thoughts: Embodiment and Moving Image Culture. University of California Press, 2004.
– "Introduction: History Happens." *The Persistence of History: Cinema, Television, and the Modern Event,* edited by Vivian Sobchack, Routledge, 1996, pp. 1–14.
Tomàs i Freixa, Jordi, and Albert Beorlegui i Tous (with the collaboration of Joaquim Romaguera i Ramió). *El Cinema Amateur a Catalunya*. Generalitat de Catalunya, 2009.
Triana Toribio, Nuria. *Spanish Film Cultures: The Making and Unmaking of Spanish Cinema*. Palgrave, BFI, 2016.
Un cos al bosc. Directed by Joaquim Jordà, performances by Rossy de Palma, Ricard Borràs, Núria Prims, and Pep Molina, Filmax, 1996.
Unión de Cineastas. "¿Qué es Unión de Cineastas?" nd. https://www.uniondecineastas.es/nosotros. Accessed 5 April 2018.
Vidal, Belén. "The Cinephilic Citation in the Essay Films by José Luis Guerin and Isaki Lacuesta." *Journal of Spanish Cultural Studies*, vol. 15, no. 3, 2015, pp. 373–93.
Villamediana, Daniel. "De la Escuela de Barcelona al Máster de la Pompeu Fabra: un recorrido sin senda." *El batallón de las sombras*, edited by Alfonso Crespo, Ediciones GPS, 2006, pp. 39–45.

Contributors

Eva Bru-Dominguez is a lecturer in Catalan and Hispanic Studies at the Department of Modern Languages and Cultures, Bangor University (United Kingdom). Her main research interest is the representation of the body in Catalan visual culture and literature. She is the author of *Beyond Containment: Corporeality in Mercè Rodoreda's Literature* (2013) and has published on Catalan cinema and the work of visual and performance artist Marcel·lí Antúnez. She is currently working on the project "Dislocations: The Catalan Body in the Contemporary Global Imaginary," which explores the ways in which notions of identity, society, and culture specific to the Catalan context are conveyed in contemporary visual culture.

Josep Maria Català Domenech got his PhD in Communication Sciences at the Universitat Autònoma in Barcelona. He also holds a BA in Modern and Contemporary History from the Universitat of Barcelona and a Master of Arts in Film Theory from San Francisco State University in California. He has received several awards, including the Premio Fundesco for *La violación de la mirada* (1993), the Essay Price in Irún's XXVII Certamen Literario for *Elogio de la paranoia* (1996), and the 2001 AEHC (Asociación Española de Historiadores de Cine) Price. He also obtained a special mention in the Prize "Escritos sobre Arte" awarded by Fundación Arte y Derecho for *Pasión y conocimiento* (first edition, 2007). He has co-edited the volume *Imagen, memoria y fascinación: Notas sobre el documental en España* (2001) and edited *Cine de pensamiento: Formas de la imagen tecno-estética* (2014). Besides these awarded texts, he has also written *La puesta en imágenes* (2001), *La imagen compleja* (2006), *La forma de lo real* (2008), *Pasión y conocimiento: El nuevo realismo melodramático* (2009), *La imagen interfaz: Representación audiovisual y conocimiento en la era de la complejidad* (2010), *El murmullo de las imágenes: Imaginación,* *documental y silencio* (2012), *Estética del ensayo: De Montaigne a Godard* (2014), and *La gran espiral: Capitalismo y paranoia* (2016). He currently teaches Visual Studies at the Univeristat Autònoma in Barcelona, where he directs the Master in Creative Documentary. He was the Dean of Communication Sciences at the UAB from 2010 to 2016.

Josetxo Cerdán is professor of film and media studies at the Universidad Carlos III de Madrid, where he is also a member of the research group Tecmerin and the University Institute of Spanish Cinema. From 2018 to 2022 he was the director of Filmoteca Española (Spanish Film Archive).

Ignasi Gozalo-Salellas (PhD, University of Pennsylvania) is an assistant professor at Bryn Mawr College and an affiliated professor at the Open University of Catalonia (UOC). He has previously taught at Ohio State University and the University of Pennsylvania. He is currently working on a book entitled *Visual Hegemonies in Early Democratic Spain* and he co-authored the interview compilation volume *El síntoma Trump* (2019). He specializes in contemporary Iberian visual cultures, with expertise in media studies, focussing on the politics and aesthetics of visual archives. His articles have been published in *Boundary 2*, *MLN*, *Hispanic Review*, *Hispanófila*, and *452°F*, among others. Besides his academic career, he is a film-maker and media contributor with broad and extensive experience in television, documentaries, and new media. He has published in Spanish media outlets such as *La Maleta de Portbou*, *CTXT*, *Público*, *La Marea*, *FronteraD*, and *Espill*.

Miguel Fernández Labayen is Miguel Fernández Labayen is an associate professor in the department of Communication and Media Studies at Universidad Carlos III de Madrid, where he is also a member of the research group Tecmerin and the University Institute of Spanish Cinema. He has curated film and video programs for the Centre de Cultura Contemporània de Barcelona (cccb), the Instituto Cervantes, Anthology Film Archives and the Filmoteca de Galicia-Centro Galego de Artes da Imaxe (CGAI) among many others. He has curated film programs for Centro de Cultura Contemporánea de Barcelona, Seville European Film Festival, and Instituto Cervantes among others.

Jaume Martí-Olivella is an associate professor in the Languages, Literatures and Cultures Department at the University of New Hampshire. He is the co-founder of CINE-LIT, a leading international conference on Hispanic cinema and literature in North America. He is also co-founder and former president of the North American Catalan Society (NACS) and the International Federation of Catalan Associations (FIAC). He has published *Basque Cinema: An Introduction* (2003) and *Basque Cinema: History of An In/Visibility* (2020). He has co-edited the volumes *Spain Is (Still) Different: Tourism and Discourse in Spanish Identity* (2008) and *The Fantastic Other* (1998). He has also co-edited five *CINE-LIT Proceedings* (1992, 1995, 1998, 2001, 2003), two special issues of *Latin American Issues* entitled "The Caribbean(s) Redefined" (1997) and "(De)Constructing the Mexican-American Border" (1998), and two special issues of *Catalan Review* entitled "Woman, History and Nation in the Works of Montserrat Roig and Maria Aurèlia Capmany (1993) and "Homage to Mercè Rodoreda" (1988). He has also published many articles on Hispanic cinema and cultural studies. Currently, he is completing a book manuscript entitled *Documenting Catalonia: New Documentary Schools in Catalan Cinema* and is co-editor of the present volume.

Steven Marsh is a professor of Spanish film and head of the Department of Hispanic and Italian Studies at the University of Illinois at Chicago. He is joint editor of *Gender and Spanish Cinema* (2004) and the author of *Popular Spanish Film Under Franco: Comedy and the Weakening of the State* (2005). In 2014 he edited a special issue of *The Journal of Spanish Cultural Studies* on Spanish film and spectrality. His work has appeared in journals in Spain, the UK, the USA, Chile, France, and Australia. His latest monograph is titled *Spanish Film against Itself: Cosmopolitanism, Experimentation, Militancy* (2020) and recently appeared in Spanish as *El cine español contra sí mismo: Cosmopolitismo, experimentación, militancia* (2022). He was one of the founding editors of the journal *Studies in Hispanic Cinemas*, he is on the advisory committee of *Libros en Acción*, and he is a member of the editorial collective of the *Journal of Spanish Cultural Studies*.

Sara Nadal-Melsió is a NYC-based Catalan writer, curator, and teacher. Presently writer-in-residence at the Slought Foundation in Philadelphia, she has taught at the University of Pennsylvania, Princeton University, SOMA in Mexico City, and New York University. Her essays have appeared in various academic journals, edited volumes, and museum catalogs. She is the co-author of *Alrededor de / Around*, and the editor of two special issues on cinema, *The Invisible Tradition: Avant-Garde Catalan Cinema under Late Francoism* and *Anachronism and the Militant Image: Temporal Disturbances of the Political Imagination*. She also has co-curated a survey of Allora & Calzadilla's work for the Fundació Tàpies in Barcelona and has written a book essay about it, "To Be All Ears, To Be in the World: Acoustic Relation in Allora & Calzadilla," as well as edited a companion volume on the Puerto Rican crisis, *A Modest Proposal: Puerto Rico's Crucible*. Her book *Politically Red*, written in collaboration with Eduardo Cadava, is forthcoming this fall with MIT Press and her *Europe and the Wolf: Political Variations on a Musical Concept* is forthcoming with Zone Books.

Anton Pujol is an associate professor at the University of North Carolina at Charlotte. He teaches Literature and Translation in both the undergraduate and the master's program in the Department of Languages and Culture Studies. He graduated from the Universitat Autònoma de Barcelona and he later earned a PhD at the University of Kansas in Spanish Literature. He also holds an MBA from the University of Chicago, with a focus on economics and international finance. He has recently published articles in *Translation Review*, *Catalan Review*, *Studies in Hispanic Cinemas*, *Anales de la Literatura Española Contemporánea*, and *Arizona Journal of Hispanic Cultural Studies*, among others. His translation of Don Mee Choi's *DMZ Colony* (2020 National Book Award for Poetry) was published in 2022. Currently, he serves as dramaturge for the Mabou Mines company opera adaptation of Lluïsa Cunillé's play *Barcelona, mapa d'ombres*, directed and adapted by Mallory Catlett with a musical score by Mika Karlsson.

Àngel Quintana teaches cinema history and theory at the Universitat de Girona. He has been invited to teach at Université Paris III, Université de Lausanne, Universidad de los Andes, Bogotá, and at FLACSO, Buenos Aires. He is a film critic for *El Punt/Avui*, the cultural suplement *Cultura/s* in *La Vanguardia*, and for the journal *Caiman: Cuadernos de cine*. He has published several books on cinema: *El cine italiano 1943–1961: Del neorrealismo a la modernidad* (1998), *Fábulas de lo visible: El cine como creador de realidades* (2003), awarded the AEHC [Associació Espanyola d'Historiadors del cinema] Prize), *Virtuel?* (2007), and *Después del cine* (2011). He has also written several monographs on Roberto Rossellini, Jean Renoir, Federico Fellini, and Olivier Assayas. He has been the PI on several research projects, the latest being "Presència i representació de la dona en el cinema dels orígens." He is the co-director of the seminar "Antecedents i orígens del cinema."

Esteve Riambau has a PhD in medicine and worked as a nephrologist until 1989. He also holds a PhD in Communication Sciences and teaches Audiovisual Communications at the Universitat Autònoma in Barcelona. He has been invited to teach at Escuela de Cine in San

Antonio de los Baños, Cuba, and in the following universities: Paris III, Rome, Stanford, San Francisco State, and UCLA. Since 2010, he has been the director of Filmoteca de Catalunya, and has been on the board of FIAF (2012–17). Alongside Elisabet Cabeza, he has co-directed two feature films: *La doble vida del faquir* (2005) and *Màscares* (2009). With Alex Gorina he has co-authored the TV series *La gran il·lusió: Relat intermittent del cinema català* (2018). He has paid special attention to the multifaceted figure of Orson Welles, who is featured in four volumes as well as in his work as co-screenwriter of the documentary *Orson Welles al país del Quixot* (2000) and as director and adapter of the play *Obediently Yours, Orson Welles* (2008), which was the runner up in the Max theatre prize. Since the seventies, he has been a film critic for several publications, both national (*Fotogramas, Dirigido por, Archivos de la Filmoteca, Avui*) and international (*Cinema Nuovo, Cahiers du Cinéma, Cineaste, Cahiers de la Cinémathèque*). He has published forty books on cinema history, including monographs on international film-makers. The biography *Ricardo Muñoz Suay: Una vida en sombras* (2007) was awarded the Comillas and the Academia del Cine Español prizes. Specialist on French cinema, he has coordinated three volumes of *Historia General del Cine* (1995–8) and is the co-author of *Historia del cine español* (1995) and the *Diccionario de cine español* (1998). Alongside Casimiro Torreiro, he has written the following books: *Guionistas en el cine español: Quimeras, picarescas y pluriempleo* (1998) – which got an award by the Academia del Cine Español – *La Escuela de Barcelona: El cine de la "gauche divine"* (1999), and *Productoress en el cine español: Estado, dependencias y mercado* (2008), which was awarded the AEHC prize.

Agustín Rico-Albero is senior lecturer in Spanish and Film at the University of Hertfordshire, where he teaches Spanish Language and Culture, European and Latin American Film, and also contributes to the master's (online) program in Global Film and Television, teaching a course on global screen violence. Previously he taught Spanish and Film at the University of Auckland and the University of Leicester, where he completed his PhD in Film Studies with a thesis entitled "Representations of Violence in Contemporary Spanish Cinema." He has participated in numerous international workshops, symposiums, and conferences dedicated to Catalan and Spanish film. He is the author of several works on Spanish film studies including contributions to the *Directory of World Cinema Spain* (2011) and a chapter on adolescent cinema and violence for *(Re)viewing Creative, Critical and Commercial Practices in Contemporary Spanish Cinema* (2014). Since 2011 he has been a Fellow of the Higher Education Academy (UK).

Teresa M. Vilarós is professor of Hispanic studies and affiliated professor of film studies at Texas A&M University. She previously held a Sixth Century Professorship Chair at the University of Aberdeen and taught at Duke University and the University of Wisconsin-Madison. She is co-founder and co-editor of the *Journal of Spanish Cultural Studies*; current executive member of the MLA Forum on Sephardic Studies; and former executive member and chair of the MLA Forum on Catalan Studies. Her research interests focus on Spanish and Catalan modern/contemporary visual and cultural studies, with a strong focus on psychoanalytical theory and critical and political thought. She has published extensively on the cultural and social effects of the years of the political transition in Spain; on the middle years of the Francoist dictatorship, analysing the use of media and visual technologies in the sixties by the state as a means of biopolitical control; on Catalan film and media, especially on film-maker Albert Serra; on La Escuela de Barcelona experimental film; and on Catalan and Spanish literature of the Marrano register. Her seminal book *El mono del desencanto: Una crítica cultural de la transición española* came out in a second edition in 2018.

Index

Page numbers with (f) refer to figures.

abduction, definition of, 150; European conference, 22, 147, 155
About Children (Jordà). *See* De Nens/ De niños
acoustic processes, 125, 129, 142, 143
Adorno, Theodor, 129
aesthetics: in cinema, 6, 7, 8, 9, 10, 20, 21, 126, 136, 137; and discontinuities, 21, 22. *See also* sound
affect, 27, 28, 117; definitions of, 260; narrative of affects, 255, 256, 260–77
Africa, 18, 52, 73, 74, 111n11; influence on Jacinto Esteva, 68, 70, 72n5, 75, 76
Aguilar, Gonzalo, 322, 324
Agustí, Ignacio, *Mariona Rebull*, 180, 181(f)
Allen, Woody, *Vicky, Cristina, Barcelona*, 45
Almendros, Néstor, 5, 66
Almodóvar, Pedro, *Todo sobre mi madre*, 45
Altaió, Vocemç, as Giacomo Casanova, 189, 192(f), 194(f)
alternative cinema, 3, 4, 50

Althusser, Louis, *Ideología y aparatos ideológicos del Estado*, 93
Álvarez, Mercedes, 65; critique of Recha's *El cielo sube*, 268
Amat, Jordi, 158, 165–6
amateur cinema, 15, 31–2, 49, 258; history of, 307–9
anachronism, strategic use of in film, 20, 134, 174–5, 177
Angulo, Jesús, 258, 268
animation, 21, 22, 26, 146–7, 148, 241; definition of, 147–8n2
anti-globalization movement, 114–15, 119
Aranda, Vicente, 65, 80, 305; *Fata Morgana*, 8, 30, 286, 293
art/artistic cinema, 4, 5, 8, 11, 13, 15, 16, 19, 46, 81, 212, 258, 259
Assemblea de Catalunya, 20
Attali, Jacques, and composition technologies, 139
Aubert, Jean-Paul, 287, 295; *Seremos Mallarmé. La Escuela de Barcelona: Una apuesta modernista*, 8, 28, 274
audiovisual technique, 19, 28, 45, 47, 49, 82, 83, 86, 87n7, 236, 268, 300, 301, 310, 311

340 Index

auteur cinema, 14–15, 32, 50, 54, 58, 235, 285; and Barcelona 1992, 46, 49
autonomy/*autonomía*, 19, 136; influence on film, 104–5, 111, 149, 164; and social transformation, 94–5, 95n11, 96, 103, 106, 116
avant-garde, 229, 236, 252; aesthetic concept of, 213, 216–17; artistic and literary, 8, 30n6, 51, 128, 132, 140, 148, 177n12, 221, 255; cinema, 5, 11, 13, 15, 31, 25, 26, 50, 58, 145, 148, 158, 176, 214, 233, 295, 302, 305, 307, 309, 310; and *Dau al Set*, 26, 130n6, 233, 235; directors, 50, 51, 52, 306; dislocation of, 132; and EdB, 5, 8, 9, 13, 14–15, 16, 17, 20, 21, 24–5, 145, 158, 172, 213, 232, 234, 259; European, 32, 232, 233; and Grup de Treball (Work Group), 132–3, 134; new, 27, 31, 52; post-avant-garde, 24, 213, 217; principles of, 9, 10; second wave of, 140; provocation legacy of, 52, 53, 57

Bach, Johann Sebastian, 128, 130n6, 190; and European identity, 127, 142; *Goldberg Variations*, 134, 148; discovery of *Saint Matthew's Passion*, 137–8, 138(f), 140; music of in *Die Stille vor Bach*, 135–40; sonata played by Carles Santos, 129–30; as theatrical subject in *La pantera imperial*, 131; *The Well-Tempered Clavier*, 129–30n5, 130
Badiou, Alain, 127, 143
Balló, Jordi, 58
Barcelona, and urban politics, 43, 44, 45, 88–90, 92
Barcelona Film School (Escola de Barcelona, EdB), 3, 5–6, 9, 255, 295, 309; aesthetics of, 5, 6, 7, 8, 9, 10, 232, 233, 234, 241, 284, 292–3, 295; apolitical principals of, 30, 284, 287, 294; artistic rebellion and autonomy, 149; and the avant-garde, 5, 9, 13, 15, 16, 20, 145, 172, 232, 233, 259, 295, 305; break with Madrid, 5–6; choosing Stéphane Mallarmé over Victor Hugo, 8, 65, 66, 214, 215; cinematic techniques of, 21, 27, 28–9, 234; film-makers/directors of, 5, 6, 7, 11, 12, 14, 18, 25, 30, 31, 32, 80–1, 82, 148–9, 214–15, 252, 258, 259, 275, 285–6, 294, 305–6; films of, 7, 18, 290, 392; and formalism, 24; history of, 65–7; "invisible tradition" of, 24, 158, 158n12; legacy of, 65–77, 145; maverick directors of, 17, 49, 50–8; neglect of EdB films, 7, 12; and the post-avant-garde, 24, 214; and ruptures in Spanish cinema, 274, 295; style of, 214; use of non-professional actors, 5, 9, 284, 274, 291; use of violence, 290; the younger generation of, 12, 13, 16
Barcelona Olympic Games (Barcelona 1992), 14, 17, 46, 88; and the media, 42–3; and the "olympic impulse," 43; Portabella's *Pont de Varsòvia*, 51
Barcelona School. *See* Barcelona Film School
Baroja, Pío, *La busca*, 300
Baroque, 191, 198; aesthetics, 129–30n5; libertine thinkers, 199, 199n33; musical concept of the "wolf," 20, 126
Bardem, Juan Antonio, 4
Barker, Jennifer, 235, 241; *Tactile Eye*, 249
Baugh, Bruce, 262

Bazin, André, 8
Beautiful Youth (Rosales): cinematic devices/style and, 292, 293, 294–5; popular digital technology in, 292; pornography and sexual exploitation, 292; as portrayal of youth during economic and political crisis, 291, 292, 293–5; and the post-financial crisis, 291–2; and social violence, 293; spectators' experiences of, 293, 294–5; story of, 292; use of professional actors, 294
Bellmunt, Francesc, *El complot dels anells*, 48
Benjamin, Walter, 56, 190, 216, 220, 223
Berlanga, Luis García, 4
Bingham, Adam, 10, 15
biopolitics, in film, 19, 104, 116
body without organs (BwO), 27, 264, 265, 266
Bofill, Ricardo, 66; *Cercles*, 67
Bohigas, Oriol, 88
Bordwell, David, *Narration in the Fiction Film*, 16
Bosch, Lolita, *Lolita Kiseljak*, 25, 231
bourgeoisie, Barcelona, 73; Catalan, 6, 25, 178; cinema, 32; and hegemony of the piano, 140–1
Brecht, Bertolt, 150; and distanciation, 107; and theatricality, 12, 146, 147, 150, 164–5
bricoleur, 30, 31–2, 33, 301. *See also* Lacuesta, Isaki
Brossa, Joan, 26, 51, 57, 130n6, 148, 184, 233
Bruno, Giuliana, 26, 240–1
Buñuel, Luis, *Viridiana*, 51, 176n11
Burgos trial (*el proceso de Burgos*), 22, 23, 171, 173, 174, 175, 176, 177, 178, 179

Cadena, Jordi, 13, 14, 50, 233, 283; style in directing *Elisa K*, 234, 238, 241, 246, 247, 252
Cadena, Jordi, films of: *Elisa K*, 25–6, 231–52; *Es quan dormo que hi veig clar*, 56–7, 233
Cage, John, 130n6, 140
Campo, Isa, 300; collaboration with Isaki Lacuesta, 304, 310, 311, 325
Camps, Francisco Ruiz, 73
Camus, Mario, 4
Capmany, Maria Aurèlia, 67, 111
Casanova, Giacomo: *Histoire de ma vie*, 23; life and death of, 189n28; representation of in Serra's *Història de la meva mort*, 187–99
Catalan cinema, 3–4, 6, 7, 15; absent during Barcelona 1992, 45–6; and audiovisual schools, 49; effects of economic crisis on, 283; focus of films on memory and history, 232, 233; history of its culture, 301, 305–11; post-Barcelona 1992 emergence of, 55, 57–8, 283; pre-Olympic Games, 46–8; repression under Franco, 4, 10. *See also* amateur cinema
Catalan culture: and Barcelona 1992, 44–5; influence of Conselleria de Cultura de la Generalitat de Catalunya, 46; under Franco, 4, 10
Catalan directors, 8, 12, 14, 236; gender of, 13, 34; and the invisible tradition, 24; as mavericks, 17, 49, 50–8
Catalan film-makers, 10, 13, 15, 28, 308; auteurist generation of, 14; characteristics of, 275; disruptive aesthetics and, 284; Nous Directors Catalans, 47, 56; and stylistic emancipation, 284; younger generation of, 15, 18, 47, 49, 55, 69

Catalan Independence Process, 20, 22, 145
Catalonia, 30; and 2008 economic crisis, 28–9, 283, 293; pro-independence movement, 167n19, 168n20, 284, 292; queer community in, 33–4
"cenesthesia," 261, 262; defined, 259
censorship of film under Franco 4, 65, 74; of Esteva's films, 66, 67; of Portabella's film, 171n1
Chávarri, Jaime, *El desencanto*, 72, 76
Cineastas Contra la Orden (CCO), 304, 311–12, 314
cine club culture, 31, 307
Cinema Law, the, resistance to 311–13
cinema noir, 48
"citizen spectator," 82, 86. *See also* spectators
coenaesthesia, 27, 261
Colbi, Jordi, "Matar al Cobi," 44
Colebrook, Claire, 262, 273
Colell, Judith, 13, 14, 283; style in directing *Elisa K*, 235, 245, 247, 251, 252
Colell, Judith, films of: *El domini dels sentits*, 248; *Elisa K*, 25–6, 231–52
Colman, Felicity, 260, 272
comedy genre, 33, 48
Communist Party (Italian), 18, 104–5, 111
Conde, José Antonio Nieves, 4
Conselleria de Cultura de la Generalitat de Catalunya, 46
Conversaciones de Salamanca (Conference), 4
Cox, Anna, 234, 241
Creed, Barbara, 249
Cuscó i Clarasó, Joan, 257
Cussó-Ferré, Manuel, 57; *L'última frontera*, 50, 56

Dante Alighieri, *Divine Comedy*, 24, 195, 208, 211–12, 215, 217, 222
Dau al Set (avant-garde group), 26, 233, 235
Dawson, Tom, 289
Deleuze, Gilles, 10–11, 27, 28, 127, 255, 263; and body without organs, 27, 264, 265, 266; body's longitude and latitude, 261; *Cinema 1: L'image-mouvement*, 268–9, 274; *Cinema 2: L'image-temps*, 138, 268; concept of affect, 260, 261, 262, 274, 275; *Expressionism in Philosophy: Spinoza*, 274; *Kafka: Toward a Minor Literature*, 11; ruptures in ways of seeing, 273–4
Delgado, Manuel, 73, 88–9, 90, 90–1n8
democracy, growth of, 43, 98; and consensus, 154–5; and public discourse, 19, 97, 106, 119; as represented in Jordà's film, 102–3; return to, 66, 68, 93; stagnation of, 22
de Moraga, Miguel, and Barcelona 1992, 44–5
demos, 103n1, 106, 116, 117–18, 119; definition of, 117; and discourse, 110, 113, 114; and lack of discourse, 116, 118
De nens/De niños (Jordà), 18, 19; and the role of institutional power in the Raval paedophilia trial, 86–94
Derrida, Jacques, 12, 173n4, 177, 196; *Spectres of Marx*, 183
de Sade, Marquis, 194, 196–7, 198, 199
de Senillosa, Anotonio, 66
Diamante, Julio, 65
Die Stille vor Bach (Portabella), 20, 50, 148; dislocation and dissonance in European culture, 126, 134–6,

137–8; as post-Franco avant-garde cinema, 132–4; use of music and sound as aesthetic artefact, 136–7; use of myths or fables in, 137
dislocation, 20, 134–5
dissonance, 20, 21; as symbol of resistance, 126–7, 128; in Santos's *La pantera imperial*, 131
Ditirambo (Suárez), 9
D'Lugo, Marvin, 5, 7
documentary cinema/genre, 17, 24, 33–4, 50, 55–6, 58, 67–8, 69, 82n4, 283; and citizen spectator, 82, 86; complexity of images, 207; exploring history and memory, 232–3; narrative genres, 17; Jordá's treatment of *El encargo del cazador*, 72–6; and situationism, 80–1, 82. *See also* essay film
d'Ors, Eugeni, *Oceanografia del tedi*, 27, 55, 255. See also *Oceanography of Tedium*
Dracula, 23. *See also* Franco, Jesús; *Història de la meva mort*; *Vampir. Cuadecuc*; vampires/vampire movies
Durán, Carles, *Cada vez que…*, 9
Durand, Gilbert, 222; and iconoclastic imagery, 216; symbol and allegory, 212

Eakin, Emily, 261
Eceiza, Antxon, 65
economic crisis, 292, 293; brutal effect of, 28–9; effect on cultural industries, 283, 284, 311; and the Sinde Law, 312
EdB (Escola de Barcelona). *See* Barcelona Film School
El cielo sube (Recha), 27–8, 55, 255; adaptation and filming of d'Ors's *Oceanografia del tedi*, 257–8;

cinematic language of, 274, 275, 276–7; critiques of cinematic style, 267–9, 273, 274; depictions of cenesthesia, 259–60; differences between novel and film, 258, 270–2; and the avant-garde of the EdB, 259; and narrative of affects, 255, 256, 260–77; spectators' expectations of, 259, 270, 272, 275; visual style of, 258–9, 272–3, 275; unconventional aesthetic of, 267; use of Deleuze's time-image, affection-image, and "espace quelconque," 268–71, 272, 274–5
El encargo del cazador (Jordà), 18; as documentary of Jacinto Esteva's life, 69, 71–6
Eliot, T.S., 24; and meaning of images versus visions, 208–9, 210, 217
Elisa K (Cadena and Colell), 25–6, 283; aesthetics of, 236, 245; brutality of mechanical toys and rides, 241, 242(f), 243; cinematic language of, 235; and diegetic worlds, 237, 243, 251; eruption of traumatic memory, 247–8; the gaze and act of gazing, 240, 243, 245, 246(f), 252; the mise en abyme in, 237, 238(f), 243; the mise en scène in, 236, 239, 239(f), 244, 251; optical and haptic cinematic techniques of, 231–2, 235, 247, 248, 252; relationship to Barcelona School, 234; references to Martin Luther King, 237–8, 246; and spectrality, 239(f), 239–40; structure of film in two parts, 234–5, 238, 245, 246, 247; trauma and loss of memory in, 232, 233, 238, 239–40, 245, 248, 252; use of doors, windows, mirrors, and

water as metaphors, 236, 237, 239, 240, 243–4, 244(f), 246, 250, 251; visual strategies for depicting trauma of rape, 238, 239, 240, 244, 245, 245(f), 247–8, 249–50, 250(f), 251, 251(f), 252, 252(f)
Elola, Joseba, 284
Elsaesser, Thomas, 12, 32, 231, 236, 237, 238, 240, 243, 324
erotic cinema, 48–9
Escudero, José María García, 4, 65
Espriu, Salvador, 179, 180n18; *Rona de mort a Sinera*, 179, 179(f)
essay film, 19; form of, 103, 108, 120; and Jean Rouch, 111n11; as response to crisis/crises, 118–20. *See also* documentary cinema/genre
Esteban, Manel, 73
Esteva, Dària, 18, 52; preservation of father's films, 77; production of *El encargo del cazador*, 70, 71, 76–7
Esteva, Grewe Jacinto, 8, 18, 65; art exhibition in Madrid, 70; censorship of films, 66, 67; connection to Africa, 18, 52, 67, 69, 70, 73, 74, 75, 76; death of, 70, 71, 77
Esteva, Grewe Jacinto, films of: *Autour des salines*, 66; *Dante no es únicamente severo*, 8–9, 18, 27, 52, 65, 258; *Después del diluvio*, 67; *Día de los Muertos*, 66; *El encargo del cazador*, 69–76; *La isla de las lágrimas/Del Arca de Noé al Pirata Rhodes*, 67; *Le Fils de Marie*, 67; *Lejos de los árboles*, 29, 66, 290; *Metamorfosis*, 67; *Mozambique*, 67; *Notes sur l'émigration. Espagne 1960*, 66
Europe: art cinema of, 15, 307; artistic currents of, 6; French Revolution, 192, 193, 197; influence of, 7, 20; musical and cultural legacy of, 126, 130, 140, 141; new cinemas of, 9, 10, 15; neo-liberalism in, 110n8, 141–2n11; New Abduction of Europe Conference, 22, 147, 155, 157, 159–63; political uncertainty and change in, 132, 133, 134, 135, 136, 137, 142; sovereignty of and discontinuity, 20, 21, 125, 126, 127, 134; and Situationist movement, 81n3; transnational cinema of, 31
European Union, 133, 138, 141, 150
Expósito, Marcelo, 97; *Primero de Mayo (la ciudad-fábrica)*, 119

Fanés, Fèlix, 130n6, 148, 288, 307
Farré, Ignasi P., 47; *Un submarí a les estovalles*, 48
Fecé, José Luis, 56
Fernández, David, 167
Filmoteca de Catalunya, 18
Flaubert, Gustave, 255, 256, 257, 259; writing style of, 276
Flem, Lydia, *Casanova: The Man Who Really Loved Women*, 194–5, 197
Foix, J.V., 13, 56, 57
Font, Domènc, 164
form, cultural and political, 103, 105, 109, 111. *See also* essay film
Foster, Hal, 216–17
Foucault, Michel, 12, 115, 160; influence on film, 19, 83, 95, 98
Franco, General Francisco, 22, 23, 68, 133, 153, 187; censorship under, 4, 65, 66, 67, 74; and the Francoist establishment, 5–6; mausoleum in Valle de los Caídos, 22, 148, 152; opposition to, 18; repression of Catalan culture, 4, 5, 10, 19, 65; in Portabella's films, 22–3, 51, 171n1;

promotion of Spanish tourism, 66; as vampire figure, 22–3, 172, 174, 178, 180, 181, 185, 186, 187

Francoism, 21, 22, 23, 52, 166, 174, 183, 184, 232, 293, 309; anti-Francoism, 51, 73, 128, 155; political prisoners of, 128–9; and Spanish Transition, 33, 103, 141–2n11, 145, 146; and social turmoil in Spain, 171–2, 173; "state of exception" imposed, 171

Franco, Jesús, 176; *Count Dracula*, 172, 173, 177, 184, 185, 186, 189

Free Cinema, 5

French Nouvelle Vague, 5, 9, 28, 65, 66, 214, 268, 295

Freud, Lucian, 248

Galt, Rosalind, 172, 172n2, 176n11, 235–6, 274

Garay, Jesús, 50, 53, 57, 65; *La banyera*, 54; *Els de davant*, 54; *Manderley*, 54; *Més enllà de la passió*, 54; *Nemo*, 54

Garcés, Marina, 95, 114n12, 159, 160–1, 162, 167

Gardel, Carlos, 96n12, 116

Gas, Mario, 107, 110

gauche divine, 67

gaze, 19, 25, 34, 58, 82, 90, 146, 162, 163, 188, 208, 215, 220, 221, 240, 243, 245, 246(f), 252, 309, 322; anthropological, 302; God-like, 326; of happiness, 300; mythical, 299, 302–3; political, 21, 147, 148, 151, 152, 157, 168. See also ways of seeing

Generalitat (Catalan government), 43, 47, 52, 168n20, 301, 307, 309

Gianetti, Louis, 146

Glen, John, *Cristobal Colón, el descubrimiento*, 45

González, Itziar, 159, 160, 161–2

Gormezano, Gerard, 57; *El vent de l'illa*, 55

Goya, Francisco, 71, 194, 197

Grau, Jordi, 8

Guattari, Félix, 11, 27, 255, 261; and body without organs, 27, 264, 265, 266; and body's longitude and latitude, 261; concept of affect, 260, 262, 263, 274, 275; *Kafka: Toward a Minor Literature*, 11

Gubern, Román, 5, 13, 14, 307

Guerín, José Luis, 12, 13, 14, 17, 24, 50, 57, 58, 65, 68, 239, 275, 313; aesthetics of, 215; on death and suicide, 224, 225–8; dual space function of documentaries, 208; the gaze and act of gazing, 208, 215, 221, 223, 224–5, 229; letters to and from Jonas Mekas, 220, 225, 226; the process of seeing, 208; representations of the past, 216, 220; use of melancholic style, 209, 220, 223–4, 225, 226, 227, 228; visionary images of, 212, 217, 219–20, 222–3, 225, 228

Guerín, José Luis, films of: *En construcción*, 24, 68, 92, 93, 216, 227, 228; *En la ciudad de Sylvia*, 25, 216; *Innisfree*, 50, 55–6, 216, 225; *La dama de Corinto. Un esbozo cinematográfico*, 216; *Los motivos de Berta*, 25, 55, 209, 216, 225; *Recuerdos de una mañana*, 25, 216, 227, 228; *Tren de sombras*, 56, 216, 225, 227, 228; *Unas fotos en la ciudad de Sylvia*, 25, 216, 222, 224

Guerra, Carles, 52, 87, 92; interview with Jordà, 104, 108

Gunning, Tom, and "cinema attractions," 234, 241

Hagener, Malte, 12, 31, 32, 231, 236, 237, 238, 240, 243, 307, 324
haptic and optical techniques, 25, 26, 192; definition of, 231, 248; in *Elisa K*, 231–2, 235, 247, 248, 252
harmony, 20; of sound, 126, 129–30, 142. *See also* "wolf"
Harvey, David, 18
Heaven Rises (Recha). See *El cielo sube*
Heller-Roazen, Daniel, *The Fifth Hammer: Pythagoras and the Disharmony of the World*, 126
Heredero, Carlos, 28, 310; critique of Racha's *El cielo sube*, 268, 269, 274; critique of Racha's film style, 267–8, 274
Hermosa juventud (Rosales). See *Beautiful Youth*
Herzog, Amy, 11–12, 268
Higginbotham, Virginia, 5
Hill, David W., 154–5
Hispanic Review's "The Barcelona School," 9–10, 146–7n2, 158n12
Histoire de ma vie (Casanova), 23, 189, 189n28, 190, 191
Història de la meva mort (Serra): cinematic filming of, 191, 191n30; and desire, 189, 193, 194, 197, 198; figure of the baroque libertine in, 189, 192, 194, 195, 196, 197, 198–9, 199n33; figure of Dracula in, 187, 188, 189, 190, 192, 193, 194, 196, 197; figure of Giacomo Casanova in, 187, 188, 189, 190, 191, 192, 192(f), 197; humour in, 187; as infrapolitical film, 187, 193, 196, 199; philosophies of Kant and Sade in, 192, 194, 196, 197, 198, 199; Lacanian phantasy and pleasure in, 188, 189, 192, 194, 195; spectral qualities, of, 187, 188, 190, 192, 193, 194, 195, 196, 198; transformation of Casanova into Dracula, 190, 192, 193, 194, 195(f), 196, 197, 198–9; union of sound and image, 193, 194(f); use of Marrano register, 187, 188, 193, 196, 199; use of time, 187, 188, 189–90, 193
history, 96, 174, 184, 190, 193, 194, 198, 223, 265, 329; of cinema, 210, 212, 236, 238, 240, 251, 283, 295, 304, 305–22, 327; of cultural theory, 103; of Europe, 133–4, 135, 137; of family, 232–3; and historical time, 3, 13, 14, 15, 17, 22, 26, 31, 69; importance of, 9; of labour, 107, 117; lack of, 52; and memory, 19, 34, 252; and memory of spaces, 93; neglect of, 8, 10; oral, 116; of Spain, 300, 303; of Spanish democracy, 98, 102
Horace, *Odes*, 256–7, 266
horror genre, 29, 172nn2–3, 249, 309–10
Hours of the Day, The (Rosales): acting process and narrative friction, 290, 291; auteur's view of a serial killer, 288, 289; cinematic devices/style and, 287–8, 289, 291; fragmented mode of storytelling, 288; minutiae of killer's daily life, 287, 288, 289, 290, 291; psychokiller and violence, 286, 287, 288, 289–90; as "social problem melodrama," 285–6; spectators' experience of, 286, 288, 289–90, 291; use of diegetic sound, 289–90
Huertas, Eliseu, 189, 195(f)
Hugo, Victor, 8, 65, 66, 68, 214, 215; as a visionary, 217–19
human body, as cartography, 32–3, 324–5, 326–7
Hunter's Request, The. See *El encargo del cazador*

Iglesias, Eulalia, 16
images: in documentaries, 207–9; as new way of seeing, 210–12; as passive allegory, 210, 212
Indignados (or 15-M) Movement, 20, 22, 32, 106, 119, 145, 156, 312, 314–17
industrial cinema, 32, 46, 310
Informe general II: El nuevo rapto de Europa (Portabella), 21, 22, 151; continuities with *Informe general sobre*, 158–68; and definition of abduction, 150, 155; New Abduction of Europe conference in, 147–8, 157; and political transition, 145, 146, 151–2, 153, 155–7; use of animation in, 146–7
Informe general sobre algunas cuestiones de interés para una proyección pública (Portabella), 21, 151; continuities with *Informe general II*, 158–68; as political dialogue, 145, 148; and radical language, 149
infrapolitical cinema, 175, 177, 178, 179, 180, 181, 185, 186, 187, 193, 196, 197, 199; definition of, 174; and Marxism, 183, 184
Institute of Cinema and Audiovisual Arts (ICAA), 47, 304, 311, 317
Instituto de Investigaciones y Experiencias Cinematográficas (IIEC), 4
international/local film festivals: Berlin, 47, 50–1, 53; Cannes, 54, 56, 66, 313; and Catalan films, 305, 306, 309, 310–11, 318, 321; evolution of festivals in Sitges, 309–10; importance of for directors, 17, 31, 58; Rotterdam, 151; San Sebastián, 31, 32, 312; Venice, 313

(in)visible tradition, 3, 7, 10, 12, 14, 16, 24, 29, 158, 233, 285

Jordà, Joaquim, 5, 8, 9, 13, 25, 31, 57, 58, 214; comment on Recha's films, 268; critical role in EdB, 14, 17, 24, 50, 66, 68–9, 284, 291, 305–6; death of, 80, 113; distancing from EdB, 73, 74, 80; documentaries of, 68–9, 119; exile in Italy, 67, 68, 104; production of Esteva's *El encargo del cazador*, 69, 71–6; obituary for Jacinto Esteva, 71; as screenwriter for film and television, 80; situationist films and documentaries, 80, 81, 82–94; teaching documentary film, 68; as "Unknown director," 96
Jordà, Joaquim, films of: *Dante no es únicamente severo*, 8–9, 18, 27, 52, 65, 258; *De nens/De niños*, 18, 19, 69, 80, 82, 86–94; *Il perchè del dissenso*, 67; *El encargo del cazador*, 18, 50, 52, 111n11; *Lenin vivo*, 67, 105; *Maria Aurèlia Capmany parla d'Un lloc entre els morts*, 67; *Más allá del espejo*, 80n1; *Més enllà del mirall/Más allá del espejo*, 69; *Mones com la Becky*, 18, 19, 68, 80, 82, 83–5; *Morir de dia*, 80n1; *Numax presenta…*, 19, 68, 94–6; *Portogallo, paese tranquilo*, 67, 105, 111n11; *Spezziamo le catene*, 67; *Un cos al bosc/Un cuerpo en el bosque*, 69; *Veinte años no es nada*, 18, 19, 69, 80, 82, 94–8, 105, 111–18
Jordan, Barry, 15

Kafka, Franz, 11; *The Trial*, 186
Kant, Immanuel, 136, 192, 192n31, 194, 196, 197, 198
King, Martin Luther, 238, 239, 246

Klee, Paul, 190, 322
Kristeva, Julia, 249

"la apertura," 4
labour: artistic, 103n1, 130, 131, 132, 133; changes in market for, 113–14; conditions of, 104; and factory work, 111, 119; unions, 94–5
Lacan, Jacques, 189; and "logic of phantasy," 23, 188, 188n27, 189, 192, 194
Lacuesta, Isaki, 13, 14, 16, 30–1, 65, 68, 214, 239, 275; anthropological perspective on means of production, 300, 301, 302; argument with Guardans of ICAA, 304, 311; and the avant-garde, 302; as *bricoleur*, 31–2, 33, 301, 302–4, 309, 311, 324, 329; cinematic devices/style of, 299, 300, 309, 323–4, 325, 326, 328–9; conflict with film critics, 312–14; collaboration with Isa Campo, 304, 310, 311, 317, 325, 326; correspondence with Naomi Kawase, 304, 305; creative body of work, 301, 302, 306; experiential orientation, 300; film festival circuit and awards, 305, 310; founding of La Termita Films, 304; Golden Shell film award, 31, 32, 33, 312–13, 317; inclusion of human bodies, people, and characters, 324–9; involvement in Indignados Movement, 32, 312, 314, 315, 317; member of Cineastas Contra la Orden (CCO), 304, 311; and popular culture, 302; and primitive art, 302, 303; publication of online blog, 313; and public persona, 300, 301, 304, 312–14; resources for sexual and gender diversity, 323–4; three political films on the discourse of vindication, 315–22
Lacuesta, Isaki, films of: *Besar-te com un home*, 323; *Cravan vs. Cravan*, 31, 302, 310, 325, 326; *Entre dos aguas*, 31, 32, 33, 299, 304, 325, 327–8; *I Tupamaros ci parlano*, 315, 318; *La leyenda del tiempo*, 31, 32, 33, 299, 302, 325, 327–8; *La matança del porc*, 301, 312, 315, 317, 318; *La propera pell*, 33, 304, 323; *La repetición*, 301; *Las variaciones Marker*, 299; *Los condenados*, 304, 315; *Los pasos dobles*, 31, 32, 312; *Lugares que no existen. Goggle Earth 1.0 Marte en la tierra*, 301, 325–6, 328; *Murieron por encima de sus posibilidades*, 32, 315, 317, 318; *Ressonàncies Magnètiques*, 310; *Soldats anòmims*, 314; *Teoría de los cuerpos*, 32, 325
language, cinematic, 7, 17, 149, 172, 233, 235, 275–6
Las horas del día (Rosales). See *Hours of the Day, The*
Lee, Christopher, 196; in *Count Dracula*, 173, 178
Lefebvre, Henri, 19
Left, the, 92–3n9; and the Entesa dels Catalans, 51; opposition to Franco, 18, 51, 74, 105; and political dialogue, 145
Lévi-Strauss, Claude, 12; *La pensée sauvage*, 302; mythical thought and artistic creation, 302–3; notion of *bricoleur*, 30, 31, 301, 303, 311
Llorente, Ángel, 6
Losilla, Carlos, 275, 284
Luchetti, Francesc, 153, 164, 165, 166
Luna, Bigas: *Bilbao*, 53; *Caniche*, 53; *Jamón, Jamón*, 49; *Los amantes de Lulú*, 49
Lunati, Montserrat, 232

Madrid cinema, 4, 5, 29, 45, 46, 47, 49, 57, 65; directors of, 285; and dissident cinema, 65. *See also* Catalan cinema
Mallarmé, Stéphane, 8, 214, 215
Markers, Chris, 299; *Sans Soleil*, 299–300
Marks, Laura U., 12, 25, 231, 235, 247, 248
Marrano register, 179, 183, 187, 193, 196–7, 199
Marsh, Steven, 15, 127, 293
Martí, Octavi, *Verónica L. (Una dona al meu jardí)*, 50, 52
Martí-Olivella, Juame, 7, 232, 235, 242
Marx, Karl, 68; and influence on film, 132, 174; and concept of the spectre, 183, 184
maverick directors. *See* Catalan directors: as mavericks
media, 19, 71, 99, 291; and Barcelona 1992, 43–4; new media, 231, 248; and Raval trial, 86, 87, 92, 93; resistance of the 15-M movement to, 311, 312–13
Mekas, Jonas, 210, 213, 219, 220, 225, 226
melancholy, 24–5, 223, 225, 227, 228; definition of, 224
memory, 25, 92, 93; disputing versions of, 118; films about, 232n1; loss of, 232, 233–52; role in documentaries, 94–8
Mendelssohn, Felix: and discovery of Bach's *Saint Matthew's Passion*, 137; music in *Die Stille vor Bach*, 135, 140
metaphors, 20, 21, 76, 88, 110, 112, 163, 166, 214, 215, 236–7, 240, 243, 244, 249
militant cinema, 14, 17, 18, 19, 32, 103–20; definition of, 104

Minguet, Joan M., 308–9
minimalism, 17, 28–9
minor/minoritarian position, 11
Mira, Alberto, 5
Miró, Joan, 51, 148
Miró Law, and funding of films, 46–7, 49
mise en abyme, 237, 243
mise en scène, 82, 84, 85, 108, 127, 147, 155, 156, 159, 166, 244, 251, 290, 291, 325; definition of, 146, 236, 325
modernism/modernity, 7–8, 11, 45, 193, 215, 293; cinema of, 299, 322; failure of, 24, 190, 209, 227; industrial, 178, 180, 184; musical, 130; postmodern, 232; and vanguard movement, 212–13
Mones com la Becky (Jordà), 18, 19, 68; as documentary on psychiatry and mental illness, 83–5
Moniz, Egas, 68, 84
Monkeys Like Becky. See *Mones com la Becky*
Montalbán, Manuel Vázquez, criticism of Barcelona 1992, 43–4
Moreiras, Alberto: and the infrapolitical, 174; and the Marrano register, 179
Moreno-Caballud, Luis, 95
Morgan-Tamosunas, Rikki, 15
Muybridge, Eadweard, 234, 240

Nadal-Melsió, Sara, 10
Nancy, Jean-Luc, 126, 139nn9–10, 143
Nazi Germany, 21, 53–4, 107, 137, 150
Negri, Toni, 19, 105, 115n14
neighbourhoods, and corruption, 69, 86, 92, 93; and memory, 92, 93; and urban reform, 88–91, 91n9

neo-liberalism, 30, 81, 87, 110, 113, 115, 119, 142, 150, 293
neorealism, 8, 227; Italian, 4, 65, 268, 269
New Spanish Cinema ("el Nuevo cine Español"), 4, 5, 285
Numax presenta... (Jordà), 19, 34, 68, 69; as a democratic film, 102–3; and performativity, 109–10; revisiting the factory experience, 97–8; use of theatricality in, 107–9, 111; and the workers behind the Numax factory strike, 94–6, 105–6, 118
Numax Presents.... See *Numax presenta...*
Nunes, José María, 6, 8, 57, 65, 73

observational techniques, 56, 82, 87, 207
Oceanography of Tedium (D'Ors), 255; affect and sensorial experiences, 261–3, 264, 266, 271, 275, 276; and anti-Cartesian principle, 261; description of story, 255–6; Noucentisme style of humorous, nonsensical, elitist language, 257, 259, 266; publication of, 255; and tedium, 256, 264, 265; termination of affect, 264, 265, 266
Ojeda, Joaquín, writer/director on *El cielo sube* (Recha), 257, 258
Orsini bombings, 180, 181, 181(f)
O'Sullivan, Simon, 263, 271, 273

Padrós, Antoni, 65; and the Spanish Transition, 52–3; *L'home precís*, 52; *Lock Out*, 52; *Shirley Temple Story*, 52; *Verónica L. (Una dona al meu jardí)*, 50, 52
Pàmies, Sergi, 92–3
Partido Popular, 29, 292

Patino, Basilio Martín, 4, 65
Pedraza, Pilar, 53
performative approach/intervention, 8, 19, 26, 82, 86, 88, 102, 108–9, 111, 118, 126, 132, 143, 150, 156
piano, 148; and Europe's cultural identification, 140–1; as symbol of dissonance and dislocation, 20, 128–9, 134
Picasso, Pablo, *Guernica*, 21, 146–7, 148
Picazo, Miguel, 4, 65
politics: crises in, 120; dichotomy of, 154; filmic engagement in, 119; grassroots, 119
Pompeu Fabra University (Barcelona), 13, 17, 30, 34, 50, 58, 68, 81, 306
Pons, Ventura, 33–4; *La rosa del bar*, 48; *Què t'hi jugues, Mari Pili?*, 48
Portabella, Pere, 7, 8, 57, 65, 66, 73, 145, 306; arrest under Franco, 128; artistic and political practices of, 141, 142, 174n7, 177n12, 183, 240, 287, 288; cinematic language of, 149–50; cinematic vision of, 14, 143; collaboration with Carles Santos, 132, 133; continuities between the two *Informes*, 158–68; critical role in EdB, 17, 285–6; founder of Films 59 productions, 51; and radical theatricality, 145–6, 153, 164; and the Spanish Transition, 51, 148
Portabella, Pere, films of: *Dante no es únicamente severo*, 9, 27, 66, 258; *Die Stille vor Bach*, 20, 50, 126, 132–40, 148; *El sopar*, 158n13; *Es quan dormo que hi veig clar*, 26; *Informe general II: El nuevo rapto de Europa*, 21, 22, 141–2n11, 145,

146–7, 148, 150–1, 152, 153, 154–8, 291; *Informe general sobre algunas cuestiones de interés para una proyección pública*, 21, 145, 148, 149, 151, 153, 155, 291; *No compteu amb els dits*, 27, 67, 176n10, 258; *Nocturno 29*, 9, 30, 258, 293; *Pont de Varsòvia*, 15, 50, 51, 137, 148; *Umbracle*, 173–4n6, 183, 287; *Vampir.Cuadecuc*, 22, 29, 171–87, 286
Porter i Moix, Miquel, 31; and history of cinema, 306–7
power: institutional, 82, 83, 88; political, 4, 43, 54, 89, 91n9, 92, 93; resistance to, 91–2n9, 92, 98–9, 113
Prévost, Clovis, *Miró sculpteur*, 140
primitive/primitivism technique, 3, 241, 258, 302–3
provocation, in avant-garde film, 52–3, 67
psychiatry and mental illness, 19, 68, 75, 76, 82–5. See also *Mones com la Becky*
public/private sphere, 22, 26, 81, 125, 127, 153, 154, 155, 159, 160, 161
public square, 22, 114, 119, 159n14, 160, 162, 163
pueblo/people, and representation of, 322–3

queer cinema, 33, 323
Quintana, Àngel, 154

Rabal, Benito, 75–6
Rancière, Jacques, 110; concept of dissensus, 12, 21–2, 103n1, 154–5, 167; definition of politics, 108–9; and Deleuzian aesthetics, 276
Rascaroli, Laura, 119–20
Raunig, Gerald, 119

Raval (Spain): and pedophilia trial, 69, 87–91; and urban reform, 91–2
realism, 289; debates of, 56, 285; hyperrealism, 257; impressions of, 237; as major European tradition, 285; neo-realism, 268, 269; romantic and visionary realism, 214; social realism, 66
Recha, Marc, 13, 14, 17, 58, 65, 214; choosing *Oceanografia del tedi* for first film, 257–8; critique of cinematic style of, 267–9; differences between novel and film, 258. See also *El cielo sube*
Recha, Marc, films of: *El cielo sube*, 27–8, 55, 255, 257–77; *La Maglana*, 267; *Pau i el seu germà*, 68; *La por d'abocar-se*, 267; *El zelador*, 267
Regueiro, Francisco, 4
Reil, Johann Christian, and "cenesthesia," 259
Reina Sofía museum (Madrid), 22, 52; as setting for Portabella's *Informe general II*, 146, 147–8, 155, 156, 157, 159, 162, 163
Resina, Joan Ramon, 6; and Barcelona culture, 44; *La vocació de modernitat de Barcelona: Auge i declivi d'una imatge urbana*, 44
Riambau, Esteve, *La Escuela deBarcelona: El cine de la "gauche divine,"* 7
Rimbaud, Arthur, 214, 215, 216, 223–4, 229
Rosales, Jaime, 13, 14, 28–9; and avant-garde cinema, 295; cinematic conventions of, 286, 295; and creating auteur cinema, 285; portrayal of the minutiae of everyday life, 285; use of urban spaces and economic depression,

287; winner of Goya award, 286. See also *Beautiful Youth*; *Hours of the Day, The*

Rosales, Jaime, films of: *Girasoles silvestres*, 283; *Hermosa juventud*, 29–30, 283, 285, 291–5; *Las horas del día*, 29, 285, 286–91; *Petra*, 283; *Le soledad*, 283, 286; *Sueño y silencio*, 283; *Tiro en la cabeza*, 283, 285, 286

Ross, Alex, 8

Rouch, Jean, 111n11, 326

Salgot, Josep Antoni, 57

Salvador, Santiago, and the Orsini bombings, 180, 181, 181(f), 182(f)

Santos, Carles, 56, 149, 164, 175, 183n20; artistic and political practices of, 141, 142; collaboration with Pere Portabella, 132, 133; and "Pianos intervinguts," 128n3, 129; performance of Bach sonata as prisoner under Franco, 128–30; use of Bach in *La pantera imperial*, 131

Santos, Carles, films of: *Miró sculpteur*, 140; ¡*Visca el piano!*, 20, 126, 132

Saura, Carlos, 4; *La caza*, 285; *Marathon*, 45

Schiele, Egon, 247

Scott, Ridley, *1492*, 45

Seitz, Matt Zoller, 15

Serra, Albert, 13, 14, 65, 214, 236, 276. See also *Història de la meva mort*

Serra, Albert, films of: *Història de la meva mort*, 23, 187–99; *Honor de Cavalleria*, 15, 236; *Quixòtic/Honor de cavalleria*, 192

Silence before Bach, The (Portabella). See *Die Stille vor Bach*

Simón, Carla, 34

Singer, Irving, 243

Sitges film festivals, evolution of, 309–10

Sitney, Adam, 221

"situated lives," 81

situationist cinema, 18, 19, 140; definition of, 81n2; European Situationist movement, 81n3; of Joaquim Jordá, 80, 81, 82–94, 98–9

Smith, Daniel, 266

Sobchack, Vivian, 12, 25, 325; *The Address of the Eye*, 231, 236

Socrates, 127; *Phaedrus*, 116

Solé, Albert, *Bucarest, la memòria perduda*, 232

Soler, Llorenç, 65

sound: and aesthetic production, 8, 126, 143; and composition of music, 131, 135, 138, 139, 141, 142; diegetic, 19, 26, 134, 138, 173, 237, 243, 244, 251, 293; dissonance and resilience of, 20, 21, 126–9; in EdB films, 12, 16, 68, 109, 115–16; original sound negative (OSN), 173n5

Spanish cinema, 258, 274; effects of economic crisis on, 283; and filmmakers, 285, 318, 325–6

Spanish Civil War (1938–9), 4, 21, 153, 178, 180, 184

Spanish Guardia Civil (Civil Guard), 5

Spanish Transition, 19, 48, 49, 51, 53, 91, 94, 96, 103, 105, 148, 232

spectators, 231, 234, 236, 237, 238, 241, 285; expectations of, 8, 12, 16, 26, 87, 259; experiences of, 27, 28, 88, 286, 288, 289–90, 291, 293, 294–5; citizen spectator, 82, 86; and the senses, 231, 232, 235; visions of, 82, 86, 211

spectral, 120; genealogy, 3; cinema, 153, 172, 173, 177, 181, 184–6, 187;

and deconstructive criticism, 12, 22; haunting, 166; historiography, 3; poetics, 17; presence, 218; spectral Marxist, 183, 184
spectrality, 22, 23, 151–2, 152nn7–8, 174, 187, 188, 190, 192, 193, 194, 197, 234, 239–40
Spinoza, Baruch, 27, 174, 255, 274; anti-Cartesian philosophy of, 260, 261; body and mind as continuum, 261; concepts of *affectus* and *affectio*, 260; *Ethics*, 261, 264
Story of My Death. See *Història de la meva mort*
Suárez, Gonzalo, 66; *Ditirambo*, 9
Subirana, Carla, *Nedar*, 232
subjectivity, 82, 106; repoliticization of, 94–6
Summers, Manuel, 4
surrealism, 76, 148, 216
symbolism: and allegory, 212, 213; and euphoria and happiness, 99; function of, 12, 24, 222, 228; of love, 225; political, 147, 148, 152; and the real, 81, 188; of understanding, 231; and violence, 88
Symbolists, 226

Tàpies, Antoni, 51, 57
Taylor, Diana, 26, 248
technology, 24, 129–30n5, 210, 325; audiovisual, 236; cinematic, 212, 217, 240; digital, 209, 283; piano as, 140
Tedium. See *Oceanography of Tedium*
television, 12, 51, 52, 58, 66, 72, 82; directors working in, 55, 75; influence on EdB, 8; influence on national imagery, 46
temporality and place, and political agency, 126–7
testimonial cinema, 84, 87, 114

theatrical cinema, 12, 33, 84–5, 87, 107; in *Numax presenta...*, 107–9; Portabella's radical theatricality, 145–6, 153, 164
time-image, 11, 28, 32, 114, 177, 268, 272, 274, 322
time out of joint, 187, 188
Torreiro, Casimiro, 69–70; *La Escuela de Barcelona: El cine de la "gauche divine,"* 7
Truffaut, François, *Les quatre cents coups*, 299
Twenty Years Is Nothing. See *Veinte años no es nada*

University Pompeu Fabra. See Pompeu Fabra University
urban reform, 44, 87, 88–91; and the Special Plan of Interior Reform, 91

Vallcorba, Jaume, 27, 257
Vampir.Cuadecuc (Portabella), 22, 29, 188, 189, 190, 193, 196, 198; anachronism as strategy, 177; definition of "cuadecuc," 184–5; humour in, 174–5, 176; image of the clapperboard, 175, 175(f), 176, 177, 178, 186; image of Dracula as Franco, 22, 172, 173–4n6; as infrapolitical film, 174, 175–6, 177, 178–9, 180, 183, 184, 186; and the Marxist spectre, 183, 184, 185; and social turmoil in Spain (1970), 171–2, 173, 174; as spectral cinema, 172, 173, 174, 185; and time/timelessness, 173, 174, 175, 177, 178, 180, 184, 185, 186
vampires/vampire movies: as B-rated movies, 176; popularity of genre, 172, 173–4n6; as stand-in for General Franco, 22, 172, 173–4n6; strategies of the genre,

175–6; vampire/phantom fantasy, 188. *See also* Dracula
vanguard movement, 212–13
Veinte años no es nada (Jordà), 18, 19, 69, 80, 82, 94, 102, 111; and discourse of precariousness, 113–14; as retrospective of individual workers' stories, 112–14, 115–18; as retrospective of the Numax strike, 96–8, 105, 112
Vergés, Rosa, *Boom boom*, 48
Vilaseca, David, *Deleuze no es únicamente severo: Time and Memory in the Films of the Escola de Barcelona*, 10
Villaronga, Agustí, 17, 57, 65; *El niño de la luna*, 50, 54; *Tras el cristal*, 47, 50, 53–4
violence in films, 29–30, 53–4, 66, 68; psycho-killer in *The Hours of the Day*, 286–91; rape and trauma in *Elisa K*, 25, 240, 243–4, 246, 247, 249; social violence in *Beautiful Youth*, 293–4
vision/visionary: and new technologies, 210; the processes of Victor Hugo, 217–19; as a way of seeing, 208–9, 210, 211, 220, 221

¡*Visca el piano!* (Santos), 20; and dissonance in, 126, 132

ways of seeing: and new technologies, 209; ruptures in, 273–4; through the camera lens, 208. *See also* images; vision/visionary
"wolf," 141; Baroque term for dissonant and resilient sound, 20, 126; and Carles Santos's performance of Bach, 126–8, 129; and cinematic dissonance, 127–8
women: intellectual activists in *Informe general II*, 158–63; roles in *Numax presente…*, 95–6, 109, 110n9; roles in *Veinte años no es nada*, 111
Workers Autonomy, and the Numax strike, 94–6, 105
working-class, and economic crisis, 29; and organized action, 103, 105, 106, 113

Žižek, Slavoj, 24, 99n13, 186; and symbolic functions, 12, 221–2
Zunzunegui, Santos, 51; "Extraterritorial Portabella," 8

Toronto Iberic

CO-EDITORS: Robert Davidson (Toronto) and Frederick A. de Armas (Chicago)

EDITORIAL BOARD: Josiah Blackmore (Harvard); Marina Brownlee (Princeton); Anthony J. Cascardi (Berkeley); Justin Crumbaugh (Mt Holyoke); Emily Francomano (Georgetown); Jordana Mendelson (NYU); Joan Ramon Resina (Stanford); Enrique García Santo-Tomás (U Michigan); H. Rosi Song (Durham); Kathleen Vernon (SUNY Stony Brook)

1 Anthony J. Cascardi, *Cervantes, Literature, and the Discourse of Politics*
2 Jessica A. Boon, *The Mystical Science of the Soul: Medieval Cognition in Bernardino de Laredo's Recollection Method*
3 Susan Byrne, *Law and History in Cervantes'* Don Quixote
4 Mary E. Barnard and Frederick A. de Armas (eds.), *Objects of Culture in the Literature of Imperial Spain*
5 Nil Santiáñez, *Topographies of Fascism: Habitus, Space, and Writing in Twentieth-Century Spain*
6 Nelson R. Orringer, *Lorca in Tune with Falla: Literary and Musical Interludes*
7 Ana M. Gómez-Bravo, *Textual Agency: Writing Culture and Social Networks in Fifteenth-Century Spain*
8 Javier Irigoyen-García, *The Spanish Arcadia: Sheep Herding, Pastoral Discourse, and Ethnicity in Early Modern Spain*
9 Stephanie Sieburth, *Survival Songs: Conchita Piquer's* Coplas *and Franco's Regime of Terror*
10 Christine Arkinstall, *Spanish Female Writers and the Freethinking Press, 1879–1926*
11 Margaret E. Boyle, *Unruly Women: Performance, Penitence, and Punishment in Early Modern Spain*

12 Evelina Gužauskytė, *Christopher Columbus's Naming in the* diarios *of the Four Voyages (1492–1504): A Discourse of Negotiation*
13 Mary E. Barnard, *Garcilaso de la Vega and the Material Culture of Renaissance Europe*
14 William Viestenz, *By the Grace of God: Francoist Spain and the Sacred Roots of Political Imagination*
15 Michael Scham, *Lector Ludens: The Representation of Games and Play in Cervantes*
16 Stephen Rupp, *Heroic Forms: Cervantes and the Literature of War*
17 Enrique Fernandez, *Anxieties of Interiority and Dissection in Early Modern Spain*
18 Susan Byrne, *Ficino in Spain*
19 Patricia M. Keller, *Ghostly Landscapes: Film, Photography, and the Aesthetics of Haunting in Contemporary Spanish Culture*
20 Carolyn A. Nadeau, *Food Matters: Alonso Quijano's Diet and the Discourse of Food in Early Modern Spain*
21 Cristian Berco, *From Body to Community: Venereal Disease and Society in Baroque Spain*
22 Elizabeth R. Wright, *The Epic of Juan Latino: Dilemmas of Race and Religion in Renaissance Spain*
23 Ryan D. Giles, *Inscribed Power: Amulets and Magic in Early Spanish Literature*
24 Jorge Pérez, *Confessional Cinema: Religion, Film, and Modernity in Spain's Development Years, 1960–1975*
25 Joan Ramon Resina, *Josep Pla: Seeing the World in the Form of Articles*
26 Javier Irigoyen-García, *"Moors Dressed as Moors": Clothing, Social Distinction, and Ethnicity in Early Modern Iberia*
27 Jean Dangler, *Edging toward Iberia*
28 Ryan D. Giles and Steven Wagschal (eds.), *Beyond Sight: Engaging the Senses in Iberian Literatures and Cultures, 1200–1750*
29 Silvia Bermúdez, *Rocking the Boat: Migration and Race in Contemporary Spanish Music*
30 Hilaire Kallendorf, *Ambiguous Antidotes: Virtue as Vaccine for Vice in Early Modern Spain*
31 Leslie J. Harkema, *Spanish Modernism and the Poetics of Youth: From Miguel de Unamuno to* La Joven Literatura
32 Benjamin Fraser, *Cognitive Disability Aesthetics: Visual Culture, Disability Representations, and the (In) Visibility of Cognitive Difference*
33 Robert Patrick Newcomb, *Iberianism and Crisis: Spain and Portugal at the Turn of the Twentieth Century*
34 Sara J. Brenneis, *Spaniards in Mauthausen: Representations of a Nazi Concentration Camp, 1940–2015*

35 Silvia Bermúdez and Roberta Johnson (eds.), *A New History of Iberian Feminisms*
36 Steven Wagschal, *Minding Animals in the Old and New Worlds: A Cognitive Historical Analysis*
37 Heather Bamford, *Cultures of the Fragment: Uses of the Iberian Manuscript, 1100–1600*
38 Enrique García Santo-Tomás (ed.), *Science on Stage in Early Modern Spain*
39 Marina S. Brownlee (ed.), *Cervantes' Persiles and the Travails of Romance*
40 Sarah Thomas, *Inhabiting the In-Between: Childhood and Cinema in Spain's Long Transition*
41 David A. Wacks, *Medieval Iberian Crusade Fiction and the Mediterranean World*
42 Rosilie Hernández, *Immaculate Conceptions: The Power of the Religious Imagination in Early Modern Spain*
43 Mary L. Coffey and Margot Versteeg (eds.), *Imagined Truths: Realism in Modern Spanish Literature and Culture*
44 Diana Aramburu, *Resisting Invisibility: Detecting the Female Body in Spanish Crime Fiction*
45 Samuel Amago and Matthew J. Marr (eds.), *Consequential Art: Comics Culture in Contemporary Spain*
46 Richard P. Kinkade, *Dawn of a Dynasty: The Life and Times of Infante Manuel of Castile*
47 Jill Robbins, *Poetry and Crisis: Cultural Politics and Citizenship in the Wake of the Madrid Bombings*
48 Ana María Laguna and John Beusterien (eds.), *Goodbye Eros: Recasting Forms and Norms of Love in the Age of Cervantes*
49 Sara J. Brenneis and Gina Herrmann (eds.), *Spain, the Second World War, and the Holocaust: History and Representation*
50 Francisco Fernández de Alba, *Sex, Drugs, and Fashion in 1970s Madrid*
51 Daniel Aguirre-Oteiza, *This Ghostly Poetry: History and Memory of Exiled Spanish Republican Poets*
52 Lara Anderson, *Control and Resistance: Food Discourse in Franco Spain*
53 Faith S. Harden, *Arms and Letters: Military Life Writing in Early Modern Spain*
54 Erin Alice Cowling, Tania de Miguel Magro, Mina García Jordán, and Glenda Y. Nieto-Cuebas (eds.), *Social Justice in Spanish Golden Age Theatre*
55 Paul Michael Johnson, *Affective Geographies: Cervantes, Emotion, and the Literary Mediterranean*
56 Justin Crumbaugh and Nil Santiáñez (eds.), *Spanish Fascist Writing: An Anthology*

57 Margaret E. Boyle and Sarah E. Owens (eds.), *Health and Healing in the Early Modern Iberian World: A Gendered Perspective*
58 Leticia Álvarez-Recio (ed.), *Iberian Chivalric Romance: Translations and Cultural Transmission in Early Modern England*
59 Henry Berlin, *Alone Together: Poetics of the Passions in Late Medieval Iberia*
60 Adrian Shubert, *The Sword of Luchana: Baldomero Espartero and the Making of Modern Spain, 1793–1879*
61 Jorge Pérez, *Fashioning Spanish Cinema: Costume, Identity, and Stardom*
62 Enriqueta Zafra, *Lazarillo de Tormes: A Graphic Novel*
63 Erin Alice Cowling, *Chocolate: How a New World Commodity Conquered Spanish Literature*
64 Mary E. Barnard, *A Poetry of Things: The Material Lyric in Habsburg Spain*
65 Frederick A. de Armas and James Mandrell (eds.), *The Gastronomical Arts in Spain: Food and Etiquette*
66 Catherine Infante, *The Arts of Encounter: Christians, Muslims, and the Power of Images in Early Modern Spain*
67 Robert Richmond Ellis, *Bibliophiles, Murderous Bookmen, and Mad Librarians: The Story of Books in Modern Spain*
68 Beatriz de Alba-Koch (ed.), *The Ibero-American Baroque*
69 Deborah R. Forteza, *The English Reformation in the Spanish Imagination: Rewriting Nero, Jezebel, and the Dragon*
70 Olga Sendra Ferrer, *Barcelona, City of Margins*
71 Dale Shuger, *God Made Word: An Archaeology of Mystic Discourse in Early Modern Spain*
72 Xosé M. Núñez Seixas, *The Spanish Blue Division on the Eastern Front, 1941–1945: War, Occupation, Memory*
73 Julia Domínguez, *Quixotic Memories: Cervantes and Memory in Early Modern Spain*
74 Anna Casas Aguilar, *Bilingual Legacies: Father Figures in Self-Writing from Barcelona*
75 Julia H. Chang, *Blood Novels: Gender, Caste, and Race in Spanish Realism*
76 Frederick A. de Armas, *Cervantes' Architectures: The Dangers Outside*
77 Michael Iarocci, *The Art of Witnessing: Francisco de Goya's Disasters of War*
78 Esther Fernández and Adrienne L. Martín (eds.), *Drawing the Curtain: Cervantes's Theatrical Revelations*
79 Emiro Martínez-Osorio and Mercedes Blanco (eds.), *The War Trumpet: Iberian Epic Poetry, 1543–1639*
80 Christine Arkinstall, *Women on War in Spain's Long Nineteenth Century: Virtue, Patriotism, Citizenship*

81 Ignacio Infante, *A Planetary Avant-Garde: Experimental Literature Networks and the Legacy of Iberian Colonialism*
82 Enrique Fernández, *The Image of Celestina: Illustrations, Paintings, and Advertisements*
83 Maryanne L. Leone and Shanna Lino (eds.), *Beyond Human: Decentring the Anthropocene in Spanish Ecocriticism*
84 Jennifer Nagtegaal, *Politically Animated: Non-fiction Animation from the Hispanic World*
85 Anton Pujol and Jaume Martí-Olivella (eds.), *Catalan Cinema: The Barcelona Film School and the New Avant-Garde*